murach's
jQuery

Zak Ruvalcaba

Anne Boehm

murach's
jQuery

Zak Ruvalcaba

Anne Boehm

MIKE MURACH & ASSOCIATES, INC.

4340 N. Knoll Ave. • Fresno, CA 93722

www.murach.com • murachbooks@murach.com

Editorial team

Authors: Zak Ruvalcaba
Anne Boehm

Editor: Mike Murach

Cover design: Zylka Design

Production: Maria Spera

Books for web developers

Murach's Dreamweaver CC 2014

Murach's HTML5 and CSS3 (3rd Edition)

Murach's JavaScript (2nd Edition)

Murach's jQuery (2nd Edition)

Murach's PHP and MySQL (2nd Edition)

Murach's Java Servlets and JSP (3rd Edition)

Murach's ASP.NET Web Programming with C#

Murach's ASP.NET Web Programming with VB

Books on core Java, C#, and Visual Basic

Murach's Java Programming (4th Edition)

Murach's Android Programming

Murach's C#

Murach's Visual Basic

Books for database programmers

Murach's MySQL (2nd Edition)

Murach's SQL Server 2012 for Developers

Murach's Oracle SQL and PL/SQL for Developers (2nd Edition)

For more on Murach books, please visit us at www.murach.com

Printed in the United States of America

10 9 8 7 6 5 4 3 2 1
ISBN: 978-1-890774-91-2

Content

Expanded contents

Section 3 jQuery UI essentials

Section 4 Ajax, JSON, and APIs

Introduction

jQuery is a free, open-source, JavaScript library that provides dozens of methods that make JavaScript programming easier. Beyond that, the jQuery methods are coded and tested for cross-browser compatibility, so they will work in all browsers. Those are just two of the reasons why jQuery is used by more than 60% of the million most-visited websites today.

In fact, you can think of jQuery as one of the four technologies that every web developer should master: HTML, CSS, JavaScript, and jQuery. But don't forget that jQuery is actually JavaScript, and to use jQuery you need to know some JavaScript. That's one of the reasons jQuery has been so hard to learn.

That's why this book starts with a four-chapter tutorial and reference section on JavaScript. Then, this book uses our unique methods to present all of the jQuery, jQuery UI (User Interface), Ajax, JSON, and jQuery Mobile skills that you are likely to need on the job. And it always presents these skills in the context of useful, real-world applications.

What this book does

- To make sure you have all of the JavaScript skills that you need for using jQuery, the four chapters in section 1 of this book present a crash course in those skills. If you already know JavaScript, you can skim this section, although you're sure to pick up a few new skills along the way. If you have programming experience in another language, this section will get you up-to-speed with JavaScript. And if you're a programming novice, you'll have to work a little harder, but this section will get you off to a good start.

- Once you have the JavaScript skills that you need, the five chapters of section 2 present the core jQuery skills that every web developer should have. Chapter 5 gets you off to a fast start with those skills, and the next four chapters focus on effects and animations, the many plugins that are available for jQuery, creating your own plugins, working with forms and data validation, and using the DOM manipulation and transversal methods. When you complete this section, you will have a solid set of jQuery skills and you can go on to any of the sections that follow.

- Besides the core jQuery library, jQuery provides the jQuery UI (User Interface) library. This library helps you build advanced features with just a few lines of code, and the two chapters in section 3 show you how to make the best use of jQuery UI. That includes the use of widgets like tabs, accordions, and datepickers...interactions like draggable, droppable, and sortable...and effects like color and class transitions.

- Next, the three chapters in section 4 show you how to use Ajax and JSON to get data from a server and add it to a web page without reloading the entire web page. They show you how to use the APIs for websites like Flickr and Google Maps. And they show you how to use HTML5 APIs like Geolocation, Web Storage, and Web Workers.

- The last section of this book shows you how to use jQuery Mobile to develop mobile websites. This requires little or no programming, and it's a great alternative for established websites when rebuilding the site with Responsive Web Design is impractical.

Why you'll learn faster and better with this book

Like all our books, this one has features that you won't find in competing books. That's why we believe you'll learn faster and better with our book than with any other. Here are a few of those features.

- Because section 1 presents a complete subset of the JavaScript that you need for using jQuery, you will be able to understand all of the JavaScript that's used in the jQuery applications in this book. In contrast, most jQuery books don't teach JavaScript, so you often need to refer to other sources when you don't understand the JavaScript that they use in their examples.

- If you page through this book, you'll see that all of the information is presented in "paired pages," with the essential syntax, guidelines, and examples on the right page and the perspective and extra explanation on the left page. This helps you learn faster by reading less...and this is the ideal reference format when you need to refresh your memory about how to do something.

- To show you how jQuery works, this book presents dozens of complete jQuery applications that range from the simple to the complex. To see how that works, take a quick look at the four applications that are presented in chapter 5, the first jQuery chapter: Email List, FAQs, Image Swaps, and Image Rollovers. These applications also show how our paired pages make it easy to study the relationships between the HTML, CSS, and JavaScript code.

- Of course, this book also presents dozens of short examples, so it's easy to find an example that shows you how to do what you want to do. Even better, our paired pages make it much easier to find the example that you're looking for than in traditional books where the examples are embedded in the text. Incidentally, all of the examples in this book use HTML5 and CSS3, so they illustrate the best web development practices of today.

- As you proceed through this book, you will learn how to use almost all of the selectors, methods, and event methods that jQuery provides. That means that you can use this book as a reference that will help you parse the code in any jQuery application. So, although no one book can present every type of jQuery application, this book prepares you to understand any application that you encounter on the job, on websites, or in other books.

- Like our other books, this one has exercises at the end of each chapter that give you hands-on experience by letting you practice what you've learned. These exercises also encourage you to experiment and to apply what you've learned in new ways.

What software you need

To develop JavaScript and jQuery applications, you can use any text editor. However, a text editor that includes syntax coloring and auto-completion will help you develop applications more quickly and with fewer errors. That's why we recommend Aptana Studio 3 for both Windows and Mac OS users. Although Aptana is free, it provides many powerful features.

Then, to test a web page, we recommend that you do your primary testing with Google's Chrome browser. As you will see, this browser's developer tools have excellent features for testing and debugging your jQuery applications. After you test and debug with Chrome, you can test your sites with any browser that your visitors will be using.

If you decide to use Aptana, chapter 1 presents a short tutorial that will get you started right. And to help you install Aptana and Chrome, appendix A provides the website addresses and procedures that you need for both Windows and Mac systems.

How our downloadable files can help you learn

If you go to our website at www.murach.com, you can download all the files that you need for getting the most from this book. That includes:

- the files for all of the applications in this book
- the files that you will use as the starting points for the exercises in the book
- the files that provide the solutions to the exercises

These files let you test, review, and copy the code. In addition, if you have any problems with the exercises, the solutions are there to help you over the learning blocks, which is an essential part of the learning process. And sometimes, the solutions will show you a more elegant way to handle a problem, even when you've come up with a solution that works. Here again, appendix A shows you how to download and install these files.

Support materials for trainers and instructors

If you're a corporate trainer or a college instructor who would like to use this book for a course, we offer these supporting materials: (1) a complete set of PowerPoint slides that you can use to review and reinforce the content of the book; (2) instructional objectives that describe the skills a student should have upon completion of each chapter; (3) test banks that measure mastery of those skills; (4) extra exercises and projects that prove mastery; and (5) solutions to the extra exercises and projects.

To learn more about these materials, please go to our website at www.murachforinstructors.com if you're an instructor. Or if you're a trainer, please go to www.murach.com and click on the *Courseware for Trainers* link, or contact Kelly at 1-800-221-5528 or kelly@murach.com.

Companion books

Since jQuery, HTML, and CSS are so tightly linked, the best web developers not only master jQuery, but also HTML5 and CSS3. To that end, you'll find that *Murach's HTML5 and CSS3* is the perfect companion to this jQuery book. With these two books at your side, you'll be able to develop web pages that use HTML5, CSS3, and jQuery the way the best professionals do.

If you want to learn more about JavaScript so you can do the type of client-side programming that jQuery doesn't provide for, we also recommend *Murach's JavaScript*. It presents all of the JavaScript skills that aren't presented in this jQuery book, including how to use regular expressions, how to create and use your own objects, and much more. It is also a great reference.

If you're looking for a way to create web pages using a visual interface instead of coding all the HTML and CSS from scratch, we've found Dreamweaver CC to be a terrific tool. So our book, *Murach's Dreamweaver CC*, teaches you how to use it to develop websites as quickly and effectively as possible. That includes two chapters on using features that relate to jQuery, like dragging-and-dropping jQuery UI widgets and effects to enhance a web page or adding jQuery Mobile components to create a separate website for mobile devices.

To find out more about our new books and latest editions, please go to our website at www.murach.com. There, you'll find the details for all of our books, including complete tables of contents.

Please let us know how this book works for you

From the start of this project, we had two goals. First, we wanted to improve upon the first edition of this book to help you learn even faster and better. Second, we wanted to make sure that this book presents all of the jQuery, jQuery UI, and jQuery Mobile skills that you are likely to need on the job.

Now, we hope we've succeeded. We thank you for buying this book. We wish you all the best with your jQuery development. And if you have any comments, we would appreciate hearing from you.

Zak Ruvalcaba, Author
zak@modulemedia.com

Anne Boehm, Author
anne@murach.com

Section 1

JavaScript essentials for jQuery users

The four chapters in this section present the JavaScript essentials that jQuery users need to know. First, chapter 1 presents the concepts and terms that you need for developing JavaScript and jQuery applications. It also shows you how to use the Aptana IDE that we recommend for developing these applications.

Then, in chapter 2, you'll learn how to use a subset of the JavaScript language that includes all of the skills that you'll need for developing jQuery applications like the ones in this book. In chapter 3, you'll learn how to use JavaScript for DOM scripting, along with some other JavaScript skills that jQuery users need. Last, in chapter 4, you'll learn the skills for testing and debugging JavaScript applications. As you'll see in that chapter, these skills also apply to jQuery applications.

When you complete this section, you'll have the JavaScript skills that you need for developing jQuery applications. Then, you can read the chapters in the sections 2 and 3 to master jQuery and jQuery UI. You can read the chapters in section 4 to learn how to use Ajax, JSON, the APIs for websites like Flickr and Google Maps, and the HTML5 Geolocation, Web Storage, and Web Workers APIs. And you can read the chapters in section 5 to learn how to use jQuery Mobile to develop mobile websites.

1

Introduction to web development

This chapter presents the background concepts, terms, and skills that you need for developing JavaScript and jQuery applications. That includes a quick review of the HTML and CSS skills that you need. That also includes a quick tutorial on how to use Aptana Studio 3, which is the IDE that we recommend for developing JavaScript applications.

If you have some web development experience, you should be able to go through this chapter quickly by skimming the topics that you already know. But if you're new to web development, you should take the time to master the concepts and terms of this chapter.

How a web application works

A web application consists of many components that work together as they bring the application to your computer or mobile device. Before you can start developing JavaScript applications, you should have a basic understanding of how these components work together.

The components of a web application

The diagram in figure 1-1 shows that web applications consist of *clients* and a *web server*. The clients are the computers, tablets, and mobile devices that use the web applications. They access the web pages through *web browsers*. The web server holds the files that make up a web application.

A *network* is a system that allows clients and servers to communicate. The *Internet* is a large network that consists of many smaller networks. In a diagram like the one in this figure, the "cloud" represents the network or Internet that connects the clients and servers.

In general, you don't need to know how the cloud works. But you should have a general idea of what's going on.

To start, networks can be categorized by size. A *local area network* (*LAN*) is a small network of computers that are near each other and can communicate with each other over short distances. Computers in a LAN are typically in the same building or adjacent buildings. This type of network is often called an *intranet*, and it can be used to run web applications for use by employees only.

In contrast, a *wide area network* (*WAN*) consists of multiple LANs that have been connected. To pass information from one client to another, a router determines which network is closest to the destination and sends the information over that network. A WAN can be owned privately by one company or it can be shared by multiple companies.

An *Internet service provider* (*ISP*) is a company that owns a WAN that is connected to the Internet. An ISP leases access to its network to companies that need to be connected to the Internet.

The components of a web application

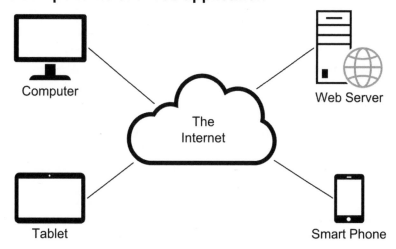

Computer

The Internet

Web Server

Tablet

Smart Phone

Description

- A web application consists of clients, a web server, and a network.

- The *clients* use programs known as *web browsers* to request web pages from the web server. Today, the clients can be computers, smart phones like the iPhone, or tablets like the iPad.

- The *web server* returns the pages that are requested to the browser.

- A *network* connects the clients to the web server.

- An *intranet* is a *local area network* (or *LAN*) that connects computers that are near each other, usually within the same building.

- The *Internet* is a network that consists of many *wide area networks* (*WANs*), and each of those consists of two or more LANs. Today, the Internet is often referred to as "the Cloud", which implies that you really don't have to understand how it works.

- An *Internet service provider* (*ISP*) owns a WAN that is connected to the Internet.

Figure 1-1   The components of a web application

How static web pages are processed

A *static web page* like the one in figure 1-2 is a web page that doesn't change each time it is requested. This type of web page is sent directly from the web server to the web browser when the browser requests it. You can spot static pages in a web browser by looking at the extension in the address bar. If the extension is .htm or .html, the page is a static web page.

The diagram in this figure shows how a web server processes a request for a static web page. This process begins when a client requests a web page in a web browser. To do that, the user can either type the address of the page into the browser's address bar or click a link in the current page that specifies the next page to load.

In either case, the web browser builds a request for the web page and sends it to the web server. This request, known as an *HTTP request*, is formatted using the *HyperText Transfer Protocol* (HTTP), which lets the web server know which file is being requested.

When the web server receives the HTTP request, it retrieves the requested file from the disk drive. This file contains the *HTML (HyperText Markup Language)* for the requested page. Then, the web server sends the file back to the browser as part of an *HTTP response*.

When the browser receives the HTTP response, it *renders* (translates) the HTML into a web page that is displayed in the browser. Then, the user can view the content. If the user requests another page, either by clicking a link or typing another web address into the browser's address bar, the process begins again.

A static web page at http://www.modulemedia.com/ourwork/index.html

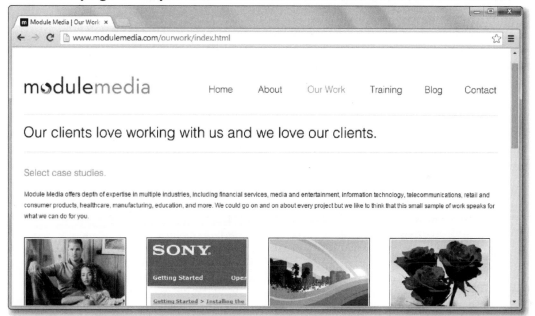

How a web server processes a static web page

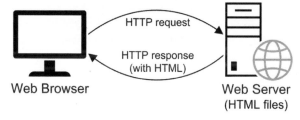

Web Browser

HTTP request

HTTP response
(with HTML)

Web Server
(HTML files)

Description

- *Hypertext Markup Language* (*HTML*) is the language used to define the web pages of an application.

- A *static web page* is an HTML document that's stored on the web server and doesn't change. The filenames for static web pages have .htm or .html extensions.

- When the user requests a static web page, the browser sends an *HTTP request* to the web server that includes the name of the file that's being requested.

- When the web server receives the request, it retrieves the HTML for the web page and sends it back to the browser as part of an *HTTP response*.

- When the browser receives the HTTP response, it *renders* the HTML into a web page that is displayed in the browser.

Figure 1-2   How static web pages are processed

How dynamic web pages are processed

A *dynamic web page* like the one in figure 1-3 is a page that's created by a program or script on the web server each time it is requested. This program or script is executed by an *application server* based on the data that's sent along with the HTTP request. In this example, the HTTP request identified the book that's shown. Then, the program or script retrieved the image and data for that book from a *database server*.

The diagram in this figure shows how a web server processes a dynamic web page. The process begins when the user requests a page in a web browser. To do that, the user can either type the address of the page into the browser's address bar, click a link that specifies the dynamic page to load, or click a button that submits a form that contains the data that the dynamic page should process.

In each case, the web browser builds an HTTP request and sends it to the web server. This request includes whatever data the application needs for processing the request. If, for example, the user has entered data into a form, that data will be included in the HTTP request.

When the web server receives the HTTP request, the server examines the file extension of the requested web page to identify the application server that should process the request. The web server then forwards the request to the application server that processes that type of web page.

Next, the application server retrieves the appropriate program or script from the hard drive. It also loads any form data that the user submitted. Then, it executes the script. As the script executes, it generates the HTML for the web page. If necessary, the script will request data from a database server and use that data as part of the web page it is generating. The processing that's done on the application server can be referred to as *server-side processing*.

When the script is finished, the application server sends the dynamically generated HTML back to the web server. Then, the web server sends the HTML back to the browser in an HTTP response.

When the web browser receives the HTTP response, it renders the HTML and displays the web page. Note, however, that the web browser has no way to tell whether the HTML in the HTTP response was for a static page or a dynamic page. It just renders the HTML.

When the page is displayed, the user can view the content. Then, when the user requests another page, the process begins again. The process that begins with the user requesting a web page and ends with the server sending a response back to the client is called a *round trip*.

A dynamic web page at amazon.com

How a web server processes a dynamic web page

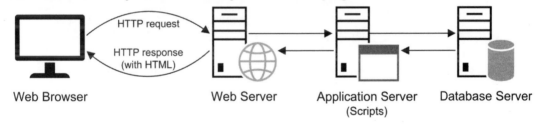

Web Browser   Web Server   Application Server   Database Server
                                              (Scripts)

Description

- A *dynamic web page* is a web page that's generated by a program or script that is running on a server.

- When a web server receives a request for a dynamic web page, it looks up the extension of the requested file to find out which *application server* should process the request.

- When the application server receives a request, it runs the specified script. Often, this script uses the data that it gets from the web browser to get the appropriate data from a *database server*. This script can also store the data that it receives in the database.

- When the application server finishes processing the data, it generates the HTML for a web page and returns it to the web server. Then, the web server returns the HTML to the web browser as part of an HTTP response.

Figure 1-3   How dynamic web pages are processed

How JavaScript and jQuery are used for client-side processing

In contrast to the server-side processing that's done for dynamic web pages, *JavaScript* is a *scripting language* that provides for *client-side processing*. In the web page in figure 1-4, for example, JavaScript is used to change the images that are shown without using server-side processing.

To make this work, all of the required images are loaded into the browser when the page is requested. Then, if the user clicks on one of the color swatches below a shirt, the shirt image is changed to the one with the right color. This is called an *image swap*. Similarly, if the user moves the mouse over a shirt, the image showing the front of the shirt is replaced with an image showing the back of the shirt. This is called an *image rollover*.

The diagram in this figure shows how JavaScript processing works. When a browser requests a web page, both the HTML and the related JavaScript are returned to the browser by the web server. Then, the JavaScript code is executed in the web browser by the browser's *JavaScript engine*. This takes some of the processing burden off the server and makes the application run faster. Often, JavaScript is used in conjunction with dynamic web pages, but it is also commonly used with static web pages.

Besides image swaps and rollovers, there are many other uses for JavaScript. For instance, another common use is to validate the data that the user enters into an HTML form before it is sent to the server for processing. This is called *data validation*, and that saves unnecessary trips to the server. Other common uses of JavaScript are to run slide shows and carousels and to provide information in tabs or accordions.

When you think of JavaScript, though, you also need to think of jQuery. That's because *jQuery* is a JavaScript library that makes it easier to do functions like image swaps, rollovers, and slide shows. As you read this section, then, just remember that jQuery is JavaScript, so most of what applies to JavaScript also applies to jQuery. Then, in the next section, you'll learn how to use jQuery, and you'll quickly see why it's so popular.

A web page with image swaps and rollovers

How JavaScript fits into this architecture

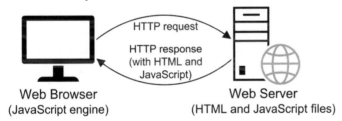

Three of the many uses of JavaScript and jQuery

- Data validation
- Image swaps and rollovers
- Slide shows

Description

- *JavaScript* is a *scripting language* that is run by the *JavaScript engine* of a web browser and controls the operation of the browser.

- When the browser requests an HTML page that contains JavaScript or a link to a JavaScript file, both the HTML and the JavaScript are loaded into the browser.

- Because JavaScript runs on the client, not the server, its functions don't require a trip back to the server. This helps an application run more efficiently.

- *jQuery* is a JavaScript library that makes it easier to do many of the common functions that JavaScript is used for.

Figure 1-4   How JavaScript and jQuery are used for client-side processing

The components
of a JavaScript application

When you develop a JavaScript application, you use HTML to define the content and structure of the page. You use CSS to format that content. And you use JavaScript to do the client-side processing. This is illustrated by the Email List application that is presented in the next three figures.

Figure 1-5 starts with the user interface for the application. It asks the user to make three entries and then click on the Join our List button. The asterisks to the right of the text boxes for the entries indicate that these entries are required.

When the user clicks on the button, JavaScript checks the entries to make sure they're valid. If they are, the entries are sent to the web server for server-side processing. If they aren't, messages are displayed so the user can correct the entries. This is a common type of JavaScript application called *data validation* that saves a trip to the server when the entries are invalid.

You might have noticed that the user interface in this figure isn't much to look at. This is what a plain HTML document with no formatting looks like. In the next figure, you'll see what this interface looks like after some CSS is applied.

The HTML

HyperText Markup Language (*HTML*) is used to define the content and structure of a web page. In figure 1-5, you can see the HTML for the Email List application. In general, this book assumes that you are already familiar with HTML, but here are a few highlights.

First, note that this document starts with a DOCTYPE declaration. This declaration is the one you'll use with HTML5, and you must code it exactly as it's shown here. If you aren't already using HTML5, you can see that this declaration is much simpler than the declaration for earlier versions of HTML. In this book, all of the applications use HTML5.

Second, in the head section of the HTML document, you can see a meta element that specifies that UTF-8 is the character encoding that's used for the page. Then, there is an HTML comment indicating that any link, style, and script elements go here in the head element. In the next figure, you'll see a link element that specifies the CSS file that should be used to format this HTML. And in the figure after that, you'll see a script element that specifies the JavaScript file that should be used to process the user's entries.

Third, in the body section, you can see the use of a main element. That is one of the HTML5 elements that we'll be using throughout this book. Within this element, you can see the use of h1, form, label, input, and span elements.

In this book, as you've just seen, we refer to *HTML elements* like the <link>, <script>, <main>, and <h1> elements as the link, script, main, and h1 elements. However, to prevent confusion when referring to one-letter elements like p and a elements, we enclose the letters in brackets, as in the <p> element or the <a> element.

The HTML file in a browser with no CSS applied to it

The code for the HTML file named index.html

```html
<!DOCTYPE html>
<html>
<head>
    <meta charset="UTF-8">
    <title>Join Email List</title>
    <!-- link, style, and script elements go here -->
</head>
<body>
    <main>
        <h1>Please join our email list</h1>
        <form id="email_form" name="email_form"
            action="join.html" method="get">
            <label for="email_address1">Email Address:</label>
            <input type="text" id="email_address1" name="email_address1">
            <span id="email_address1_error">*</span><br>

            <label for="email_address2">Re-enter Email Address:</label>
            <input type="text" id="email_address2" name="email_address2">
            <span id="email_address2_error">*</span><br>

            <label for="first_name">First Name:</label>
            <input type="text" id="first_name" name="first_name">
            <span id="first_name_error">*</span><br>

            <label> </label>
            <input type="button" id="join_list" value="Join our List">
        </form>
    </main>
</body>
</html>
```

Description

- *HTML* (*HyperText Markup Language*) is used to define the structure and content of a web page.

- To add CSS and JavaScript files to a web page, you code link and script elements in the head element. To embed CSS and JavaScript in a page, you code style and script elements.

Figure 1-5   The HTML for a web page

In practice, you'll often hear *elements* called *tags* so you can think of them as synonyms. In this book, we occasionally use the term *tag*, especially when referring to an opening tag like <h1> or a closing tag like </h1>.

The CSS

Not long ago, HTML documents were coded so the HTML not only defined the content and structure of the web page but also the formatting of that content. However, this mix of structural and formatting elements made it hard to edit, maintain, and reformat the web pages.

Today, *Cascading Style Sheets* (*CSS*) let you separate the formatting from the content and structure of a web page. As a result, the formatting that was once done with HTML should now be done with CSS.

In figure 1-6, then, you can see the link element that links the external CSS file to the HTML. As you saw in figure 1-5, this link element goes in the HTML head element. You can also see how this CSS has changed the appearance of the page in the browser.

After that, you can see the CSS that's used to format the HTML in the last figure. Here again, this book assumes that you are already familiar with CSS, but here is a quick description of what this CSS is doing.

In the rule set for the body element, the font-family property sets the font for the entire document, the background-color property sets the color for the body of the page to white, and the margin property centers the body in the browser window. Then, the width property sets the width of the body to 670 pixels, the border property puts a blue border around the body, and the padding property adds space between the content and the border. This is typical CSS for the applications in the book, just to make them look better.

Similarly, the rule sets for the h1, label, and input elements are intended to make these elements look better. Here, the rule set for the h1 element sets the font color to blue. Then, the rule set for the labels floats them left so the text boxes will be to their right. This rule set also sets the width of the labels to 11 ems, and it aligns the text for the labels on the right. Next, the rule set for the input elements sets the left margin so there's space between the labels and the text boxes, and it sets the bottom margin so there's space after each label and text box.

Last, the rule set for the span elements sets the text color to red. When the HTML page is first loaded, these span elements only contain asterisks (*) to indicate that these entries are required. But the JavaScript changes those asterisks to error messages if the related entries are invalid, and it removes the asterisks if the related entries are valid.

The web page in a browser after CSS has been applied to it

The link element in the HTML head element that applies the CSS file

```
<link rel="stylesheet" href="email_list.css">
```

The code for the CSS file named email_list.css

```
body {
    font-family: Arial, Helvetica, sans-serif;
    background-color: white;
    margin: 0 auto;
    width: 670px;
    padding: 0 2em 1em;
    border: 3px solid blue;
}
h1 {
    color: blue;
}
label {
    float: left;
    width: 11em;
    text-align: right;
}
input {
    margin-left: 1em;
    margin-bottom: .5em;
}
span {
    color: red;
}
```

Description

- *Cascading Style Sheets* (*CSS*) are used to control how web pages are displayed by specifying the fonts, colors, borders, spacing, and layout of the pages.

Figure 1-6   The CSS for the web page

The JavaScript

Figure 1-7 shows how this application looks in a browser if the JavaScript finds any invalid data after the user clicks the Join our List button. Here, you can see that error messages are displayed to the right of the user entries for the second and third text boxes. In other words, the JavaScript has actually changed the contents of the span elements.

When JavaScript changes the HTML for a page, it is called *DOM scripting*. That's because the JavaScript is actually changing the *Document Object Model* (or *DOM*) that's generated by the browser when the page is loaded. This DOM represents all of the elements and attributes that are coded in the HTML. Then, when JavaScript changes any aspect of the DOM, the change is immediately made to the browser display too.

After the browser display, this figure shows the script element that links the external JavaScript file to the HTML. This script element goes in the HTML head element.

Then, this figure shows the JavaScript for this application. Since you are going to learn how all of this code works in the next two chapters, you may want to skip over this code right now. But if you have any programming experience, it may be worth taking a quick look at it. In that case, here are a few highlights.

To start, this code consists of three functions: a $ function, a joinList function that is executed when the user clicks on the button, and a function that is run after the DOM has been loaded into the browser. Then, in the joinList function, you can see four if statements with else clauses that provide most of the logic for this application.

Here, you can see that the if-else structures are similar to those in any modern programming language like Java, C#, or PHP. You can also see that declaring a variable (var) and assigning a value to it is done in a way that's similar to the way that's done in other programming languages.

What's different about JavaScript is that it provides methods and properties that let you modify the DOM. For instance, the $ function uses the getElement-ById method to get the object with the id that's passed to the function. Then, the first statement in the joinList function uses the $ function to get the object that represents the first text box in the HTML. This statement also uses the value property to get the value that the user entered into that text box.

Later, the first if statement checks if that value is an empty string (""). If it is, it means the user didn't make an entry, and the JavaScript replaces the * in the span element for that text box with an error message. To do that, it uses this code:

```
$("email_address1_error").firstChild.nodeValue =
    "This field is required.";
```

Although this code may look daunting right now, you'll see that it's all quite manageable. You'll also come to realize that DOM scripting is where JavaScript get its power.

The web page in a browser with JavaScript used for data validation

The script element in the HTML head element that adds the JavaScript file

```
<script src="email_list.js"></script>
```

The code for the JavaScript file named email_list.js

```javascript
var $ = function (id) {
    return document.getElementById(id);
}
var joinList = function () {
    var emailAddress1 = $("email_address1").value;
    var emailAddress2 = $("email_address2").value;
    var isValid = true;

    if (emailAddress1 == "") {
        $("email_address1_error").firstChild.nodeValue =
            "This field is required.";
        isValid = false;
    } else { $("email_address1_error").firstChild.nodeValue = ""; }

    if (emailAddress1 != emailAddress2) {
        $("email_address2_error").firstChild.nodeValue =
            "This entry must equal first entry.";
        isValid = false;
    } else { $("email_address2_error").firstChild.nodeValue = ""; }

    if ($("first_name").value == "") {
        $("first_name_error").firstChild.nodeValue =
            "This field is required.";
        isValid = false;
    } else { $("first_name_error").firstChild.nodeValue = ""; }

    if (isValid) {
        // submit the form if all entries are valid
        $("email_form").submit(); }
}
window.onload = function () {
    $("join_list").onclick = joinList;
    $("email_address").focus();
}
```

Figure 1-7   The JavaScript for the web page

The HTML skills that you need for this book

Although this book assumes that you are already familiar with HTML, the next three topics present a quick review of the HTML skills that you're going to need for this book. If you don't already have these skills and you can't pick them up from the topics that follow, we recommend that you use *Murach's HTML5 and CSS3* as a reference while you're learning JavaScript.

How to use the HTML5 semantic elements

All of the applications in this book use the *HTML5 semantic elements* whenever they're appropriate. If you aren't already using them or at least familiar with them, figure 1-8 summarizes what you need to know.

In particular, the applications in this book use the main, section, aside, and nav elements. That makes it easier to apply CSS to these elements because you don't have to code id attributes that are used by the CSS. Instead, you can apply the CSS to the elements themselves.

Be aware, however, that older browsers like IE7 and IE8 won't recognize the HTML5 semantic elements, which means that you won't be able to use CSS to apply formatting to them. So, if you want your HTML5 and CSS to work in older browsers, you need to provide a workaround. You'll learn how to do that in figure 1-16.

The primary HTML5 semantic elements

Element	Contents
header	The header for a page.
main	The main content of a page. Can only appear once per page, and cannot be the child of an article, aside, footer, header, or nav element.
section	A generic section of a document that doesn't indicate the type of content.
article	A composition like an article in the paper.
aside	A portion of a page like a sidebar that is related to the content that's near it.
nav	A portion of a page that contains links to other pages or placeholders.
figure	An image, table, or other component that's treated as a figure.
footer	The footer for a page.

A page that's structured with header, main, and footer elements

```
<body>
    <header>
        <h1>San Joaquin Valley Town Hall</h1>
    </header>
    <main>
        <p>Welcome to San Joaquin Valley Town Hall. We have some
            fascinating speakers for you this season!</p>
    </main>
    <footer>
        <p>&copy; San Joaquin Valley Town Hall.</p>
    </footer>
</body>
```

The page displayed in a web browser

San Joaquin Valley Town Hall

Welcome to San Joaquin Valley Town Hall. We have some fascinating speakers for you this season!

© San Joaquin Valley Town Hall.

Description

- HTML5 provides new *semantic elements* that you should use to structure the contents of a web page. Using these elements can be referred to as *HTML5 semantics*.

- All of the HTML5 elements are supported by the modern browsers. They will also work in older browsers if you provide for cross-browser compatibility as shown in figure 1-16.

- This book also uses standard HTML elements like h1 and h2 elements for headings, img elements for images, <a> elements for links, and <p> elements for paragraphs.

Figure 1-8   How to use the HTML5 semantic elements

How to use the div and span elements

If you've been using HTML for a while, you are certainly familiar with the div element. It has traditionally been used to divide an HTML document into divisions that are identified by id attributes. Then, CSS can use the ids to apply formatting to the divisions.

But now that HTML5 is available, div elements shouldn't be used to structure a document. Instead, they should only be used when the HTML5 semantic elements aren't appropriate.

Note, however, that div elements are often used in JavaScript applications. If, for example, a main element contains three h2 elements with each followed by a div element, JavaScript can be used to display or hide a div element whenever the heading that precedes it is clicked. This structure is illustrated by the first example in figure 1-9. Here, you'll notice that an id is assigned to the main element, even though that element can only be used once on a page. Although this id isn't necessary, it makes the JavaScript code for this application easier to read. You'll see how this application works in chapter 3.

Similarly, span elements have historically been used to identify portions of text that can be formatted by CSS. By today's standards, though, it's better to use elements that indicate the contents of the elements, like the cite, code, and <q> elements.

But here again, span elements are often used in JavaScript applications, as shown by the second example in this figure. In fact, you've just seen this in the Email List application. In that application, JavaScript puts the error messages in the appropriate span elements.

The div and span elements

Element	Description
div	A block element that provides a container for other elements.
span	An inline element that lets you identify text that can be formatted with CSS.

Div elements in the HTML for a JavaScript application

```
<main id="faqs">
    <h1>jQuery FAQs</h1>
    <h2>What is JavaScript?</h2>
    <div>
        // contents
    </div>
    <h2>What is jQuery?</h2>
    <div>
        // contents
    </div>
    <h2>Why is jQuery becoming so popular?</h2>
    <div>
        // contents
    </div>
</main>
```

Span elements in the HTML for a JavaScript application

```
<label for="email_address1">Email Address:</label>
<input type="text" id="email_address1" name="email_address1">
<span id="email_address1_error">*</span><br>

<label for="email_address2">Re-enter Email Address:</label>
<input type="text" id="email_address2" name="email_address2">
<span id="email_address2_error">*</span><br>

<label for="first_name">First Name:</label>
<input type="text" id="first_name" name="first_name">
<span id="first_name_error">*</span>
```

Description

- Before HTML5, div elements were used to define the structure within the body of a document. The ids for these div elements were then used by the CSS to apply formatting to the elements.

- Today, the HTML5 semantic elements are replacing div elements. That makes the structure of a page more apparent. However, you will still use div elements to define blocks of code that are used in JavaScript applications.

- Before HTML5, span elements were often used to identify portions of text that you could apply formatting to.

- Today, a better practice is to use specific elements to identify content. However, you will still use span elements for some JavaScript applications, like the Email List application in figures 1-5 through 1-7.

Figure 1-9   How to use the div and span elements

How to use the basic HTML attributes

Figure 1-10 presents the HTML *attributes* that are commonly used in JavaScript applications. You should already be familiar with the *id attribute* that identifies one HTML element and with *class attributes* that can be applied to more than one HTML element. You should also be familiar with the *for attribute* that relates a label to an input element and with the *title attribute* that can be used to provide a tooltip for an element.

When you use JavaScript, you will commonly use the *name attribute* so the server-side code can access the data that is submitted to it. You will sometimes add or remove class attributes to change the formatting of elements. And you will sometimes use title attributes to provide text that's related to elements.

In practice, you usually use the same value for the id and name attributes of an element. For instance, the example in this figure uses "email" as the value of both the id and name attributes for the text box. That makes it easier to remember the attribute values.

The basic HTML attributes

Attribute	Description
`id`	Specifies a unique identifier for an element that can be referred to by CSS.
`class`	Specifies one or more class names that can be referred to by CSS, and the same name can be used for more than one element. To code more than one class name, separate the class names with spaces.
`name`	Specifies a unique name for an element that is commonly used by the server-side code and can also be used by the JavaScript code.
`for`	In a label element, this attribute specifies the id of the control that it applies to.
`title`	Specifies additional information about an element. For some elements, the title appears in a tooltip when the user hovers the mouse over the element.

HTML that uses these attributes

```html
<body>
    <h1>San Joaquin Valley Town Hall</h1>
    <h2 class="first_h2">Welcome to San Joaquin Valley Town Hall.</h2>
    <p>Please enter your e-mail address to subscribe to our
        newsletter.</p>
    <form id="email_form" name="email_form"
            action="join.html" method="get">
        <label for="email">E-Mail: </label>
        <input type="text" id="email" name="email"
                title="Enter e-mail address here.">
        <input type="button" value="Subscribe">
    </form>
</body>
```

The HTML in a web browser with a tooltip displayed for the text box

San Joaquin Valley Town Hall

Welcome to San Joaquin Valley Town Hall.

Please enter your e-mail address to subscribe to our newsletter.

E-Mail: [   ]   [Subscribe]

[Enter e-mail address here.]

Description

- An *attribute* consists of an attribute name, an equals sign, and the value of the attribute enclosed in either single or double quotation marks.
- The *id* and *class attributes* are commonly used to apply CSS formatting,
- The *name attribute* is commonly used by the server-side code to access the data that is sent to it, but this attribute can also be used by the JavaScript code for a page.
- The *for attribute* in a label element is used to identify the control that it applies to.

Figure 1-10   How to use the basic HTML attributes

The CSS skills that you need for this book

Although this book assumes that you are already familiar with CSS, the next three topics present a quick review of the CSS skills that you're going to need for this book. If you don't already have these skills and you can't pick them up from the topics that follow, we recommend that you use *Murach's HTML5 and CSS3* as a reference while you're learning JavaScript.

How to provide the CSS styles for an HTML page

Figure 1-11 shows the two ways that you can include CSS styles for an HTML document. First, you can code a link element in the head section of an HTML document that specifies a file that contains the CSS for the page. This is referred to as an *external style sheet*, and this is the method that's used for most of the applications in this book.

Second, you can code a style element in the head section that contains the CSS for the page. This can be referred to as *embedded styles*. In general, it's better to use external style sheets because that makes it easier to use them for more than one page. However, embedded styles can be easier to use for simple applications like the ones in this book because you don't need to create an extra file.

In some cases, you may want to use two or more external style sheets for a single page. You may even want to use both external style sheets and embedded styles for a page. In these cases, the styles are applied from the first external style sheet to the last one and then the embedded styles are applied.

Two ways to provide styles

Use an external style sheet by coding a link element in the head section

```
<link rel="stylesheet" href="styles/main.css">
```

Embed the styles in the head section

```
<style>
    body {
        font-family: Arial, Helvetica, sans-serif;
        font-size: 87.5%; }
    h1 { font-size: 250%; }
</style>
```

The sequence in which styles are applied

- Styles from an external style sheet
- Embedded styles

A head element that includes two external style sheets

```
<head>
    <title>San Joaquin Valley Town Hall</title>
    <link rel="stylesheet" href="../styles/main.css">
    <link rel="stylesheet" href="../styles/speaker.css">
</head>
```

The sequence in which styles are applied

- From the first external style sheet to the last

Description

- When you use *external style sheets*, you separate content (HTML) from formatting (CSS). That makes it easy to use the same styles for two or more pages.

- If you use *embedded styles*, you have to copy the styles to other documents before you can use them in those documents.

- If more than one rule for the same property is applied to the same element, the last rule overrides the earlier rules.

- When you specify a relative URL for an external CSS file, the URL is relative to the current file.

Figure 1-11   How to provide CSS styles for an HTML page

How to code the basic CSS selectors

Figure 1-12 shows how to code the basic *CSS selectors* for applying styles to HTML elements. To start, this figure shows the body of an HTML document that contains a main and a footer element. Here, the two <p> elements in the main element have class attributes with the value "blue". Also, the <p> element in the footer has an id attribute with the value "copyright" and a class attribute with two values: "blue" and "right". This means that this element is assigned to two classes.

The four rule sets in the first group of examples are *type selectors*. To code a type selector, you just code the name of the element. As a result, the first rule set in this group selects the body element. The second rule set selects the main element. The third rule set selects the h1 element. And the fourth rule set selects all <p> elements.

In these examples, the first rule set changes the font for the body, and all of the elements within the body inherit this change. This rule set also sets the width of the body and centers it in the browser. Then, the second rule set puts a border around the main element and puts some padding inside the border. It also makes the main element a block element. This is necessary for IE because it doesn't treat the main element as a block element.

The third rule set that uses a type selector sets the margins for the heading. In this case, all the margins are set to zero except for the bottom margin. Last, the rule set for the paragraphs sets the margins for the top, bottom, and left side of the paragraphs. That's why the paragraphs in the main element are indented.

The rule set in the second group of examples uses an *id selector* to select an element by its id. To do that, the selector is a pound sign (#) followed by the id value that uniquely identifies an element. As a result, this rule set selects the <p> element that has an id of "copyright". Then, its one rule sets the font size for the paragraph to 90% of the default size.

The two rule sets in the last group of examples use *class selectors* to select HTML elements by class. To do that, the selector is a period (.) followed by the class name. As a result, the first rule set selects all elements that have been assigned to the "blue" class, which are all three <p> elements. The second rule set selects any elements that have been assigned to the "right" class. That is the paragraph in the footer. Then, the first rule set sets the color of the font to blue and the second rule set aligns the paragraph on the right.

One of the key points here is that a class attribute can have the same value for more than one element on a page. Then, if you code a selector for that class, it will be used to format all the elements in that class. In contrast, since the id for an element must be unique, an id selector can only be used to format a single element.

As you probably know, there are several other selectors that you can use with CSS. But the ones in this figure will get you started. Then, whenever an application in this book requires other selectors, the selectors will be explained in detail.

HTML that can be selected by element type, id, or class

```
<body>
    <main>
        <h1>The Speaker Lineup</h1>
        <p class="blue">October 19: Jeffrey Toobin</p>
        <p class="blue">November 16: Andrew Ross Sorkin</p>
    </main>
    <footer>
        <p id="copyright" class="blue right">Copyright SJV Town Hall</p>
    </footer>
</body>
```

CSS rule sets that select by element type, id, and class

Four elements by type

```
body {
    font-family: Arial, Helvetica, sans-serif;
    width: 400px;
    margin: 1em auto; }
main {
    display: block;
    padding: 1em;
    border: 2px solid black; }
h1 { margin: 0 0 .25em; }
p { margin: .25em 0 .25em 3em; }
```

One element by ID

```
#copyright { font-size: 90%; }
```

Elements by class

```
.blue { color: blue; }
.right { text-align: right; }
```

The elements displayed in a browser

Description

- You code a selector for all elements of a specific type by naming the element. This is referred to as a *type selector*.
- You code a selector for an element with an id attribute by coding a pound sign (#) followed by the id value. This is known as an *id selector*.
- You code a selector for an element with a class attribute by coding a period followed by the class name. Then, the rule set applies to all elements with that class name. This is known as a *class selector*.

Figure 1-12   How to code the basic CSS selectors

How to code CSS rule sets

Figure 1-13 presents the CSS for the Email List application that was presented earlier in this chapter. This is typical of the CSS for the applications in this book. Since the focus of this book is on JavaScript, not CSS, the CSS for the book applications is usually limited. For instance, the CSS in this example doesn't require id or class selectors.

Just to make sure we're using the same terminology, this CSS contains six *rule sets*. Each rule set consists of a selector, a set of braces { }, and one or more *rules* within the braces. Also, each rule consists of a *property name*, a colon, the value or values for the property, and an ending semicolon.

For instance, the first rule set is for the body element. It consists of six rules that set the font, background color, margins, width, padding, and border for the body. Here, the margin rule sets the top and bottom margins to zero and the left and right margins to "auto", which means the body will be centered in the browser window. In addition, the padding rule sets the top padding to zero, the left and right padding to 2 ems, and the bottom padding to 1 em. (An *em* is a typesetting term that is approximately equal to the width of a capital letter M.)

The second rule set is for the h1 element, and its one rule sets the color of the font to blue. The third rule set is for the label elements, and the fourth rule set is for the input elements. The third rule set floats the labels to the left of the input elements, sets the labels to a width of 11 ems, and aligns the text in the labels on the right. Then, the fourth rule set sets the left margin of the input elements to 1 em so there's separation between the labels and text boxes, and it sets the bottom margin to .5 em so there's some vertical spacing between the rows of labels and input elements.

The last rule set is for the span elements that follow the input elements. It just sets the color of the text in these elements to red because these elements will display the error messages for the application.

Beyond this brief introduction to CSS, this book will explain any of the CSS that is relevant to the JavaScript for an application. So for now, if you understand the rule sets in this figure, you're ready to continue.

The CSS file for a typical application in this book

```css
body {
    font-family: Arial, Helvetica, sans-serif;
    background-color: white;
    margin: 0 auto;
    width: 670px;
    padding: 0 2em 1em;
    border: 3px solid blue;
}
h1 {
    color: blue;
}
label {
    float: left;
    width: 11em;
    text-align: right;
}
input {
    margin-left: 1em;
    margin-bottom: .5em;
}
span {
    color: red;
}
```

Description

- Because the focus of this book is on JavaScript, not CSS, the CSS that's used in this book is usually simple. We just apply enough CSS to make each application look okay and work correctly.

- In fact, for most of the applications in this book, you won't have to understand the CSS so it won't even be shown. Whenever the CSS is critical to the understanding of the JavaScript application, though, it will be explained in detail.

- At the least, you should know that the CSS for an HTML document consists of one or more *rule sets*. Each of these rule sets starts with the selector for the rule set followed by a set of braces { }. Within the braces are one or more rules.

- You should also know that each CSS *rule* consists of a *property name*, a colon, the value or values for the property, and a semicolon.

Figure 1-13   How to code CSS rule sets

How to test a JavaScript application

Next, you'll learn how to test a JavaScript application. To do that, you run the HTML for the web page that uses the JavaScript.

How to run a JavaScript application

When you develop a JavaScript application, you're usually working on your own computer or your company's server. Then, to run the application, you use one of the four methods shown in figure 1-14. Of the four, it's easiest to run the HTML page from the IDE that you're using to develop the HTML, CSS, and JavaScript files. You'll learn more about that in a moment.

Otherwise, you can open the HTML file from your browser. To do that, you can press Ctrl+O to start the Open command. Or, you can find the file using the file explorer for your system and double-click on it. If you're using Windows, for example, you can find the file using Windows Explorer. That will open the page in your system's default browser. Of course, you can also run a new page by clicking on the link to it in the current page.

After an application has been uploaded to an Internet web server, you can use the second set of methods in this figure to run the application. The first way is to enter a *Uniform Resource Locator* (*URL*) into the address bar of your browser. The second way is to click on a link in one web page that requests another page.

As the diagram in this figure shows, the URL for an Internet page consists of four components. In most cases, the *protocol* is HTTP. If you omit the protocol, the browser uses HTTP as the default.

The second component is the *domain name* that identifies the web server that the HTTP request will be sent to. The web browser uses this name to look up the address of the web server for the domain. Although you can't omit the domain name, you can often omit the "www." from the domain name.

The third component is the *path* where the file resides on the server. The path lists the folders that contain the file. Forward slashes are used to separate the names in the path and to represent the server's top-level folder at the start of the path. In this example, the path is "/ourwork/".

The last component is the name of the file. In this example, the file is named index.html. If you omit the filename, the web server will search for a default document in the path. Depending on the web server, this file will be named index.html, default.htm, or some variation of the two.

The web page at c:/javascript/book_apps/ch01/email_list/index.html

Four ways to run an HTML page that's on your own server or computer

- Use the Ctrl+O shortcut key combination to start the Open command from your browser. Then, browse to the HTML file for the application and double-click on it.
- Use the file explorer on your system to find the HTML file and double-click on it.
- Use the features of your text editor or IDE.
- Click on a link in the current web page to load the next web page.

Two ways to run an HTML page that's on the Internet

- Enter the URL of the web page into the browser's address bar.
- Click on a link in the current web page to load the next web page.

The components of an HTTP URL on the Internet

What happens if you omit parts of a URL

- If you omit the protocol, the default of http:// will be used.
- If you omit the filename, the default document name for the web server will be used. This is typically index.html, default.htm, or some variation.

Description

- When you are developing JavaScript applications, you usually store them on your own computer instead of the Internet. So when you test the applications, you run them from your own computer.
- Later, after the applications are deployed to your Internet web server, you can run the applications from the Internet.

Figure 1-14   How to run a JavaScript application

How to find errors in your code

As you enter and test even the simplest of applications, you're likely to have errors in your code. When that happens, the JavaScript may not run at all, or it may run for a short while and then stop. That's why figure 1-15 shows you how to find the errors in your code.

As this figure shows, if a JavaScript application doesn't run or stops running, you start by opening the *developer tools*. Although there are several ways to do that, you'll use the F12 key most of the time. That's why the developer tools for Chrome and other browsers are often referred to as the *F12 tools*.

Next, you open the Console panel of the developer tools to see if there's an error message. In this figure, the console shows a message for an error that occurred when the user started the Email List application, clicked on the Join our List button, and nothing happened. Then, if you click on the link to the right of the error message, the JavaScript source code is displayed with the statement that caused the error highlighted. In this case, the problem is that "email_address" should be "email_address2" since that's the id of the second text box in the HTML.

Since jQuery is a JavaScript library, this technique also works for jQuery applications. However, if the error occurs on a statement that's in the jQuery library, it means that there is something wrong in the JavaScript that called the jQuery method. In chapter 4, you'll learn more about testing and debugging, but this technique will be all that you need until your applications get more complicated.

Chrome with an open Console panel that shows an error

The Sources panel after the link in the Console panel has been clicked

How to open or close Chrome's developer tools

- To open the developer tools, press F12 or Ctrl+Shift+I. Or, click on the Menu button in the upper right corner of the browser, and select More Tools→Developer Tools.

- To close the developer tools, click on the X in the upper right corner of the tools panel or press F12.

How to find the JavaScript statement that caused the error

- Open the Console panel by clicking on the Console tab. You should see an error message like the one above along with the line of code that caused the error.

- Click on the link to the right of the error message that indicates the line of code. That will open the Sources panel with the portion of JavaScript code that contains the statement displayed and the statement highlighted.

Description

- Chrome's *developer tools* provide some excellent debugging features, like identifying the JavaScript statement that caused an error.

- Because you usually start the developer tools by pressing the F12 key, these tools are often referred to as the *F12 tools*.

Figure 1-15   How to find errors in your code

How to provide cross-browser compatibility

If you want your website to be used by as many visitors as possible, you need to make sure that your web pages are compatible with as many browsers as possible. That's known as *cross-browser compatibility*. That means you should test your applications on as many browsers as possible, including the five browsers in the table in figure 1-16. This table shows the variance in the levels of HTML5 compatibility for these browsers, which is significant.

Today, all modern browsers support the HTML5 semantic elements so you shouldn't have any problems with those browsers. It's the older browsers that you may need to be concerned about, especially IE7 and IE8 because they still represent a significant portion of the market. That's why this figure presents a workaround for making your applications work with these older browsers.

This workaround is called the *JavaScript shiv*. It ensures that the HTML5 elements will work with older browsers. To implement it, you code the first script element shown in this figure within the head element for a page. This shiv loads a JavaScript file into the web page that provides HTML5 compatibility with older browsers.

While you're learning, you won't need to test your web pages on old browsers. That's why the JavaScript shiv isn't used by any of the applications in this book. For production applications, though, you usually do need to provide for compatibility with older browsers. As you will see in chapter 4, you can test for compatibility with older versions of IE by using the developer tools for the current version of IE.

Just so you're aware of it, this figure also shows how to use the normalize.css style sheet to fix minor browser differences. To do that, you download the style sheet and include it as the first style sheet for all of your web pages. In this book, though, it isn't used for any of the applications so you might see some occasional variances between browsers. In that case, you may want to try using this style sheet to see whether it resolves the variances.

By the way, IE11 still doesn't support the HTML5 main element. To provide support for this element, though, you just need to use CSS to set its display property to block, as shown in the example in figure 1-12. Or, you can use the JavaScript shiv or the normalize.css style sheet to fix this problem.

The current browsers and their HTML5 ratings

Browser	Release	HTML5 Test Rating
Google Chrome	43	526
Opera	29	519
Mozilla Firefox	38	467
Apple Safari	8	396
Internet Explorer	11	336

The website for these ratings

`http://www.html5test.com`

The code that includes the JavaScript shiv for HTML5 compatibility

`<script src="http://html5shiv.googlecode.com/svn/trunk/html5.js"></script>`

What the shiv does

- A JavaScript *shiv* (or *shim*) forces older browsers, like Internet Explorer 7 and 8, to recognize the HTML5 semantic elements and let you apply CSS to these elements.

- The effect of the shiv is to add the HTML5 semantic elements to the DOM in the browser and also to add a CSS rule set that tells the browser to treat the HTML5 elements as block elements instead of inline elements.

The URL for downloading the normalize.css style sheet

http://necolas.github.io/normalize.css/

What the normalize.css style sheet does

- Normalize.css is a style sheet that makes minor adjustments to browser defaults so all browsers render HTML elements the same way.

- For instance, the normalize.css style sheet sets the margins for the body of the document to zero so there's no space between the body and the edge of the browser window. The normalize.css style sheet also sets the default font family for the document to sans-serif.

Description

- Today, there are still differences in the way that different browsers handle HTML and CSS. As a developer, though, you want your web pages to work on as many different web browsers as possible. This is referred to as *cross-browser compatibility*.

- At this writing, you still need to provide workarounds for IE7 and IE8, but you shouldn't need to provide for other old browsers. However, you do need to provide for the main element in all current versions of IE.

- Eventually, all browsers will support HTML5 and CSS3 so the workarounds won't be necessary.

- To provide browser compatibility, you can use the *JavaScript shiv* and the *normalize.css style sheet*. However, neither are used in the applications for this book.

- Today, you can use the developer tools for IE11 to emulate older versions of IE, which makes it easier to test whether your applications run correctly in those browsers.

Figure 1-16   How to provide cross-browser compatibility

How to use Aptana to develop JavaScript applications

Because HTML, CSS, and JavaScript are just text, you can use any text editor to create the files for a JavaScript application. However, a better editor or an *Integrated Development Environment* (*IDE*) can speed development time and reduce coding errors. That's why we recommend Aptana Studio 3. It is a free IDE that runs on Windows, Mac OS, and Linux, and it can greatly improve your productivity.

In appendix A of this book, you can learn how to install Aptana. You can also learn how to use Aptana for the common development functions in the topics that follow. If you prefer to use another editor, you can skip these topics. But even then, you may want to browse these topics because they will give you a good idea of what an IDE should be able to do. They may also encourage you to give Aptana a try.

How to create or import a project

In Aptana, a *project* consists of the folders and files for a complete web application. Once you create a project, it's easier to work with its folders and files, to create new files for the project, and so forth.

To create a project, you use the first command in figure 1-17 and complete the dialog boxes. The result is a named project that starts with the top-level folder for the application. Then, you can easily access the folders and files for the application by using the App Explorer window that's shown in the next figure.

To make it easier to work with the applications for this book, we recommend that you import them into one Aptana project that includes all of the book applications. To do that, you can use the second procedure in this figure. The dialog boxes in this figure import the downloaded book applications at this location

`c:/murach/jquery/book_apps`

into a project named jQuery Book Apps. Once that's done, you can easily access the applications by using the App Explorer window.

The dialog boxes for importing a project in Aptana 3.4 or later

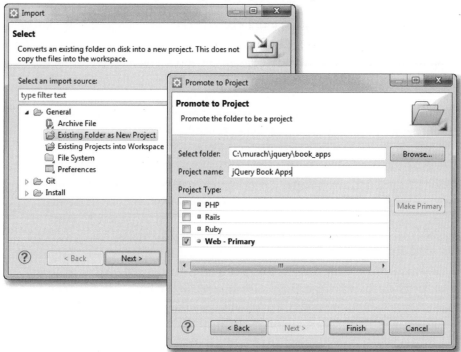

How to create a new project

- Use the File→New→Web Project command.

How to import a project with Aptana 3.4 or later

- Use the File→Import command to display the Import dialog box, click on Existing Folder as New Project, and click Next.
- In the Promote to Project dialog box, browse to the top-level folder for the application, enter a project name, and click the Finish button.

Description

- Aptana works the best when you set up projects for the web applications that you're developing and maintaining.
- In general, each Aptana *project* should contain the folders and files for one web application. For this book, however, you can set up one project for all of the book applications, one project for all exercises, and one project for all exercise solutions.

Figure 1-17   How to create or import a project in Aptana

How to work with files

Figure 1-18 shows how to open or close an HTML, CSS, or JavaScript file after you've created a project. Here, the JavaScript Book Apps project is shown in the App Explorer window on the left side of Aptana. If you have created more than one project, you can switch from one to another by using the drop-down project list that's at the top of the App Explorer window.

Once you have the correct project open, you can drill down to the file that you want to open by clicking on the ◢ symbols for the folders. In this example, the ch01 and email_list folders have been expanded so you can see the four files for the Email List application. Then, to open a file, you just double-click on it.

When you open a file in Aptana, it is opened in a new tab. This means that you can have several files open at the same time and move from one to another by clicking on a tab. This makes it easy to switch back and forth between the HTML, CSS, and JavaScript files for a web page. This also makes it easy to copy code from one file to another.

If you want to open a file that isn't part of a project, you can do that by using one of the methods shown in this figure. First, you can use the Project Explorer window to locate the file on your computer and then double-click on it. Second, you can use the File→Open File command to open a file.

To close one or more files, you can use one of the three methods shown in this figure. This makes it easy to close all of the files except the ones that you're currently working with. And that helps you avoid the mistake of making a change to the wrong file.

This figure ends by showing how to start a new file. Most important is to name the file with the appropriate extension (.html, .css, or .js) depending on whether it is going to be an HTML, CSS, or JavaScript file. Then, Aptana will know what type of file it is, and its editor will be adjusted to the syntax of that type of file when it is opened.

As you work with Aptana, you'll see that it has the same type of interface that you've used with other programs. So if you want to do something that isn't presented in this chapter, try right-clicking on an item to see what menu options are available. Check out the other buttons in the toolbar. See what's available from the drop-down menus. With a little experimentation, you'll find that this program is not only powerful, but also easy to use.

Before you go on, you should notice the two yellow triangles with exclamation marks in them to the left of lines 1 and 5 in the JavaScript file. As you'll learn in the next figure, Aptana uses these markers to indicate warnings. In this case, Aptana thinks that a semicolon is needed after the closing brackets on lines 3 and 28. This isn't required, though, and most programmers don't include these semicolons.

Aptana with the App Explorer shown and a JavaScript file in the second tab

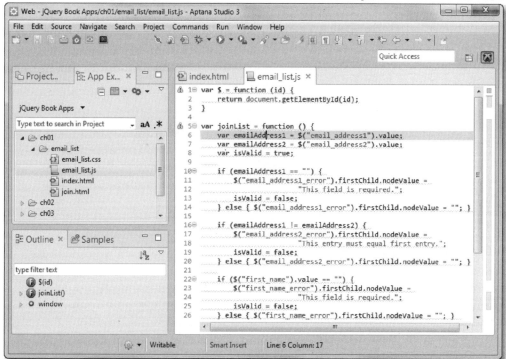

How to open a file within a project

- Use the drop-down list in Aptana's App Explorer to select the project. Then, locate the file in the App Explorer and double-click on it.

Two ways to open a file that isn't in a project

- Use the Project Explorer to locate the file, and double-click on it.
- Use the File→Open File command.

How to close one or more files

- To close one file, click on the X in the tab for the file.
- To close all of the files except one, right click on the tab you don't want to close and select Close Others.
- To close all of the files, right click on any tab and select Close All.

How to start a new file

- To start an HTML, CSS, or JavaScript file, select the File→New→File command. Then, in the New File dialog box, select the folder that the file should be stored in, enter a filename for the new file with an extension (.html, .css, or .js), and click the Finish button.
- To start a new file from another file, use the File→Save As command to save the file with a new name.

Figure 1-18   How to work with files in Aptana

How to edit a file

Figure 1-19 shows how to edit a JavaScript file with Aptana, but editing works the same for HTML and CSS files. When you open a file with an html, css, or js extension, Aptana knows what type of file you're working with so it can use color to highlight the syntax components. The good news is that color coding is also used for CSS that's in a style element of an HTML document or JavaScript that's in a script element of an HTML document.

As you enter a new line of code, the auto-completion feature presents lists of words that start with the letters that you've entered. This type of list is illustrated by this figure. Here, the list shows the JavaScript choices after the letter *t* has been entered. Then, you can select a word and press the Tab key to insert it into your code.

This also works with HTML and CSS entries. If, for example, you type <s in an HTML document, Aptana presents a list of the elements that start with s. Then, if you select one of the elements, Aptana finishes the opening tag and adds the closing tag. This feature also works when you start an attribute.

Similarly, if you enter # to start a CSS rule set, Aptana presents a list of the ids that can be used in an id selector. If you enter *b* to start a rule, Aptana presents a list of the properties that start with b. And if you start an entry for a property value, Aptana will present a list of values. In short, this is a powerful feature that can help you avoid many entry errors.

Beyond that, Aptana provides error markers and warning markers that help you find and correct errors. In this figure, for example, you can see two error markers and a warning marker. Then, to get the description for a marker, you can hover the mouse over the marker.

As you're editing, you may want to enlarge the editing area by closing the side pane and restoring that pane later on. Or you may want to close the Project Explorer, as shown in this figure, because you don't use it often. To work with the panes and the Explorers, you can use the third set of procedures in this figure.

Last, if you want to change the colors that are used by the editor, you can use the fourth procedure in this figure. In this book, we use the Dreamweaver theme, but you can experiment with other themes until you find one that you like. If you click the Apply button after you select a theme, you can see the colors that are used in the window behind the dialog box. Then, if you like the colors, you can click the OK button to close the dialog box.

Aptana with an auto-completion list for a JavaScript entry

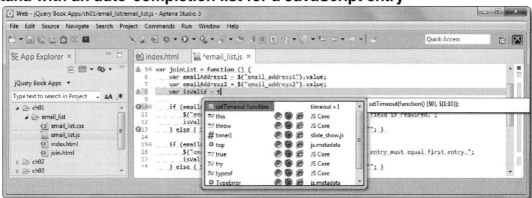

How to use the auto-completion feature

- The auto-completion feature displays a list of items that start with what you've typed. To insert one of those items, double-click on it or use the arrow keys to highlight it and press the Tab key.

- For some JavaScript statements, like an if statement, the editor will insert a snippet that contains the starting code including parentheses and braces.

How to identify the errors that are marked by the Aptana editor

- An error marker is a red circle that contains a white X at the start of a line. A warning marker is a yellow triangle that contains an exclamation mark. These markers are displayed as you enter and edit code.

- To get the description for an error or warning marker, hover the mouse over the marker.

How to hide and restore the Project and App Explorers

- To hide the Project or App Explorer, click on the X in its tab. To display the Project or App Explorer, use the Window→Show View→App Explorer or Project Explorer command.

- To hide the pane on the left side of the window, click on its minimize button. To restore the pane, click on the Restore icon at the top of the vertical bar that's to the left or right of the editing window.

How to set the colors that are used to highlight the syntax

- Use the Window→Preferences command to open the Preferences dialog box.

- Click on Aptana Studio, and then click on Themes to display the Themes dialog box.

- Choose a theme from the Editor Theme list. (This book uses the Dreamweaver theme.)

Description

- Aptana provides many features that make it easier to enter and edit JavaScript code.

- Aptana provides many ways to display the panes for its many features.

Figure 1-19   How to edit a file in Aptana

How to run a JavaScript application

Figure 1-20 shows how to run a JavaScript application from Aptana. To do that, you open the HTML file for the application. Or, if the HTML file is already open, you click on its tab to select it as shown in this figure. Then, you click on the Run button. This opens the default browser and runs the file in that browser. You can also run an HTML file in another browser using the drop-down list to the right of the Run button.

Before you run a JavaScript application, you need to save any changes to the HTML file and its related files. To do that, you can click on the Save or Save All button in the toolbar. If you don't save the files before you click the Run button, though, you'll get a warning message with an option that will save the files for you.

When you run a JavaScript application this way, a new browser or browser tab is opened each time you click the Run button. So, if you click on the Run button 10 times for an application, 10 browsers or tabs will be opened.

Another way to do this, though, is to run an application the first time by clicking on the Run button. Then, after you find and fix the errors in Aptana, you can click on the Save All button in Aptana to save the changes, switch to the browser, and click on the Reload or Refresh button in the browser to reload the application with the changes. That way, you use the same tab or Browser instance each time you test the application.

Aptana's Run button

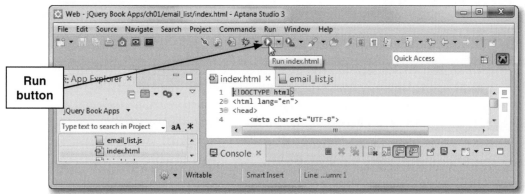

The web page in Chrome

How to run a JavaScript application from Aptana

- Before you run a file, you should save any changes that you've made to it or any of its related files. To do that, you can click on the Save or Save All button in the toolbar.

- To run a JavaScript application in the default browser, open the HTML file for the application, select its tab, and click on the Run button. (The Run button won't work if the HTML file isn't the one that's selected.)

- To run a JavaScript application in another browser, select the tab for its HTML file, click the down-arrow to the right of the Run button, and select the browser.

Description

- When you test an application, you run its HTML page. Then, you can note the errors, fix the errors in Aptana, save the changes, and run the page again.

- Every time you run a page from Aptana, another browser instance or browser tab is opened. Another alternative is to save the corrected files in Aptana, switch to the browser, and click its Reload or Refresh button. That way, another browser or tab isn't opened.

Figure 1-20   How to run a JavaScript application from Aptana

Perspective

This chapter has presented the background concepts and terms that you need for developing JavaScript applications. Now, if you're comfortable with everything that you've learned, you're ready for chapter 2.

But what if you aren't comfortable with your HTML and CSS skills? First, we recommend that you keep going in this book because you don't have to be an HTML or CSS expert to develop JavaScript applications. Second, we recommend that you get a copy of *Murach's HTML5 and CSS3*, because every web developer should eventually master HTML5 and CSS3.

Terms you should know

client	CSS (Cascading Style Sheets)
web browser	DOM scripting
web server	Document Object Model (DOM)
network	HTML5 semantic elements
intranet	HTML5 semantics
local area network (LAN)	attribute
Internet	id attribute
wide area network (WAN)	class attribute
Internet service provider (ISP)	name attribute
HTML (HyperText Markup	for attribute
Language)	title attribute
static web page	external style sheet
HTTP request	embedded styles
HTTP (HyperText Transfer Protocol)	CSS selector
HTTP response	type selector
render a web page	id selector
dynamic web page	class selector
application server	rule set
database server	rule
server-side processing	property name
round trip	URL (Uniform Resource Locator)
JavaScript	protocol
JavaScript engine	domain name
scripting language	path
client-side processing	developer tools
image swap	F12 tools
image rollover	cross-browser compatibility
data validation	JavaScript shiv
jQuery	IDE (Integrated Development
HTML element	Environment)
tag	Aptana project

Summary

- A web application consists of clients, a web server, and a network. *Clients* use *web browsers* to request web pages from the web server. The *web server* returns the requested pages.

- A *local area network* (*LAN*) connects computers that are near to each other. This is often called an *intranet*. In contrast, the *Internet* consists of many *wide area networks* (*WANs*).

- To request a web page, the web browser sends an *HTTP request* to the web server. Then, the web server gets the HTML for the requested page and sends it back to the browser in an *HTTP response*. Last, the browser *renders* the HTML into a web page.

- A *static web page* is a page that is the same each time it's retrieved. In contrast, the HTML for a *dynamic web page* is generated by a server-side program or script, so its HTML can change from one request to another.

- *JavaScript* is a *scripting language* that is run by the *JavaScript engine* of a web browser. It provides for *client-side processing*. *jQuery* is a JavaScript library that makes it easier to code many common functions.

- JavaScript is commonly used to modify the *Document Object Model* (*DOM*) that's built for each web page when it is loaded. This is referred to as *DOM scripting*. When the DOM is changed, the browser immediately changes its display so it reflects those changes.

- *HTML* (*HyperText Markup Language*) is the language that defines the structure and contents of a web page. *CSS* (*Cascading Style Sheets*) is used to control how the web pages are formatted.

- You can view a web page that's on your own computer or server or on an Internet server. To view a web page on an Internet server, you can enter the *URL* (*Uniform Resource Locator*) that consists of the *protocol*, *domain name*, *path*, and filename into a browser's address bar.

- To find errors when a JavaScript or jQuery application stops running or doesn't run at all, you can use Chrome's *developer tools* (or *F12 tools*).

- When you develop a JavaScript application, you need to provide for *cross-browser compatibility*. That means you have to test your applications on all modern browsers as well as older versions of those browsers.

- To provide compatibility with older browsers like IE7 and IE8, you can use the *JavaScript shiv* for the HTML5 semantic elements.

- To develop JavaScript applications, you can use a text editor or an *Integrated Development Environment* (*IDE*). For this book, we recommend Aptana Studio 3 because it's powerful, free, and runs on Windows, Mac, and Unix systems.

Before you do the exercises for this book...

Before you do the exercises for this book, you should download and install the Chrome browser as well as the applications for this book. If you're going to use Aptana, you should also download and install that product. The procedures for installing the software and applications for this book are in appendix A.

Exercise 1-1   Run the Email List application

In this exercise, you'll run the Email List application that's presented in figures 1-5, 1-6, and 1-7.

1. Start Chrome if it isn't already open. Then, open this HTML file:

    `c:\murach\jquery\book_apps\ch01\email_list\index.html`

2. To test what happens when you don't enter any data, just click the Join our List button without entering any data. Then, you can see the error messages that are displayed.

3. Enter an email address in the first text box and invalid data in the second text box and click the Join our List button to see what error messages are displayed.

4. Enter valid data for all three text boxes and click on the button. Then, the data is submitted for processing and a new web page is displayed.

Exercise 1-2   Run other section 1 applications

This exercise has you run the applications presented in chapter 3. These applications will give you some idea of what you'll able to do when you complete this section.

1. Open this file in the Chrome browser:

    `c:\murach\jquery\book_apps\ch03\faqs\index.html`

    Then, click on one of the headings to display the text for it, and click the heading again to hide the text.

2. Open this file in the Chrome browser:

    `c:\murach\jquery\book_apps\ch03\image_swap\index.html`

    Then, click on the small images to see the large image get swapped.

3. Open this file in the Chrome browser:

    `c:\murach\jquery\book_apps\ch03\slide_show\index.html`

    Watch the slide show.

Exercise 1-3   Get started with Aptana

This exercise is for readers who are going to use Aptana with this book. It guides you through the process of creating projects that provide easy access to the book applications and exercises that you've downloaded.

Create the projects

1. Start Aptana, and use the procedure in figure 1-17 to create a project for the book applications that are stored in this folder:

   `c:\murach\jquery\book_apps`

   This project should be named jQuery Book Apps, and the entries for the last dialog box should be just like those in this figure.

2. Use the same procedure to create a project named jQuery Exercises for the exercises that are stored in this folder:

   `c:\jquery\exercises`

   as well as a project named jQuery Solutions for the exercise solutions that are stored in this folder:

   `c:\murach\jquery\solutions`

Test the Email List application

3. Use the drop-down list in the App Explorer to select the jQuery Exercises project. This provides access to all of the exercises that are in this book.

4. Click on the ◢ symbol before ch01 to display the email_list folder, and click on the ◢ symbol for the email_list folder to display the files for the Email List application.

5. Double-click on the file named index.html to open that file. Then, click the Run button in the toolbar to run the application in the default browser. That will automatically switch you to that browser.

6. Switch back to Aptana, and click on the down arrow to the right of the Run button. If the drop-down list offers Internet Explorer, click on it to run the application in that browser. Then, return to Aptana.

Edit the JavaScript code

7. In the App Explorer, double click on the file named email_list.js to open that file, and note the colors that are used for syntax highlighting.

8. If you don't like the colors that are used, use the procedure in figure 1-19 to change them.

9. In the JavaScript file, delete the right parenthesis in the first line of code. This should display two error markers. Then, hover the mouse over the markers to display the error descriptions. This illustrates Aptana's error-checking feature. Now, undo the change that you made. (To undo a change with the keyboard, press Ctrl+Z.)

10. In the JavaScript file, after the third statement that starts with var, start a statement on a new line with these characters:

    ```
    if (e
    ```

    This should display a list of the possible entries that start with the letter *e*. Here, you can see that emailAddress1 and emailAddress2 are included in the list. These are the variables that are created by the first two var statements, and this illustrates Aptana's auto-completion feature. Now, undo this change.

11. Enter this statement on a new line that comes right before the last line of the JavaScript code, which consists of just a right brace (}):

    ```
    alert("The DOM has now been built");
    ```

    In other words, this statement will become the second last line in the file.

12. To test the statement that you've added, click on the Save All button in the toolbar to save your changes. Then, switch to your browser and click on the Reload or Refresh button to run the application with this change. This should display a dialog box that you can close by clicking on its OK button. After that, the application should work the same as it did before.

13. If you're curious, do more experimenting on your own. Then, close the files and exit from Aptana.

2

A JavaScript subset for jQuery users

This chapter presents the JavaScript skills that you need for using jQuery. If you already know how to program in JavaScript, you can just skim this chapter to make sure you have the required skills. If you don't know JavaScript, but know how to program in another language, this chapter should get you up-to-speed with JavaScript. And if you don't have any programming experience, you can think of this chapter as a crash course in JavaScript.

The basics of JavaScript

The first three figures in this chapter get you started with JavaScript programming. If you already know how to use a language like Java or PHP, you'll quickly see the similarities.

How to include JavaScript in an HTML document

Figure 2-1 presents two ways to include JavaScript in an HTML document. As you saw in the last chapter, one way is to code the JavaScript in a separate *external file*. Then, you code a script element in the head section of the HTML document to include that file.

In the script element, the src attribute is used to refer to the external file. For this element, you can also code a type attribute with the value "text/javascript" to tell the browser what kind of content the file contains. But with HTML5, that attribute is no longer needed because the assumption is that all files that are referred to in script elements contain JavaScript.

In the example in this figure, the src attribute refers to a file named calculate_mpg.js. The assumption here is that this file is in the same folder as the HTML file. Otherwise, you need to code a relative URL that provides the right path for the file. If, for example, the JavaScript file is in a folder named javascript and that folder is in the same folder as the HTML file, the src attribute would be coded this way:

```
<script src="javascript/calculate_mpg.js"></script>
```

This works the same as it does for any other file reference in an HTML document.

The second way to include JavaScript in an HTML document is to code the JavaScript within the script element in the head section. This can be referred to as *embedded JavaScript*. Note, however, that the application will work the same whether the JavaScript is embedded in the head section or loaded into the head section from an external file.

The benefit of using an external file is that it separates the JavaScript from the HTML. Another benefit is that it makes it easier to re-use the code in other pages or applications.

The benefit of using embedded JavaScript is that you don't have to switch between the HTML and JavaScript files as you develop the application. In the examples in this book, you'll see both uses of JavaScript.

Two attributes of the script element

Attribute	Description
`src`	Specifies the location (source) of an external JavaScript file.
`type`	With HTML5, this attribute can be omitted. If you code it, use "text/javascript" for JavaScript code.

A script element in the head section that loads an external JavaScript file

```
<script src="calculate_mpg.js"></script>
```

A script element that embeds JavaScript in the head section

```
<head>
    ...
    <script>
        alert("The Calculate MPG application");
        var miles = prompt("Enter miles driven");
        miles = parseFloat(miles);
        var gallons = prompt("Enter gallons of gas used");
        gallons = parseFloat(gallons);
        var mpg = miles/gallons;
        mpg = parseInt(mpg);
        alert("Miles per gallon = " + mpg);
    </script>
</head>
```

Description

- A script element in the head section of an HTML document is commonly used to identify an *external JavaScript file* that should be included with the page.

- A script element in the head section can also contain the JavaScript statements that are included with the page. This can be referred to as *embedded JavaScript.*

- If you code more than one script element in the head section, the JavaScript is included in the sequence in which the script statements appear.

- When a script element in the head section includes an external JavaScript file, the JavaScript in the file runs as if it were coded in the script element.

- Some programmers prefer to place their script elements at the bottom of the page, just before the closing body tag. This can make a page seem to load faster, but the JavaScript won't run until after the page is loaded.

Figure 2-1   How to include JavaScript in an HTML document

How to code JavaScript statements

The *syntax* of JavaScript refers to the rules that you must follow as you code statements. If you don't adhere to these rules, your web browser won't be able to interpret and execute your statements.

Figure 2-2 summarizes the rules for coding *JavaScript statements*. The first rule is that JavaScript is case-sensitive. This means that uppercase and lowercase letters are treated as different letters. For example, *salestax* and *salesTax* are treated as different names.

The second rule is that JavaScript statements must end with a semicolon. If you don't end each statement with a semicolon, JavaScript won't be able to tell where one statement ends and the next one begins.

The third rule is that JavaScript ignores extra whitespace in statements. Since *whitespace* includes spaces, tabs, and new line characters, this lets you break long statements into multiple lines so they're easier to read.

Be careful, though, to follow the guidelines in this figure about where to split a statement. If you don't split a statement at a good spot, JavaScript will sometimes try to help you out by adding a semicolon for you, and that can lead to errors.

Within your JavaScript coding, you can use *comments* to add descriptive notes that are ignored by the JavaScript engine. Later on, these comments can help you or someone else understand the code whenever it needs to be modified.

The example in this figure shows how comments can be used to describe or explain portions of code. At the start, a *block comment* describes what the application does. This kind of comment starts with /* and ends with */. Everything that's coded between the start and the end is ignored by the JavaScript engine when the application is run.

The other kind of comment is a *single-line comment* that starts with //. In the example, the first single-line comment describes what the JavaScript that comes before it on the same line does. In contrast, the second single-line comment takes up a line by itself. It describes what the function that comes after it does.

In addition to describing JavaScript code, comments can be useful when testing an application. If, for example, you want to disable a portion of the JavaScript code, you can enclose it in a block comment. Then, it will be ignored when the application is run. This can be referred to as *commenting out* a portion of code.

Later, after you test the rest of the code, you can enable the commented out code by removing the markers for the start and end of the block comment. This can be referred to *uncommenting*.

A block of JavaScript code with the comments highlighted

```
/* this application validates a user's entries for joining
   our email list */
var $ = function (id) {                        // the standard $ function
    return document.getElementById(id);
}
// this function gets and validates the first user entry
var joinList = function () {
    var emailAddress1 = $("email_address1").value;
    var emailAddress2 = $("email_address2").value;

    if (emailAddress1 == "") {
        alert("Email Address is required.");
    } else {
        $("email_form").submit();
    }
}
```

The basic syntax rules

- JavaScript is case-sensitive.
- Each JavaScript statement ends with a semicolon.
- JavaScript ignores extra whitespace within statements.

How to split a statement over two or more lines

- Split a statement after:
    - an arithmetic or relational operator such as +, -, *, /, =, ==, >, or <
    - an opening brace ({), bracket ([ ), or parenthesis
    - a closing brace (})
- Do not split a statement after:
    - an identifier, a value, or the *return* keyword
    - a closing bracket ( ]) or closing parenthesis

How to code comments

- For a *single-line comment*, code two slashes followed by the comment.
- For a *block comment*, enclose the comment in /* and */ symbols.

Description

- *Whitespace* refers to the spaces, tab characters, and return characters in the code, and it is ignored by the compiler. As a result, you can use spaces, tab characters, and return characters to format your code so it's easier to read.
- In some cases, JavaScript will try to correct what it thinks is a missing semicolon by adding a semicolon at the end of a split line. To prevent this, follow the guidelines above for splitting a statement.
- During testing, comments can be used to *comment out* (disable) portions of code that you don't want tested. Then, you can remove the comments when you're ready to test those portions.

Figure 2-2   How to code JavaScript statements

How to create identifiers

Variables, functions, objects, properties, methods, and events must all have names so you can refer to them in your JavaScript code. An *identifier* is the name given to one of these components.

Figure 2-3 shows the rules for creating identifiers in JavaScript. Besides the first three rules, you can't use any of the JavaScript *reserved words* (also known as *keywords*) as an identifier. These are words that are reserved for use within the JavaScript language.

In addition to the rules, you should give your identifiers meaningful names. That means that it should be easy to tell what an identifier refers to and easy to remember how to spell the name. To create names like that, you should avoid abbreviations. If, for example, you abbreviate the name for monthly investment as mon_inv, it will be hard to tell what it refers to and hard to remember how you spelled it. But if you spell it out as monthly_investment, both problems are solved.

To create an identifier that has more than one word in it, many JavaScript programmers use a convention called *camel casing*. With this convention, the first letter of each word is uppercase except for the first word. For example, monthlyInvestment and taxRate are identifiers that use camel casing.

The alternative is to use underscore characters to separate the words in an identifier. For example, monthly_investment and tax_rate use this convention. If the standards in your shop specify one of these conventions, by all means use it. Otherwise, you can use whichever convention you prefer...but be consistent.

In this book, we use underscore notation for the ids and class names in the HTML and camel casing for all JavaScript identifiers. That way, it will be easier for you to tell where the names originated.

A JavaScript function with the identifiers highlighted

```
var processEntries = function() {
    var investment = parseFloat( $("investment").value );
    var rate = parseFloat( $("annual_rate").value );
    var years = parseInt( $("years").value );
    $("future_value").value = calculateFV(investment,rate,years);
}
```

Rules for creating identifiers

- Identifiers can only contain letters, numbers, the underscore, and the dollar sign.
- Identifiers can't start with a number.
- Identifiers are case-sensitive.
- Identifiers can't be the same as *reserved words*.

Valid identifiers in JavaScript

```
subtotal        index_1             $
taxRate         calculate_click     $log
```

Camel casing versus underscore notation

```
taxRate             tax_rate
calculateClick      calculate_click
emailAddress        email_address
```

Reserved words in JavaScript

```
abstract    else         instanceof    switch
boolean     enum         int           synchronized
break       export       interface     this
byte        extends      long          throw
case        false        native        throws
catch       final        new           transient
char        finally      null          true
class       float        package       try
const       for          private       typeof
continue    function     protected     var
debugger    goto         public        void
default     if           return        volatile
delete      implements   short         while
do          import       static        with
double      in           super
```

Naming recommendations

- Use meaningful names for identifiers. That way, your identifiers aren't likely to be reserved words.
- Be consistent: Either use camel casing (taxRate) or underscores (tax_rate) to identify the words within the variables in your scripts.

Description

- *Identifiers* are the names given to variables, functions, objects, properties, and methods.
- In *camel casing*, all of the words within an identifier except the first word start with capital letters.

Figure 2-3   How to create identifiers

How to use primitive data types to work with data

When you develop JavaScript applications, you frequently work with data, especially the data that users enter into the controls of a form. In the topics that follow, you'll learn how to work with the three types of JavaScript data.

The primitive data types

JavaScript provides for three *primitive data types*. The *number data type* is used to represent numerical data. The *string data type* is used to store character data. And the *Boolean data type* is used to store true and false values. This is summarized in figure 2-4.

The number data type can be used to represent either integers or decimal values. *Integers* are whole numbers, and *decimal values* are numbers that can have one or more decimal digits. The value of either data type can be coded with a preceding plus or minus sign. If the sign is omitted, the value is treated as a positive value. A decimal value can also include a decimal point and one or more digits to the right of the decimal point.

As the last example of the number types shows, you can also include an exponent when you code a decimal value. If you aren't familiar with this notation, you probably won't need to use it because you won't be working with very large or very small numbers. On the other hand, if you're familiar with scientific notation, you already know that this exponent indicates how many places the decimal point should be moved to the right or left. Numbers that use this notation are called *floating-point numbers.*

To represent string data, you code the *string* within single or double quotation marks (quotes). Note, however, that you must close the string with the same type of quotation mark that you used to start it. If you code two quotation marks in a row without even a space between them, the result is called an *empty string*, which can be used to represent a string with no data in it.

To represent Boolean data, you code either the word *true* or *false* with no quotation marks. This data type can be used to represent one of two states.

Examples of number values

```
15                  // an integer
-21                 // a negative integer
21.5                // a decimal value
-124.82             // a negative decimal value
-3.7e-9             // floating-point notation for -0.0000000037
```

Examples of string values

```
"JavaScript"        // a string with double quotes
'String Data'       // a string with single quotes
""                  // an empty string
```

The two Boolean values

```
true                // equivalent to true, yes, or on
false               // equivalent to false, no, or off
```

The number data type

- The *number data type* is used to represent an integer or a decimal value that can start with a positive or negative sign.

- An *integer* is a whole number. A *decimal value* can have one or more decimal positions to the right of the decimal point.

- If a result is stored in a number data type that is larger or smaller than the data type can store, it will be stored as the value Infinity or -Infinity.

What you need to know about floating-point numbers

- In JavaScript, decimal values are stored as *floating-point numbers*. In that format, a number consists of a positive or negative sign, one or more significant digits, an optional decimal point, optional decimal digits, and an optional exponent.

- Unless you're developing an application that requires the use of very large or very small numbers, you won't have to use floating-point notation to express numbers. If you need to use this notation, however, it is illustrated by the last example of number values above.

The string data type

- The *string data type* represents character (*string*) data. A string is surrounded by double quotes or single quotes. The string must start and end with the same type of quotation mark.

- An *empty string* is a string that contains no characters. It is entered by typing two quotation marks with nothing between them.

The Boolean data type

- The *Boolean data type* is used to represent a *Boolean value*. A Boolean value can be used to represent data that has two possible states: true or false.

Figure 2-4   The primitive data types

How to code numeric expressions

A *numeric expression* can be as simple as a single value or it can be a series of operations that result in a single value. In figure 2-5, you can see the operators for coding numeric expressions. If you've programmed in another language, these are probably similar to what you've been using. In particular, the first four *arithmetic operators* are common to most programming languages.

Most modern languages also have a *modulus operator* that calculates the remainder when the left value is divided by the right value. In the example for this operator, 13 % 4 means the remainder of 13 / 4. Then, since 13 / 4 is 3 with a remainder of 1, 1 is the result of the expression.

In contrast to the first five operators in this figure, the increment and decrement operators add or subtract one from a variable. To complicate matters, though, these operators can be coded before or after a variable name, and that can affect the result. To avoid confusion, then, we recommend that you only code these operators after the variable names and only in simple expressions like the one that you'll see in the next figure.

When an expression includes two or more operators, the *order of precedence* determines which operators are applied first. This order is summarized in the table in this figure. For instance, all multiplication and division operations are done from left to right before any addition and subtraction operations are done.

To override this order, though, you can use parentheses. Then, the expressions in the innermost sets of parentheses are done first, followed by the expressions in the next sets of parentheses, and so on. This is typical of all programming languages, as well as basic algebra, and the examples in this figure show how this works.

Common arithmetic operators

Operator	Description	Example	Result
+	Addition	`5 + 7`	`12`
-	Subtraction	`5 - 12`	`-7`
*	Multiplication	`6 * 7`	`42`
/	Division	`13 / 4`	`3.25`
%	Modulus	`13 % 4`	`1`
++	Increment	`counter++`	adds 1 to counter
--	Decrement	`counter--`	subtracts 1 from counter

The order of precedence for arithmetic expressions

Order	Operators	Direction	Description
1	`++`	Left to right	Increment operator
2	`--`	Left to right	Decrement operator
3	`* / %`	Left to right	Multiplication, division, modulus
4	`+ -`	Left to right	Addition, subtraction

Examples of precedence and the use of parentheses

```
3 + 4 * 5           // Result is 23 since the multiplication is done first
(3 + 4) * 5         // Result is 35 since the addition is done first

13 % 4 + 9          // Result is 10 since the modulus is done first
13 % (4 + 9)        // Result is 0  since the addition is done first

100 + 100 * 2       // Result is 300 since the multiplication is done first
100 + (100 * 2)     // Result is still 300 since the multiplication is first
```

Description

- To code a *numeric expression*, you can use the *arithmetic operators* to operate on two or more values.

- The *modulus operator* returns the remainder of a division operation.

- An arithmetic expression is evaluated based on the *order of precedence* of the operators.

- To override the order of precedence, you can use parentheses.

- Because the use of increment and decrement operators can be confusing, we recommend that you only use these operators in expressions that consist of just a variable name followed by the operator, as shown in the next figure.

Figure 2-5   How to code numeric expressions

How to work with numeric variables

A *variable* stores a value that can change as the program executes. When you code a JavaScript application, you frequently declare variables and assign values to them. Figure 2-6 shows how to do both of these tasks with numeric variables.

To *declare* a numeric variable in JavaScript, code the *var* (for variable) keyword followed by the identifier (or name) that you want to use for the variable. To declare more than one variable in a single statement, code *var* followed by the variable names separated by commas. This is illustrated by the first group of examples in this figure.

To assign a value to a variable, you code an *assignment statement*. This type of statement consists of a variable name, an *assignment operator* like =, and an expression. Here, the expression can be a *numeric literal* like 74.95, a variable name like subtotal, or an arithmetic expression. When the equals sign is the operator, the value of the expression on the right of the equals sign is stored in the variable on the left and replaces any previous value in the variable. The use of this operator is illustrated by the second group of examples.

The second operator in the table in this figure is the += operator, which is a *compound assignment operator*. It modifies the variable on the left of the operator by adding the value of the expression on the right to the value of the variable on the left. When you use this operator, the variable must already exist and have a value assigned to it. The use of this operator is illustrated by the third group of examples.

The fourth group of examples shows three different ways to increment a variable by adding one to it. As you will see throughout this book, this is a common JavaScript requirement. In this group, the first statement assigns a value of 1 to a variable named counter.

Then, the second statement in this group uses an arithmetic expression to add 1 to the value of the counter, which shows that a variable name can be used on both sides of the equals sign. The third statement adds one to the counter by using the += operator.

The last statement in this group uses the increment operator shown in the previous figure to add one to the counter. This illustrates our recommendation for the use of increment and decrement operators. Here, the numeric expression consists only of a variable name followed by the increment operator, and it doesn't include an assignment operator.

The last group of examples illustrates a potential problem that you should be aware of. Because decimal values are stored internally as floating-point numbers, the results of arithmetic operations aren't always precise. In this example, the salesTax result, which should be 7.495, is 7.495000000000001. Although this result is extremely close to 7.495, it isn't equal to 7.495, which could lead to a programming problem if you expect a comparison of the two values to be equal. The solution is to round the result, which you'll learn how to do later in this chapter.

The most useful assignment operators

Operator	Description
=	Assigns the result of the expression to the variable.
+=	Adds the result of the expression to the variable.

How to declare numeric variables without assigning values to them

```
var subtotal;                              // declares one variable
var investment, interestRate, years;       // declares three variables
```

How to declare variables and assign values to them

```
var subtotal = 74.00;           // subtotal = 74.00
var salesTax = subtotal * .1;   // salesTax = 7.4
```

How to code compound assignment statements

```
var subtotal = 74.95;           // subtotal = 74.95
subtotal += 20.00;              // subtotal = 94.95
```

Three ways to increment a variable named counter by 1

```
var counter = 1;                // counter = 1
counter = counter + 1;          // counter now = 2
counter += 1;                   // counter now = 3
counter++;                      // counter now = 4
```

A floating-point result that isn't precise

```
var subtotal = 74.95;           // subtotal = 74.95
var salesTax = subtotal * .1;   // salesTax = 7.495000000000001
```

Description

- A *variable* stores a value that can change as the program executes.

- To *declare* a variable, code the keyword *var* and a variable name. To declare more than one variable in a single statement, code *var* and the variable names separated by commas.

- To assign a value to a variable, you use an *assignment statement* that consists of the variable name, an *assignment operator*, and an expression. When appropriate, you can declare a variable and assign a value to it in a single statement.

- Within an expression, a *numeric literal* is a valid integer or decimal number that isn't enclosed in quotation marks.

- If you use a plus sign in an expression and both values are numbers, JavaScript adds them. If both values are strings, JavaScript concatenates them as shown in the next figure. And if one value is a number and one is a string, JavaScript converts the number to a string and concatenates.

- When you do some types of arithmetic operations with decimal values, the results aren't always precise, although they are extremely close. That's because decimal values are stored internally as floating-point numbers. The only problem with this is that an equality comparison may not return true.

Figure 2-6   How to work with numeric variables

How to work with string and Boolean variables

To declare a string or Boolean variable, you use techniques that are similar to those you use for declaring a numeric variable. The main difference is that a *string literal* is a value enclosed in quotation marks, while a numeric literal isn't. Besides that, the + sign is treated as a *concatenation operator* when working with strings. This means that one string is added to the end of another string.

This is illustrated by the first two groups of examples in figure 2-7. In the second group, the first statement assigns string literals to the variables named firstName and lastName. Then, the next statement concatenates lastName, a string literal that consists of a comma and a space, and firstName. The result of this concatenation is

`Hopper, Grace`

which is stored in a new variable named fullName.

In the third group of examples, you can see how the += operator can be used to get the same results. When the expressions that you're working with are strings, this operator does a simple concatenation.

In the fourth group of examples, though, you can see what happens if the += operator is used with a string and a numeric value. In that case, the number is converted to a string and then the strings are concatenated.

The fifth group of examples shows how you can use *escape sequences* in a string. Three of the many escape sequences that you can use are summarized in the second table in this figure. These sequences let you put characters in a string that you can't put in just by pressing the appropriate key on the keyboard. For instance, the \n escape sequence is equivalent to pressing the Enter key in the middle of a string. And the \' sequence is equivalent to pressing the key for a single quotation mark.

Escape sequences are needed so the JavaScript engine can interpret code correctly. For instance, since single and double quotations marks are used to identify strings in JavaScript statements, coding them within the strings would cause syntax errors. But when the quotation marks are preceded by escape characters (\), the JavaScript engine can interpret them correctly.

The last example in this figure shows how to create and assign values to Boolean variables. Here, a variable named isValid is created and a value of false is assigned to it.

The concatenation operator for strings

Operator	Example	Result
+	`"Grace " + "Hopper"`	`"Grace Hopper"`
	`"Months: " + 120`	`"Months: 120"`

Escape sequences that can be used in strings

Operator	Description
`\n`	Starts a new line in a string.
`\"`	Puts a double quotation mark in a string.
`\'`	Puts a single quotation mark in a string.

How to declare string variables without assigning values to them

```
var zipCode;                          // declares one variable
var lastName, state, zipCode;         // declares three variables
```

How to declare string variables and assign values to them

```
var firstName = "Grace", lastName = "Hopper"; // assigns two string values
var fullName = lastName + ", " + firstName;   // fullName is "Hopper, Grace"
```

How to code compound assignment statements with string data

```
var firstName = "Grace", lastName = "Hopper";
var fullName = lastName;               // fullName is "Hopper"
fullName += ", ";                      // fullName is "Hopper, "
fullName += firstName;                 // fullName is "Hopper, Grace"
```

How to code compound assignment statements with mixed data

```
var months = 120;
message = "Months: ";
message += months;                     // message is "Months: 120"
```

How escape sequences can be used in a string

```
var message = "A valid variable name\ncannot start with a number.";
var message = "This isn\'t the right way to do this.";
```

How to declare Boolean variables and assign values to them

```
var isValid = false;                   // Boolean value is false
```

Description

- To assign values to string variables, you can use the + and += operators, just as you use them with numeric variables.

- To *concatenate* two or more strings, you can use the + operator.

- Within an expression, a *string literal* is enclosed in quotation marks.

- *Escape sequences* can be used to insert special characters within a string like a return character that starts a new line or a quotation mark.

- If you use a plus sign in an expression and both values are strings, JavaScript concatenates them. But if one value is a number and one is a string, JavaScript converts the number to a string and concatenates the strings.

Figure 2-7   How to work with string and Boolean variables

How to use objects to work with data

In addition to working with data using the primitive data types, JavaScript provides for working with data using objects. You'll learn about some of the objects for working with data in just a minute. But first, you need to know the basic skills for working with any object.

How to use objects, methods, and properties

In simple terms, an *object* is a collection of methods and properties. A *method* performs a function or does an action. A *property* is a data item that relates to the object. When you develop JavaScript applications, you will often work with objects, methods, and properties.

To get you started with that, figure 2-8 shows how to use the methods and properties of the *window object*, which is a common JavaScript object. To *call* (execute) a method of an object, you use the syntax in the summary after the first table. That is, you code the object name, a *dot operator* (period), the method name, and any *parameters* that the method requires within parentheses.

In the syntax summaries in this book, some words are italicized and some aren't. The words that aren't italicized are keywords that always stay the same, like *alert*. You can see this in the first table, where the syntax for the alert method shows that you code the word *alert* just as it is in the summary. In contrast, the italicized words are the ones that you need to supply, like the string parameter you supply to the alert method.

In the first example after the syntax summary, you can see how the alert method of the window object is called:

```
window.alert("This is a test of the alert method");
```

In this case, the one parameter that's passed to it is "This is a test of the alert method". So that message is displayed when the alert dialog box is displayed.

In the second example, you can see how the prompt method of the window object is called. This time, though, the object name is omitted. For the window object (but only the window object), that's okay because the window object is the *global object* for JavaScript applications.

As you can see, the prompt method accepts two parameters. The first one is a message, and the second one is an optional default value for a user entry. When the prompt method is executed, it displays a dialog box like the one in this figure. Here, you can see the message and the default value that were passed to the method as parameters. At this point, the user can change the default value or leave it as is, and then click on the OK button to store the entry in the variable named userEntry. Or, the user can click on the Cancel button to cancel the entry.

To access a property of an object, you use a similar syntax. However, you code the property name after the dot operator as illustrated by the second syntax summary. Unlike methods, properties don't require parameters in parentheses. This is illustrated by the statement that follows the syntax. This statement uses the alert method of the window object to display the location property of the window object.

Common methods of the window object

Method	Description
`alert(string)`	Displays a dialog box that contains the string that's passed to it by the parameter along with an OK button.
`prompt(string, default)`	Displays a dialog box that contains the string in the first parameter, the default value in the second parameter, an OK button, and a Cancel button. When the user enters a value and clicks OK, that value is returned as a string. Or if the user clicks Cancel, null is returned, which indicates that the value is unknown.

The syntax for calling a method of an object

`objectName.methodName(parameters)`

A statement that calls the alert method of the window object

```
window.alert("This is a test of the alert method");
```

A statement that calls the prompt method with the object name omitted

```
var userEntry = prompt("This is a test of the prompt method", 100);
```

The prompt dialog box that's displayed

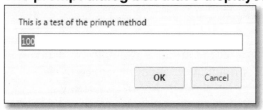

One property of the window object

Property	Description
`location`	The URL of the current web page.

The syntax for accessing a property of an object

`objectName.propertyName`

A statement that displays the location property of the window object

```
alert(window.location);    // Displays the URL of the current page
```

Description

- An *object* has *methods* that perform functions that are related to the object as well as *properties* that represent the data or attributes that are associated with the object.

- When you *call* a method, you may need to pass one or more *parameters* to it by coding them within the parentheses after the method name, separated by commas.

- The *window object* is the *global object* for JavaScript, and JavaScript lets you omit the object name and *dot operator* (period) when referring to the window object.

Figure 2-8   How to use objects, methods, and properties

How to use the window and document objects

Figure 2-9 starts by presenting one method of the *document object*. This getElementById method gets the object that represents an HTML element. It requires one parameter, which is the id for the element.

You can see how this works in the first set of examples, which starts with the HTML for two label elements and two input elements with their type attributes set to "text". That means that the input elements are displayed in a web page as text boxes, and users can enter values into these text boxes.

This HTML is followed by two JavaScript statements that use getElementById methods to return the objects for the elements with "miles" and "gallons" as their ids. Those of course are the objects for the two text boxes. In the next figure, you'll see how you can use those objects to get the data that the user has entered into the textboxes.

The second table in this figure summarizes the parseInt and parseFloat methods that are available through the window object. The parseInt method converts a string to an integer, and the parseFloat method converts a string to a decimal value. If the string can't be converted to a number, the value *NaN* is returned. NaN means "Not a Number"

These methods are needed because the values that are returned by the prompt method and the values that the user enters into text boxes are treated as strings. These methods are illustrated by the second group of examples. For this group, assume that the default value in the prompt method isn't changed by the user. As a result, the first statement in this group stores 1234.567 as a string in a variable named miles. Then, the second statement in this group converts the string to an integer value of 1234.

Note that the object name isn't coded before the method name in these examples. That's okay because window is the global object of JavaScript. Note too that the parseInt method doesn't round the value. It just removes, or truncates, any decimal portion of the string value.

The next two statements in this group illustrate the use of the parseFloat method. This time, a string value of 24.675 is converted to a numeric value of 24.675.

The last two statements in this group show what happens when the parseInt or parseFloat method is used to convert a value that isn't a number. In that case, both of these methods return the value NaN.

Note, however, that these methods can convert values that consist of one or more numeric characters followed by one or more nonnumeric characters. In that case, these methods simply drop the nonnumeric characters. For example, if a string contains the value 72.5%, the parseFloat method will convert it to a decimal value of 72.5. These methods will also trim leading or trailing spaces from a number.

One method of the document object for getting HTML objects

Method	Description
`getElementById(id)`	Gets the HTML element that has the id that's passed to it and returns that element.

Examples of the getElementById method

The HTML for a text box and a button

```
<label for="miles">Miles Driven:</label>
<input type="text" id="miles" name="miles"><br>
<label for"gallons">Gallons of Gas:</label>
<input type="text" id="gallons" name="gallons"><br>
```

The JavaScript that gets the objects for the text boxes

```
var miles = document.getElementById("miles");
var gallons = document.getElementById("gallons");
```

Two methods of the window object for working with numbers

Method	Description
`parseInt(string)`	Converts the string that's passed to it to an integer data type and returns that value. If it can't convert the string to an integer, it returns NaN.
`parseFloat(string)`	Converts the string that's passed to it to a decimal data type and returns that value. If it can't convert the string to a decimal value, it returns NaN.

The parsing that's done by the parse methods

- Only the first number in the string is returned.
- Leading and trailing spaces are removed.
- If the first character cannot be converted to a number, NaN is returned.

Examples of parse methods

```
var miles = prompt("Enter Miles Driven", 1234.567);
miles = parseInt(miles);                        // miles = 1234
var gallons = prompt("Enter Gallons of Gas", 24.675);
gallons = parseFloat(gallons);                  // gallons = 24.675

var message = "Hello out there!";
message = parseFloat(message);                  // message = NaN
```

Description

- The *document object* is the object that lets you work with the Document Object Model (DOM) that represents all of the HTML elements of the page.
- The getElementById method is commonly used to get the object for an HTML element.
- *NaN* is a value that means "Not a Number". It is returned by the parseInt and parseFloat methods when the value that's being parsed isn't a number.

Figure 2-9   How to use the window and document objects

How to use Textbox and Number objects

The Textbox object is one of the DOM objects. It represents a text box that is used to get input from the user or display output to the user. The first two tables in figure 2-10 summarize one of its methods and two of its properties. Then, this figure shows the HTML code for two text boxes that have "first_name" and "sales_amount" as their ids.

The first group of examples in this figure shows two ways to get the value from the text box with "first_name" as its id. To do that with two statements, the first statement uses the getElementById method of the document object to get the Textbox object for that text box. Then, the second statement uses the value property of the Textbox object to get the value that the user entered into the text box.

In practice, though, you would do that with just one statement by using *method chaining*, or just *chaining*. In that case, a single statement first uses the getElementById method to get the Textbox object, and then uses the value property of the Textbox object to get the value from the text box. In other words, you combine the use of the two methods into a single statement.

The second group of examples takes chaining to a third level. Without chaining, it takes three statements to get a valid number from a text box. First, the getDocumentById method gets the Textbox object for the text box with sales_amount as its id. Second, the value property of the Textbox object gets the value that the user entered into the text box. Third, the parseFloat method of the window object converts the string value to a decimal number. If the user entry is a valid number, this stores the number in the salesAmount variable, so it becomes a Number object.

With chaining, though, this requires only one statement. Code like this is sometimes called *fluent,* because it's more like a sentence and thus more readable to a human eye. It can also make your code shorter, and shorter code is usually easier to understand. You'll want to be careful with this, though. Like a run-on sentence in a book, if you get to the end of the statement and can't remember what the beginning was doing, you might have chained too much.

The third table in this figure summarizes the toFixed method of a Number object. When a user enters a valid number in a text box and the parseInt or parseFloat method is used to parse it before it is stored in a variable, the variable becomes a Number object. Then, you can use the toFixed method of that Number object to round the number to a specific number of decimal places.

This is illustrated by the first statement in the last group of examples. This statement takes chaining to a fourth level by adding the toFixed method to the chain. As a result, the number that's stored in the salesAmount variable is rounded to two decimal places. Some might consider this an example of chaining taken too far.

The last two statements in this group present two more examples of chaining. The first one shows how to assign a value to a text box. In this case, the value is an empty string, which in effect clears the text box of any data. The second statement shows how to move the focus to a text box.

One method of the Textbox object

Method	Description
`focus()`	Moves the cursor into the text box, but doesn't return anything.

Two properties of the Textbox object

Property	Description
`value`	A string that represents the contents of the text box.
`disabled`	A Boolean value that controls whether the text box is disabled.

One method of the Number object

Method	Description
`toFixed(digits)`	Returns a string representation of the number after it has been rounded to the number of decimal places in the parameter.

HTML tags that define two text boxes

```
<input type="text" id="first_name">
<input type="text" id="sales_amount">
```

How to use the value property to get the value from a text box

Without chaining

```
var firstName = document.getElementById("first_name");
firstName = firstName.value;
```

With chaining

```
var firstName = document.getElementById("first_name").value;
```

How to use the parseFloat method to get a number value from a text box

Without chaining

```
var salesAmount = document.getElementById("sales_amount");
salesAmount = salesAmount.value;
salesAmount = parseFloat(salesAmount);
```

With chaining

```
var salesAmount = parseFloat(document.getElementById("sales_amount").value);
```

Other examples of chaining

```
var salesAmount =
    parseFloat(document.getElementById("sales_amount").value).toFixed(2);

document.getElementById("first_name").value = "";   // clear a text box
document.getElementById("first_name").focus();      // move focus to a text box
```

Description

- When you use the getElementById method to get a text box, the method returns a Textbox object. Then, you can use its value property to get the value in the box.

- When you store a numeric value in a variable, a Number object is created. Then, you can use the Number methods with the variable.

Figure 2-10   How to use Textbox and Number objects

How to use Date and String objects

When you store a numeric or string value in a variable, it is automatically converted to a Number or String object. This lets you use the properties and methods of the Number and String objects without having to explicitly create the objects.

However, there isn't a primitive data type for dates. As a result, you need to create a Date object before you can use its methods. To do that, you can use the syntax shown in figure 2-11. When you create a Date object, it is initialized with the current date and time, which is the date and time on the user's computer.

After you create a Date object, you can use the methods in this figure to work with it. These methods are illustrated by the first group of examples, assuming that the date is March 9, 2015. Here, the toDateString method converts the date to a string. The getFullYear method gets the four-digit year from the date. The getDate method gets the day of the month. And the getMonth method gets the month, counting from 0, not 1. As a result, the getMonth method returns 2 for March, not 3.

This figure also presents one property and five methods of a String object. Then, the last group of examples presents some statements that show how these properties work. For example, the second statement uses the toUpperCase method to convert a string to uppercase, and the third statement uses the length property to get the number of characters in a string.

The last two statements show how the indexOf and substr methods of a String object can be used to extract a substring from a string. Here, the indexOf method is used to get the position (index) of the first space in the string, counting from zero. Since the space is in the sixth position, this method returns 5. Then, the substr method gets the substring that starts at the first position and has a length of 5. As a result, this method returns "Grace".

It's important to note the difference between the substr and substring methods. If you start from the first position, as in the example, there is no difference. In that case, both methods will return "Grace". However, if you start anywhere else, you'll get different results depending on which method you use.

For example, if you start at the third position (with an index of 2), the substr method will still return five characters, and you'll get the string "ace H". The substring method, on the other hand, will stop at the sixth position (with an index of 5). This means it will only return 3 characters, the string "ace".

The syntax for creating a JavaScript object and assigning it to a variable

```
var variableName = new ObjectType();
```

A statement that creates a Date object

```
var today = new Date();
```

A few of the methods of a Date object

Method	Description
`toDateString()`	Returns a string with the formatted date.
`getFullYear()`	Returns the four-digit year from the date.
`getDate()`	Returns the day of the month from the date.
`getMonth()`	Returns the month number from the date. The months are numbered starting with zero. January is 0 and December is 11.

Examples that use a Date object

```
var today = new Date();            // creates Date object with current date
alert ( today.toDateString() );    // displays Mon Mar 09 2015 on 3/9/2015
alert ( today.getFullYear() );     // displays 2015
alert ( today.getDate() );         // displays 9
alert ( today.getMonth() );        // displays 2, not 3 for March
```

One property of a String object

Method	Description
`length`	Returns the number of characters in the string.

A few of the methods of a String object

Method	Description
`indexOf(search,position)`	Searches for the first occurrence of the search string starting at the position specified or zero if position is omitted. If found, it returns the position of the first character, counting from 0. If not found, it returns -1.
`substr(start,length)`	Returns the substring that starts at the specified position (counting from zero) and contains the specified number of characters.
`substring(start,stop)`	Returns the substring that starts at the specified position (counting from zero) and stops at the specified position (counting from zero).
`toLowerCase()`	Returns a new string with the letters converted to lowercase.
`toUpperCase()`	Returns a new string with the letters converted to uppercase.

Examples that use a String object

```
var name = "Grace Hopper";
var nameUpper = name.toUpperCase();      // nameUpper = "GRACE HOPPER"
var nameLength = name.length;            // nameLength = 12
var index = name.indexOf(" ");           // index = 5
var firstName = name.substr(0, index);   // firstName = "Grace"
```

Description

- To create a Date object and assign it to a variable, use the syntax shown above.
- When you store a string value in a variable, a String object is automatically created.

Figure 2-11   How to use Date and String objects

How to code control statements

Like all programming languages, JavaScript provides *control statements* that let you control how information is processed in an application. These statements include if statements as well as looping statements. Before you can learn how to use these statements, though, you need to learn how to code conditional expressions, so we'll start there.

How to code conditional expressions

Figure 2-12 shows you how to code *conditional expressions* that use the six *relational operators*. A conditional expression returns a value of true or false based on the result of a comparison between two expressions. If, for example, the value of lastName in the first expression in the first table is "Harrison", the expression will return false. Or, if the value of rate in the last expression is 10, the expression will return true (because 10 / 100 is .1 and .1 is greater than or equal to 0.1).

In addition to using the relational operators to code a conditional expression, you can use the global isNaN method. This method determines whether a string value is a valid numeric value, as illustrated by the next set of examples. To use this method, you pass a parameter that represents the string value that should be tested. Then, this method returns true if the value can't be converted to a number or false if it can be converted.

To code a *compound conditional expression*, you use the *logical operators* shown in the second table in this figure to combine two conditional expressions. If you use the AND operator, the compound expression returns true if both expressions are true. If you use the OR operator, the compound expression returns true if either expression is true. If you use the NOT operator, the value returned by the expression is reversed. For instance, !isNaN returns true if the parameter is a number, so isNaN(10) returns false, but !isNaN(10) returns true.

Note that the logical operators in this figure are shown in their order of precedence. That is the order in which the operators are evaluated if more than one logical operator is used in a compound expression. This means that NOT operators are evaluated before AND operators, which are evaluated before OR operators. Although this is normally what you want, you can override this order by using parentheses.

In most cases, the conditional expressions that you use are relatively simple so coding them isn't much of a problem. In the rest of this chapter, you'll see some of the types of conditional expressions that are commonly used.

The relational operators

Operator	Description	Example
==	Equal	`lastName == "Hopper"` `testScore == 10`
!=	Not equal	`firstName != "Grace"` `months != 0`
<	Less than	`age < 18`
<=	Less than or equal	`investment <= 0`
>	Greater than	`testScore > 100`
>=	Greater than or equal	`rate / 100 >= 0.1`

The syntax of the global isNaN method

`isNaN(expression)`

Examples of the isNaN method

```
isNaN("Hopper") // Returns true since "Hopper" is not a number
isNaN("123.45") // Returns false since "123.45" can be converted to a number
```

The logical operators in order of precedence

Operator	Description	Example
!	NOT	`!isNaN(age)`
&&	AND	`age > 17 && score < 70`
||	OR	`isNaN(rate) || rate < 0`

How the logical operators work

- Both tests with the AND operator must be true for the overall test to be true.
- At least one test with the OR operator must be true for the overall test to be true.
- The NOT operator switches the result of the expression to the other Boolean value. For example, if an expression is true, the NOT operator converts it to false.
- To override the order of precedence when two or more logical operators are used in a conditional expression, you can use parentheses.

Description

- A *conditional expression* uses the *relational operators* to compare the results of two expressions.
- A *compound conditional expression* joins two or more conditional expressions using the *logical operators*.
- The isNaN method tests whether a string can be converted to a number. It returns true if the string is not a number and false if the string is a number.

Note

- Confusing the assignment operator (=) with the equality operator (==) is a common programming error.

Figure 2-12 How to code conditional expressions

How to code if statements

If you've programmed in other languages, you won't have any trouble using JavaScript if statements. Just study figure 2-13 to get the syntax and see how the conditions are coded. But if you're new to programming, let's take it slower.

An *if statement* lets you control the execution of statements based on the results of conditional expressions. In a syntax summary like the one in this figure, the brackets [ ] indicate a portion of the syntax that is optional. As a result, this summary means that each if statement must start with an *if clause*. Then, it can have one or more *else if clauses*, but they are optional. Last, it can have an *else clause*, but that clause is also optional.

To code the if clause, you code the keyword *if* followed by a conditional expression in parentheses and a block of one or more statements inside braces. If the conditional expression is true, this block of code will be executed and any remaining clauses in the if statement will be skipped over. If the conditional expression is false, the next clause that follows will be executed.

To code an else if clause, you code the keywords *else if* followed by a conditional expression in parentheses and a block of one or more statements inside braces. If the conditional expression is true, its block of code will be executed and any remaining clauses in the if statement will be skipped over. This will continue until one of the else if expressions is true or they all are false.

To code an else clause, you code the keyword *else* followed by a block of one or more statements inside braces. This code will only be executed if all the conditional expressions in the if and else if clauses are false. If those expressions are false and there isn't an else clause, the if statement won't execute any code.

The first example in this figure shows an if statement with an else clause. If the value of the age variable is greater than or equal to 18, the first message will be displayed. Otherwise, the second message will be displayed.

The second example shows an if statement with two else if clauses and an else clause. If the rate is not a number, the first message is displayed. If the rate is less than zero, the second message is displayed. If the rate is greater than 12, the third message is displayed. Otherwise, the message in the else clause is displayed.

The third example shows an if statement with a compound conditional expression that tests whether the value of the userEntry variable is not a number or whether the value is less than or equal to zero. If either expression is true, a message is displayed. If both expressions are false, nothing is done because this if statement doesn't have else if clauses or an else clause.

The fourth set of examples shows two ways to test whether a Boolean variable is true. Here, both statements are evaluated the same way. That's because a condition that is coded as just a Boolean variable is tested to see whether the variable is equal to true. In practice, this condition is usually coded the way it is in the second statement, with just the name of the variable.

The fifth set of examples is similar. It shows three ways to test whether a Boolean variable is false. Here again, the last statement illustrates the way this condition is usually coded: !isValid.

The syntax of the if statement

```
if ( condition-1 ) { statements }
[ else if ( condition-2 ) { statements }
  ...
  else if ( condition-n ) { statements } ]
[ else { statements } ]
```

An if statement with an else clause

```
if ( age >= 18 ) {
    alert ("You may vote.");
} else {
    alert ("You are not old enough to vote.");
}
```

An if statement with else if and else clauses

```
if ( isNaN(rate) ) {
    alert ("You did not provide a number for the rate.");
} else if ( rate < 0 ) {
    alert ("The rate may not be less than zero.");
} else if ( rate > 12 ) {
    alert ("The rate may not be greater than 12.");
} else {
    alert ("The rate is: " + rate + ".");
}
```

An if statement with a compound conditional expression

```
if ( isNaN(userEntry) || userEntry <= 0 ) {
    alert ("Please enter a number greater than zero.");
}
```

Two ways to test whether a Boolean variable is true

```
if ( isValid == true ) { }
if ( isValid ) { }                 // same as isValid == true
```

Three ways to test whether a Boolean variable is false

```
if ( isValid == false ) { }
if ( !isValid == true ) { }
if ( !isValid ) { }                // same as !isValid == true
```

Description

- An *if statement* always has one *if clause*. It can also have one or more *else if clauses* and one *else clause* at the end.

- The statements in a clause are executed when its condition is true. Otherwise, control passes to the next clause. If none of the conditions in the preceding clauses are true, the statements in the else clause are executed.

- If necessary, you can code one if statement within the if, else if, or else clause of another if statement. This is referred to as *nesting if statements*.

Figure 2-13   How to code if statements

How to code while, do-while, and for loops

Figure 2-14 starts by presenting the syntax of the *while statement* that is used to create *while loops*. This statement executes the block of code that's in the loop while its conditional expression is true.

The example that follows this syntax shows how a while loop can be used to add the numbers 1 through 5. Before the while statement starts, a variable named sumOfNumbers is set to zero, a variable named numberOfLoops is set to 5, and a variable named counter is set to 1. Then, the condition for the while statement says that the while loop should be repeated as long as the counter value is less than or equal to the numberOfLoops value.

Within the while loop, the first statement adds the counter value to the sumOfNumbers variable. Then, the counter is increased by 1. As a result, this loop is executed five times, one time each for the counter values 1, 2, 3, 4, and 5. The loop ends when the counter is no longer less than or equal to 5, which is when the counter value equals 6.

This example is followed by the syntax for the *do-while statement* that is used to create *do-while loops*. This is like the while statement, but its condition is tested at the end of the loop instead of at the start. As a result, the statements in the loop are always executed at least once.

This statement is illustrated by the example that follows the syntax. This loop keeps going while the user's entry isn't a number (isNaN). Within the loop, a prompt statement gets the user's entry, the entry is parsed, and an if statement displays an error message if the entry isn't a number. This loop continues until the user enters a number.

This example is followed by the syntax for the *for statement* that is used to create *for loops*. This type of loop is easier to code when the progress of the loop depends on a value that is incremented each time through the loop. Within the parentheses of a for statement, you initialize a *counter* (or *index*) variable that will be used within the loop. Then, you code a condition that determines when the loop will end. Last, you code an expression that specifies how the counter should be incremented.

The example in this figure shows how this works. This for loop calculates the future value of an investment amount ($10,000) at a specific interest rate (7.0%) for a specific number of years (10). Here, *i* is used as the name for the counter variable, which is a common coding practice. Then, the loop continues as long as this index is less than or equal to the number of years, and the index is incremented by 1 each time through the loop. In other words, the statement in the loop is executed once for each of the 10 years.

Within the loop, this expression is used to calculate the interest for the year

```
futureValue * annualRate / 100
```

Then, the += operator adds the interest to the futureValue variable. Note here that the annualRate needs to be divided by 100 for this calculation to work right (7.0 / 100 = .07).

The syntax of a while loop

```
while ( condition ) { statements }
```

A while loop that adds the numbers from 1 through 5

```
var sumOfNumbers = 0;
var numberOfLoops = 5;
var counter = 1;
while (counter <= numberOfLoops) {
    sumOfNumbers += counter;      // adds counter to sumOfNumbers
    counter++;                    // adds 1 to counter
}
alert(sumOfNumbers);             // displays 15
```

The syntax of a do-while loop

```
do { statements } while ( condition );
```

A do-while loop that gets a user entry until it is a number

```
do {
    var investment = prompt("Enter investment amount as xxxxxx.xx", 10000);
    investment = parseFloat(investment);
    if ( isNaN(investment) ) {
        alert("Investment must be a number");
    }
}
while ( isNaN(investment) );
```

The syntax of a for loop

```
for ( counterInitialization; condition; incrementExpression ) {
    statements
}
```

A for loop that calculates the future value of an investment

```
var investment = 10000, var annualRate = 7.0, var years = 10;
var futureValue = investment;
for ( var i = 1; i <= years; i++ ) {
    futureValue += futureValue * annualRate / 100;
}
alert (futureValue);             // displays 19672
```

Description

- The *while statement* creates a *while loop* that contains a block of code that is executed while its condition is true. This condition is tested at the beginning of the loop, and the loop is skipped if the condition is false.

- The *do-while statement* creates a *do-while* loop that contains a block of code that is executed while its condition is true. However, its condition is tested at the end of the loop instead of the beginning, so the code in the loop will always be executed at least once.

- The *for statement* is used when you need to increment or decrement a counter that determines how many times the *for loop* is executed.

- Within the parentheses of a for statement, you code an expression that initializes a *counter* (or *index*) variable, a conditional expression that determines when the loop ends, and an increment expression that indicates how the counter should be incremented or decremented each time through the loop.

Figure 2-14   How to code while, do-while, and for loops

How to work with arrays

The next two figures present the basic skills for working with arrays. As you will see, arrays are commonly used in JavaScript applications.

How to create and use arrays

An *array* is an object that contains one or more items called *elements*. Each of these elements can be a primitive data type or an object. The *length* of an array indicates the number of elements that it contains.

Figure 2-15 shows two ways to create an array. When you use the first method, you use the *new* keyword followed by the Array object name to create an array with the number of elements that is indicated by the length parameter. This length must be a whole number that is greater than or equal to zero. If you don't specify the length, the array will be empty.

When you use the second method, you just code a set of brackets. This gives you the same result that you get with the first method and no parameter, an empty array.

To refer to the elements in an array, you use an *index* that ranges from zero to one less than the number of elements in an array. In an array with 12 elements, for example, the index values range from 0 to 11.

To use an index, you code it within brackets after the name of the array. In this figure, all of the examples use literal values for the indexes, but an index can also be a variable that contains an index value, as you'll see shortly. If you try to access an element that hasn't been assigned a value, the value of undefined will be returned.

The last two examples in this figure show how to work with the array's length property. The length property returns the number of elements in an array. In the first example, the length property is stored in a variable for later use.

In the second example, the length property is used as the index of a new element. Since this property will always be 1 more than the highest index used in the array, this adds the new element at the end of the array.

The syntax for creating an array

Using the new keyword with the Array object name
```
var arrayName = new Array(length);
```

Using the brackets literal
```
var arrayName = [];
```

The syntax for referring to an element of an array
```
arrayName[index]
```

The syntax for getting the length property of an array
```
arrayName.length
```

How to add values to an array
```
var totals = [];
totals[0] = 141.95;
totals[1] = 212.25;
totals[2] = 411;
```

How to refer to the elements in an array
```
totals[2]          // refers to the third element - 411
totals[1]          // refers to the second element - 212.25
```

How to determine how many elements are in an array
```
var count = totals.length;          // 3
```

How to add a value to the end of an array
```
totals[totals.length] = 135.75;     // adds a fourth element, index = 3
```

Description
- An *array* can store one or more *elements*. The *length* of an array is the number of elements in the array.
- One way to create an array is to use the new keyword, the name of the object (Array), and an optional length parameter.
- The other way to create an array is to code a set of brackets.
- To refer to the elements in an array, you use an *index* where 0 is the first element, 1 is the second element, and so on.
- One way to add an element to the end of an array is to use the length property as the index.

Figure 2-15   How to create and use arrays

How to use for loops to work with arrays

For loops are commonly used to process one array element at a time by incrementing an index variable. Figure 2-16 shows how this works.

The first example in this figure shows how to create an array and fill it with the numbers 1 through 10. First, the code creates an empty array named numbers. Then, an index variable named i is used to loop through the first ten elements of the array by using values that range from 0 to 9. In the body of this loop, one is added to the value in i and the result is stored in the element. As a result, 1 is stored in the element at index 0, 2 is stored in the element at index 1, and so on.

Next, this example displays the values in the array. First, it creates an empty string named numbersString. Then, it uses a for loop to access the elements in the array. In the for loop, the length property of the array is used to control how many times the loop executes. This allows the same code to work with arrays of different lengths. Inside the for loop, the value in the element and a space are concatenated to the end of numbersString. Finally, numbersString is displayed, which shows the ten numbers that were stored in the array.

The next example in this figure shows how to use for loops to add the totals in an array and to display those totals. First, the code puts four values into an array named totals. Then, a for loop adds the four totals in the array to a variable named sum. Last, a for loop concatenates the four totals in the array to a string variable, and those totals and the sum are displayed when the loop ends.

Code that puts the numbers 1 through 10 into an array

```
var numbers = [];
for (var i = 0; i < 10; i++) {
    numbers[i] = i + 1;
}
```

Code that displays the numbers in the array

```
var numbersString = "";
for (var i = 0; i < numbers.length; i++) {
    numbersString += numbers[i] + " ";
}
alert (numbersString);
```

The message that's displayed

Code that puts four totals in an array

```
var totals = [];
totals[0] = 141.95;
totals[1] = 212.25;
totals[2] = 411;
totals[3] = 135.75;
```

Code that sums the totals in the array

```
var sum = 0;
for (var i = 0; i < totals.length; i++) {
    sum += totals[i];
}
```

Code that displays the totals and the sum

```
var totalsString = "";
for (var i = 0; i < totals.length; i++) {
    totalsString += totals[i] + "\n";
}
alert ("The totals are:\n" + totalsString + "\n" + "Sum: " + sum);
```

The message that's displayed

Description

- When you use a for loop to work with an array, you can use the counter for the loop as the index for the array.

Figure 2-16   How to use for loops to work with arrays

How to use functions

When you develop JavaScript applications, you need to handle *events* like a user clicking on a button. To do that, you need to code and call functions that handle the events. As you will see, you can also use functions in other ways.

How to create and call a function

A *function* is a block of statements that performs an action. It can receive *parameters* and return a value by issuing a *return statement*. Once you've defined a function, you can call it from other portions of your JavaScript code. As figure 2-17 shows, JavaScript provides for two kinds of functions.

To create a *function expression*, you code the keyword *var* followed by the name of the variable that will store the function. Then, you code an assignment operator, the keyword *function*, a list of parameters in parentheses, and a block of code in braces. The parentheses are required even if there are no parameters.

Functions that are coded this way are called function expressions because they're assigned to a variable, and they usually aren't named. That's why you'll sometimes see them called *anonymous functions*.

Note in the syntax summary that there's a semicolon in square brackets [ ] after the closing brace, which means the semicolon is optional. Nevertheless, some IDEs like Aptana issue a warning if you omit the semicolon. That makes sense because you have to code a semicolon after other types of assignment statements. In this book, though, these optional semicolons have been omitted.

To *call* a function expression, you code the name of the variable that the function is stored in, followed by the parameters in parentheses. Then, the function uses the data that's passed to it in the parameters as it executes its block of code. Here again, the parentheses are required even if there are no parameters.

The first example in this figure creates a function that's stored in a variable named $. This is a commonly-used function that takes one parameter, which is the value of the id attribute of an HTML element. This function returns an object that represents the HTML element. In this example, the statement that calls the function gets the object for an HTML text box with "email_address1" as its id, and then uses the value property of that object to store the value that the user entered in a variable.

The second example creates a function with no parameters that's stored in a variable named showYear. It displays an alert dialog box that gives the current year. Note that the statement that calls this function includes an empty set of parentheses.

Next, this figure shows how to code a *function declaration*. As the syntax shows, a function declaration isn't stored in a variable, and its name is coded after the keyword *function* and before the parameters. The one benefit of a function declaration is that it can be coded before or after any statements that call it. In contrast, a function expression must be coded before any statements that call it.

The example after the syntax shows a function named calculateTax that requires two parameters and returns a value. It calculates sales tax, rounds it to two decimal places, and returns that rounded value to the statement that called it.

The syntax for a function expression

```
var variableName = function(parameters) {
    // statements that run when the function is executed
}[;]
```

A function expression with one parameter that returns a DOM element

```
var $ = function (id) {
    return document.getElementById(id);
}
```

A statement that calls the $ function

```
var emailAddress1 = $("email_address1").value;
```

A function expression with no parameters that doesn't return a value

```
var showYear = function() {
    var today = new Date();
    alert( "The year is " + today.getFullYear() );
}
```

A statement that calls the showYear function

```
showYear();
```

The syntax for a function declaration

```
function functionName (parameters) {
    // statements that run when the function is executed
}
```

A function declaration with two parameters that returns a value

```
function calculateTax ( subtotal, taxRate ) {
    var tax = subtotal * taxRate;
    tax = tax.toFixed(2);
    return tax;
}
```

A statement that calls the calculateTax function

```
var subtotal = 85.00, var taxRate = 0.05;
var salesTax = calculateTax( subtotal, taxRate ); // calls the function
```

Description

- A *function* is a block of code that can be *called* by other statements in the program. When the function ends, the program continues with the statement after the calling statement.

- A *function expression* is stored in a variable and is referred to by the variable name. It must be coded before any statement that calls it.

- A *function declaration* is another way to code a function, but it doesn't have to be coded before any statement that calls it.

- A function can require that one or more *parameters* be *passed* to it when the function is called. To return a value to the statement that called it, a function uses a *return statement*.

Figure 2-17   How to create and call a function

In the calling statement, you can see how the parameters are passed to the function. In this case, the variable names for these values are the same as the parameter names in the function, but that isn't necessary. What is required is that the calling statement must pass parameters with the same data types and in the same sequence as the parameters in the function.

When and how to use local and global variables

Scope in a programming language refers to the visibility of variables and functions. That is, it tells you where in your program you are allowed to use the variables and functions that you've defined.

When you use JavaScript, *local variables* are variables that are defined within functions. They have *local scope*, which means that they can only be used within the functions that define them. In contrast, *global variables* are variables that are defined outside of functions. These variables have *global scope*, so they can be used by any function without passing them to the function as parameters.

The first example in figure 2-18 illustrates the use of a local variable. Here, the calculateTax function creates a variable named tax and returns that variable to the calling statement. Then, that statement can store the variable in another variable. Note, however, that a statement outside of the function can't refer to the variable named tax without causing an error. That's because it has local scope.

In contrast, the second example first creates a global variable named tax. Then, the function calculates the sales tax and stores the result in that global variable. As a result, the function doesn't have to return the tax variable. Instead, a statement outside of the function can refer to the variable because it is global.

Although it may seem easier to use global variables than to pass data to a function and return data from it, global variables often create problems. That's because any function can modify a global variable, and it's all too easy to misspell a variable name or modify the wrong variable, especially in large applications. That in turn can create debugging problems.

In contrast, the use of local variables reduces the likelihood of naming conflicts. For instance, two functions can use the same names for local variables without causing conflicts. That means fewer errors and debugging problems.

To complicate the use of variables, the JavaScript engine assumes that a variable is global if you accidentally omit the var keyword when you declare it. This is illustrated by the third example in this figure. Here, the var keyword is missing before the first assignment statement, so tax is assumed to be a global variable. This is a weakness of JavaScript that you need to be aware of because it can lead to coding errors. If, for example, you misspell the name of a variable that you've already declared when you code an assignment statement, it will be treated as a new global variable.

To address this problem, JavaScript provides a mode of operation called *strict mode*. To use strict mode, you code the strict mode directive shown in this figure at the start of your JavaScript code. Then, the JavaScript engine in a modern browser will throw an error if a variable name is used before it has been declared. That alerts you to the problem and forces you to fix it.

A function that uses a local variable named tax

```
var calculateTax = function ( subtotal, taxRate ) {
    var tax = subtotal * taxRate;      // tax is a local variable
    tax = tax.toFixed(2);
    return tax;
}
alert("Tax is " + tax);                // causes an error
```

A function that uses a global variable named tax

```
var tax;                               // tax is a global variable
var calculateTax = function ( subtotal, taxRate ) {
    tax = subtotal * taxRate;
    tax = tax.toFixed(2);
}
alert("Tax is " + tax);                // does not cause error
```

A function that inadvertently uses a global variable named tax

```
var calculateTax = function ( subtotal, taxRate ) {
    tax = subtotal * taxRate;  // no var keyword so tax is treated as global
    tax = tax.toFixed(2);
}
alert("Tax is " + tax);                // does not cause error but it should!
```

The same function in strict mode

```
"use strict";                          // the strict mode directive
var calculateTax = function ( subtotal, taxRate ) {
    tax = subtotal * taxRate;          // in strict mode so error is thrown
    tax = tax.toFixed(2);
}
alert("Tax is " + tax);                // causes an error
```

Best coding practices

- Use local variables whenever possible.
- Use strict mode.
- Declare the variables for a function at the start of the function.

Discussion

- The *scope* of a variable or function determines what code has access to it.
- Variables that are created inside a function are *local variables*, and local variables can only be referred to by the code within the function.
- Variables created outside of functions are *global variables*, and the code in all functions has access to all global variables.
- If you forget to code the var keyword in a variable declaration, the JavaScript engine assumes that the variable is global. This can cause debugging problems.
- When you're coding in strict mode, if you forget to code the var keyword in a variable declaration or if you misspell a variable name that has been declared, the JavaScript engine will throw an error.
- The *strict mode* directive goes at the top of a file or function, before any other code.

Figure 2-18   When and how to use local and global variables

Note, however, that this feature isn't supported by older browsers like IE7, IE8, and IE9. In this case, that's okay, because if you fix the problems in a modern browser, the problems won't be there for older browsers either.

With that in mind, figure 2-18 summarizes the best coding practices for working with variables. First, use local variables whenever possible. Second, always use strict mode. Third, declare the variables that are used by a function at the start of the function, before you use them.

How to attach an event handler to an event

The table in figure 2-19 summarizes some of the events that are commonly handled by JavaScript applications. For instance, the load event of the window object occurs when the browser finishes loading the HTML for a page and building the DOM for it. The click event of a button object occurs when the user clicks on the button. And the mouseover action of an element like a heading or link occurs when the user hovers the mouse over the element.

After this table, you can see the syntax for *attaching* a function to an event. To do that, you code the object name, a dot, and the event name preceded by the word *on*. Then, you code an equals sign followed by the name of the variable for the function expression that's going to handle the event.

The first example in this figure starts with a function expression that can be used as an *event handler*. This function is stored in a variable named joinList, and all it does is display a message. In an actual application, of course, this function would perform the actions needed for handling the event.

This function expression is followed by a JavaScript statement that attaches the joinList function to the click event of a button that has "submit_button" as its id. To do that, this statement first uses the $ function that you saw in figure 2-17 to get the object for the button. This is followed by the dot operator and the event name preceded by *on* (onclick). Then, the result is set equal to the variable name (joinList) for the function that will be used as the event handler.

Note here that you don't code the parentheses after the name of the variable that's used for the function, as in figure 2-17. That's because you're attaching the event handler, not calling it. As a result, the function will be called when the event is fired. In contrast, if you were to put parentheses after joinList, the function would be called right away, and the function wouldn't be attached to the event.

The next statement in this example attaches the joinList event handler to the double-click event of a text box that has text_box_1 as its id. This means that the same event handler will be used for two different events. Here again, you don't code the parentheses when you attach the function.

The last example in this figure illustrates how to create an event handler and attach it to the window.onload event in one step. This is a common way to attach event handlers to events, especially the onload event, as you'll see in the next figure.

Common events

Object	Event	Occurs when...
`window`	`load`	The document has been loaded into the browser.
`button`	`click`	The button is clicked.
`control or link`	`focus`	The control or link receives the focus.
	`blur`	The control or link loses the focus.
`control`	`change`	The user changes the value in the control.
	`select`	The user selects text in a text box or text area.
`element`	`click`	The user clicks on the element.
	`dblclick`	The user double-clicks on the element.
	`mouseover`	The user moves the mouse over the element.
	`mousein`	The user moves the mouse into the element.
	`mouseout`	The user moves the mouse out of the element.

The syntax for attaching an event handler

```
objectVariable.oneventName = eventHandlerName;
```

An event handler named joinList

```
var joinList = function() {
    alert("The statements for the function go here");
}
```

How to attach the event handler to the click event of a button

```
$("submit_button").onclick = joinList;
```

How to attach the event handler to the double-click event of a text box

```
$("text_box_1").ondblclick = joinList;
```

How to create and attach an event handler in one step

```
window.onload = function() {
    alert("This is the window onload event handler function.");
}
```

Description

- An *event handler* is a function that's executed when an *event* occurs, so it "handles" the event. As a result, you code an event handler just like any other function.

- To *attach* an event handler to an event, you must first specify the object and the event that triggers the event handler. Then, you assign the event handler function to that event.

- When you code the event for an event handler, you precede the event name with *on*. So, for example, onclick is used for the click event.

- You can create a function expression as an event handler and then attach it to an event. This is useful when you want to use the same function for more than one event, as shown above. When you do it this way, you don't code the parentheses after the variable name.

- You can also create and attach an event handler function in one step, as in the last example above. This is commonly done for the load event as you'll see in the next figure.

Figure 2-19   How to attach an event handler to an event

How to use an onload event handler
to attach the other event handlers

When do you attach an event handler like the one in the previous figure? You attach it after all the HTML has been loaded into a user's browser and the DOM has been built. To do that, you code an event handler for the load event of the window object as shown in figure 2-20.

In the HTML for this example, you can see a label, a text box, a label that contains one space, and a button. This simple application is supposed to display a message when the button is clicked or when the user changes the value in the text box.

In the JavaScript code, you can see three function expressions. The first one is stored in a variable named $. This function uses the getElementById method of the document object to get an element object when the id of an HTML element is passed to it. This is a standard function that makes it easy to get an element object without coding the document.getElementById method every time.

The second function is the event handler for the click event of the button, and the third function is the event handler for the change event of the text box. Both of these functions just display a message.

The fourth function is the event handler for the load event. It is used to attach the other event handlers to the click and change events. Note that this function starts with

`window.onload`

so it is attached to the load event of the window object. As a result, this event handler is executed after the page is loaded and the DOM has been built.

Within this event handler are the two statements that attach the other event handlers. The first one attaches the joinList handler to the click event of the button. The second one attaches the changeValue handler to the change event of the text box. Both of these statements use the $ function to get the object that the event applies to, which makes the code easier to read and understand.

Incidentally, the event handler for the window.onload event can do more than assign functions to events. In fact, it can do whatever needs to be done after the DOM is loaded. You'll see this illustrated throughout this book.

The web browser after the Email Address has been changed

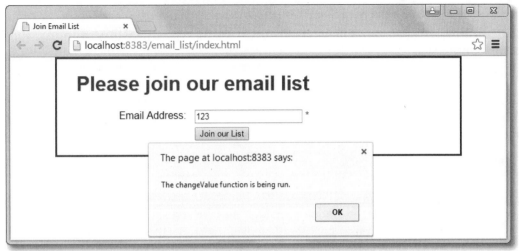

The HTML

```
<h1>Please join our email list</h1>
<label for="email_address">Email Address:</label>
<input type="text" id="email_address" name="email_address"><br>
<label> </label>
<input type="button" id="join_list" value="Join our List"><br>
```

The JavaScript

```
// the $ function
var $ = function (id) {
    return document.getElementById(id);
}
// the event handler for the click event of the button
var joinList = function () {
    alert("The joinList function is being run.");
}
// the event handler for the change event of the text box
var changeValue = function () {
    alert("The changeValue function is being run.");
}
// the event handler for the load event that attaches two event handlers
window.onload = function () {
    $("join_list").onclick = joinList;          // attaches 1st handler
    $("email_address").onchange = changeValue;  // attaches 2nd handler
}
```

Description

- The event handler for the onload event of the window object can be used to attach the event handlers for other events after the DOM has been built.

Figure 2-20   How to use an onload event handler to attach the other event handlers

The Future Value application

To show you how all of the skills in this chapter can be used in a simple application, the next two figures present the Future Value application. This application gets the user entries for investment amount, yearly interest rate, and number of years. Then, it calculates the future value of the investment amount, rounds it to two decimal places, and displays it in the fourth text box on the page.

The HTML and CSS

Figure 2-21 shows the HTML for the Future Value application. In the head section of the HTML, the link element identifies the style sheet file that will be used for this application and the script element identifies the JavaScript file that will be used for this application. That means that both the HTML and JavaScript are in external files.

In the main element in the body, you can see the h1 element for the page followed by five sets of label and input elements. The first four input elements have the type attribute set to "text", which means that the elements are displayed as text boxes. The fifth input element has its type attribute set to "button", which means its click event can be used to start the calculation.

In the input element for the fourth text box, you should note that the disabled attribute has been turned on. This attribute shades a text box and also disables it so the user can't enter data into it.

In this figure, the CSS isn't shown, but it provides the alignment of the labels, text boxes, and buttons. It also centers the application in the web browser and puts a border around it.

The Future Value application

Future Value Calculator

Total Investment: `10000`
Annual Interest Rate: `7.5`
Number of Years: `10`
Future Value: `20610.32`
`Calculate`

The HTML (index.html)

```html
<!DOCTYPE html>
<html>
<head>
    <meta charset="UTF-8">
    <title>Future Value Calculator</title>
    <link rel="stylesheet" href="future_value.css">
    <script src="future_value.js"></script>
</head>
<body>
    <main>
        <h1>Future Value Calculator</h1>

        <label for="investment">Total Investment:</label>
        <input type="text" id="investment"><br>

        <label for="rate">Annual Interest Rate:</label>
        <input type="text" id="annual_rate"><br>

        <label for="years">Number of Years:</label>
        <input type="text" id="years"><br>

        <label for="future_value">Future Value:</label>
        <input type="text" id="future_value" disabled><br>

        <label> </label>
        <input type="button" id="calculate" value="Calculate"><br>
    </main>
</body>
</html>
```

Figure 2-21   The HTML for the Future Value application

The JavaScript

Figure 2-22 shows the JavaScript for the Future Value application. Here, you can see that strict mode is declared, all the variables have local scope, and the variables for each function are declared at the start of the function. These are all best coding practices.

You should also note the sequence of the functions. Here, the first function is the $ function. The second function is the calculateFV function, which calculates the future value of the investment amount. The third function is the processEntries function, which calls both the $ function and the calculateFV function. And the fourth function is the event handler for the load event, which attaches the processEntries function and moves the focus to the first text box.

In short, each function only calls functions that precede it in the code. Also, each function is assigned to a variable whose name consists of a verb and a noun that describes what the function does.

In the processEntries function, the user entries are retrieved using the $ function and then parsed into the investment, rate, and years variables. Then, an if statement tests whether any of the three entries is invalid because it isn't a number. If so, an error message is displayed. However, if all three entries are numbers, the one statement in the else clause calls the calculateFV function and passes it the entries.

The calculateFV function calculates the future value by using a for loop that is done once for each of the years that the user has specified. Within the loop, the interest for the year is calculated by multiplying the current value of the investment by the interest rate. Then, the result is added to the investment amount by using the += operator. When the loop finishes, the future value is rounded to two decimal places, and the value is returned to the calling statement. Then, that statement stores the value in the value property of the text box with "future_value" as its id.

When the web page is loaded, the onload event handler is executed first, even though it comes last in the script. It attaches the event handler for the click event of the Calculate button. After that, the browser waits until the user clicks on that button. Then, the processEntries function validates the entries, calls the calculateFV function if the entries are valid, and displays the result when it is returned.

In this application, the calculateFV function illustrates the use of a function that isn't an event handler. Because this function is short, you could delete this function and put the statements that calculate and round the future value into the else clause of the processEntries function. But moving its code into a separate function like this simplifies the code in the calling function.

The JavaScript (future_value.js)

```javascript
"use strict";
var $ = function (id) {
    return document.getElementById(id);
}
var calculateFV = function(investment, rate, years) {
    var futureValue = investment;
    for (var i = 1; i <= years; i++ ) {
        futureValue += futureValue * rate / 100;
    }
    futureValue = futureValue.toFixed(2);
    return futureValue;
}
var processEntries = function() {
    var investment = parseFloat( $("investment").value );
    var rate = parseFloat( $("annual_rate").value );
    var years = parseInt( $("years").value );

    if (isNaN(investment) || isNaN(rate) || isNaN(years)) {
        alert("One or more entries is invalid");
    }
    else {
        $("future_value").value = calculateFV(investment, rate, years);
    }
}
window.onload = function () {
    $("calculate").onclick = processEntries;
    $("investment").focus();
}
```

Best practices

- Strict mode is declared.

- All of the variables have local scope and are declared at the start of the functions that use them.

- The name of all the variables that have functions assigned to them consist of a verb and a noun that describe what the functions do. Function declarations should be given names like this too.

- All of the functions are coded before the functions that call them. That's required for function expressions.

Figure 2-22   The JavaScript for the Future Value application

Perspective

This chapter has presented the JavaScript skills that you need for developing jQuery applications. These are the skills that are used in the jQuery applications in this book. Now, if you feel comfortable with these skills, you're ready to go on to the next chapter.

But what if you don't feel comfortable with your JavaScript skills at this point? First, do the exercises at the end of this chapter and review the solutions. You may find that you know more than you think. Second, keep going anyway, and use this chapter as a reference whenever you don't understand the JavaScript that's used in a jQuery application. Third, get a copy of *Murach's JavaScript*. It's the tutorial and on-the-job reference that every jQuery developer needs.

Terms you should know

external JavaScript file	assignment statement	while statement
embedded JavaScript	assignment operator	do-while statement
whitespace	numeric literal	for statement
comment	concatenate	loop counter
block comment	string literal	loop index
single-line comment	escape sequence	array
comment out	object	array element
identifier	method	array length
keyword	property	array index
camel casing	call a method	function
primitive data type	dot operator (dot)	function expression
number data type	parameter	call a function
integer	window object	return statement
decimal value	global object	parameter
floating-point number	document object	function declaration
string data type	method chaining	scope
string	chaining	local variable
empty string	control statement	local scope
Boolean data type	conditional expression	global variable
numeric expression	relational operator	global scope
arithmetic operator	compound conditional	strict mode
order of precedence	expression	event
variable	logical operator	event handler
declare a variable	if statement	attach an event handler

Summary

- The JavaScript for an HTML document is commonly coded in an *external JavaScript file* that's identified by a script element. However, the JavaScript can also be *embedded* in a script element in the head of a document.

- JavaScript statements end with semicolons. JavaScript *comments* can be *block* or *single-line*. JavaScript *identifiers* are case-sensitive, and they should be coded with either *camel casing* or underscore notation.

- JavaScript provides three *primitive data types*. The *number data type* provides for both *integers* and *decimal values*. The *string data type* provides for character (*string*) data. And the *Boolean data type* provides for true and false values.

- When you assign a value to a number *variable*, you can use *numeric expressions* that include *arithmetic operators*, variable names, and *numeric literals*.

- When you assign a value to a string variable, you can use *string expressions* that include *concatenation operators*, variable names, and *string literals*. Within a string literal, you can use *escape sequences* to provide special characters.

- JavaScript provides many *objects* that provide *methods* and *properties* that you can *call* or refer to in your applications. Since the *window object* is the *global object* for JavaScript, you can omit it when referring to its methods or properties.

- The Textbox, Number, Date, and String objects provide methods and properties for text boxes, number data types, dates, and string data types. When working with the methods and properties of these objects, you often use *method chaining*.

- When you code a *conditional expression*, you can use *relational operators*, the global isNaN method, and *logical operators*. The primary control statements in JavaScript are the *if*, *while*, *do-while*, and *for statements*.

- An *array* can store one or more *elements* that you can refer to by the *indexes* of the elements. The *length* property of the array holds the number of elements in the array. To process the elements in an array, you can use a for loop.

- A *function* consists of a block of code that is executed when the function is *called*. The function can require one or more *parameters* that are passed to it by the calling statement.

- A *function expression* is stored in a variable and usually isn't named, while a *function declaration* is given a name but isn't stored in a variable.

- *Local variables* are defined within a function and can only be accessed by statements within the function. *Global variables* are defined outside of all functions and can be accessed by any of the other code.

- *Strict mode* is a JavaScript feature that causes the JavaScript engine to throw an error if a variable name is used before it has been declared.

- An *event handler* is a function that is called when an *event* like clicking on a button occurs. To make this work, the function must be *attached* to the event.

Before you do the exercises for this book...

If you haven't already done so, you should install the Chrome browser and install the downloads for this book as described in appendix A.

Exercise 2-1   Enhance the Future Value application

In this exercise, you'll enhance the Future Value application in two ways. One will be to provide better data validation. The other will be to add a clear button:

Do all of the testing for this exercise in Chrome. Then, if you have any problems as you test your enhancements, refer back to figure 1-15, which shows how to find JavaScript errors when you're using Chrome.

Test the application

1. Open your text editor or IDE, and open these files:

   ```
   c:\jquery\exercises\ch02\future_value\index.html
   c:\jquery\exercises\ch02\future_value\future_value.js
   ```

   Then, review the JavaScript code to see that it's the same as in figure 2-22.

2. Test this application in Chrome with valid data to see how it works. When you click the Calculate button, the correct result should be displayed.

3. Test the data validation routine by entering invalid data. Note that one error message is displayed in an alert dialog box no matter which entry is invalid.

Enhance the data validation

4. Enhance the data validation so it displays a different error message for each type of entry:

   Investment amount must be > 0 and <= 100000
   Interest rate must be > 0 and <= 15
   Number of years must be > 0 and <= 50

   Do this with one if statement that consists of one if clause that tests the first entry, two else if clauses that test the next two entries, and an else clause that calls the calculateFV function.

Add other enhancements

5. Change the calculateFV function from a function expression to a function declaration. Then, note that the application works the same as it did before.

6. Add a Clear Entries button below the Calculate button. To do that, copy the HTML for the label and input elements for the Calculate button, and paste it after the input element for the Calculate button. Then, modify the HTML for the Clear Entries button so it has a unique id and the right value attribute.

7. Add a function expression that clears the entries in the four text boxes, and assign it to a variable named clearEntries. Then, add a statement in the onload event handler that attaches the clearEntries function to the click event of the Clear Entries button.

8. Add a statement to the onload event handler that attaches the clearEntries function to the double-click event of the investment text box. Then, test this change.

See what can happens when you remove strict mode

9. Change the next to last statement in the calculateFV function as follows so the variable name is misspelled as *futurevalue* instead of *futureValue*.

    ```
    var futureValue = investment;
    for (var i = 1; i <= years; i++ ) {
        futureValue += futureValue * rate / 100;
    }
    futurevalue = futureValue.toFixed(2);
    ```

10. Test this application with valid entries, and note that it doesn't work. Then, press F12 to display the developer tools, click on the Console tab, and see this error message:

    ```
    futurevalue is not defined
    ```

    Then, click on the link to the right of the message to go to the statement that causes the error. This shows that strict mode prevents the declaration of a variable without using the var keyword.

11. Delete the strict mode declaration, and test again. This time, the application works, but the result isn't rounded. That's because the JavaScript engine treated futurevalue as a new variable.

12. Restore the strict mode declaration and return the variable name to future-Value. Then, test again to make sure the application is working.

Exercise 2-2   Build a Miles Per Gallon application

If you would like to try writing the JavaScript code for an application from scratch, this exercise guides you through the process of building a Miles Per Gallon application that looks like this:

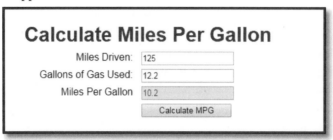

Do all of the testing for this exercise in Chrome. Then, if you have any problems as you test your enhancements, refer back to figure 1-15, which shows how to find JavaScript errors when you're using Chrome.

Open and review the starting files

1. Open your text editor or IDE, and open this file:

    `c:\jquery\exercises\ch02\mpg\index.html`

2. Run the application to see that the HTML provides for the user interface, but nothing works. Then, review the JavaScript in the script element, and note that it contains just the strict mode declaration.

Create the functions

3. Create the standard $ function.

4. Create a new function expression that's assigned to a variable named calculateMPG. This function should have two parameters that receive the user's entries: miles driven and gallons of gas used. It should calculate the miles per gallon by dividing miles by gallons and then round the result to one decimal place.

5. Create the event handler for the click event of the Calculate MPG button. This handler should be a function expression that's assigned to a variable named processEntries. It should get the user entries with no data validation, call the calculateMPG function, and store the returned result in the third text box.

6. Create an event handler for the onload event that attaches the processEntries function to the click event of the Calculate button. This handler should also move the focus to the first text box.

7. Test this application with valid entries, and debug until this works correctly.

Add data validation

8. Add data validation that displays appropriate error messages in an alert dialog box if either entry is invalid. You decide what the error messages should be and how thorough the validation tests should be.

3

How to script the DOM with JavaScript

This chapter presents some of the skills for DOM scripting with JavaScript. As you read this chapter, though, keep in mind that most DOM scripting is done with jQuery because it's much easier. As a result, your focus should be more on the concepts than the coding details. If you're new to JavaScript, this chapter will also give you a chance to get more familiar with how JavaScript can be used for building applications.

DOM scripting properties and methods

To start, this chapter shows you how to use some of the properties and methods of the DOM for DOM scripting. These are defined by the *DOM Core specification* that is implemented by all current browsers.

DOM scripting concepts

Figure 3-1 presents the DOM scripting concepts that you need to understand before you start DOM scripting. First, the *Document Object Model*, or *DOM*, is built as an HTML page is loaded into the browser. Second, you can use JavaScript or jQuery to change the DOM. Third, as soon as the DOM is changed, the web page is updated to reflect those changes. That's the magic of *DOM scripting*.

As the HTML and diagram in this figure show, the DOM contains *nodes* that represent all of the HTML elements and attributes for the page. Besides the *element nodes* that are represented by ovals in this diagram, the DOM includes *text nodes* that hold the data for the HTML elements. In this diagram, these text nodes are rectangles. For instance, the first text node contains the text for the title element in the head section: "Join Email List". The one to the right of that contains the text for the h1 element in the body: "Please join our email list". And so on.

For simplicity, this diagram only includes the element and text nodes, but the DOM also contains *attribute nodes*, and each attribute node can have a text node that holds the attribute value. Also, if the HTML includes comments, the DOM will include *comment nodes*.

If you study the table in this figure, you can see that an element node can have element, text, and comment nodes as child nodes. An attribute node can have a text node as a child node. And a text node can't have a child node. Even though an attribute node is attached to an element node, it isn't considered to be a child node of the element node.

The properties and methods for working with DOM nodes are defined by a specification called an *interface*. In the topics that follow, you'll learn how to work with the properties and methods of the Node, Document, and Element interfaces.

As you work with these interfaces, you'll come across terms like *parent*, *child*, *sibling*, and *descendant*. These terms are used just as they are in a family tree. In the diagram in this figure, for example, the form element is the parent of the label, input, and span elements, and the label, input, and span elements are children of the form element. The label, input, and span elements are also siblings because they have the same parent. Similarly, the h1 and form elements are children of the body element, and the h1, form, label, input, and span elements are all descendants of the body element.

You should also be able to see these relationships in the HTML for a web page. In the HTML in this figure, for example, the indentation clearly shows the children and descendants for each element.

The code for a web page

```
<!DOCTYPE html>
<html>
<head>
    <title>Join Email List</title>
</head>
<body>
    <h1>Please join our email list</h1>
    <form id="email_form" name="email_form" action="join.html" method="get">
        <label for="email_address">Email Address:</label>
        <input type="text" id="email_address">
        <span id="email_error">*</span><br>
    </form>
</body>
</html>
```

The DOM for the web page

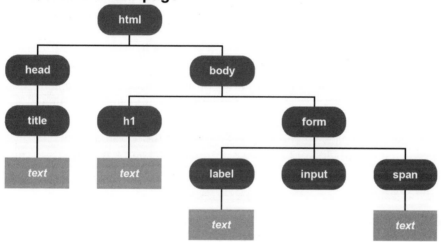

The DOM nodes that you commonly use

Type	Description
Document	Root node of the DOM. It can only have one Element node as a child node.
Element	An element in the web page. It can have Element, Text, and Comment nodes as child nodes.
Attr	An attribute of an element. Although it is attached to an Element node, it isn't considered a child node. It can have a Text node as a child node.
Text	The text for an element or attribute. It can't have a child node.

DOM scripting concepts

- The *DOM* (*Document Object Model*) is a hierarchical collection of *nodes* in the web browser's memory that represents the current web page. The DOM for a web page is built as the page is loaded by the web browser.

- To modify the DOM, you can use the properties and methods that are defined by the *DOM Core specification*.

- Whenever the DOM is changed, the web browser displays the results of the change.

Figure 3-1   DOM scripting concepts

The properties of the Node interface

Figure 3-2 describes six properties that you can use for working with nodes. These properties are defined by the Node interface. All the examples in this figure assume the use of the $ function that gets an element by id.

The first example shows how to use the firstChild and nodeValue properties to get the text of an HTML element. In this case, this statement will store an asterisk (*) in the variable named errorText if the statement is run before the node is changed. That's because this node is set to the asterisk by the HTML.

If you refer back to the diagram in the previous figure, you can see that the firstChild property is needed to get the text node for the span element. Then, the nodeValue property gets the text from that text node.

The second example shows how to use the firstChild and nodeValue properties to put text into the text node of an HTML element. This is how the Email List application of the last chapter put the error messages in the span elements that follow the text boxes.

The third example shows how to use three properties of the input element with "email_address" as its id to set the text for the span element that follows it to an empty string. First, the nextElementSibling property gets the span element that is the next sibling of the input element. Then, the firstChild and nodeValue properties get the text.

For all of these examples, you need to make sure that the text node contains a text value when it initially loads. Otherwise, the element won't have a firstChild property. You'll learn more about this later on in this chapter.

Some of the properties of the Node interface

Property	Description
nodeValue	For a Text, Comment, or Attribute node, this property returns the text that's stored in the node. Otherwise, it returns a null value.
parentNode	Returns a Node object for the parent node of the current node if one exists. Otherwise, this property returns a null value.
childNodes	Returns an array of Node objects representing the child nodes of the current node. If this node doesn't have child nodes, the array contains no elements.
firstChild	Returns a Node object for the first child node. If this node doesn't have child nodes, this property returns a null value.
lastChild	Returns a Node object for the last child node. If this node doesn't have child nodes, this property returns a null value.
nextElementSibling	Returns a Node object for the next sibling. If this node doesn't have a sibling element that follows it, this property returns a null value.

HTML that contains element and text nodes

```
<body>
    <h1>Please join our email list</h1>
    <form id="email_form" name="email_form" action="join.html" method="get">
        <label for="email_address">Email Address:</label>
        <input type="text" id="email_address">
        <span id="email_error">*</span><br>
        <label> </label>
        <input type="button" id="join_list" value="Join our List">
    </form>
</body>
```

How to get the text of an HTML element with "email_error" as its id

```
var errorText = $("email_error").firstChild.nodeValue;
```

How to set the text of an HTML element with "email_error" as its id

```
$("email_error").firstChild.nodeValue = "Entry is invalid.";
```

How to set the text of an HTML element without using its id

```
$("email_address").nextElementSibling.firstChild.nodeValue = "";
```

Description

- An *interface* describes the properties and methods for an object.
- When *DOM scripting*, you often use the properties of the Node interface. Some of the most useful properties are summarized in the table above.
- In the examples above, the $ sign calls the standard $ function that gets the element that has the id that's passed to it as the parameter.

Figure 3-2   The properties of the Node interface

The methods of the Document and Element interfaces

The first table in figure 3-3 summarizes three methods that are in both the Document and Element interfaces. All three of these methods return arrays. For instance, the getElementsByTagName method returns an array that contains all of the Element nodes with the specified tag name.

If these methods are used with the document object, they get all of the elements in the document. This is illustrated by the first example that gets all of the <a> elements in the document and puts them in an array named links.

If these methods are used with an element as the object, they get all of the elements that are descendants of that element. For instance, the first statement in the second example gets the element with "image_list" as its id. Then, the second statement gets an array of all of the li elements that are descendants of the image_list element.

The second table in this figure summarizes some of the methods of the Element interface that work with attributes. For instance, the third example in this figure uses the hasAttribute method to find out whether an element has a class attribute. If it does, it uses the getAttribute method to get the value of that attribute.

The fourth example shows how to use the setAttribute method to set an attribute. Here, the second statement sets the class attribute to "open". When this method is used, if the class doesn't already exist, the method creates it. Then, the last example in this figure uses the removeAttribute method to remove the class attribute.

Common methods of the Document and Element interfaces

Method	Description
getElementsByTagName(*tagName*)	Returns an array of all Element objects descended from the document or element that have a tag that matches the specified tag.
getElementsByName(*name*)	Returns an array of all Element objects descended from the document or element that have a name attribute that matches the specified name.
getElementsByClassName(*classNames*)	Returns an array of all Element objects descended from the document or element that have a class attribute with a name or names that match the parameter. The classNames parameter can be a single name or a space-separated list of class names.

Common methods of the Element interface

Method	Description
hasAttribute(*name*)	Returns true if the Element has the attribute specified in name.
getAttribute(*name*)	Returns the value of the attribute specified in name or an empty string if an attribute of that name isn't set.
setAttribute(*name, value*)	Sets the attribute specified in name to the specified value. If the attribute doesn't already exist, it creates the attribute too.
removeAttribute(*name*)	Removes the attribute specified in name.

How to create an array of all <a> tags in a document

```
var links = document.getElementsByTagName("a");
```

How to create an array of all li tags within a ul element (image_list)

```
var list = document.getElementById("image_list");
var items = list.getElementsByTagName("li");
```

How to test for and get an attribute

```
var list = document.getElementById("image_list");
if ( list.hasAttribute("class") ) {
    var classAttribute = list.getAttribute("class"));
}
```

How to set an attribute

```
var list = document.getElementById("image_list");
list.setAttribute("class", "open");
```

How to remove an attribute

```
var list = document.getElementById("image_list");
list.removeAttribute("class");
```

Description

- The methods of the Document and Element interfaces let you get arrays of elements.

- The methods of the Element interface also let you work with attributes.

Figure 3-3   The methods of the Document and Element interfaces

The Email List application

The next two figures show how the properties and methods of the Node, Document, and Element interfaces are used in a simple DOM scripting application that we call the Email List application. Here, three text boxes are used to get entries from the user. Then, when the user clicks on the Join our List button, the entries are validated. If all three entries are valid, the form is submitted to the server. If any of the entries are invalid, error messages are displayed to the right of the related text boxes.

The HTML

Figure 3-4 shows the HTML for this application. It contains a form element that contains three sets of label, input, and span elements. Here, the input elements have the type attribute set to "text" so they are rendered as text boxes. The span elements that follow contain single asterisks to show that the elements are required, and the span elements receive the error messages if the related entries are invalid.

These elements are followed by another label and input element. But this time, the type attribute for the input element is "button" so it is rendered as a button.

Notice that the span elements don't have id attributes to identify them. Instead, the JavaScript will modify the contents of these elements by using the nextElementSibling properties of the input elements to refer to the span elements and then the firstChild property to refer to the text node within the span elements.

Remember, though, that for this to work, the HTML must give each span element a starting value. Otherwise, the firstChild property will be null. In this case, the starting values are asterisks, but they could be non-breaking spaces ( ) if you want the starting values to appear empty.

The Email List application in a web browser

Please join our email list

Email Address:	ben@yahoo.com
Re-enter Email Address:	ben@yahoo	This entry must equal first entry.
First Name:		This field is required.
	Join our List

The HTML file for the page

```html
<!DOCTYPE html>
<html>
<head>
    <title>Join Email List</title>
    <link rel="stylesheet" href="email_list.css">
    <script src="email_list.js"></script>
</head>
<body>
    <main>
        <h1>Please join our email list</h1>
        <form id="email_form" name="email_form"
            action="join.html" method="get">

            <label for="email_address1">Email Address:</label>
            <input type="text" id="email_address1" name="email_address1">
            <span>*</span><br>

            <label for="email_address2">Re-enter Email Address:</label>
            <input type="text" id="email_address2" name="email_address2">
            <span>*</span><br>

            <label for="first_name">First Name:</label>
            <input type="text" id="first_name" name="first_name">
            <span>*</span><br>

            <label> </label>
            <input type="button" id="join_list" value="Join our List">

        </form>
    </main>
</body>
</html>
```

Figure 3-4   The HTML for the Email List application

The JavaScript

Figure 3-5 presents the JavaScript for this application. At the start of the joinList function, you can see that four variables are declared. The first three use the standard $ function to store the objects for the three text boxes on the form in variables named emailAddress1, emailAddress2, and firstName. The fourth variable is a Boolean variable that indicates whether all the user entries are valid (isValid = true) or whether one or more of the entries are invalid (isValid = false).

This is followed by three if statements that check the three entries for validity. For instance, the first if statement checks whether the value of the first email address entry is equal to an empty string (""). If so, this statement places an error message in the span element after the input element:

```
emailAddress1.nextElementSibling.firstChild.nodeValue =
    "This field is required.";
```

Then, it sets the isValid variable to false. Otherwise, the else clause uses a similar statement to put an empty string into the span element to show that the entry is valid.

The next two if statements use similar coding to test for validity and put error messages into the span elements for invalid entries. They are followed by one more if statement that checks whether the isValid variable is equal to true. If it is, the submit method of the form is used to submit the form to the server for processing. But if the isValid variable is false, nothing is done so the user can correct the invalid entries.

The JavaScript for the Email List application

```javascript
"use strict";
var $ = function (id) {
    return document.getElementById(id);
}
var joinList = function () {
    var emailAddress1 = $("email_address1");
    var emailAddress2 = $("email_address2");
    var firstName = $("first_name");
    var isValid = true;

    // validate the first entry
    if (emailAddress1.value == "") {
        emailAddress1.nextElementSibling.firstChild.nodeValue =
            "This field is required.";
        isValid = false;
    } else {
        emailAddress1.nextElementSibling.firstChild.nodeValue = "";
    }

    // validate the second entry
    if (emailAddress2.value == "") {
        emailAddress2.nextElementSibling.firstChild.nodeValue =
            "This field is required.";
        isValid = false;
    } else if (emailAddress1.value != emailAddress2.value) {
        emailAddress2.nextElementSibling.firstChild.nodeValue =
            "This entry must equal first entry.";
        isValid = false;
    } else {
        emailAddress2.nextElementSibling.firstChild.nodeValue = "";
    }

    // validate the third entry
    if (first_name.value == "") {
        first_name.nextElementSibling.firstChild.nodeValue =
            "This field is required.";
        isValid = false;
    } else {
        first_name.nextElementSibling.firstChild.nodeValue = "";
    }

    // submit the form if all entries are valid
    if (isValid) {
        $("email_form").submit();
    }
}
window.onload = function () {
    $("join_list").onclick = joinList;
    $("email_address1").focus();
}
```

Figure 3-5   The JavaScript for the Email List application

The FAQs application

Now, you'll see how DOM scripting can be used in another type of application. We call this the FAQs (Frequently Asked Questions) application, and you can see its user interface in figure 3-6.

Here, if the user clicks on a heading with a plus sign before it, the text below it is displayed and the plus sign is changed to a minus sign. Similarly, if the user clicks on a heading with a minus sign before it, the text below it is hidden and the minus sign is changed to a plus sign. The user can display the text below all three headings at the same time, and the user can hide the text below all three headings at the same time. Areas of content like this that can be hidden or displayed by the user are often referred to as *collapsible panels*.

The HTML and CSS

In the HTML in this figure, you can see that each of the questions is coded in an <a> element within an h2 element, and each h2 element is followed by a div element that contains the answer. Note that the href attributes in these elements are coded as # signs so these links don't go anywhere.

Because <a> elements are coded within the h2 elements, a user can tab from one heading to the next. Then, when a user tabs to a heading and presses the Enter key, the effect is the same as clicking on the heading. This makes this app easier to use for motor-impaired users who can't handle a mouse.

In the CSS, you can see that both the focus and hover pseudo-classes are set to the color blue. That way, the <a> elements will look the same whether the user hovers the mouse over a link or tabs to the link.

Next, look at the two rule sets for the h2 elements. The first one applies to all h2 elements, and it applies a background property that includes an image named plus.png. This image is displayed just once (no-repeat) to the left of the element and it is vertically centered.

The second rule set for the h2 elements applies to elements that have a class property set to "minus". This rule set applies a background property like the one for all h2 elements, but this time it uses an image named minus.png. That's the image that's used when the text below a heading is displayed.

Now, look at the two rule sets for the div elements. The first one sets the display property to none, which hides the contents of the div element. In contrast, the second rule set applies to div elements that have a class attribute set to "open". It sets the display property to block, which means that the contents of the div element are displayed.

With the HTML and CSS set up this way, all the JavaScript has to do is add and remove these classes as the user clicks on a heading. If, for example, the user clicks on the middle h2 heading when the application starts and its text is hidden, the JavaScript needs to add a class attribute with the value "minus" for the clicked h2 element and add a class attribute with the value "open" for its sibling div element.

The FAQs application in a browser

JavaScript FAQs

− **What is JavaScript?**

  JavaScript is a browser-based programming language that makes web pages
  more responsive and saves round trips to the server.

＋ **What is jQuery?**

＋ **Why is jQuery becoming so popular?**

The HTML

```html
<body>
    <main id="faqs">
        <h1>JavaScript FAQs</h1>
        <h2><a href="#">What is JavaScript?</a></h2>
        <div>
            <p>JavaScript is a programming language that's built into the
                major web browsers. It makes web pages more responsive and
                saves round trips to the server.</p>
        </div>
        <h2><a href="#">What is jQuery?</a></h2>
        <div>
            <p>jQuery is a library of the JavaScript functions that you're
                most likely to need as you develop websites.</p>
        </div>
        <h2><a href="#">Why is jQuery becoming so popular?</a></h2>
        <div>
            <p>Three reasons:</p>
            <ul>
                <li>It's free.</li>
                <li>It lets you get more done in less time.</li>
                <li>All of its functions are cross-browser compatible.</li>
            </ul>
        </div>
    </main>
</body>
```

The CSS

```css
a {
    color: black;
    text-decoration: none; }
a:focus, a:hover {
    color: blue; }
h2 {
    background: url(images/plus.png) no-repeat left center; }
h2.minus {
    background: url(images/minus.png) no-repeat left center; }
div {
    display: none; }
div.open {
    display: block; }
```

Figure 3-6   The HTML and CSS for the FAQs application

The JavaScript

Figure 3-7 shows the JavaScript for this application. In chapter 5, you'll learn how jQuery makes coding this application much easier. But this will give you a basis for comparison.

Here, the event handler for the onload event attaches the event handlers for each of the h2 elements. To do that, its first statement gets the object for the element that has "faqs" as its id. That's the main element in the HTML code. Then, the second statement uses the getElementsByTagName method to get an array of the h2 elements within that element. This array is stored in a variable named h2Elements.

This is followed by a for statement that attaches an event handler to each h2 element. To do that, its loop is executed once for each element in the h2Elements array. The only statement in this loop attaches the event handler named "toggle" to the click event of the current h2 element in the array.

The onload event handler ends by setting the focus to the <a> element in the first h2 element in the array of h2 elements. It does that with this code:

```
h2Elements[0].firstChild.focus();
```

This refers to the first child of the first h2 element in the array (index zero), which is its <a> element.

Now, look at the toggle function that is the event handler for the click event of each h2 element. The first statement within this function declares a new variable named h2 and assigns the *this* keyword to it. This is the critical statement in this function, because the this keyword refers to the h2 element that was clicked.

The second statement in the toggle function gets the div element below the current h2 element by using the nextElementSibling method. Then, the if statement that follows tests whether the h2 element has a class attribute. If it does, it removes that attribute. If it doesn't, it adds a class attribute with a value of "minus". That means that the CSS will change the background image from a plus sign to a minus sign, or vice versa.

Then, the second if statement uses similar code to add an "open" class to the div element if it doesn't have one and to remove the class if it does have one. And that means that the CSS will change the display property from none to block, or vice versa.

Now that you've reviewed this code, you should note that it will work for any number of h2 and div elements that are defined by the HTML. You should also note that the div elements can contain whatever HTML elements the application requires, including img, <a>, and list elements. This application should also give you some idea of what JavaScript and DOM scripting can do.

The JavaScript for the FAQs application

```
var $ = function (id) { return document.getElementById(id); };

// the event handler for the click event of each h2 element
var toggle = function () {
    var h2 = this;                      // this refers to the clicked h2 tag
    var div = h2.nextElementSibling;    // div = h2's sibling div

    // toggle + and - image in h2 elements by adding or removing a class
    if (h2.hasAttribute("class")) {
        h2.removeAttribute("class");
    } else {
        h2.setAttribute("class", "minus");
    }

    // toggle div visibility by adding or removing a class
    if (div.hasAttribute("class")) {
        div.removeAttribute("class");
    } else {
        div.setAttribute("class", "open");
    }
};

window.onload = function () {
    // get the h2 tags
    var faqs = $("faqs");
    var h2Elements = faqs.getElementsByTagName("h2");

    // attach event handler for each h2 tag
    for (var i = 0; i < h2Elements.length; i++ ) {
        h2Elements[i].onclick = toggle;
    }
    // set focus on first h2 tag's <a> tag
    h2Elements[0].firstChild.focus();
};
```

Notes

- The first two statements in the onload event handler create an array of the h2 elements in the main element with "faqs" as its id.

- The for loop in the onload event handler is executed once for each of the h2 elements. It attaches the toggle event handler to the onclick event of each h2 element.

- In the code for the toggle event handler, the *this* keyword refers to the h2 element that has been clicked.

Figure 3-7   The JavaScript for the FAQs application

DOM scripting skills for links and images

The next two figures present two DOM scripting skills that you need for working with links and images: how to cancel the default action of an event and how to preload images to improve performance.

How to cancel the default action of an event

The table in figure 3-8 presents some of the common *default actions* for the click event of HTML elements. For instance, the default action for clicking on a link is to load the page or go to the placeholder that's specified by the href attribute of the link. Similarly, the default action for clicking on a submit or reset button in a form is to submit or reset the data in the form.

For some applications, though, you don't want the default actions to occur. Then, you need to cancel those actions. Unfortunately, this introduces a browser-compatibility problem, because older versions of IE work differently than DOM-compliant browsers like Firefox, Safari, Opera, and Chrome.

The good news is that jQuery provides a single preventDefault method that works in all browsers. As a result, you may never need to use JavaScript to cancel the default action. So for now, the concept in this figure is more important than the coding details.

The first example in this figure shows how easy it is to cancel a default action in a DOM-compliant browser. In these browsers, an event object is created whenever an event occurs, and this object is automatically passed to the event handler. This object contains information about the event and provides a method that lets you control the behavior of the event.

To access this event, you code a parameter in the function for the event handler as shown in the first example. In this case, evt is used as the parameter name, and it will receive the event object when the handler is called. Then, to cancel the default action, you use the preventDefault method of the event object that the parameter represents.

For older versions of IE, though, you need to use the code in the second example. To get the event object, you use the window.event property instead of getting the object as a parameter. Then, you set the returnValue property of the event object to false to prevent the default action from occurring.

To make your applications compatible with both types of browsers, you combine the two techniques as shown in the third example. Here, the function has a parameter that will receive the event object in a DOM-compliant browser. Then, the first if statement in the function tests the evt parameter to see if the event object is undefined. This works because if the object is undefined, a false value is returned. In that case, the browser is IE, so this code assigns the event object in the window.event property to the evt parameter. Otherwise, the browser is DOM-compliant, so the evt parameter already contains the event object.

Common default actions for the click event

Tag	Default action for the click event
a	Load the page or go to the placeholder in the href attribute.
input	Submit the form if the type attribute is set to submit.
input	Reset the form if the type attribute is set to reset.
button	Submit the form if the type attribute is set to submit.
button	Reset the form if the type attribute is set to reset.

DOM-compliant code that cancels the default action

```
var eventHandler = function (evt) {
    evt.preventDefault();
}
```

IE code that cancels the default action

```
var eventHandler = function () {
    var evt = window.event;
    evt.returnValue = false;
}
```

Browser-compatible code that cancels the default action

```
var eventHandler = function (evt) {
    // If the event object is not sent, get it
    if (!evt) { evt = window.event; )     // for IE

    // Cancel the default action
    if (evt.preventDefault) {
        evt.preventDefault();             // for most browsers
    }
    else {
        evt.returnValue = false;          // for IE
    }
}
```

Description

- In some JavaScript applications, you need to cancel the *default action* of an event.
- All browsers except older IE browsers pass an event object to the first parameter of the event handler, but IE stores the event object in the global window.event property.
- All browsers except older IE browsers provide a preventDefault method for the event object. When called, this method prevents the default action of the event from occurring.
- In contrast, older IE browsers provide a property named returnValue in the event object. When set to false, this property prevents the default action of the event from occurring.
- Since jQuery provides a browser-compatible preventDefault method, you may never need to use JavaScript for this purpose.

Figure 3-8   How to cancel the default action of an event

Then, the second if statement tests the evt parameter to see if the preventDefault method of the event object is defined. If it is, this code calls the preventDefault method. If it isn't, this code sets the returnValue property to false.

How to preload images

In DOM scripting applications that load an image in response to a user event, the image isn't downloaded until the JavaScript code changes the src attribute of the img element that will display the changed image. For large images or slow connections, this can cause a delay while the browser loads the image.

To solve this problem, your application can download the images before the user event occurs. This is known as *preloading images*. Although this may result in a longer delay when the page is initially loaded, the user won't encounter any delays when using the application.

Figure 3-9 shows how to preload an image. First, you use the new keyword to create an Image object and store it in a variable. This creates an empty Image object. Then, you set the src property to the URL of the image that you want to preload. This causes the web browser to preload the image.

The example in this figure shows how to preload the images for all the links on a page. This assumes that the href attribute in each link contains the location of each image that needs to be preloaded. First, the getElementsByTagName method is used to get an array of all the links, and this array is stored in a variable named links. Then, a for loop is used to process each link in the array.

Within the loop, the first statement assigns the current link to the link variable, and the second statement creates a new Image object. Then, the third statement sets the src property of the Image object to the href property of the link. This preloads the image. As a result, all of the images will be preloaded when the loop finishes.

How to create and preload an Image object

How to create an Image object

```
var image = new Image();
```

How to preload an image in an Image object

```
image.src = "image_name.jpg";
```

How to preload all images referenced by the href attributes of <a> tags

```
var links = document.getElementsByTagName("a");
var i, link, image;
for ( i = 0; i < links.length; i++ ) {
    link = links[i];
    image = new Image();
    image.src = link.href;
}
```

Description

- When an application *preloads images*, it loads all of the images that it's going to need when the page loads, and it stores these images in the web browser's cache for future use.

- If the images aren't preloaded, they are retrieved from the server as needed. In some cases, that can cause a noticeable delay.

- When you use the new keyword to create an Image object, the object is empty. Then, when you set the src attribute of this object, the web browser preloads the image identified by that attribute.

Figure 3-9   How to preload images

The Image Swap application

To show the use of the two skills you've just learned, figure 3-10 illustrates an *image swap* application. Here, the main image is swapped whenever the user clicks on one of the small (thumbnail) images. In this example, the user has clicked on the sixth thumbnail so the larger version of that image is displayed. In this application, the caption above the large image is also changed as part of the image swap, but that isn't always done in image swaps.

The HTML and CSS

In the HTML for this application, img elements are used to display the six thumbnail images. However, these elements are coded within <a> elements so the images are clickable and they can receive the focus. In the <a> elements, the href attributes identify the images to be swapped when the links are clicked and the title attributes provide the text for the related captions. In this case, both the <a> elements and the img elements are coded within a ul element.

After the ul element, you can see the h2 element for the caption and the img element for the main image on the page. The contents of the h2 element provides the caption for the first image, and the src attribute of the img element provides the location for the first image. That way, when the application first starts, the first caption and image are displayed.

The two ids that are used by the JavaScript are highlighted here. First, the id of the h2 element is set to "caption" so the JavaScript can change the caption. Second, the id of the main img element is set to "image" so the JavaScript can change the image.

For the motor-impaired, this HTML provides accessibility by coding the img elements for the thumbnails within <a> elements. That way, the user can access the thumbnail links by pressing the Tab key, and the user can swap the image by pressing the Enter key when a thumbnail has the focus, which starts the onclick event handler.

Of note in the CSS for this page is the rule set for the li elements. As this figure shows, their display properties are set to inline so the thumbnail images go from left to right instead of from top to bottom. Also, the padding to the right of each item is set to 10 pixels to provide space between the thumbnail images.

The user interface for the Image Swap application

The HTML

```
<main>
    <h1>Ram Tap Combined Test</h1>
    <ul id="image_list">
        <li><a href="images/h1.jpg" title="James Allison: 1-1"
            <img src="thumbnails/t1.jpg" alt=""></a></li>
        <li><a href="images/h2.jpg" title="James Allison: 1-2">
            <img src="thumbnails/t2.jpg" alt=""></a></li>
        <li><a href="images/h3.jpg" title="James Allison: 1-3">
            <img src="thumbnails/t3.jpg" alt=""></a></li>
        <li><a href="images/h4.jpg" title="James Allison: 1-4">
            <img src="thumbnails/t4.jpg" alt=""></a></li>
        <li><a href="images/h5.jpg" title="James Allison: 1-5">
            <img src="thumbnails/t5.jpg" alt=""></a></li>
        <li><a href="images/h6.jpg" title="James Allison: 1-6">
            <img src="thumbnails/t6.jpg" alt=""></a></li>
    </ul>
    <h2 id="caption">James Allison 1-1</h2>
    <p><img src="images/h1.jpg" alt="" id="image"></p>
</main>
```

The CSS for the li elements

```
li {
    padding-right: 10px;
    display: inline;
}
```

Figure 3-10   The user interface, HTML, and CSS for the Image Swap application

The JavaScript

Figure 3-11 presents the JavaScript for this application. In chapter 5, you'll learn how to code this application with jQuery, which makes this much easier. But the JavaScript shows what needs to be done to get this application to work, and you'll need some of this code in a jQuery version of this application.

In the onload event handler, the first statement gets the object for the ul element (image_list). Then, the second statement gets an array of the <a> elements within the image list and saves it in a variable name imageLinks. After that, the code processes each of the links in the array using a for loop.

Within the for loop, each link is retrieved and the event handler named "swap" is attached to its click event. In addition, the image that's identified by the href attribute of the link is preloaded. To do that, the href attribute is assigned to the src attribute of a new Image object.

The onload event handler ends by moving the focus to the first <a> element. To do that, the focus method is called on the first element in the array of links.

Now, look at the swap function that's the event handler for the click event of each link. Note here that the function has an evt parameter that will receive the event object for the current link in a DOM-compliant browser. To get the current link (the one that was clicked), the first statement in the function uses the this keyword. Then, the next two statements get the h2 element for the caption and the img element that displays the swaps. These objects are for the nodes in the DOM.

After that, the src attribute in the image node is changed to the href attribute of the current link, and the value of the first child of the caption node is changed to the title attribute of the link. Later, when the application is run and the user clicks on a thumbnail, these statements will change the DOM so the image and caption are immediately changed in the display.

This event handler ends by cancelling the default action of the event for the link using the code in figure 3-8. Since the default event is to display the file identified by the href attribute, cancelling this action is essential. Otherwise, clicking on a link would display the image that's specified by the href attribute in a new browser window or tab. Remember, though, that jQuery offers a preventDefault method that is browser compatible.

The JavaScript for the Image Swap application

```javascript
$ = function (id) {
    return document.getElementById(id);
}

var swap = function(evt) {
    var link = this;
    var captionNode = $("caption");
    var imageNode = $("image");

    imageNode.src = link.getAttribute("href");
    captionNode.firstChild.nodeValue = link.getAttribute("title");

    // Cancel the default action of the event
    if (!evt) { evt = window.event; }
    if ( evt.preventDefault ) {
        evt.preventDefault();              // DOM compliant code
    }
    else {
        evt.returnValue = false;
    }
}

window.onload = function () {
    var listNode = $("image_list");
    var imageLinks = listNode.getElementsByTagName("a");

    // Process image links
    var i, linkNode, image;
    for ( i = 0; i < imageLinks.length; i++ ) {

        // Attach event handler
        linkNode = imageLinks[i];
        linkNode.onclick = swap;

        // Preload image
        image = new Image();
        image.src = linkNode.getAttribute("href");
    }
    imageLinks[0].focus();
}
```

Figure 3-11   The JavaScript for the Image Swap application

How to use timers

Timers let you execute functions after a specified period of time. These timers are provided by web browsers, and they are often used in DOM scripting applications like slide shows. Here, you'll learn about the two types of timers.

How to use a one-time timer

The first type of timer calls its function only once. To create this type of timer, you use the global setTimeout method that's shown in figure 3-12. Its first parameter is the function that the timer calls. Its second parameter is the number of milliseconds to wait before calling the function.

When you use the setTimeout method to create a timer, this method returns a reference to the timer that's created. Then, if necessary, you can use this reference to cancel the timer. To do that, you pass this reference to the clearTimeout method.

The examples in this figure use a one-time timer to hide a message in a heading at the top of the page after a delay of five seconds. It does that by setting the class attribute of the heading to "closed". That hides the heading because the CSS for this class sets the display property to none.

In the first example of JavaScript code, the onload event handler creates a timer that calls the hideMessage function after a delay of 5 seconds (5000 milliseconds). In the hideMessage function, the setAttribute method is used to set the class attribute for the heading to "closed". After that, the hideMessage function uses the clearTimeout method to cancel the timer. That isn't necessary, but it's okay to do since the timer won't be used again.

In the second example of JavaScript code, the function that's called is embedded in the first parameter of the setTimeout method. Look closely to see how this is coded. After the left parenthesis of the setTimeout method, the entire function is coded followed by a comma. Then, the second parameter is coded as 5000. Although this is more complicated than the coding in the first example, you'll often see parameters with embedded functions like this. This also avoids the need for the global timer variable that the first example requires.

Two methods for working with a timer that calls a function once

```
setTimeout( function, delayTime )      // creates a timer
clearTimeout ( timer )                 // cancels a timer
```

The FAQs application with a first heading that is hidden after 5 seconds

Still under construction!

jQuery FAQs

✦ What is jQuery?

The HTML for the heading

```
<h1 id="startup_message">Still under construction!</h1>
```

The CSS for the heading when the class attribute is "closed"

```
#startup_message.closed { display: none; }
```

How to use a named one-time timer to hide the first heading

```
// declare a global variable so it can be accessed by the function
var timer;                // declare the timer variable

// create a timer that calls the hideMessage function once
window.onload = function () {
    timer = setTimeout(hideMessage, 5000);
}
// create the function that the timer calls
// when the class attribute is set to closed, the css hides the element
var hideMessage = function () {
    $("startup_message").setAttribute("class", "closed");
    clearTimeout(timer);
}
```

How to embed the timer function in the first parameter of the setTimeout method

```
window.onload = function () {
    var timer = setTimeout(
        function () {                        // the start of the first parameter
            $("startup_message").setAttribute("class", "closed");
            clearTimeout(timer);
        },
        5000);                              // the second parameter
}
```

Description

- The setTimeout method creates a *timer* that calls the specified function once after the specified delay in milliseconds. This method returns a reference to the new timer that can be used to cancel the timer.

- The clearTimeout method cancels the timer that was created with the setTimeout method.

- When you embed a timer function, you avoid the need for global variables.

Figure 3-12   How to use a one-time timer

How to use an interval timer

The second type of timer calls its function repeatedly. To create this type of timer, you use the global setInterval method shown in figure 3-13. Its first parameter is the function to be called. Its second parameter is the time interval between function calls. To cancel this type of timer, you pass the timer to the clearInterval method.

The example in this figure shows how to use an interval timer to create a counter that is incremented every second. This timer is coded within the onload event handler.

Before the timer is created, a counter variable is declared with a starting value of zero. Then, the setInterval method is used to create a timer. Here, the first parameter is the function that updates the counter variable and displays the updated counter value on the web page. The second parameter sets the interval to 1000 milliseconds, so the web page is updated every second.

When you use the setInterval method to create a timer, the timer waits for the specified interval to pass before calling the function the first time. So, if you want the function to be called immediately, you need to call the function before you create the timer.

Once you create an interval timer, you can't modify it. However, you can cancel the old timer and create a new one that works the way you want it to. This has the same effect as modifying the original timer.

Two methods for working with a timer that calls a function repeatedly

```
setInterval( function, intervalTime )    // creates a timer
clearInterval ( timer )                  // cancels a timer
```

The FAQs application with a counter at the bottom

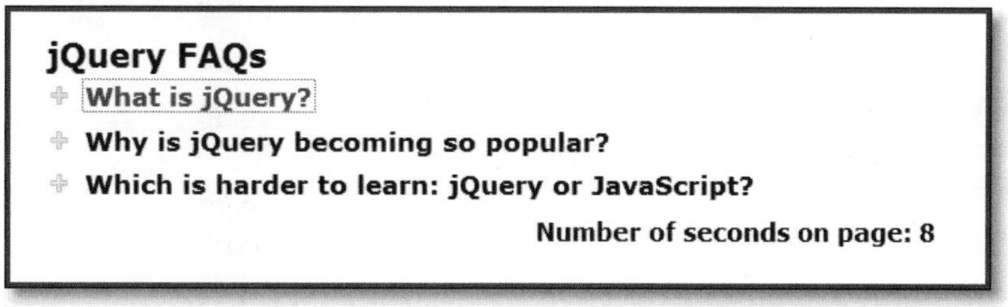

jQuery FAQs

✦ What is jQuery?

✦ Why is jQuery becoming so popular?

✦ Which is harder to learn: jQuery or JavaScript?

Number of seconds on page: 8

The HTML for the counter

```
<h3>Number of seconds on page: <span id="counter">0</span></h3>
```

The JavaScript for the interval timer that updates the counter

```
window.onload = function () {
    // create a timer that calls a function every second
    var counter = 0;
    var timer = setInterval(
        function () {                          // the start of the first parameter
            counter++;
            document.getElementById("counter").firstChild.nodeValue
                = counter;
        },
        1000 );                                // the second parameter
}
```

Description

- The setInterval method creates a timer that calls a function each time the specified interval in milliseconds has passed.

- The setInterval method returns a reference to the new timer that can be used by the clearInterval method to cancel the timer.

- Although you can't modify an interval timer, you can cancel it and create a new one that works the way you want it to.

Figure 3-13   How to use an interval timer

The Slide Show application

Figure 3-14 shows how to use an interval timer in a Slide Show application. When the user starts this application, it displays a new caption and image every two seconds.

The HTML and CSS

If you look at the HTML, you can see that five img elements are coded within a div element. These are the images that will be displayed by the slide show.

The h2 and img elements that precede the div element are used to display the caption and image for the slide show. The starting content of the h2 element provides the caption for the first slide, which is the same as the value of the alt attribute for the first image in the div element. The starting src attribute of the image provides the location of the first slide, which is the same as the src attribute of the first image in the div element. That way, the first caption and slide are displayed when the application starts.

To keep this application simple, no controls are provided for stopping the slide show or moving through the slides manually. As a result, this slide show doesn't meet the best standards for usability or accessibility.

Of note in the CSS is the rule set for the img elements within the div element. Since the purpose of these elements is to provide the captions and image locations for the slide show, the images shouldn't be displayed. That's why their display properties are set to none.

The Slide Show application with the third image displayed

The HTML

```
<main>
    <h1>Fishing Slide Show</h1>
    <h2 id="caption">Casting on the Upper Kings</h2>
    <img id="slide" src="images/casting1.jpg" alt="">
    <div id="slides">
        <img src="images/casting1.jpg" alt="Casting on the Upper Kings">
        <img src="images/casting2.jpg" alt="Casting on the Lower Kings">
        <img src="images/catchrelease.jpg"
            alt="Catch and Release on the Big Horn">
        <img src="images/fish.jpg" alt="Catching on the South Fork">
        <img src="images/lures.jpg" alt="The Lures for Catching">
    </div>
</main>
```

The CSS for the ul element

```
#slides img { display: none; }
```

Figure 3-14   The user interface, HTML, and CSS for the Slide Show application

The JavaScript

Figure 3-15 presents the JavaScript for this application. In chapter 6, you'll learn how to do this with jQuery, which is much easier. But the use of the timer is JavaScript code that works the same when you use jQuery.

In this figure, you can see that the onload event handler starts by declaring variables that contain the nodes for the div element, the h2 element for the caption, and the img element for the slide show. Then, the getElementsByTagName method is used to create an array named slides that contains one object for each img element in the div element.

At this point, the onload event handler starts the slide show. To do that, it creates an interval timer with a function that's embedded in the first parameter and 2000 (2 seconds) as the second parameter. It is the embedded function that displays the next slide when the interval time is up.

Within this function, the variable named imageCounter determines which slide in the slides array will be displayed next. The first statement in this loop adds one to the imageCounter, and then uses the modulus operator (%) to get the remainder when the imageCounter property is divided by the length of the slides array. This means the imageCounter property will range from 0 through one less than the length of the array.

If, for example, the slides array contains 5 images, the counter values will range from 0 through 4 (1%5=1; 2%5=2; 3%5=3; 4%5=4, 5%5 = 0; 6%5=1, and so on). So, if the imageCounter value is used as the index of the slides array, the function will loop through the elements of the array and the index will never be larger than 4.

After the value of the imageCounter variable is set, the second statement in this function uses the imageCounter as the index for the slides array and stores that image object in the image variable. The third statement sets the src attribute of the image node to the src attribute of the image object. And the last statement sets the text for the caption node to the alt attribute of the image object. As soon as these changes are made to the DOM, the image and caption are changed in the browser display.

You might notice that this code doesn't set up any event handlers for user events. Instead, the slide show is driven by the interval timer, which issues timer events. Then, after each time interval passes, the function in the first parameter is executed again, which changes the src attribute of the img element in the DOM and the text of the h2 element.

You might also notice that this code doesn't preload the images for the slide show. That's because an img element is included in the HTML for each of these images, and that means that these images are loaded by default even though they're hidden.

The JavaScript for the Slide Show application

```javascript
var $ = function (id) {
    return document.getElementById(id);
}

window.onload = function () {
    var slidesNode = $("slides");
    var captionNode = $("caption");
    var imageNode = $("slide");

    var slides = slidesNode.getElementsByTagName("img");

    // Start slide show
    var image, imageCounter = 0;
    var  timer = setInterval(
        function () {
            imageCounter = (imageCounter + 1) % slides.length;
            image = slides[imageCounter];
            imageNode.src = image.src;
            captionNode.firstChild.nodeValue = image.alt;
        },
        2000);
}
```

Figure 3-15   The JavaScript for the Slide Show application

Perspective

Now that you've completed this chapter, you should know how to use JavaScript for some common DOM scripting applications like image swaps and slide shows. If some of this has been confusing, that's because this is both complicated and difficult.

The good news is that jQuery makes it much easier to develop DOM scripting applications like the ones you've just seen. Even better, you now have all the JavaScript skills that you need for using jQuery, and those skills will make it easier for you to learn jQuery. Before you learn jQuery, though, the next chapter presents the skills for testing and debugging JavaScript and jQuery applications.

Terms

DOM Core specification	comment node
DOM (Document Object Model)	interface
DOM scripting	collapsible panel
DOM node	default action
element node	preloading an image
text node	image swap
attribute node	timer

Summary

- The *Document Object Model*, or *DOM*, is built when a page is loaded into a browser. It consists of various types of *nodes*.

- In the DOM, *element nodes* represent the elements in an HTML document and *text nodes* represent the text within those elements. The DOM can also contain *attribute nodes* with text nodes that store the attribute values as well as *comment nodes*.

- JavaScript provides properties and methods for the objects of the DOM that are described in the *DOM Core Specification*. These include the properties and methods that are described by the Node, Document, and Element *interfaces*.

- For some JavaScript applications, you need to cancel the *default action* of an event, like clicking on a link or a button.

- For applications like *image swaps*, it's good to *preload* the images. That way, the page may take longer to load, but the image changes will take place immediately.

- Browsers provide two different types of *timers*. A one-time timer executes a function just once after the specified interval of time. An interval timer executes a function each time the specified interval passes.

Exercise 3-1   Enhance the Future Value application

In this exercise, you'll enhance the Future Value application of chapter 2 with data validation that provides error messages like this:

Do the testing for this exercise in Chrome. Then, if you have any problems as you test your enhancements, refer back to figure 1-15 to help find your error.

Test the application

1. Open your text editor or IDE, and open the HTML and JavaScript files in this folder:

    `c:\jquery\exercises\ch03\future_value\`

2. Review the HTML code to see that span elements have been added after the text boxes, and review the JavaScript code to see that it's the same as in figure 2-22.

3. Test this application to remind yourself how it works. Then, delete the data validation code and test with valid data to make sure the calculation still works.

Enhance the data validation

4. Add data validation for the first field that tests for three condition and displays one of the following messages to the right of its text box:

    This field is required
    Must be numeric
    Must be > 0 and <= 100000

    In other words, your code needs to test (1) whether the user has made an entry, (2) whether the entry is a number, and (3) whether a numeric entry is in the right range. (Feel free to copy and modify any code from the Email List application for this chapter.)

5. Add the data validation for the second and third fields. But this time, just test that each entry is numeric and within the range shown above, and display the message shown above if it isn't. This should be easy once you have the data validation for the first field working right.

6. Enhance the application so the text box for future value is set to an empty string if the user tries to do the calculation for an invalid set of entries after getting the future value for a valid set of entries.

Exercise 3-2   Experiment with the FAQs application

This exercise will give you a chance to better understand the FAQs application by forcing you to work with its code.

1. Use your text editor or IDE to open the HTML and JavaScript files in this folder:

   `c:\jquery\exercises\ch03\faqs\`

   Then, test this application to see how it works, and review its code.

2. Change this application so the toggle event handler is attached to the <a> elements within the h2 elements instead of to the h2 elements themselves. Be sure to change the code within the toggle event handler so it works with an <a> element instead of an h2 element.

3. Test the application. When you do, clicking on the headings should work, but clicking on the plus or minus signs before them shouldn't work.

Exercise 3-3   Review the other chapter applications

If you have any questions about how any of the applications in this chapter work, you'll find them all in this folder:

   `c:\jquery\exercises\ch03\`

That way, you can test them, modify them, and experiment with them until you completely understand how they work. Besides the complete applications presented in this chapter, you'll find another one in a folder named faqs_timers that uses the timers shown in figures 3-12 and 3-13.

4

How to test and debug a JavaScript or jQuery application

As you build a JavaScript application, you need to test it to make sure that it performs as expected. Then, if there are any problems, you need to debug your application to correct those problems. This chapter shows you how to do both.

But remember that jQuery is a JavaScript library that consists of JavaScript functions and statements. As a result, all of the skills that you learn in this chapter apply to jQuery applications as well as JavaScript applications.

An introduction to testing and debugging

When you *test* an application, you run it to make sure that it works correctly. As you test the application, you try every possible combination of input data and user actions to be certain that the application works in every case. In other words, the goal of testing is to make an application fail.

When you *debug* an application, you fix the errors (*bugs*) that you discover during testing. Each time you fix a bug, you test again to make sure that the change you made didn't affect any other aspect of the application.

Typical test phases for a JavaScript application

When you test an application, you typically do so in phases, like the three that are summarized in figure 4-1.

In the first phase, you test the application with valid data. To start, you can enter the data that you would expect a user to enter. Before you're done, though, you should enter valid data that tests the limits of the entries.

In the second phase, you test the application with invalid data. That way, you can make sure that all of the error messages are displayed correctly, and that the application doesn't fail due to invalid data entries.

In the third phase, you go all out to make the application fail by testing every combination of data and user action that you can think of. That should include random actions like pressing the Enter key or clicking the mouse at the wrong time or place.

The three types of errors that can occur

As you test an application, three types of errors can occur. *Syntax errors* violate the rules for coding JavaScript statements. These errors are detected by the JavaScript engine as a page is loaded into the browser. As you learned in chapter 1, some syntax errors are also detected by IDEs like Aptana. Syntax errors are the easiest to fix, because web browsers and IDEs provide error messages that help you do that.

A *runtime error* occurs after a page has been loaded and the application is running. Then, when a statement can't be executed, the JavaScript engine *throws an exception* (or *error*) that stops the execution of the application.

Logic errors are errors in the logic of the coding: an arithmetic expression that delivers the wrong result, using the wrong relational operator in a comparison, and so on. To illustrate, the Miles Per Gallon application in this figure has a logic error. Here, you can see that the second entry is empty and the result of the calculation is NaN, but the calculation shouldn't be done at all if one of the entries is empty. Could it be a problem with the if statement?

The Calculate MPG application with a logic error

Calculate Miles Per Gallon

Miles Driven:	273
Gallons of Gas Used:	
Miles Per Gallon	NaN

[Calculate MPG]

The goal of testing

- To find all errors before the application is put into production.

The goal of debugging

- To fix all errors before the application is put into production.

Typical test phases

- Test the application with valid input data to make sure the results are correct.
- Test the application with invalid data to make sure that the proper error messages are displayed and that the application doesn't fail.
- Try everything you can think of to make the application fail, like unusual or unexpected combinations of user actions.

The three types of errors that can occur

- *Syntax errors* violate the rules for how JavaScript statements must be written. These errors are caught by the JavaScript engine as a page is loaded into the web browser.
- *Runtime errors* occur after a page is loaded and the application is being run. When a runtime error occurs, the JavaScript engine throws an error that stops the execution of the application.
- *Logic errors* are statements that don't cause syntax or runtime errors, but produce the wrong results.

Description

- To *test* a JavaScript application, you run it to make sure that it works properly no matter what data you enter or what events you initiate.
- When you *debug* an application, you find and fix all of the errors (*bugs*) that you find when you test the application.

Figure 4-1   An introduction to testing and debugging

Common JavaScript errors

Figure 4-2 presents some of the coding errors that are commonly made as you write a JavaScript application. If you've been doing the exercises, you most likely have encountered several of these errors already. Now, if you study this figure, you'll have a better idea of what to watch out for.

If you're using a good text editor or IDE, you can avoid most of these errors by noting the error markers and warnings that are displayed as you enter the code. For instance, Aptana will help you avoid most of the errors in the first two groups in this figure. However, it won't help you avoid the errors in the third group.

The fourth group in this figure addresses the problem with floating-point arithmetic that was mentioned in chapter 2. In brief, JavaScript uses the IEEE 754 standard for floating-point numbers, and this standard can introduce inexact results, even for simple calculations. Although these results are extremely close to the exact results, they can cause problems, especially in comparisons. For instance, the number 7.495 is not equal to 7.495000000000001.

To get around this problem, you can round the result as shown by the examples. Here, the first statement rounds the salesTax value to two decimal places by using the toFixed method of the number. In this case, the result is stored as a string because the toFixed method returns a string.

In contrast, the second statement gets the rounded result and then uses the parseFloat method to store it as a number. Which approach you use depends on whether you need the result to be a string or a number.

The last group in this figure illustrates the type of problem that can occur when JavaScript assumes that a variable is global. In this example, the salesTax variable is declared properly by using the var keyword. But the next statement misspells salesTax as salestax when it tries to assign a rounded and parsed value to salesTax. As a result, salestax is treated as a global variable, and the rounded and parsed value goes into salestax, not salesTax, which of course causes a bug.

As you learned in chapter 2, though, you can avoid that type of error by declaring strict mode for all of your JavaScript files. Then, the JavaScript engine will throw an error if you use a variable before it's declared, so you'll have to fix the error. Otherwise, an error like this will go undetected, which may lead to a difficult debugging problem.

Common syntax errors

- Misspelling keywords, like coding getElementByID instead of getElementById.
- Omitting required parentheses, quotation marks, or braces.
- Not using the same opening and closing quotation mark.
- Omitting the semicolon at the end of a statement.
- Misspelling or incorrectly capitalizing an identifier, like defining a variable named salesTax and referring to it later as salestax.

Problems with HTML references

- Referring to an attribute value or other HTML component incorrectly, like referring to an id as salesTax when the id is sales_tax.

Problems with data and comparisons

- Not testing to make sure that a user entry is the right data type before processing it.
- Not using the parseInt or parseFloat method to convert a user entry into a numeric value before processing it.
- Using one equal sign instead of two when testing for equality.

Problems with floating-point arithmetic

- The number data type in JavaScript uses floating-point numbers, and that can lead to arithmetic results that are imprecise. For example,

```
var salesAmount = 74.95;
salesTax = salesAmount * .1;                  // result is 7.495000000000001
```

- One way to fix this potential problem is to round the result to the right number of decimal places. If necessary, you can also convert it back to a floating-point number:

```
salesTax = salesTax.toFixed(2)                // result is 7.50 as a string
salesTax = parseFloat(salesTax.toFixed(2));   // result is 7.50 as a number
```

Problems with undeclared variables that are treated as global variables

- If you don't declare strict mode and you assign a value to a variable that hasn't been declared, the JavaScript engine treats it as a global variable, as in this example:

```
var calculateTax = function (subtotal, taxRate) {
    var salesTax = subtotal * taxRate;           // salesTax is local
    salestax = parseFloat(salesTax.toFixed(2));  // salestax is global
    return salesTax;             // salesTax isn't rounded but salestax is
}
```

- The solution to this type of problem is to always declare strict mode.

Description

- When the JavaScript engine in a browser comes to a JavaScript statement that it can't execute, it *throws an exception* (or *error*) and skips the rest of the JavaScript statements.

Figure 4-2   Common JavaScript errors

How top-down coding and testing can simplify debugging

One way to simplify debugging is to code and test just a small portion of code at a time. This can be referred to as *top-down coding and testing* or just *top-down testing*. The implication is that you test the most important operations first and work your way down to the least important operations and the finishing touches.

This is illustrated by the example in figure 4-3. Here, the first testing phase consists of 15 lines of code that provide an event handler for the click event of the Calculate button. However, that event handler doesn't do any data validation. It just calculates the future value of the investment amount, which is the essence of this application.

Then, phase 2 adds to this code by doing the data validation for just the first entry. Phase 3 adds the data validation for the other two entries. And phase 4 adds finishing touches like moving the focus to the first text box when the application starts.

The result is that you're testing a small amount of code at a time. That makes debugging easy because you know that any errors were introduced by the lines of code that you've just added. This also makes developing an application more enjoyable because you're making continuous progress without the frustration of complex debugging problems.

The user interface for a Future Value application

> ### Future Value Calculator
>
> Investment Amount: `1375000`
> Annual Interest Rate: `5.5`
> Number of Years: `7`
> Future Value: `2000184`
>
> [Calculate]

Testing phase 1: No data validation

```
var $ = function (id) { return document.getElementById(id); }
var calculateFV = function(investment,rate,years) {
    var futureValue = investment;
    for (var i = 1; i <= years; i++ ) {
        futureValue += futureValue * rate / 100;
    }
    futureValue = futureValue.toFixed(2);
    return futureValue;
}
var processEntries = function() {
    var investment = parseFloat( $("investment").value );
    var rate = parseFloat( $("annual_rate").value );
    var years = parseInt( $("years").value );
    $("future_value").value = calculateFV(investment,rate,years);
}
window.onload = function () {
    $("calculate").onclick = processEntries;
}
```

Testing phase 2: Add data validation for just the first entry

```
if (isNaN(investment) || investment <= 0 || investment > 100000) {
    alert("Investment amount must be > 0 and <= 100000"); }
else {
    // the call to the future value calculation from phase 1
}
```

Testing phase 3: Add data validation for the other entries

```
// Add data validation for the other entries
```

Testing phase 4: Add the finishing touches

```
// Add finishing touches like moving the focus to the first text box
```

Discussion

- When you use *top-down coding and testing*, you start by coding and testing a small portion of code. Then, you build on that base by adding an operation or two at a time and testing after each addition.

- This simplifies debugging because you know that any errors are caused by the code that you've just added.

Figure 4-3   How top-down coding and testing can simplify debugging

How to debug with Chrome's developer tools

In chapter 1, you were introduced to the Console panel of Chrome's *developer tools* as a way to find errors. Besides that, though, Chrome offers some excellent debugging features for more complicated problems.

Since Chrome's developer tools are relatively easy to use, the topics that follow don't present the procedures for using all of its features. Instead, they present the skills that you're going to use the most. Then, if you decide that you want to use some of the other features, you can experiment with them on your own.

How to use Chrome to find errors

As figure 4-4 shows, there are several ways to open and close the developer tools, but most of the time you'll use the F12 key. That's why the developer tools for Chrome and other browsers are often referred to as the *F12 tools*.

One of the primary uses of Chrome's developer tools is to get error messages when a JavaScript application throws an error and stops running. To get the error message, you open the developer tools and click on the Console tab to display the Console panel, which will show the error message. Then, you can click on the link to the right of the message to switch to the Sources panel and the JavaScript code for the statement in error will be highlighted.

In the example in this figure, the problem is that the first *isNaN* in the statement is spelled wrong. It is *isNan* when it should be *isNaN*. This shows how easy it can be to find an error. Often, the statement that's highlighted isn't the one that caused the error, but at least you have a clue that should help you find the actual error.

Incidentally, the error message that's displayed is for the first error that's detected, but there can be other errors in the code. To catch them, you have to correct the first error and run the application again. Then, if there are other errors, you repeat the process until they're all fixed and the application runs to completion.

When you're debugging a jQuery application, the error statement may be in the jQuery library instead of your JavaScript code. Because you can assume that all of the jQuery code is thoroughly tested, that means the error must be in the way your JavaScript code called a jQuery method. Then, if the cause of the error isn't obvious, you may need to use one of the other techniques in this chapter to find the cause error.

Chrome with an open Console panel that shows an error

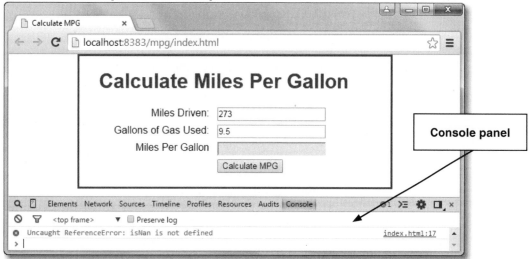

The Sources panel after the link in the Console panel has been clicked

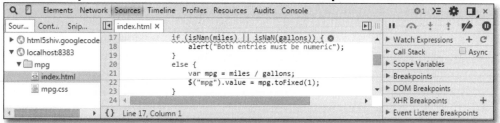

How to open or close Chrome's developer tools

- To open the develop tools, press F12 or Ctrl+Shift+I. Or, click on the Menu button in the upper right corner of the browser, and select More Tools→Developer Tools.

- To close the developer tools, click on the X in the upper right corner of the tools panel or press F12.

How to find the JavaScript statement that caused the error

- Open the Console panel by clicking on the Console tab. You should see an error message like the one above along with the line of code that caused the error.

- Click on the link to the right of the error message that indicates the line of code. That will open the Sources panel with the portion of JavaScript code that contains the statement displayed and the statement highlighted.

Description

- Chrome's *developer tools* provide some excellent debugging features. These tools are often referred to as the *F12 tools* because you can access them by pressing the F12 key.

- When you're debugging a jQuery application, the error statement may be in the jQuery library. Then, you have to figure out how your JavaScript code led to the error.

Figure 4-4   How to use Chrome's developer tools to find errors

How to use breakpoints and step through your code

A *breakpoint* is a point in your code at which the execution of your application will be stopped. Then, you can examine the contents of variables to see if your code is executing as expected. You can also *step through* the execution of the code from that point on. These techniques can help you solve difficult debugging problems.

Figure 4-5 shows you how to set breakpoints, step through the code, and view the contents of variables. In this example, you can see that a breakpoint has been set on line 6 of the Email List application.

When you run your application, it will stop at the first breakpoint that it encounters and highlight the line of code next to the breakpoint. While your code is stopped, you can hover your mouse over a variable name in the center pane of the Sources panel to display the current value of that variable.

At a breakpoint, you can also view the current variables in the Scope Variables pane on the right side of the panel. That pane has two sections, Local and Global. The Local section contains the variables that are used by the function that is being executed.

You can also see the values of other variables and expressions by clicking the plus sign to the right of Watch Expressions at the top of the pane and typing the variable name or expression that you want to watch. In this example, the expression "$("first_name").value" has been added as a Watch Expression, and its current value is an empty string.

To step through the execution of an application after a breakpoint is reached, you can use the Step Into, Step Over, and Step Out buttons. These buttons are just above the Watch Expressions pane. Or, you can press the keys associated with these operations, as shown in the table in this figure.

If you repeatedly click or press Step Into, you will execute the code one line at a time and the next line to be executed will be highlighted. After each line of code is executed, you can use the Local or Watch Expressions pane to observe any changes in the variables.

As you step through an application, you can use Step Over if you want to execute a called function without taking the time to step through it. Or, you can use Step Out to step out of a function that you don't want to step all the way through. Both of these can also be used to avoid stepping through the code in the jQuery library.

When you want to return to normal execution, you can use Resume. Then, the application will run until the next breakpoint is reached.

These are powerful debugging features that can help you find the causes of serious debugging problems. Stepping through an application is also a good way to understand how the code in an existing application works. If, for example, you step through the statements in any of the applications of the last chapter, you'll get a better idea of how they work.

A breakpoint in the Sources panel

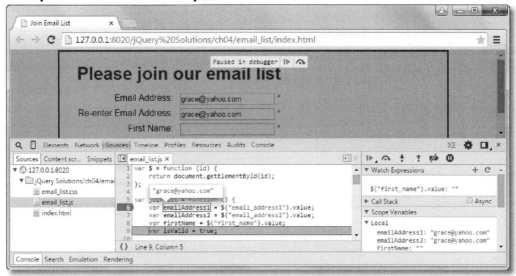

How to set or remove a breakpoint in the Sources panel

- Click on the Sources tab to display the Sources panel. Then, click on the JavaScript file that you want to debug.

- In the center pane, click on a line number in the bar to the left of a statement. This will either add a breakpoint or remove an existing one.

The buttons and keys for stepping through the JavaScript code

Button	Key	Description
Step Into	F11	Step through the code one line at a time.
Step Over	F10	Run any called functions without stepping through them.
Step Out	SHIFT+F11	Execute the rest of a function without stepping through it.
Resume	F8	Resume normal execution.

How to view the current data values at each step

- Hover the mouse pointer over a variable name in the center pane.

- View the current variables in the Scope Variables→Local section of the right-hand pane.

- Click the plus sign in the Watch Expressions section of the right-hand pane and type the variable name or expression that you want to watch.

Description

- You can set a *breakpoint* on any line except a blank line. When the JavaScript engine encounters a breakpoint, it stops before executing the statement at the breakpoint.

- A dark blue arrow around the line number marks a breakpoint, and a light blue highlight marks the next statement to be executed as you *step through* your code.

- When debugging a jQuery application, you usually step over any functions in the jQuery library.

Figure 4-5   How to use breakpoints and step through your code

Other debugging methods

Because Chrome has excellent developer tools, you should use them for most of your debugging. Here, though, are other debugging methods that you should be aware of.

How to debug in Internet Explorer

Sometimes things that work fine in the other major browsers won't work in Internet Explorer, especially in the older IE versions. As a result, you should always test your applications in a standard browser like Chrome as well as in IE. Then, if you have problems with IE, you can use its developer tools to help you debug them.

That's why figure 4-6 shows how to use the developer tools for the current version of IE. If you experiment with them, you'll see that when an error occurs, the Debugger panel is displayed with the statement in error highlighted and an error message displayed. You can also set breakpoints and step through statements using techniques similar to those you use in Chrome. In this figure, for example, a breakpoint has been set on line 6 and the next statement to be executed is the one on line 8.

One of the unique features of the IE developer tools is that they let you emulate earlier versions of IE, like IE7, 8, 9, and 10. To do that, you use the Emulation tab as described in this figure. Then, you can test your applications in these versions of the browsers, which should give you a strong indication of what (if any) compatibility problems you're going to encounter.

Remember, though, that these versions are only emulators. They are not the actual browsers. As a result, if you need to make sure that your applications are going to work on these older browsers, you need to test your applications on the actual browsers.

Internet Explorer in debugging mode

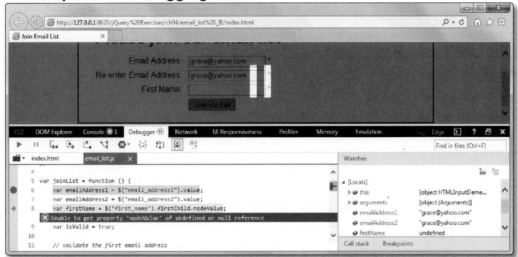

How to display or hide the developer tools

- Press F12. Or, click on the Settings icon (the gear) in the upper right corner of the browser, and then click on F12 Developer Tools.

How to find a JavaScript error

- Open the developer tools and run the application. When an error occurs, the Debugger panel is displayed, the statement in error is highlighted, and an error message is displayed.

How to set breakpoints and step through an application

- To set a breakpoint, click in the space to the left of a statement in the Debugger panel.
- To step through the statements, use the buttons below the tabs or press the keys shown in figure 4-5.

How to test applications in older versions of IE

- Click on the Emulation tab in the developer tools. Then, select the version that you want to use from the Documents Mode list. When the session ends, IE returns to its default mode.

Description

- IE along with its older versions is most likely to cause compatibility problems. That's why you always need to test your applications in IE.
- If you have problems when testing with IE, you can use its developer tools for debugging, which are similar to Chrome's.
- One of the features of the IE developer tools is that they let you emulate older versions of IE, like IE7, 8, 9, and 10. This makes it easy to test your applications in the older browsers, although these are only approximations to the actual browsers.
- When debugging a jQuery application, you usually step over any functions in the jQuery library.

Figure 4-6   How to debug in Internet Explorer

How to trace the execution of your JavaScript code

When you *trace* the execution of an application, you determine the sequence in which the statements in the application are executed. An easy way to do that is to add statements to your code that log messages or variable values at key points in the code. You can then view this information in the Console panel of Chrome's developer tools.

To add messages and variable values to the Console panel, you use the console.log method as illustrated by the example in figure 4-7. Here, the first log statement that's highlighted lets you know that the calculateMpg function has been started. The second and third log statements display the user entries for miles and gallons to make sure the two statements that precede it have worked correctly. The fourth log statement lets you know that the else clause of the if statement has been started. And the fifth log statement lets you know the value of the mpg calculation, both to be sure that the statement that preceded it worked correctly, and to see the calculated value before it's rounded.

When you use this technique, you usually start by adding just a few log statements to the code. Then, if that doesn't help you solve the problem, you can add more. Often, this is all you need for solving simple debugging problems, and this is quicker than setting breakpoints and stepping through the code.

One situation where tracing is better than stepping through code is when you're dealing with code that's executed many times. Say you've got an error that occurs somewhere inside a loop that performs a calculation on each element of an array with 1000 elements. Then, it would be daunting to step through the entire array to find the calculation that fails. With the console.log method, though, you can send the loop's index and the element's value to the console on each iteration, and then look at the complete log when the script has stopped running.

You can also use the alert method to trace the execution of an application. This has the benefit of displaying the trace data directly in the browser, rather than having to open the Console panel. But it has the drawback of being intrusive.

In the example in this figure, for instance, you would need to close an alert dialog box 5 times each time you ran the calculateMpg function. That may not seem like much, but that can quickly become annoying, especially if you're tracing something extensive. Imagine tracing the loop that I just described with alert statements! Of course, if you just want to check one or two values, the alert method might be all that you need.

JavaScript with five statements that trace the execution of the code

```javascript
var calculateMpg = function () {
    console.log("calculateMpg function has started");
    var miles = parseFloat($("miles").value);
    var gallons = parseFloat($("gallons").value);
    console.log("miles = " + miles);
    console.log("gallons = " + gallons);

    if (isNaN(miles) || isNaN(gallons)) {
        alert("Both entries must be numeric");
    }
    else {
        console.log("The data is valid and the calculation is next");
        var mpg = miles / gallons;
        console.log("mpg = " + mpg);
        $("mpg").value = mpg.toFixed(1);
    }
};
```

The messages in the Console panel of Chrome's developer tools

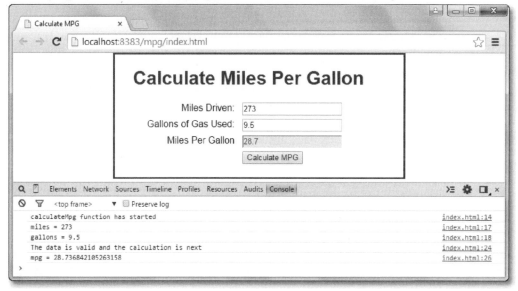

Description

- A simple way to *trace* the execution of a JavaScript application is to insert console.log methods at key points in the code. Then, the messages that you specify in these methods are displayed in the Console panel.

- The log statements can display messages that indicate what portion of the code is being executed or display the values of variables.

- You can also use the alert method for tracing, but the resulting popups can be intrusive, especially if you're tracing something extensive like a loop.

Figure 4-7   How to trace the execution of your JavaScript code

How to view the source code

Occasionally, when nothing seems to be working right as you test an application, you may want to view the source code for the application. That will at least confirm that you're testing the right files.

To view the HTML source code, you can use one of the techniques in figure 4-8. Be aware, however, that the HTML source code is the code that is initially loaded into the browser, so it doesn't reflect any changes made to the DOM by the JavaScript.

In this figure, for example, the JavaScript code has changed the text in the span elements after the text boxes. If you were to look at the HTML source code, though, you would see that the span elements still contain asterisks. In other words, the HTML source code doesn't reflect any changes made to the DOM by DOM scripting.

Luckily, you can use the Elements panel in Chrome's developer tools to see the changes that JavaScript has made to the DOM. By using the techniques described in this figure, you can drill down into the document's elements. In this figure, for example, the Elements panel is open and the span element with the id "email_address2_error" is selected. You can tell it's selected because the line is highlighted in blue. Within the highlighted line, you can see that the span's text has changed from an asterisk to "This field is required."

In the Styles pane at the right side of the Elements panel, you can also see the CSS that has been applied to the selected element. This pane shows all of the styles that have been applied from all of the style sheets that are attached to the web page. If a style in this pane has a line through it, that means it has been overridden by another style. This pane can be invaluable when you're trying to solve complicated formatting problems with cascading style sheets.

The Elements panel after JavaScript has changed the DOM

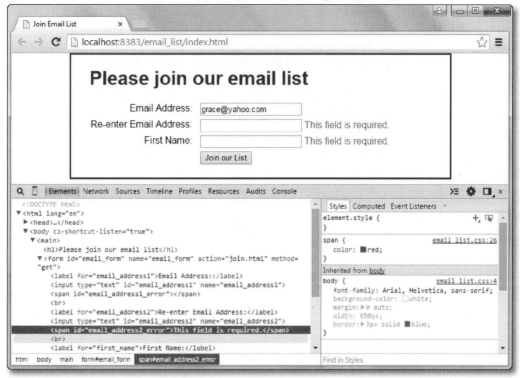

How to view the source code for a web page in any browser

- If it's available, use a menu command like View→Source or View→Page Source.
- You can also right-click on the page and select a command like Source, View Source, or View Page Source.

How to view DOM changes in the Elements panel in Chrome

- Press F12 and then click on Elements to open the Elements panel.
- Expand the HTML nodes until you get to the node you're interested in.
- Click on the node to select it. You'll see any changes made to the DOM by JavaScript, and you'll see the CSS that's applied to the element in the Styles pane to the right.

Description

- When you're debugging, it can be useful to view the page's HTML. You can do so easily in any browser, but that will only show the HTML that has been loaded into the browser and not any subsequent changes to the DOM.
- If you're using Chrome, you can use the Elements panel to see the changes to the DOM that your JavaScript has made.

Figure 4-8   How to view the source code for a web page

When and how to validate the HTML

In some cases, an HTML error will cause a JavaScript error. Then, if you suspect that might be happening, it's worth taking the time to *validate* the HTML code. To do that, you can use the technique in figure 4-9.

Suppose, for example, that you accidentally use the same id attribute for more than one element in an HTML document. Then, when the JavaScript refers to that id, it won't run correctly...although it may not throw an error. If you validate the HTML, though, the problem with duplicate ids will be identified, so you can fix the ids in the HTML as well as the JavaScript that refers to those ids.

In fact, we recommend that you validate the HTML for all of the pages in an application. Of course, this isn't necessary when you're doing exercises or developing applications for a class, but this may help you fix a problem that is affecting your JavaScript.

The home page for the W3C validator

The validation results with one error

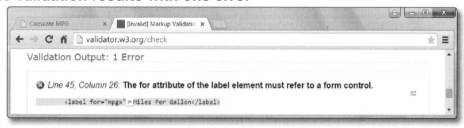

How to use the W3C Markup Validation Service

- Go to the URL that follows, identify the file to be validated, and click the Check button:

   http://validator.w3.org/

How to validate an HTML file from Aptana

- Select the file. Then, select the Commands→HTML→Validate Syntax (W3C) command.

Description

- Occasionally, an error in the HTML for a page will affect the operation of the JavaScript for that page. If you suspect that could be happening, *validating* the HTML for the page will sometimes expose the error.

- To validate the HTML for a page, you can use a program or website for that purpose. One of the most popular websites is the W3C Markup Validation Service.

- When you use the W3C Markup Validation Service, if the file you want to validate has already been uploaded to a web server, you can validate it by entering its URL on the Validate by URI tab. If the file you want to validate hasn't been uploaded to a web server, you can validate it by locating it on the Validate by File Upload tab.

- If you're using Aptana, you can validate an HTML file by using the command above.

Figure 4-9   When and how to validate an HTML file

Perspective

All too often, JavaScript and jQuery applications are put into production before they have been thoroughly tested and debugged. In the early days of JavaScript programming, that was understandable because the tools for testing and debugging were limited. Today, however, you have all the tools that you need for thoroughly debugging an application before you put it into production.

Terms

test	top-down coding and testing
debug	top-down testing
bug	developer tools
syntax error	F12 tools
runtime error	breakpoint
throw an exception	step through code
throw an error	trace
logic error	validate the HTML

Summary

- When you *test* an application, you try to make it fail. When you *debug* an application, you fix all of the problems that you discover during testing.

- When you write the code for a JavaScript application, you are likely to introduce three types of errors: *syntax errors*, *runtime errors*, and *logic errors*.

- *Top-down coding and testing* simplifies debugging because you build an application by coding and testing a small number of statements at a time.

- Chrome's *developer tools* (or *F12 tools*) can help you debug an application when it stops running. First, the Console panel displays an error message. Then, the link in the message goes to the statement that caused the error in the Sources panel.

- In the Sources panel of Chrome's developer tools, you can set *breakpoints* that stop the execution of code. Then, you can *step through* the code starting from a breakpoint and view the changes in the variables at each step.

- You can use Internet Explorer's developer tools to find errors in a way that's similar to Chrome's. IE's developer tools also let you emulate older versions of IE, like IE 7 through IE10.

- An easy way to *trace* the execution of an application is to insert console.log methods at key points in the JavaScript code. These methods log the data in Chrome's Console panel. You can also use alert methods for tracing.

- As you debug, you may occasionally want to view the HTML that has been loaded into the browser. You can also use Chrome's Elements panel to view any changes in the HTML that have been made by scripting the DOM.

- *Validating* the HTML for a page will occasionally help you debug an application.

Exercise 4-1   Use Chrome's developer tools

In this exercise, you'll use Chrome's developer tools to find a syntax error, set a breakpoint, and step through the Email List application.

1. Open the HTML and JavaScript files for the Email List application in this folder:

   `c:\jquery\exercises\ch04\email_list`

2. Run the application in Chrome, enter valid values in just the first two text boxes, and click on the Join our List button. Then, note that nothing happens.

3. Open the developer tools and use the Console panel to display the error that caused the problem, as shown in figure 4-4. Then, click the link for the error to find the statement that caused the error.

4. Switch to your text editor or IDE and fix the code. Then, test the application again.

5. In Chrome's developer tools, switch to the Sources panel. Then, if necessary, click on the email_list.js file in the Sources pane on the left to display the JavaScript code in the email_list.js file.

6. Set a breakpoint on the first statement in the joinList function, as shown in figure 4-5. Then, with valid values in just the first two text boxes, click the Join our List button. The application should stop at the breakpoint.

7. Use the Step Into button or F11 key to step through the application. At each step, notice the values that are displayed in the Local section of the Scope Variables pane. Also, hover the mouse over a variable in the JavaScript code to see what its value is.

8. Experiment with the Step Over and Step Out buttons as you step through the application. When you're through experimenting, remove the breakpoint.

Exercise 4-2   Use IE's developer tools

In this exercise, you'll use Internet Explorer's developer tools.

1. Open the HTML and JavaScript files for the Email List application in this folder:

   `c:\jquery\exercises\ch04\email_list_IE`

2. Run the application in IE, and open the developer tools so you can use them to debug the application.

3. Enter valid values in just the first two text boxes, click on the Join our List button, and notice the error message that's displayed in the Debugger panel.

4. Switch to your text editor or IDE, fix the error, and test again. The correction should be fairly obvious.

Exercise 4-3   Use other debugging methods

In this exercise, you'll use other debugging methods that you learned in this chapter.

1. Open this HTML file, and notice that it includes console.log methods for tracing the execution of this application, as shown in figure 4-7:

    `c:\jquery\exercises\ch04\mpg\index.html`

2. Run this application in Chrome, don't enter anything into the text boxes, and click on the Calculate button. Note that an error message is displayed below the button.

3. Use one of the methods in figure 4-8 to display the source code for the page, and notice that the content of the <p> element is a non-breaking space. Then, use Chrome's Elements panel to see that the content of the <p> element has been changed to the error message by DOM scripting.

4. Switch to the Console panel, and review the information in the log.

5. Enter valid values in the two text boxes, and click on the Calculate button. Then, go to the Console panel to review the new information.

6. In the JavaScript for this application, replace each console.log method with the alert method. Then, run the application to see how this works.

7. In the HTML, change the name in the for attribute of the Miles per Gallon label from *mpg* to *mpgx*. This may not be identified as an error by your text editor or IDE. Then, use one of the methods in figure 4-9 to validate the HTML for the page, which should identify this error.

Exercise 4-4   Add log statements
to the Future Value application

Console.log methods work especially well for debugging applications that require loops. In this exercise, you'll see how that can work.

1. Open the JavaScript file in this folder:

    `c:\jquery\exercises\ch04\future_value\`

2. Add console.log statements that log the values of the investment amount for each year and also after the final value has been rounded. The log should look something like this:

    ```
    Year 1 Value = 1100
    Year 2 Value = 1210
    Year 3 Value = 1331
    Year 4 Value = 1464.1
    Year 5 Value = 1610.51
    Year 6 Value = 1771.561
    Year 7 Value = 1948.7170999999998
    Rounded Value = 1948.72
    ```

3. Test the application with valid entries. Then, check the log results in the Console panel. This shows how an error in a loop can be detected.

Section 2

jQuery essentials

Now that you have the JavaScript skills that you need for using jQuery, you're ready to learn jQuery. So, in chapter 5, you'll learn a working subset of jQuery that will get you off to a fast start. And in chapter 6, you'll learn how to use the jQuery effects and animations that can bring a web page to life.

Then, in chapter 7, you'll learn how to use the many jQuery plugins that can quickly improve your productivity, and you'll also learn how to create your own plugins. In chapter 8, you'll learn how to use the jQuery features for working with forms. And in chapter 9, you'll learn how to use the DOM manipulation and traversal methods for advanced DOM scripting.

When you complete this section, you'll have all the jQuery skills that you need for developing professional web pages. You can also go on to any of the sections that follow because they are written as independent modules. If, for example, you want to learn how to use Ajax next, skip to section 4.

5

Get off to a fast start with jQuery

In this chapter, you'll quickly see how jQuery makes JavaScript programming easier. Then, you'll learn a working subset of jQuery that will get you off to a fast start. Along the way, you'll study four complete applications that will show you how to apply jQuery.

Introduction to jQuery

In this introduction, you'll learn what jQuery is, how to include it in your applications, and how jQuery, jQuery UI, and plugins can simplify JavaScript development.

What jQuery is

As figure 5-1 summarizes, *jQuery* is a free, open-source, JavaScript library that provides dozens of methods for common web features that make JavaScript programming easier. Beyond that, the jQuery functions are coded and tested for cross-browser compatibility, so they will work in all browsers.

Those are just two of the reasons why jQuery is used by more than 60% of the one million most-visited websites today. And that's why jQuery is commonly used by professional web developers. In fact, you can think of jQuery as one of the four technologies that every web developer should know how to use: HTML, CSS, JavaScript, and jQuery. But don't forget that jQuery is actually JavaScript.

The jQuery website at www.jQuery.com

What jQuery offers

- Dozens of selectors, methods, and event methods that make it easier to add JavaScript features to your web pages
- Cross-browser compatibility
- Selectors that are compliant with CSS3
- A compressed library that loads quickly so it doesn't degrade performance

Description

- *jQuery* is a free, open-source, JavaScript library that provides methods that make JavaScript programming easier.
- Today, jQuery is used by more than 60% of the one million most-visited websites, and its popularity is still growing.

Figure 5-1   What jQuery is

How jQuery can simplify JavaScript development

To show you how jQuery can simplify JavaScript development, figure 5-2 shows the jQuery for the FAQs application that you learned how to develop in chapter 3. If you're like most people, you probably found the JavaScript code for this application both complicated and confusing. That's because it is.

In contrast, the jQuery code takes about one-fourth as many lines of code. You'll also find that it is much easier to understand once you learn how to use the JQuery selectors, methods, and event methods. And you'll start learning those skills right after this introduction.

Incidentally, jQuery uses CSS selectors to select the HTML elements that the methods should be applied to. For instance,

```
$("#faqs h2")
```

is a jQuery selector for the CSS selector

```
#faqs h2
```

which selects all of the h2 elements in the element with "faqs" as its id. In fact, jQuery supports all of the CSS selectors including the CSS3 selectors, even in browsers that don't support all of the CSS3 selectors. This is another reason why developers like jQuery.

The FAQs application in a browser

jQuery FAQs

✛ **What is jQuery?**

━ **Why is jQuery becoming so popular?**

Three reasons:

- It's free.
- It lets you get more done in less time.
- All of its functions are cross-browser compatible.

✛ **Which is harder to learn: jQuery or JavaScript?**

The HTML

```html
<main id="faqs">
    <h1>jQuery FAQs</h1>
    <h2><a href="#">What is jQuery?</a></h2>
    <div>
        <p>jQuery is a library of the JavaScript functions that you're most
            likely to need as you develop websites.</p>
    </div>
    <h2><a href="#">Why is jQuery becoming so popular?</a></h2>
    <div>
        ...
    </div>
    ...
    ...
</main>
```

The critical CSS

```css
h2 { background: url(images/plus.png) no-repeat left center; }
h2.minus { background: url(images/minus.png) no-repeat left center; }
div { display: none; }
```

The jQuery for the application

```javascript
$(document).ready(function() {
    $("#faqs h2").click(function() {
        $(this).toggleClass("minus");
        if ($(this).attr("class") != "minus") {
            $(this).next().hide();
        }
        else {
            $(this).next().show();
        }
    });    // end click
});        // end ready
```

Description

- The application illustrates the use of the ready event method, a jQuery selector that's just like a CSS selector (#faqs h2"), and five jQuery methods. All of these make jQuery programming easier than JavaScript programming.

Figure 5-2   How jQuery can simplify JavaScript development

How jQuery UI and plugins can simplify JavaScript development

Besides the core jQuery library, jQuery provides the *jQuery UI* (User Interface) library. The functions in this library use the core jQuery library to build advanced features that can be created with just a few lines of code. These features include themes, effects, widgets, and mouse interactions.

For instance, the browser display in figure 5-3 shows the FAQs application as a jQuery UI widget known as an accordion. To implement this widget, you just need the three lines of JavaScript code that are highlighted, and that also applies the formatting that's shown.

To use jQuery UI, you include a jQuery UI library file in your web pages in much the same way that you include the jQuery core library. You also include a jQuery UI CSS file that provides a theme for jQuery UI. In section 3, you'll learn how to do that, and you'll learn how to use the features of jQuery UI.

Because jQuery UI can make JavaScript development even easier than it is when using jQuery, it makes sense to use jQuery UI whenever it provides an effect, widget, or mouse interaction that you need. Keep in mind, though, that jQuery UI is limited, so you'll still need jQuery for most of your web applications. As a result, you should think of jQuery UI as an add-on that you should learn how to use after you master jQuery.

Besides jQuery UI, the jQuery website provides access to dozens of *plugins* that have been developed for jQuery. These plugins provide higher-level functions like data validation and text layout that require minimal coding for their implementation. To facilitate the development of plugins, jQuery provides specifications that help standardize the way that plugins are implemented. Plugins are one more reason why developers like jQuery.

Like jQuery UI, plugins are libraries that make use of the core jQuery library. In fact, you can think of jQuery UI as a plugin. To use a plugin, you use a script element to include the plugin file in a web page, and you code that script element after the script element for the jQuery core library. In chapter 7, you'll learn how to get the most from plugins, and you'll also learn how to create your own plugins.

In practice, it makes sense to look first for a plugin that implements a feature that you want to add to a web page. If you can find one, you may be able to do in a few hours what would otherwise take a few days. Next, if you can't find a suitable plugin, it makes sense to see whether jQuery UI can facilitate the implementation of the feature. Finally, if neither a plugin nor jQuery UI can help you implement a feature, you have to use jQuery to develop it. That's why you need to master all of the jQuery skills in this section.

The FAQs application as a jQuery UI accordion

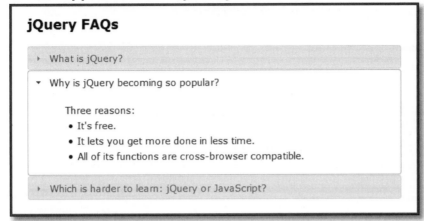

The HTML for a jQuery UI accordion

```html
<div id="accordion">
  <h3><a href="#">What is jQuery?</a></h3>
  <div> <!-- panel contents --> </div>
  <h3><a href="#">Why is jQuery becoming so popular?</a></h3>
  <div> <!-- panel contents --> </div>
  <h3><a href="#">Which is harder to learn: jQuery or JavaScript?</a></h3>
  <div> <!-- panel contents --> </div>
</div>
```

The JavaScript code for the jQuery UI accordion

```html
<script>
    $(document).ready(function() {
        $("#accordion").accordion();
    });
</script>
```

Some typical plugin functions

- Data validation
- Slide shows
- Carousels

Description

- *jQuery UI* is a free, open-source, JavaScript library that provides higher-level effects, widgets, and mouse interactions that can be customized by using themes. In section 3, you'll learn how to use jQuery UI.

- A *plugin* is a JavaScript library that provides functions that work in conjunction with jQuery to make it easier to add features to your web applications. In chapter 7, you'll learn how to use some of the most useful plugins, and you'll also learn how to create your own plugins.

- In general, if you can find a plugin or jQuery UI feature that does what you want it to do, you should use it. Often, though, you won't be able to find what you want so you'll need to develop the feature with just the core jQuery library.

Figure 5-3   How jQuery UI and plugins can simplify JavaScript development

The basics of jQuery programming

In the next four figures, you're going to learn the basics of jQuery programming. Then, you'll study an application that uses these skills. That will show you how jQuery simplifies JavaScript programming.

How to include jQuery in your web pages

If you go to the web page that's shown in figure 5-4, you'll see that it contains links that let you download various releases of the jQuery core library. The most current release at this writing is jQuery 2.1.4, and it comes in two versions. The compressed version is around 83KB. As a result, this version loads quickly into browsers, which is another reason why developers like jQuery.

The other version is uncompressed and currently about 242KB. If you download this version, you can study the JavaScript code that's used in the library. But beware, this code is extremely complicated.

Once you've downloaded the compressed version of the core library, you can include it in a web page by coding a script element like the first one in this figure. Then, if you store the file on your own computer or a local web server, you'll be able to develop jQuery applications without being connected to the Internet. For production applications, though, you'll need to deploy the file to your Internet web server.

The other way to include the jQuery library in your web applications and the one we recommend is to get the file from a *Content Delivery Network (CDN)*. A CDN is a web server that hosts open-source software, and the Google, Microsoft, and jQuery websites are CDNs for getting the jQuery libraries. In the second example in this figure, the script element uses the jQuery CDN with a URL that gets version 2.1.4 of jQuery, and that's the way all of the applications in this book include the jQuery library.

The benefit to using a CDN is that you don't have to download the jQuery file. The disadvantage is that you have to be connected to the Internet to use a CDN.

Although you might think that you should always use the most current release of jQuery, that's not necessarily the case. For example, jQuery 2.1.4 doesn't provide support for IE6, IE7, or IE8. So if you think that some of your users may be using these browsers, you'll want to use jQuery 1.11.2 instead since it's the most current release that does support these browsers. Note, however, that this release doesn't support the features that were dropped in jQuery 1.9. But if you need to provide for those features, you can use the jQuery migrate plugin.

The last example in this figure illustrates how this works. Here, the jQuery CDN is used to get release 1.11.2 of the jQuery core library as well as the migrate plugin. Because of that, the jQuery will work in older IE browsers and it will provide for jQuery features that were dropped in release 1.9.

The jQuery page for downloading the latest versions of jQuery

The current versions of jQuery

- jQuery 2.1.4 is the newest version of jQuery, but it no longer supports IE6, IE7, and IE8.
- jQuery 1.11.2 provides support for older browsers, but it doesn't support the features that were dropped in jQuery 1.9. To provide for those, you must include the migrate plugin.

How to include jQuery 2.1.4 after you've downloaded it to your computer

```
<script src="jquery-2.1.4.min.js"></script>
```

How to include jQuery 2.1.4 from a Content Delivery Network (CDN)

```
<script src="http://code.jquery.com/jquery-2.1.4.min.js"></script>
```

How to include jQuery 1.11.2 and the migrate plugin from a CDN

```
<script src="http://code.jquery.com/jquery-1.11.2.min.js"></script>
<script src="http://code.jquery.com/jquery-migrate-1.2.1.min.js"></script>
```

Description

- Each version of jQuery comes in a compressed version (min) that is relatively small and loads fast, and an uncompressed version with all of the JavaScript code in the library.
- If you include the jQuery file from a *Content Delivery Network* (*CDN*), you don't have to provide it from your own server, but then you can't work offline.
- If you include the migrate plugin with jQuery 1.11.2, jQuery will support the features of earlier versions that were dropped in jQuery 1.9.

Figure 5-4   How to include jQuery in your web pages

How to code jQuery selectors

When you use jQuery, you start by selecting the element or elements that you want to apply a jQuery method to. To do that, you can use jQuery *selectors* as shown in figure 5-5.

To code a jQuery selector, you start by coding the dollar sign ($) followed by a set of parentheses that contains a set of quotation marks. Then, within the quotation marks, you code the CSS selector for the element or elements that you want to select. This is shown by the syntax summary at the top of this figure.

The HTML and the examples that follow show how easy it is to select one or more elements with jQuery. For instance, the first selector in the first group of examples selects all <p> elements within the entire document. The second selector selects the element with "faqs" as its id. And the third selector selects all elements with "minus" as the value of its class attribute.

In the second group of examples, you can see how other types of CSS selectors are coded with jQuery. Here, you can see how descendants, adjacent siblings, general siblings, and children are coded. For instance, the first selector gets all <p> elements that are descendants of the element with "faqs" as its id. That includes all of the <p> elements in the HTML in this figure.

In contrast, the second selector gets the div elements that are adjacent siblings to the h2 elements, which includes all of the div elements. The third selector gets all <p> elements that are siblings of ul elements, which selects the one <p> element in the second div element. And the fourth selector gets all ul elements that are children of div elements, which selects the ul element in the second div element.

The third group of examples shows how to code multiple selectors. To do that, you separate them with commas, just as you do with CSS.

The syntax for a jQuery selector

```
$("selector")
```

The HTML for the elements that are selected by the examples

```
<main id="faqs">
    <h1>jQuery FAQs</h1>
    <h2 class="minus"><a href="#">What is jQuery?</a></h2>
    <div>
        <p>jQuery is a library of the JavaScript functions that you're most
            likely to need as you develop websites.
        </p>
    </div>
    <h2><a href="#">Why is jQuery becoming so popular?</a></h2>
    <div>
        <p>Three reasons:</p>
        <ul>
            <li>It's free.</li>
            <li>It lets you get more done in less time.</li>
            <li>All of its functions are cross-browser compatible.</li>
        </ul>
    </div>
</main>
```

How to select elements by element, id, and class

By element type: All <p> elements in the entire document
```
$("p")
```

By id: The element with "faqs" as its id
```
$("#faqs")
```

By class: All elements with "minus" as a class
```
$(".minus")
```

How to select elements by relationship

Descendants: All <p> elements that are descendants of the main element
```
$("#faqs p");
```

Adjacent siblings: All div elements that are adjacent siblings of h2 elements
```
$("h2 + div")
```

General siblings: All <p> elements that are siblings of ul elements
```
$("ul ~ p")
```

Children: All ul elements that are children of div elements
```
$("div > ul")
```

How to code multiple selectors

```
$("#faqs li, div p")
$("p + ul, div ~ p")
```

Description

- When you use jQuery, the dollar sign ($) is used to refer to the jQuery library. Then, you can code *selectors* by using the CSS syntax within quotation marks within parentheses.

Figure 5-5   How to code jQuery selectors

How to call jQuery methods

Once you've selected the element or elements that you want to apply a *method* to, you call the method using the syntax shown at the top of figure 5-6. This is the same way that you call a method of any object. You code the selector that gets the element or elements, the dot, the method name, and any parameters within parentheses.

To get you started with jQuery, the table in this figure summarizes some of the jQuery methods that you'll use the most. For instance, the val method without a parameter gets the value from a selected text box or other form control, and the val method with a parameter sets the value in a selected text box or other form control. The first two examples after the table show how this works.

Similarly, the text method without a parameter can be used to get the text of a selected element, and the text method with a parameter can be used to set the text of a selected element. Methods like these are often referred to as *getter* and *setter* methods. Here, the third example illustrates the setter version of the text method, which sets the text of an element to "Email address is required".

The fifth method in the table is the next method, which is used to get the next (or adjacent) sibling of an element. This method is often followed by another method. To do that, you use *object chaining*, which works just as it does with JavaScript. This is illustrated by the fourth example. Here, the next method gets the next sibling after the element that has been selected, and the text method sets the text for that sibling.

The last two methods in the table are the submit and focus methods, which are just like the JavaScript submit and focus methods. The submit method submits the data for a selected form to the server, and the focus method moves the focus to the selected form control or link.

In a moment, you'll see how these selectors and methods work in an application. But first, you need to learn how to set up the event handlers for an application.

The syntax for calling a jQuery method

```
$("selector").methodName(parameters)
```

Some common jQuery methods

Method	Description
`val()`	Get the value of a text box or other form control.
`val(value)`	Set the value of a text box or other form control.
`text()`	Get the text of an element.
`text(value)`	Set the text of an element.
`next([type])`	Get the next sibling of an element or the next sibling of a specified type if the parameter is coded.
`submit()`	Submit the selected form.
`focus()`	Move the focus to the selected form control or link.

Examples

How to get the value from a text box
```
var gallons = $("#gallons").val();
```

How to set the value for an input element
```
$("#gallons").val("");
```

How to set the text in an element
```
$("#email_address_error").text("Email address is required");
```

How to set the text for the next sibling with object chaining
```
$("#last_name").next().text("Last name is required");
```

How to submit a form
```
$("#join_list").submit();
```

How to move the focus to a form control or link
```
$("#email_address").focus();
```

Description

- To call a jQuery *method*, you code a selector, the dot operator, the method name, and any parameters within parentheses. Then, that method is applied to the element or elements that are selected by the selector.

- When you use *object chaining* with jQuery, you code one method after the other. This works because each method returns the appropriate object.

- If the selector for a method selects more than one element, jQuery applies the method to all of the elements so you don't have to code a loop to do that.

Figure 5-6   How to call jQuery methods

How to use jQuery event methods

When you use jQuery, you use *event methods* to attach event handlers to events. To do that, you use the syntax shown at the top of figure 5-7. First, you code the selector for the element that will initiate the event like a button that will be clicked. Then, you code the name of the event method that represents the event that you want to use. Last, you code a function that will be the event handler for the event within parentheses.

In the table in this figure, the two event methods that you'll use the most are summarized. The ready event is the jQuery alternative to the JavaScript load event. The ready event works better than the load event, though, because it's triggered as soon as the DOM is built, even if other elements like images are still being loaded into the browser. This means that the user can start using the web page faster.

Because the DOM usually has to be built before you can use JavaScript or jQuery, you'll probably use the ready event method in every JavaScript application that you develop. The examples in this figure show two ways to do that. In the long form, you use document as the selector for the web page followed by the dot, the method name (ready), and the function for the event handler.

In the short form, you can omit the selector and event method name and just code the function in parentheses after the dollar sign. Although this form is often used by professional developers, all of the examples in this book use the long form. That way, it's clear where the ready event handler starts.

The next example in this figure shows an event handler for the click event of all h2 elements. This is coded just like the event handler for the ready event except h2 is used as the selector and click is used as the name of the event method.

The last example in this figure shows how you code an event handler within the ready event handler. Note here that the closing brace, parenthesis, and semicolon for each event handler is critical. As you can guess, it's easy to omit one of these marks or get them out of sequence, so this is a frequent source of errors. That's why professional programmers often code inline comments after the ending marks for each event handler to identify which event handler the marks are for.

The syntax for a jQuery event method

```
$(selector).eventMethodName(function() {
    // the statements of the event handler
});
```

Two common jQuery event methods

Event method	Description
`ready(handler)`	The event handler runs when the DOM is ready.
`click(handler)`	The event handler runs when the selected element is clicked.

Two ways to code an event handler for the jQuery ready event

The long way

```
$(document).ready(function() {
    alert("The DOM is ready");
});
```

The short way

```
$(function(){                          // (document).ready is assumed
    alert("The DOM is ready");
});
```

An event handler for the click event of all h2 elements

```
$("h2").click(function() {
    alert("This heading has been clicked");
});
```

The click event handler within the ready event handler

```
$(document).ready(function() {
    $("h2").click(function() {
        alert("This heading has been clicked");
    });                                // end of click event handler
});                                    // end of ready event handler
```

Description

- To code a jQuery event handler, you code a selector, the dot operator, the name of the jQuery *event method*, and an anonymous function that handles the event within parentheses.

- The event handler for the ready event will run any methods that it contains as soon as the DOM is ready, even if the browser is loading images and other content for the page. This works better than the JavaScript onload event, which doesn't occur until all of the content for the page is loaded.

- In this book, the ready event is always coded the long way that's shown above. In practice, though, many programmers use the short way.

- When coding one event handler within another, the use of the closing braces, parentheses, and semicolons is critical. To help get this right, many programmers code inline comments after these punctuation marks to identify the ends of the handlers.

Figure 5-7   How to use jQuery event methods

The Email List application in jQuery

With that as background, you're ready to see how jQuery can be used in the Email List application that you studied in section 1. That will show you how jQuery can simplify coding.

The user interface and HTML

To refresh your memory, figure 5-8 presents the user interface and HTML for the Email List application. To use the application, the user enters text into the first three text boxes and clicks on the Join our List button. Then, the JavaScript validates the entries and displays appropriate error messages if errors are found. If no errors are found, the data in the form is submitted to the web server for processing.

In the HTML, note first the script element that loads jQuery. It is followed by the script element that identifies the file that holds the JavaScript for this application. That sequence is essential because the JavaScript file is going to use the jQuery file.

Also note that the span elements are adjacent siblings to the input elements for the text boxes. The starting text for each of these span elements is an asterisk that indicates that the text box entry is required. Later, if the JavaScript finds errors in the entries, it displays error messages in these span elements.

The user interface for the Email List application

The HTML

```html
<!DOCTYPE html>
<html>
<head>
    <meta charset="UTF-8">
    <title>Join Email List</title>
    <link rel="stylesheet" href="email_list.css">
    <script src="http://code.jquery.com/jquery-2.1.4.min.js"></script>
    <script src="email_list.js"></script>
</head>
<body>
    <main>
        <h1>Please join our email list</h1>
        <form id="email_form" name="email_form"
              action="join.html" method="get">
            <label for="email_address1">Email Address:</label>
            <input type="text" id="email_address1">
            <span>*</span><br>

            <label for="email_address2">Re-enter Email Address:</label>
            <input type="text" id="email_address2">
            <span>*</span><br>

            <label for="first_name">First Name:</label>
            <input type="text" id="first_name">
            <span>*</span><br>

            <label> </label>
            <input type="button" id="join_list" value="Join our List">
        </form>
    </main>
</body>
</html>
```

Figure 5-8   The user interface and HTML for the Email List application

The jQuery

Figure 5-9 presents the jQuery for this application. This is the code in the email_list.js file that's included by the HTML. Here, all of the jQuery is highlighted. The rest of the code is JavaScript code.

To start, you can see that an event handler for the click event of the Join our List button is coded within the event handler for the ready event. Then, if you look at the last three lines of code, you can see the ending punctuation marks for these handlers. Within the click event handler, the first two statements show how jQuery selectors and the val method can be used to get the values from text boxes.

In the first if statement, you can see how an error message is displayed if the user doesn't enter an email address in the first text box. Here, the next method gets the adjacent sibling for the text box, which is the span element, and then the text method puts an error message in that span element. This changes the DOM, and as soon as it is changed, the error message is displayed in the browser.

The next, text, and val methods are used in similar ways in the next two if statements. Then, the fourth if statement tests to see whether the isValid variable is still true. If it is, the submit method of the form is issued, which sends the data to the web server.

That ends the event handler for the click event of the Join our List button. But that handler is followed by one more statement. It moves the focus to the first text box, the one with "email_address1" as its id.

As you review this code, note that it doesn't require the standard $ function that gets an element object when the element's id is passed to it. Instead, the $ sign is used to start a jQuery selector that gets elements by their ids. This simplifies the coding.

Although this jQuery code illustrates how jQuery can simplify a data validation application, it doesn't begin to show the power of jQuery. For that, you need to learn more selectors, methods, and event methods, and then see how they can be used in other types of applications. You'll do that next.

The jQuery for the Email List application (email_list.js)

```javascript
$(document).ready(function() {
    $("#join_list").click(function() {
        var emailAddress1 = $("#email_address1").val();
        var emailAddress2 = $("#email_address2").val();
        var isValid = true;

        // validate the first email address
        if (emailAddress1 == "") {
            $("#email_address1").next().text("This field is required.");
            isValid = false;
        } else {
            $("#email_address1").next().text("");
        }

        // validate the second email address
        if (emailAddress2 == "") {
            $("#email_address2").next().text("This field is required.");
            isValid = false;
        } else if (emailAddress1 != emailAddress2) {
            $("#email_address2").next().text(
                "This entry must equal first entry.");
            isValid = false;
        } else {
            $("#email_address2").next().text("");
        }

        // validate the first name entry
        if ($("#first_name").val() == "") {
            $("#first_name").next().text("This field is required.");
            isValid = false;
        }
        else {
            $("#first_name").next().text("");
        }

        // submit the form if all entries are valid
        if (isValid) {
            $("#email_form").submit();
        }
    });     // end click
    $("#email_address1").focus();
});         // end ready
```

Figure 5-9   The jQuery for the Email List application

A working subset of selectors, methods, and event methods

The next three figures present a working subset of the most useful jQuery selectors, methods, and event methods. This is a lot to take in, but once you understand them, you'll be able to write practical jQuery applications of your own.

The most useful selectors

In figure 5-5, you were introduced to the basic selectors that you can use with jQuery. Now, figure 5-10 presents the other selectors that you're most likely to use in your jQuery applications. The only selectors of significance that are missing are ones that you'll learn about in later chapters, like the animate selector that you use with animations and the form control selectors that you use with forms.

If this summary seems daunting, just read the list and realize that these selectors let you select just about any element that you need to select. Then, make sure that you understand the examples in this figure. Later, when you need to make a specific type of selection for an application, you can refer back to this summary and to figure 5-5.

To illustrate the use of these selectors, the first example shows a selector that gets the li elements that are the first children of their parent elements. If the HTML contains more than one list, this selects the first li element of each list. The second example shows how to get the even tr (row) elements in an HTML table.

The third example shows how to use the :eq selector to get a specific element within an array of elements. If, for example, there are four <p> elements that are descendants of the "faqs" element, :eq(2) will return the third <p> element because the index values start with zero.

The last example shows a selector that gets all input elements with type attributes that have "text" as the value. In other words, this selector gets all text boxes. Note, however, that you can also get the text boxes by using this selector:

```
$("input[type=text]")
```

This just shows that you can often select the elements that you want in more than one way.

A summary of the most useful jQuery selectors

Selector	Selects
[*attribute*]	All elements with the named attribute.
[*attribute=value*]	All elements with the named attribute and value.
:contains(*text*)	All elements that contain the specified text.
:empty	All elements with no children including text nodes.
:eq(*n*)	The element at index n within the selected set.
:even	All elements with an even index within the selected set.
:first	The first element within the set.
:first-child	All elements that are first children of their parent elements.
:gt(*n*)	All elements within the selected set that have an index greater than n.
:has(*selector*)	All elements that contain the element specified by the selector.
:header	All elements that are headers (h1, h2, ...).
:hidden	All elements that are hidden.
:last	The last element within the selected set.
:last-child	All elements that are the last children of their parent elements.
:lt(*n*)	All elements within the selected set that have an index less than n.
:not(*selector*)	All elements that aren't selected by the selector.
:nth-child	All elements that are the nth children of their parent elements.
:odd	All elements with an odd index within the selected set.
:only-child	All elements that are the only children of their parent elements.
:parent	All elements that are parents of other elements, including text nodes.
:text	All input elements with the type attribute set to "text".
:visible	All elements that are visible.

Examples

How to select the li elements that are the first child of their parent element
```
$("li:first-child")
```

How to select the even tr elements of a table
```
$("table > tr:even")     // numbering starts at 0, so first tag is even
```

How to select the third descendant <p> element of an element
```
$("#faqs p:eq(2)")       // numbering starts at 0
```

How to select all input elements with "text" as the type attribute
```
$(":text")
```

Description

- Figure 5-5 and the table above summarize the selectors that you are most likely to need.

- Not included are six attribute selectors that let you select attributes with attribute values that contain specific substrings.

- In chapter 6, you'll learn about a selector that's used with animation, and in chapter 8, you'll learn about other selectors that are used for form controls.

Figure 5-10   The most useful selectors

The most useful methods

The table in figure 5-11 represents a collection of methods that are taken from several jQuery categories. For instance, the prev and next methods are DOM traversal methods. The attr, css, addClass, removeClass, and toggleClass methods are DOM manipulation methods. The hide and show methods are effect methods. And the each method is a miscellaneous method.

These are some of the most useful jQuery methods, and they will get you off to a fast start with jQuery. Then, you'll add methods to your repertoire as you read the rest of the chapters in this section. For instance, you'll learn how to use the other effect methods in chapter 6, and you'll learn how to use the other DOM transversal and manipulation methods in chapter 9.

Here again, if this table seems daunting, just read through these methods to see what's available. Then, study the examples to see how they can be used. Later, when you need a specific method for an application, you can refer back to this summary.

In the first example, the attr method is used to get the src attribute of an element with "image" as its id. The second example uses the attr method to add an src attribute to the selected element with the value that's stored in the variable named imageSource. If the element already has an src attribute, this method changes its value. The third example uses the css method to change the color property of the selected elements to blue.

In the fourth example, the addClass method is used to add a class to all of the h2 elements within the element that has "faqs" as its id. That's similar to what you've done using JavaScript.

In the last example, the each method is used to perform a function for each element in an array. In this case, the array contains all of the <a> elements within the element with "image_list" as its id, and the each method loops through these elements. As you will see, this simplifies the handling of the elements in the array.

In most cases, the jQuery methods operate on all of the selected elements. There are some exceptions, however. For example, if you use the attr method to get the value of an attribute, it will get the value only for the first selected element. Similarly, the css method will get the value of a property only for the first selected element.

A summary of the most useful jQuery methods

Method	Description
next([*selector*])	Get the next sibling of each selected element or the first sibling of a specified type if the parameter is coded.
prev([*selector*])	Get the previous sibling of each selected element or the previous sibling of a specified type if the parameter is coded.
attr(*attributeName*)	Get the value of the specified attribute from the first selected element.
attr(*attributeName, value*)	Set the value of the specified attribute for each selected element.
css(*propertyName*)	Get the value of the specified property from the first selected element.
css(*propertyName, value*)	Set the value of the specified property for each selected element.
addClass(*className*)	Add one or more classes to the selected elements and, if necessary, create the class. If you use more than one class as the parameter, separate them with spaces.
removeClass([*className*])	Remove one or more classes. If you use more than one class as the parameter, separate them with spaces.
toggleClass(*className*)	If the class is present, remove it. Otherwise, add it.
hide([*duration*])	Hide the selected elements. The duration parameter can be "slow", "fast", or a number giving the time in milliseconds. By default, the duration is 400 milliseconds, "slow" is 600 milliseconds, and "fast" is 200 milliseconds.
show([*duration*])	Show the selected elements. The duration parameter is the same as for the hide method.
each(*function*)	Run the function for each element in an array.

Get the value of the src attribute of an image
```
$("#image").attr("src");
```

Set the value of the src attribute of an image to the value of a variable
```
$("#image").attr("src", imageSource);
```

Set the value of the color property of the h2 elements to blue
```
$("h2").css("color", "blue");
```

Add a class to the h2 descendants of the "faqs" element
```
$("#faqs h2").addClass("minus");
```

Run a function for each <a> element within an "image_list" element
```
$("#image_list a").each(function() {
    // the statements of the function
});
```

Description
- The table above presents a powerful set of jQuery methods. This table adds to the methods that were presented in figure 5-6.
- In the chapters that follow, you'll learn how to use other methods, including those for effects (chapter 6), forms (chapter 8), DOM scripting and traversal (chapter 9), and Ajax and JSON (chapter 12).

Figure 5-11   The most useful methods

The most useful event methods

Figure 5-12 summarizes the most useful event methods, and this summary includes the ready and click methods that were introduced in figure 5-7. As you can see, most of these event methods provide for a single event handler that runs when the event occurs. Those event methods work like the ready and click methods, but with different events.

This is illustrated by the first example, which works just like the click event method except that it handles the double-click event. Of note here is the use of the *this* keyword within the handler. Here, it is coded as a jQuery selector, and it refers to the text box that has been double-clicked. This is similar to the way the this keyword works with JavaScript. Note that it isn't enclosed within quotation marks, even though it's a selector. What this function does is use the val method to set the value of the double-clicked text box to an empty string.

In contrast, the hover event method provides for two event handlers: one for when the mouse pointer moves into an element and another for when the mouse pointer moves out of an element. This is illustrated by the second example in this figure. Note here that the first function is the first parameter of the hover method, and it is followed by a comma. Then, the second function is the second parameter of the hover method. To end the parameters, the last line of code consists of a right parenthesis followed by a semicolon.

The hover method is typical of jQuery coding, which often requires the use of one or more functions within another function. That's why you need to code the functions in a way that helps you keep the punctuation straight. It also helps to code inline comments that mark the ends of functions and methods.

In these examples, note that when a selector gets more than one element, the event method sets up the event handler for each of the selected elements. This makes it much easier to set up event handlers with jQuery than it is with JavaScript.

The last example in this figure shows how to use the preventDefault method of the event object that's passed to the event handler to cancel the default action of the event. This jQuery method is executed in place of the preventDefault method of the browser when you include the jQuery library. Because this method is cross-browser compatible, it simplifies the JavaScript code. You'll see how this method is used in the Image Swap application that's presented later in this chapter.

A summary of the most useful jQuery event methods

Event method	Description
`ready(handler)`	The handler runs when the DOM is ready.
`unload(handler)`	The handler runs when the user closes the browser window.
`error(handler)`	The handler runs when a JavaScript error occurs.
`click(handler)`	The handler runs when the selected element is clicked.
`dblclick(handler)`	The handler runs when the selected element is double-clicked.
`mouseenter(handler)`	The handler runs when the mouse pointer enters the selected element.
`mouseover(handler)`	The handler runs when the mouse pointer moves over the selected element.
`mouseout(handler)`	The handler runs when the mouse pointer moves out of the selected element.
`hover(handlerIn, handlerOut)`	The first event handler runs when the mouse pointer moves into an element. The second event handler runs when the mouse pointer moves out.
`event.preventDefault()`	Stops the default action of an event from happening.

A handler for the double-click event of all text boxes that clears the clicked box

```
$(":text").dblclick(function () {
    $(this).val("");
});
```

A handler for the hover event of each img element within a list

```
$("#image_list img").hover(
    function() {
        alert("The mouse pointer has moved into an img element");
    },
    function() {
        alert("The mouse pointer has moved out of an img element);
    }
);      // end hover
```

A preventDefault method that stops the default action of an event

```
$("#faqs a").click(function(evt)  // the event object is named evt
{
    evt.preventDefault();           // the method is run on the event object
});                                 // end click
```

Description

- The table above presents the event methods that you'll use the most. Not included are: keydown, keypress, keyup, mousedown, mouseup, mouseleave, and mousemove.

- The preventDefault method is executed on the event object that gets passed to a function when an event occurs. You can name this object whatever you want.

Figure 5-12   The most useful event methods

Other event methods that you should be aware of

For most applications, you'll use the event methods that have already been presented. You'll also code the function or functions for the event handlers as the parameters of the event methods.

Sometimes, though, you'll want to attach event handlers in other ways, remove an event handler, or trigger an event that starts an event handler. Then, you can use the methods that are presented in the table in figure 5-13.

The on method lets you attach an event handler to one or more events. In the first set of examples, it's used to attach an event handler to the click event of an element with "clear" as its id. You can also do this using the click event method as shown here. A method like this is called a *shortcut method* because it actually uses the on method internally. In a case like this where you're attaching a single event handler, you can use either the on method or the shortcut method.

One advantage of the on method is that you can use it to attach an event handler to two different events. This is illustrated by the first statement in the second set of examples. Here, two events—click and mouseover—are included in the first parameter of the on method. That means that the event handler will be triggered whenever either of these events occurs on the selected elements.

In contrast, if you want to attach an event handler to two different events of two different elements, you can use shortcut events as shown here. Notice that because both event methods refer to the same event handler, you typically assign the event handler to a variable. Then, you can use the name of that variable as the parameter of the shortcut methods. In this example, the event handler is assigned to a variable named clearClick. Then, the click method is used to attach this event handler to an element with "clear" as its id, and the dblclick method is used to attach this event handler to all text boxes.

For some applications, you may want to remove an event handler when some condition occurs. To do that, you can use the off method, as illustrated by the third example in this figure. If the event handler is assigned to a variable, you can also name the variable on the handler parameter of the off method.

Or, if you want to remove an event handler after it runs just one time, you can use the one event method. This is illustrated by the fourth example.

If you want to initiate an event from your jQuery code, you can use the trigger method in either the long or short form, as illustrated by the fifth set of examples. Both of those examples trigger the click event of the element with "clear" as its id, which in turn causes the event handler for that event to be run.

That provides another way to run the same event handler for two different events. All you have to do is trigger the event for one event handler from another event handler. That's illustrated by the last example in this figure. There, the event handler for the double-click event of all text boxes triggers the click event of the element with "clear" as its id, and that starts the event handler.

The last two event methods in this figure, bind and unbind, are similar to the on and off methods. Because the on and off methods provide more flexibility, though, you'll want to use them instead. You've already seen how you can use on to attach two or more event handlers to an event. And in chapter 9, you'll see how these methods are particularly useful when you manipulate the DOM.

Other event methods that you should be aware of

Event method	Description
`on(`*events,* *handler*`)`	Attach an event handler to one or more events.
`off(`*events,* `[`*handler*`])`	Remove an event handler from one or more events.
`one(`*event,* *handler*`)`	Attach an event handler and remove it after it runs one time.
`trigger(`*event*`)`	Trigger the event for the selected element.
`bind(`*event,* *handler*`)`	Attach an event handler to an event.
`unbind(`*event,* `[`*handler*`])`	Remove an event handler from an event.

How to attach an event handler to an event

With the on method

```
$("#clear").on("click", function() {...});
```

With the shortcut method

```
$("#clear").click(function() {...});
```

How to attach an event handler to two different events

Of the same element

```
$("image_list img").on("click mouseover", function() {...});
```

Of two different elements

```
var clearClick = function() {...}
$("#clear").click(clearClick);
$(":text").dblclick(clearClick);
```

How to remove an event handler from an event

```
$("#clear").off("click");
```

How to attach and remove an event handler so it runs only once

```
$("#clear").one("click", function() {...});
```

How to trigger an event

With the trigger method

```
$("#clear").trigger("click");
```

With the shortcut method

```
$("#clear").click();
```

How to use the shortcut method to trigger an event from an event handler

```
$(":text").dblclick(function() {
    $("#clear").click();    // triggers the click event of the clear button
}
```

Description

- When you use a *shortcut method* to attach an event handler to an event, you're actually using the on method.

- Although you can use the bind and unbind methods to attach and remove event handlers, the on and off methods provide additional flexibility and are the preferred methods.

Figure 5-13   Other event methods that you should be aware of

Three illustrative applications

Now, to help you see how the selectors, methods, and event methods work in actual applications, this chapter presents three typical JavaScript applications.

The FAQs application in jQuery

Figure 5-14 presents the FAQs application that you studied in chapter 3, but this time it uses jQuery. When this applications starts, the div elements after the h2 elements are hidden by the CSS, and the h2 elements are preceded by a plus sign. Then, if the user clicks on an h2 element, the div element below it is displayed and the plus sign is changed to a minus sign. And if the user clicks on the heading again, the process is reversed.

The jQuery code for this application consists of a click event method that's within the ready method. This click event method sets up the event handlers for every h2 element within the section that has "faqs" as its id:

```
$("#faqs h2").click
```

Within the function for the event handler, the this keyword is used to refer to the current h2 element because that's the object of the click method. Then, the toggleClass method is used to add a class named "minus" to the h2 element if it isn't present or to remove it if it is. If you refer to the CSS for this page that's shown here, you can see that this class determines whether a plus or minus sign is displayed before the heading.

Next, an if statement is used to check the value of the class attribute of the h2 element. To do that, it uses the attr method. If the class isn't equal to "minus", it means that the div element that follows the h2 element shouldn't be displayed. Then, the statement within the if clause chains the next and hide methods to hide the div element that is a sibling to the h2 element.

If the class attribute of the h2 element is equal to "minus", it means that the div element that follows the h2 element should be displayed. Then, the statement within the else clause uses the next and show methods to show the div element that is a sibling to the h2 element.

This application begins to show the power of jQuery. Here, it takes just 11 lines of code to set up the event handlers for alternating clicks of as many h2 elements as there are in the "faqs" element. If you compare this code with the JavaScript code for this application in figure 3-17, you can get a better idea of how much this simplifies this application. In fact, since JavaScript doesn't provide for show and hide methods, the JavaScript has to use a class and CSS to hide and close the div elements.

The FAQs application in a browser

jQuery FAQs

✤ **What is jQuery?**

− **Why is jQuery becoming so popular?**
Three reasons:
  • It's free.
  • It lets you get more done in less time.
  • All of its functions are cross-browser compatible.

✤ **Which is harder to learn: jQuery or JavaScript?**

The HTML

```html
<main id="faqs">
    <h1>jQuery FAQs</h1>
    <h2><a href="#">What is jQuery?</a></h2>
    <div>
        <p>jQuery is a library of the JavaScript functions that you're most
            likely to need as you develop websites.
        </p>
    </div>
    <h2><a href="#">Why is jQuery becoming so popular?</a></h2>
    <div>
        <p>Three reasons:</p>
        <ul>
            <li>It's free.</li>
            <li>It lets you get more done in less time.</li>
            <li>All of its functions are cross-browser compatible.</li>
        </ul>
    </div>
    ...
    ...
</main>
```

The critical CSS

```css
h2 { background: url(images/plus.png) no-repeat left center; }
h2.minus { background: url(images/minus.png) no-repeat left center; }
div { display: none; }
```

The jQuery

```javascript
$(document).ready(function() {
    $("#faqs h2").click(function() {
        $(this).toggleClass("minus");
        if ($(this).attr("class") != "minus") {
            $(this).next().hide();
        }
        else {
            $(this).next().show();
        }
    });    // end click
});        // end ready
```

Figure 5-14   The FAQs application in jQuery

The Image Swap application in jQuery

Figure 5-15 presents another application that shows the power of jQuery. It is the Image Swap application that you studied in chapter 3. In short, when the user clicks on one of the thumbnail images at the top of the browser window, the caption and image below the thumbnails are changed.

In the HTML for this application, img elements are used to display the six thumbnail images. However, these elements are coded within <a> elements so the images are clickable and they can receive the focus. In the <a> elements, the href attributes identify the images to be swapped when the links are clicked, and the title attributes provide the text for the related captions. In this case, both the <a> elements and the img elements are coded within a ul element.

After the ul element, you can see the h2 element for the caption and the img element for the main image on the page. The ids of these elements are highlighted because the jQuery will use those ids as it swaps captions and images into them.

For the motor-impaired, this HTML provides accessibility by coding the img elements for the thumbnails within <a> elements. That way, the user can access the thumbnail links by pressing the Tab key, and the user can swap the image by pressing the Enter key when a thumbnail has the focus, which starts the click event.

Of note in the CSS for this page is the rule set for the li elements. Their display properties are set to inline so the images go from left to right instead of from top to bottom. Also, the padding on the right of each item is set to 10 pixels to provide space between the images.

The user interface for the Image Swap application

The HTML

```
<main>
    <h1>Ram Tap Combined Test</h1>
    <ul id="image_list">
        <li><a href="images/h1.jpg" title="James Allison: 1-1">
            <img src="thumbnails/t1.jpg" alt=""></a></li>
        <li><a href="images/h2.jpg" title="James Allison: 1-2">
            <img src="thumbnails/t2.jpg" alt=""></a></li>
        <li><a href="images/h3.jpg" title="James Allison: 1-3">
            <img src="thumbnails/t3.jpg" alt=""></a></li>
        <li><a href="images/h4.jpg" title="James Allison: 1-4">
            <img src="thumbnails/t4.jpg" alt=""></a></li>
        <li><a href="images/h5.jpg" title="James Allison: 1-5">
            <img src="thumbnails/t5.jpg" alt=""></a></li>
        <li><a href="images/h6.jpg" title="James Allison: 1-6">
            <img src="thumbnails/t6.jpg" alt=""></a></li>
    </ul>
    <h2 id="caption">James Allison 1-1</h2>
    <p><img src="images/h1.jpg" alt="" id="image"></p>
</main>
```

The CSS for the li elements

```
li {
    padding-right: 10px;
    display: inline;
}
```

Figure 5-15   The user interface, HTML, and CSS for the Image Swap application

Figure 5-16 presents the JavaScript and jQuery for this application. Within the ready event handler, the each method is used to run a function for each <a> element in the unordered list. This function preloads the images that will be swapped so they are in the browser when the user starts using the application. If an application uses many images, this can make the application run faster.

Within the function for each <a> element, the first statement creates a new Image object. Then, the second statement uses the this keyword and the attr method to set the src attribute of the Image object to the value of the href attribute in the <a> element. As soon as that's done, the image is loaded into the browser.

The each method is followed by a click event method that sets up the event handlers for the click events of the <a> elements that contain the thumbnail images. Note here that evt is coded as the parameter for the click event method, which receives the event object when the event occurs. This object will be used later to cancel the default action of each link.

The first two statements in this event handler swap the image in the main portion of the browser window. The first statement uses the this keyword and attr method to get the value of the href attribute of the <a> element. This value gives the location of the image to be swapped. Then, the second statement sets the src attribute of the main img element to this value. As soon as that's done, the image is swapped in the browser.

The next two statements work similarly. They swap the caption of the image in the main portion of the browser window. This time, the caption is taken from the title attribute of the <a> element.

The last statement in the click event handler uses the preventDefault method of the evt object that is passed to the event handler to cancel the default action of the link. If the default action isn't cancelled, clicking on the link will display the image that's referred to by the href attribute in a new window or tab, and that isn't what you want.

After the click event handler, the last statement in the ready method moves the focus to the first thumbnail image. That will make it easier for the users to tab to the thumbnails that they want to swap. To identify the first <a> element in the thumbnails, the :first-child selector is used to get the first li element of the unordered list. Then, a descendant selector is used to get the <a> element within the li element.

The JavaScript

```
$(document).ready(function() {
    // preload images
    $("#image_list a").each(function() {
        var swappedImage = new Image();
        swappedImage.src = $(this).attr("href");
    });

    // set up event handlers for links
    $("#image_list a").click(function(evt) {
        // swap image
        var imageURL = $(this).attr("href");
        $("#image").attr("src", imageURL);

        //swap caption
        var caption = $(this).attr("title");
        $("#caption").text(caption);

        // cancel the default action of the link
        evt.preventDefault();   // jQuery cross-browser method
    }); // end click

    // move focus to first thumbnail
    $("li:first-child a").focus();
}); // end ready
```

Description

- When you attach an event handler to a link, you often need to cancel the default action of the link, which is to open the page or image that's identified by its href attribute.

- To cancel the default action of a link, you can use the jQuery preventDefault method of the event object that is passed to the event handler. The jQuery version of this method is cross-browser compatible.

- To get the event object that's passed to a method, you need to code a parameter for the event handler function. You can use whatever name you want for this parameter, like evt or event. Then, you must use that name whenever you refer to the event object.

- When you use jQuery to work with images that aren't included in the HTML, preloading the images can improve the performance of the application because the user doesn't have to wait for a new image to be loaded into the browser.

- To preload an image, you create a new Image object and assign the URL for the image to the Image object's src attribute. As soon as that's done, the image is loaded into the browser.

Figure 5-16   The JavaScript for the Image Swap application

The Image Rollover application in jQuery

Figure 5-17 presents another application that shows the power of jQuery. In short, when the user hovers the mouse pointer over one of the starting images, it is replaced by another image. And when the user moves the mouse pointer out of the image, the original image is again displayed.

In the HTML for this application, img elements are coded within the li elements of an unordered list. In these img elements, the src attribute identifies the image that is displayed when the application is loaded into the browser, and the id attribute identifies the image that should be displayed when the mouse hovers over the img element.

In the JavaScript for this application, an each method is used to perform a function for each occurrence of an img element within the ul element that has "image_rollovers" as its id:

```
$("#image_rollovers img").each
```

The function for the each method starts by using the this keyword and the attr method to get the values of the src and id attributes of the current image and storing them in variables named oldURL and newURL. Remember that these attributes hold the values that locate the starting image and its rollover image. Then, as you'll see in a minute, these variables can be used to preload the rollover image and to set up the hover event handlers for each image.

The next two statements preload the rollover image by creating a new Image object and assigning the value of the newURL variable to its src attribute. As soon as the src attribute is set, the browser loads the image. Although preloading isn't essential, it can improve the user experience because the users won't have to wait for a rollover image to be loaded.

Next, the hover event method is used to set up the event handlers for the current image (this). Remember that this event method has two event handlers as its parameters. The first event handler is run when the mouse pointer moves into the element, and the second one is run when the mouse pointer moves out of the element.

In the function for the first event handler, you can see that the this keyword and the attr method are used to set the src attribute of the image to the value of the newURL variable. That causes the rollover image to be displayed. The function for the second event handler reverses this process by restoring the src attribute of the image to the value of the oldURL variable.

Of course, there's more than one way to code an application like this. For instance, you could implement this application by using the mouseover and mouseout event methods instead of the hover event method. Then, you would code the first function of the hover event as the mouseover event handler and the second function as the mouseout event handler.

Three images with the middle image rolled over

The HTML

```
<main>
    <h1>Ram Tap Combined Test</h1>
    <ul id="image_rollovers">
        <li><img src="images/h1.jpg" alt="" id="images/h4.jpg"></li>
        <li><img src="images/h2.jpg" alt="" id="images/h5.jpg"></li>
        <li><img src="images/h3.jpg" alt="" id="images/h6.jpg"></li>
    </ul>
</main>
```

The JavaScript

```
$(document).ready(function() {
    $("#image_rollovers img").each(function() {
        var oldURL = $(this).attr("src");        // gets the src attribute
        var newURL = $(this).attr("id");         // gets the id attribute

        // preload rollover image
        var rolloverImage = new Image();
        rolloverImage.src = newURL;

        // set up event handlers
        $(this).hover(
            function() {
                $(this).attr("src", newURL);     // sets the src attribute
            },
            function() {
                $(this).attr("src", oldURL);     // sets the src attribute
            }
        );                                       // end hover
    });                                          // end each
});                                              // end ready
```

Figure 5-17   The Image Rollover application in jQuery

Perspective

To get you off to a fast start, this chapter has presented a working subset of the most useful jQuery selectors, methods, and event methods. That should give you some idea of what you have to work with when you use jQuery. And you'll add to those selectors and methods as you read other chapters in this book.

The trick of course is being able to apply the right selectors, methods, and event methods to the application that you're trying to develop. To get good at that, it helps to review many different types of jQuery applications. That's why this chapter has presented four applications, and that's why you'll see many more before you complete this book.

Terms

jQuery	getter method
jQuery UI	setter method
plugin	object chaining
CDN (Content Delivery Network)	event method
selector	shortcut method
method	

Summary

- *jQuery* is a JavaScript library that provides methods that make JavaScript programming easier. These methods have been tested for cross-browser compatibility.

- *jQuery UI* and *plugins* are JavaScript libraries that use the jQuery library to build higher-level features.

- To use jQuery, you code a script element in the head section that includes the file for the jQuery core library. This file can be downloaded and stored on your computer or server, or you can access it through a *Content Delivery Network* (*CDN*).

- When you code statements that use jQuery, you use *selectors* that are like those for CSS. You also use a dot syntax that consists of the selector for one or more elements, the dot, and the name of the *method* that should be executed.

- You can use *object chaining* to call a jQuery method on the object that's returned by another method.

- To set up event handlers in jQuery, you use *event methods*. Most of these methods have one parameter that is the event handler that will be run when the event occurs. But some event methods like the hover method take two event handler parameters.

Exercise 5-1   Add a Clear button to the Email List application

In this exercise, you'll add a Clear button to the Email List application of figures 5-8 and 5-9. That will force you to create and attach another event handler.

1. Use your text editor to open the index.html and email_list.js files in this folder:

   `c:\jquery\exercises\ch05\email_list\`

2. Run the application to refresh your memory about how it works. Note that a Clear button has been added below the Join our List button, but the button doesn't work.

3. Add an event handler for the click event of the Clear button that clears all of the text boxes by setting them to an empty string (""). This can be done in one statement. To select just the text boxes, you use a selector like the one in the last example in figure 5-10. To set the values to empty strings, you use the val method like the second example in figure 5-6. Now, test this change.

4. This event handler should also put the asterisks back in the span elements that are displayed to the right of the text boxes to show that entries are required. That requires just one statement that uses the next and the text methods.

5. Add one more statement to this event handler that moves the focus to the first text box. Then, test this change.

6. Add another event handler to this application for the double-click event of any text box. This event handler should do the same thing that the event handler for the click event of the Clear button does. The easiest way to do that is to trigger the click event of the Clear button from the handler for the double-click event, as in the last example in figure 5-13.

7. Comment out the line of code that you just used to trigger the click event of the Clear button. Then, add a statement to the double-click event handler that only clears the text from the text box that the user double-clicks in. To do that, you'll have to use the this keyword, as in the first example in figure 5-12.

Exercise 5-2   Use different event methods for the Image Rollover application

This exercise asks you to modify the Image Rollover application of figure 5-17 so it uses different events for the event handlers.

1. Use your text editor to open the HTML and JavaScript files that are in this folder:

   `c:\jquery\exercises\ch05\image_rollover\`

2. Run the application to refresh your memory about how it works.

3. Comment out the hover method in the JavaScript, and rewrite the code so it uses the mouseover and mouseout event methods to implement this application. That should take about five minutes.

Exercise 5-3   Develop a Book List application

In this exercise, you'll start with the HTML and CSS for the user interface that follows. Then, you'll develop the jQuery code that makes it work.

Murach products

+ **Books for web developers**
− **Books for Java developers**
   • Murach's Java Programming (4th Edition)
   • Murach's Java Servlets and JSP (3rd Edition)
   • Murach's Oracle SQL and PL/SQL (2nd Edition)
+ **Books for .NET developers**

Development guidelines

1. You'll find the HTML, CSS, and image files for this application in this folder:

    `c:\jquery\exercises\ch05\book_list\`

    You'll also find an empty JavaScript file named book_list.js. You can add your code to this file.

2. This application works like the FAQs application you saw in this chapter, except that a list of book links is displayed below each heading. If the user clicks on one of these links, an image for the book is displayed to the right of the list. In addition, anytime the user clicks on a heading with a plus or minus sign before it, the image should no longer be displayed.

3. The HTML for the links of this application is like the HTML for the Image Swap application. However, the links for this application don't require the title attribute since no caption is displayed for the image.

4. The images that are referred to by the href attributes of the links in this application should be preloaded. To do that, you can loop through all the links in the main element. Also, be sure to cancel the default actions of the links.

5. Feel free to copy and paste code from any of the applications that are available to you. That's the most efficient way to build a new application.

IE note: If you set the src attribute of the img element to an empty string so no image is displayed when the application starts and when the user clicks on a heading, a placeholder will be displayed for this element in Internet Explorer. To avoid that, you can set the style attribute of the img element so the display property is set to "none". Then, you can set this property to "block" when you want to display an image. In chapter 9, you'll learn an easier way to set CSS properties using jQuery.

6

How to use effects
and animations

Now that you know the basics of using jQuery, this chapter presents the methods for effects and animations. Many developers like these jQuery methods the best because effects and animations are fun to develop and can add interest to a page. As you study these methods, though, remember that the primary goal of a website is usability, so make sure that your effects and animations don't detract from that goal.

Keep in mind too that it may be difficult to understand how some of these methods work until you see them in action. To help you with that, we've included most of the examples in this chapter in the downloadables for this chapter. So, you may want to run these examples as you progress through this chapter to see how they work.

How to use effects

This chapter starts by presenting the basic methods for effects that are provided by jQuery. After you learn how to use them, you'll learn how to use what the jQuery documentation refers to as custom effects. In practice, though, any illusion of movement on a web page can be referred to as *animation*, so you can think of all the examples in this chapter as animation.

The jQuery methods for effects

Figure 6-1 summarizes the jQuery methods for *effects*. These include the show and hide methods that were presented in chapter 5.

For all of the methods except the fadeTo method, the primary parameter is the duration parameter that determines how long the effect will take. If, for example, the duration parameter for the fadeOut method is 5000, the selected element or elements will be faded out over 5 seconds (5000 milliseconds). If the duration parameter is omitted, the effect takes place immediately so there is no animation.

In contrast, the fadeTo method not only requires the duration parameter but also an opacity parameter. The opacity parameter must be a value from 0 through 1, where 1 is the full (normal) opacity and 0 is invisible.

The examples in this figure show how these methods work. Here, the first example uses the fadeOut method to fade out a heading over 5 seconds. Then, the second example chains the fadeOut and slideDown methods to first fade out the heading over five seconds and then redisplay it by increasing its height over one second so it appears to slide down. As you will see, chaining is commonly used with effects to get the desired animation.

The next example shows how fadeTo methods can be chained. Here, the heading is first faded to an opacity of .2 over 5 seconds. Then, the heading is faded to an opacity of 1 over 1 second. This has the effect of the heading almost fading away completely and then being restored to its full opacity.

The last example shows how a *callback function* can be used with any of these methods. To use a callback function, you code a function as the last parameter of the method. Then, that function is called after the method finishes.

In this example, the fadeTo method is used to fade a heading to .2 opacity. Then, the callback function fades the heading back to full opacity. Note in the callback function that the this keyword is used to refer to the heading that's selected for the first fadeTo method. As you will see, though, the callback method often selects other elements for its operations.

Please note that the last two examples in this figure get the same result. However, chaining is the better way to get this result.

Before I go on, you may be interested to know that when you specify a duration with the hide or show method, the effect is implemented by changing the height, width, and opacity properties of the elements. To show an element, for example, its height, width, and opacity are increased so it appears to grow from its upper left corner. Conversely, to hide an element, its height, width, and opacity are decreased so it appears to shrink from its lower right corner.

The basic methods for jQuery effects

Method	Description
show()	Display the selected elements from the upper left to the lower right.
hide()	Hide the selected elements from the lower right to the upper left.
toggle()	Display or hide the selected elements.
slideDown()	Display the selected elements with a sliding motion.
slideUp()	Hide the selected elements with a sliding motion.
slideToggle()	Display or hide the selected elements with a sliding motion.
fadeIn()	Display the selected elements by fading them in to opaque.
fadeOut()	Hide the selected elements by fading them out to transparent.
fadeToggle()	Display or hide the selected elements by fading them in or out.
fadeTo()	Adjust the opacity property of the selected elements to the opacity set by the second parameter. With this method, the duration parameter must be specified.

The basic syntax for all of the methods except the fadeTo method

```
methodName([duration][, callback])
```

The basic syntax for the fadeTo method

```
fadeTo(duration, opacity[, callback])
```

HTML for a heading that is animated after the web page is loaded

```
<h1 id="startup_message">Temporarily under construction!</h1>
```

jQuery that fades the heading out over 5 seconds

```
$("#startup_message").fadeOut(5000);
```

jQuery that uses chaining to fade the heading out and slide it back down

```
$("#startup_message").fadeOut(5000).slideDown(1000);
```

Chaining with fadeTo methods

```
$("#startup_message").fadeTo(5000, .2).fadeTo(1000, 1);
```

jQuery with a callback function that gets the same result as the chaining

```
$("#startup_message").fadeTo(5000, .2,
    function() {                      // start callback function
        $(this).fadeTo(1000, 1);
    }                                 // end callback function
);
```

Description

- The duration parameter can be "slow", "fast", or a number giving the time in milliseconds. By default, the duration is 400 milliseconds, "slow" is 600 milliseconds, and "fast" is 200 milliseconds.

- The callback parameter is for a function that is called after the effect has finished. If more than one element is selected, the *callback function* is run once for each element.

- Chaining is commonly used with effects. This works because each effect method returns the object that it performed the effect on.

Figure 6-1   The jQuery methods for effects

The FAQs application with jQuery effects

Remember the FAQs application from the last chapter? That application used the show and hide methods without duration parameters to show and hide the answers to the questions in h2 elements. Now, figure 6-2 shows two ways that you can apply animation to that application.

The first example uses code similar to the code you saw in chapter 5. Here, when the user clicks on an h2 element, the function for the click event uses the toggleClass method to add or remove a class named "minus". Then, the div element that's adjacent to the h2 element is displayed or hidden depending on whether the h2 element includes the "minus" class. In this case, though, the show and hide methods are replaced by slideDown and fadeOut methods with duration parameters to add animation to the application.

The second example shows another way to get the same results. Just as in the first example, the function for the click event starts by using the toggleClass method to add or remove a class named "minus". Then, the slideToggle method is used to toggle the slideUp and slideDown methods on each click. This works just like the first example, except the slideUp method is used instead of the fadeOut method. It also requires fewer lines of code.

The FAQs application as the text for a heading is displayed

jQuery FAQs
✛ **What is jQuery?**

– **Why is jQuery becoming so popular?**
   Three reasons:
   • It's free.
   • It lets you get more done in less time

✛ **Which is harder to learn: jQuery or JavaScript?**

The HTML

```
<main id="faqs">
    <h1>jQuery FAQs</h1>
    <h2><a href="#">What is jQuery?</a></h2>
    <div>
        <!-- div content -->
    </div>
    <h2><a href="#">Why is jQuery becoming so popular?</a></h2>
    <div>
        <!-- div content -->
    </div>
    <h2><a href="#">Which is harder to learn: jQuery or JavaScript?</a></h2>
    <div>
        <!-- div content -->
    </div>
</main>
```

The jQuery with slideDown and fadeOut methods

```
$(document).ready(function() {
    $("#faqs h2").click(
        function() {
            $(this).toggleClass("minus");
            if ($(this).attr("class") != "minus") {
                $(this).next().fadeOut(1000);
            }
            else {
                $(this).next().slideDown(1000);
            }
        }
    );     // end click
});        // end ready
```

The jQuery with the slideToggle method

```
$(document).ready(function() {
    $("#faqs h2").click(
        function() {
            $(this).toggleClass("minus");
            $(this).next().slideToggle(1000);
        }
    );     // end click
});        // end ready
```

Figure 6-2   The FAQs application with jQuery effects

A Slide Show application with effects

To give you a better idea of how effects can be used, you will now review two different ways that a Slide Show application can be coded.

The user interface, HTML, and CSS

In figure 6-3, the screen capture shows the third slide in a slide show as it is being faded in. In the div element in the HTML, you can see that five img elements provide the slides for the show, and each of these has an alt attribute that provides the caption that is shown above the slide.

In the HTML, note that an h2 element is used for the caption, an img element is used for the slide show, and the div element that follows contains the img elements for the slides. The id attributes for these elements are "caption", "slide", and "slides", and the "caption" and "slide" elements contain the caption and slide for the first slide in the series.

In the CSS that's shown for this application, you can see that the height of the images is set to 250 pixels. In practice, all of the images for a slide show would usually be the same size, but setting the height for all of them ensures that the heights will be the same, even if the widths aren't.

Note too that the CSS sets the display property of all of the img elements in the div element named "slides" to "none". This means that those img elements will be loaded into the browser when the page is loaded, but they won't be displayed. Instead, they will be displayed one at a time as they're moved into the "slide" img element by the jQuery.

A Slide Show application with fading out and fading in

The HTML for the slide show

```
<main>
    <h1>Fishing Slide Show</h1>
    <h2 id="caption">Casting on the Upper Kings</h2>
    <img id="slide" src="images/casting1.jpg" alt="">
    <div id="slides">
        <img src="images/casting1.jpg" alt="Casting on the Upper Kings">
        <img src="images/casting2.jpg" alt="Casting on the Lower Kings">
        <img src="images/catchrelease.jpg"
            alt="Catch and Release on the Big Horn">
        <img src="images/fish.jpg" alt="Catching on the South Fork">
        <img src="images/lures.jpg" alt="The Lures for Catching">
    </div>
</main>
```

The critical CSS for the slide show

```
img {
    height: 250px;
}
#slides img {
    display: none;
}
```

Description

- The images in the "slides" div element will be used in the slide show.
- The caption for each image will come from its alt attribute.

Figure 6-3   The HTML and CSS for a slide show

Two ways to code the jQuery

It should be obvious by now that most jQuery applications can be coded in many different ways. In fact, the biggest problem when learning jQuery is figuring out how to apply jQuery to get the result that you want. That's why this book frequently shows more than one way to get a result, and that's why figure 6-4 shows two ways to code the Slide Show application.

In the first example, the code starts by creating an array of Image objects that store the src and alt attributes of the five img elements in the "slides" division of the HTML. That's done by using the each method to process each of the five elements. Within the processing loop, the attr method is used to get the src and alt attributes from each img element and store them in the src and title properties of each Image object. Then, the Image object is added to the array.

After the array has been created, the setInterval method is used to perform its function (the first parameter) every 3000 milliseconds (the second parameter). Within that function, the first statement selects the caption and fades it out over 1000 milliseconds. Then, the second statement selects the slide and fades it out. But note that this statement includes a callback function.

Within the callback function, the first statement gets a new value for the imageCounter variable, which was initially set to zero. To do that, it increases the counter value by 1 and uses the modulus operator to get the remainder that's left when the counter is divided by the length of the array. For the second slide in the show, that means the counter is increased to 1 and divided by 5 so the remainder is 1. For the fifth slide, the counter is increased to 5 and divided by 5 so the remainder is 0. Since this remainder is assigned back to the imageCounter variable, this means that variable will range from 0 to 5 as the slide show progresses.

Once the imageCounter value is set, the rest is easy. First, the nextImage variable is set to the next image in the array. Second, the src attribute for the "slide" img element is set to the src property of the next image object in the array, and that slide is faded in. Last, the text for the caption is set to the title property of the next image object in the array, and that caption is faded in.

In the second example, the code starts by setting the nextSlide variable to the first img element in the "slides" division. Then, the function for the setInterval timer fades out the starting slide and caption, just as it did in the first example. However, the code in the callback function for the fadeOut method is completely different.

It starts by testing whether the next img element in the "slides" division has a length of zero. If so, that means that there isn't a next slide, and the nextSlide variable is set to the first img element in that division. Otherwise, the next slide is set to the next img element in the "slides" division.

Once the next slide is established, the code sets variables for the next slide's src and alt attributes. Then, it uses the first variable to set the src attribute for the img element that is displaying the slide show and fades it in, and it uses the second variable to set the text for the next caption and fades that in.

This shows just two of the ways that an application like this can be coded, and you'll see a few more in subsequent chapters. When you develop any appli-

One way to code the jQuery

```
$(document).ready(function() {
    // create an array of the slide images
    var image, imageCounter = 0, imageCache = [];
    $("#slides img").each(function() {
        image = new Image();
        image.src = $(this).attr("src");
        image.title = $(this).attr("alt");
        imageCache[imageCounter] = image;
        imageCounter++;
    });
    // start slide show
    imageCounter = 0;
    var nextImage;
    setInterval(
        function () {
            $("#caption").fadeOut(1000);
            $("#slide").fadeOut(1000,
                function() {
                    imageCounter = (imageCounter + 1) % imageCache.length;
                    nextImage = imageCache[imageCounter];
                    $("#slide").attr("src", nextImage.src).fadeIn(1000);
                    $("#caption").text(nextImage.title).fadeIn(1000);
                }
            );
        },
    3000);
})
```

Another way to code the jQuery

```
$(document).ready(function() {
    var nextSlide = $("#slides img:first-child");
    var nextCaption;
    var nextSlideSource;
    // start slide show
    setInterval(
        function () {
            $("#caption").fadeOut(1000);
            $("#slide").fadeOut(1000,
                function () {
                    if (nextSlide.next().length == 0) {
                        nextSlide = $("#slides img:first-child");
                    }
                    else {
                        nextSlide = nextSlide.next();
                    }
                    nextSlideSource = nextSlide.attr("src");
                    nextCaption = nextSlide.attr("alt");
                    $("#slide").attr("src", nextSlideSource).fadeIn(1000);
                    $("#caption").text(nextCaption).fadeIn(1000);
                }
            )
        },
    3000);
})
```

Figure 6-4   Two ways to code the jQuery for the slide show

cation, one of the goals is to write code that is easy to read, maintain, and reuse in other web pages. The other is to write code that's efficient. Judging by those goals, the second example in figure 6-4 is better because its code is relatively straightforward, and it doesn't require an array of Image objects.

Regardless of how you code this application, though, you'll notice that when you run it, the captions and slides are faded out almost simultaneously, not one after the other. That's because the effects for two different elements run as soon as they're started. In this case, that means that one effect is started a few milliseconds after the other, so the fade out and in for the caption runs at almost the same time that the fade out and fade in for the slide runs.

How to stop and start a slide show

To improve the usability of a slide show, you usually provide some way for the user to stop and restart the show. Figure 6-5 shows one way to do that. It stops on the current slide when the user clicks on it, and it restarts when the user clicks on it again.

First, this code sets up an anonymous function for running the slide show and stores it in a variable named runSlideShow. If you look at the code in this function, you can see that it's the same as the code in the second example in the previous figure.

Second, this function is followed by a statement that creates a timer variable that calls the runSlideShow function every 3 seconds. Note, however, that this must be coded after the runSlideShow function because that function is an anonymous function. If this statement is coded before the function, the JavaScript engine will throw an error.

Third, the last event handler uses the click event method to cancel and restore the timer on alternate clicks of the current slide. When a slide is clicked and the timer isn't null, the function uses the clearInterval method to cancel the timer and thus stop the slide show. Otherwise, the timer is created again so the show restarts.

You'll also notice that the slide show stops on a full image, not one that is fading out or fading in. That's because the timer for the slide show isn't cancelled until the current interval ends. Also, the slide show restarts with the next image in sequence. That's because the values of the nextSlide, nextCaption, and nextSlideSource variables are retained, even though the timer has been cancelled.

Of course, there are many other ways that you can stop and restart a slide show. For instance, you could provide a stop/start button that works the same way that clicking on a slide works. You could also add next and previous buttons that would let the user manually move from one slide to the next while the slide show is stopped. Now that you know the basic code for running, stopping, and starting a slide show, you should be able to add these enhancements on your own.

The jQuery for stopping and restarting a slide show

```
$(document).ready(function() {
    var nextSlide = $("#slides img:first-child");
    var nextCaption;
    var nextSlideSource;

    // the function for running the slide show
    var runSlideShow = function() {
        $("#caption").fadeOut(1000);
        $("#slide").fadeOut(1000,
            function () {
                if (nextSlide.next().length == 0) {
                    nextSlide = $("#slides img:first-child");
                }
                else {
                    nextSlide = nextSlide.next();
                }
                nextSlideSource = nextSlide.attr("src");
                nextCaption = nextSlide.attr("alt");
                $("#slide").attr("src", nextSlideSource).fadeIn(1000);
                $("#caption").text(nextCaption).fadeIn(1000);
            }
        )
    }

    // start slide show
    var timer1 = setInterval(runSlideShow, 3000);

    // starting and stopping the slide show
    $("#slide").click(function() {
        if (timer1 != null) {
            clearInterval(timer1);
            timer1 = null;
        }
        else {
            timer1 = setInterval(runSlideShow, 3000);
        }
    });
})
```

Description

- With this code, the user can stop a slide show by clicking on a slide and restart the slide show by clicking on it again.

- So the code for the slide show doesn't have to be repeated, it is coded in an anonymous function and stored in the variable named runSlideShow.

- Because the runSlideShow function is an anonymous function, it must come before the setInterval method that calls it. Otherwise, the JavaScript engine will throw an error.

Figure 6-5   How to stop and start a slide show

How to use animation

Now that you know how to use the basic jQuery effects, you'll learn how to use what the jQuery website refers to as custom effects. We refer to these custom effects as animation, and that starts with the animate method.

How to use the basic syntax of the animate method

Figure 6-6 presents the basic syntax of the animate method. Here, the first parameter is a *properties map* that's coded in braces. This map consists of name/value pairs. For instance, the first example in this figure sets the fontSize property to 275%, the opacity property to 1, and the left property to 0. Then, the second parameter is the duration for the animation, which in the first example is 2 seconds.

When the animate method is executed, it modifies the selected element or elements by changing their properties to the ones in the properties map over the duration specified. This gives the illusion of animation.

If you look at the starting CSS for the heading that is animated in the examples, you can see that the heading starts with its font size at 75% of the browser default, its opacity at .2 (faded out), and its left position at -175 pixels, which is 175 pixels to the left of its normal position. Then, when the animate method in the first example is run, the heading's font size is increased to 275%, its opacity is increased to 1, and its left position is changed to zero, which is its normal position. Since this is done over 2 seconds, the result is an interesting animation, with the heading moving to the right and increasing in size and opacity.

Incidentally, to make this work correctly, the position property for the heading must be set to relative. That means that the settings for the left and top properties are relative to the position the element would be in with normal flow. That position has left and top properties of 0.

The second example is like the first one, but it includes a callback function. Here, the callback function selects the h2 headings on the page and then uses the next, fadeIn, and fadeOut methods to fade in and out the div elements that follow the h2 headings. The one difference in the properties map is that the left property is set to "+=175" which moves the heading 175 pixels to the right of where it started. This gets the same results as the properties map in the first example.

When you code the properties map for a function, you must obey the rules that are summarized in this figure. For instance, you either use camel casing for the property names, like fontSize instead of font-size, or you code the property names in quotation marks. You code numeric values as numbers or decimal values, but otherwise you code the values in quotation marks. And when you code a numeric value for a property like left, pixels are assumed, unless you specify the unit of measurement and enclose the entire value in quotation marks.

For some properties, like width, height, and opacity, you can use "show", "hide", or "toggle" as the property values. If, for example, you code "hide" for

The basic syntax for the animate method

```
animate({properties}[, duration][, callback])
```

An animated heading that is moving into the "faqs" section

jQuery FAQs
+ What is jQuery?
+ Why is jQuery becoming so popular?
+ Which is harder to learn: jQuery or JavaScript?

The CSS for the h1 heading

```
#faqs h1 {
    position: relative;
    left: -175px;
    font-size: 75%;
    opacity: .2;
}
```

An animate method for the h1 heading without a callback function

```
$("#faqs h1").animate(
    { fontSize: "275%", opacity: 1, left: 0 },    // the properties map
    2000
);                                                 // end animate
```

An animate method for the h1 heading with a callback function

```
$("#faqs h1").animate(
    { fontSize: "275%", opacity: 1, left: "+=175" },
    2000,
    function() {
        $("#faqs h2").next().fadeIn(1000).fadeOut(1000);
    }
);                                                 // end animate
```

Description

- When the animate method is run, the CSS properties for the selected elements are changed to the properties in the *properties map* that is coded as the first parameter of the method. The animation is done in a phased transition based on the duration parameter.

- To specify a property name in the properties map, you can use camel casing instead of the CSS hyphenation (as above) or you can enclose the property name in quotation marks.

- To specify a non-numeric property value, enclose the value in quotation marks.

- To specify a numeric property value, just code the value. For measurements, pixels are assumed. You can also use the += and -= operators with numeric values, but these expressions must be enclosed in quotation marks.

- For some properties, like width, height, and opacity, you can use "show", "hide", or "toggle" as the property values. These will show, hide, or toggle the element by setting the property appropriately.

- Although color transitions aren't handled properly by jQuery, they are by jQuery UI.

Figure 6-6   How to use the basic syntax of the animate method

the width or opacity value, it is decreased to zero. If you code "show", the width is increased to its normal width or the opacity is increased to 1. And if you code "toggle", the values toggle between the show and hide values.

Last, you should be aware that jQuery animation doesn't work right with colors. How, for example, do you change a color from orange to black over time? However, jQuery UI does provide for color animations, and you'll learn about that in section 3.

How to chain animate methods

To chain animations, you use the same technique that you use for chaining effects or any other methods. You code a dot operator after the first animate method and then code the second animate method.

This is illustrated by the first example in figure 6-7, which chains two animate methods in the click event handler for a heading. Here, the indentation and alignment of the code is meant to show that the two animate methods are chained. The first method increases the font size and opacity and moves the heading 275 pixels to the right. Then, the second method reduces the font size and moves the heading 275 pixels to the left so it's back where it started.

When you chain effects or animations for a selected element, they are placed in the *queue* for that element. Then, the effects and animations are run in sequence. This makes it easy for you to create some interesting animations.

Note, however, that animations that are coded separately are also placed in queues. This is illustrated by the second example in this figure. Here, the first statement is for one animate method that is applied to the heading (this). The second statement is for another animate method that is applied to the same heading (this). Then, when the user clicks the heading, these animations are placed in a queue and run in succession just as though they were chained, so the result is the same as for the chained methods in the first example.

Now, what happens if you click on the heading two or three times in quick succession? Either way, the animate methods are put in the queue for the heading so they will run two or three times in a row.

In contrast, the third example uses a callback function for the first animate method to provide the second animate method. Then, if the user clicks on the heading just once, it works the same as the other two examples. But if the user clicks on it twice in succession, the second click will queue the second animate method so it runs right after the first. But this may mean that the second animate method will start before the callback method of the first animate method is finished.

As you will see, the concept of queuing is important for some applications, especially when you want to stop the methods in the queue from running. Remember too that there is a separate queue for each element. That's why the fading in and fading out of the captions and slides in the Slide Show application are almost simultaneous.

A heading with two animations started by its click event

Chained animations

```
$("#faqs h1").click(function() {
    $(this).animate(
            { fontSize: "650%", opacity: 1, left: "+=275" }, 2000 )
        .animate(
            { fontSize: "175%", left: "-=275" }, 1000 );
});          // end click
```

Queued animations

```
$("#faqs h1").click(function() {
    $(this).animate(
        { fontSize: "650%", opacity: 1, left: "+=275" }, 2000 );
    $(this).animate(
        { fontSize: "175%", left: "-=275" }, 1000 );
});          // end click
```

An animation with a second animation in its callback function

```
$("#faqs h1").click(function() {
    $(this).animate(
        { fontSize: "650%", opacity: 1, left: "+=275" },
        2000,
        function() {
            $(this).animate(
                { fontSize: "175%", left: "-=275" }, 1000
            );
        }    // end function
    );
});          // end click
```

Description

- When you chain the effects and animations for an element, they are placed in a *queue* for that element and run in sequence, not at the same time.

- When separate effects and animations are started for an element, they are also placed in a queue for that element and run in sequence.

- When you use a callback function with an animate method, the callback function is run after the animation is finished.

- In some cases, a problem will occur if the user starts a second animation for an element before the callback function for the first animation has finished.

Figure 6-7   How to chain animate methods

How to use the delay, stop, and finish methods

Figure 6-8 shows how to use the delay, stop, and finish methods for effects and animations. As the first example shows, the delay method delays the start of the next animation in the queue for the number of milliseconds that are specified. Here, the fadeOut effect of the selected heading is delayed for five seconds.

In contrast, the stop method stops the animations in the queue for the selected element. This is illustrated by the second example. Here, the animation is for the hover event of the <a> elements in the HTML. This animation moves an <a> element down 15 pixels when the mouse pointer moves into the element, and it moves it back to its starting location when the mouse pointer moves out of the element.

But what if the user swipes the mouse pointer back and forth over the <a> elements several times in succession? As you've just learned, this will queue multiple animations for each <a> element that will run in succession. This will cause a bouncing effect after the user stops using the mouse, and that's not what you want.

To fix this, you can use the stop method as shown in this figure. As the summary shows, this method stops the current animation for the selected elements. In addition, when the first parameter is set to true, the queues for the elements are cleared. As a result, all of the animations for an element in the example are stopped and the queue is cleared before another animation is added to the queue. This stops the bouncing of the <a> elements, which makes the application easier to use.

The second parameter for the stop method causes the current animation to be completed immediately. For example, suppose an element is being faded in when the stop method is executed. In that case, the element is left at its current opacity. If that's not what you want, you can code true for the second parameter so the end result of the animation is displayed. In the case of the fadeIn method, that means that the element is displayed with an opacity of 1.

The finish method is similar to the stop method with both of its parameters set to true. The difference is that the properties of *all* queued animations, not just the current animation, are immediately set to their end values when you use finish.

The delay, stop, and finish methods

Method	Description
delay(*duration*)	Delay the start of the next animation in the queue.
stop([*clearQueue*] [,*jumpToEnd*])	Stop the current animation for the selected element. The two parameters are Boolean with false default values. If set to true, the first parameter clears the queue so no additional animations are run. The second parameter causes the current animation to be completed immediately.
finish([*queue*])	Stop the current animation for the selected element, clear the queue, and complete all animations for the selected elements.

HTML for a heading that is displayed when the web page is loaded

```
<h1 id="startup_message">Temporarily under construction!</h1>
```

jQuery that fades the heading out after 5 seconds

```
$("#startup_message").delay(5000).fadeOut(1000);
```

Thumbnail images with queues that are still running

The HTML for the thumbnail images

```
<ul id="image_list">
    <li><a href="images/h1.jpg" title="James Allison: 1-1"
        <img src="thumbnails/t1.jpg" alt=""></a></li>
    // four more li elements that contain thumbnail images
    <li><a href="images/h6.jpg" title="James Allison: 1-6">
        <img src="thumbnails/t6.jpg" alt=""></a></li>
</ul>
```

The CSS for the <a> elements

```
a { position: relative; }
```

The stop method stops the queued animations before starting a new one

```
$("#image_list a").hover(
    function(evt) { $(this).stop(true).animate({ top: 15 }, "fast"); },
    function(evt) { $(this).stop(true).animate({ top: 0 }, "fast"); }
); // end hover
```

Description

- The delay method in the example works as an alternative to the use of a one-time timer.

- The stop method in the example above stops the current animation for each <a> element and clears the queue. This will stop the bouncing effect that occurs when the user moves the mouse pointer rapidly back and forth over the thumbnails.

- The finish method is similar to the stop method with true coded for both parameters, except that the properties of all queued animations jump to their end values.

Figure 6-8   How to use the delay, stop, and finish methods

How to use easings with effects and animations

Figure 6-9 shows how to use easings with effects and animations. An *easing* determines the way an animation is performed. For instance, an animation can start slowly and pick up speed as it goes. Or, an animation can start or end with a little bounce.

Right now, jQuery only provides two easings: linear and swing. As you might guess, the linear easing moves an animation at a uniform speed, but the swing easing varies the speed in a way that is more interesting. Fortunately, swing is the default, so you don't need to change that.

If you want to use other easings, you need to use a plugin or jQuery UI. Both provide many different easings that you can experiment with. To show you how to use the jQuery UI easings, this figure provides the basic skills that you need, but you'll learn more about easings in section 3.

To use the jQuery UI easings, you start by coding a script element for jQuery UI. In the example in this figure, this script element gets jQuery UI from the jQuery CDN. Note that this script element must be coded after the script element for jQuery because jQuery UI uses jQuery.

Then, to use one of the easings that jQuery UI provides, you code the easing parameter for an effect or animation. The location of this parameter in each type of statement is shown in the syntax summaries at the top of this figure.

To code this parameter, of course, you need to know the names of the easings that you want to use. Perhaps the best way to find out what's available is to go to the URL that's specified at the bottom of this figure. This page of the jQuery UI website not only gives you the names of the easings, but also lets you run a demonstration of each one. That will help you select the easings that you want to use for each type of animation.

The syntax for using easing with effects and animations

The syntax for all of the basic methods except the fadeTo method

```
methodName([duration][, easing][, callback])
```

The syntax for the fadeTo method

```
fadeTo(duration, opacity[, easing][, callback])
```

The syntax for the basic animate method

```
animate({properties}[, duration][, easing][, callback])
```

A script element for getting the jQuery UI library from the jQuery CDN

```
<!-- the element for jquery ui must come after the one for jquery -->
<script src="//code.jquery.com/ui/1.11.4/jquery-ui.min.js"></script>
```

Two easings used by the FAQs application

```
$("#faqs h2").click(function() {
    $(this).toggleClass("minus");
    if ($(this).attr("class") == "minus") {
        $(this).next().slideDown(1000, "easeOutBounce");
    }
    else {
        $(this).next().slideUp(1000, "easeInBounce");
    }
});    // end click
```

Two easings for an animated heading

```
$("#faqs h1").click(function() {
    $(this).animate(
      { fontSize: "650%", opacity: 1, left: "+=275" }, 2000, "easeInExpo" )
    .animate(
      { fontSize: "175%", left: "-=275" }, 1000, "easeOutExpo" );
});    // end click
```

Description

- *Easing* refers to the way an animation is performed. jQuery provides only two easings: swing and linear. Swing is the default, and it's the animation that you usually want.

- Plugins, including jQuery UI, provide many other types of easings.

- To use an easing, you code a script element for the plugin library or jQuery UI. Then, you code the easing parameter for a method with the name of any easing that the plugin or jQuery UI supports.

- In chapter 7, you'll learn more about plugins, and in chapters 10 and 11, you'll learn more about jQuery UI.

- For a full list and demonstration of all the jQuery UI easings, you can go to:
  http://jqueryui.com/easing

Figure 6-9   How to use easings with effects and animations

How to use the advanced animate syntax and the methods for working with queues

At this point, you've probably already learned all of the methods and skills that you're going to want to use for your effects and animations. But in case you are trying to build applications that require more control over the queues, figure 6-10 presents the advanced syntax of the animate method and the methods for working with queues.

When you use the advanced syntax of the animate method, you code two parameters within braces and separated by a comma. In the first set of braces, you code the properties map just as you do in the basic syntax. In the second set of braces, you code one or more of the options that are summarized in the first table in this figure.

The first example in this figure shows how this works with three options: duration, specialEasing, and complete. Here, the duration option is like the duration parameter in the basic syntax, and the complete option is like the callback parameter in the basic syntax. However, the special easing parameter lets you specify a different easing for each property that is being animated.

Although the use of special easings may be more than you need, you should know that you can also use them with the basic syntax. That is illustrated by the second example in this figure. Here, you just code each property and its easing within brackets within the properties map.

The step option of the advanced animate method lets you run a function after each step of the animation. This makes you realize that an animation is actually broken down into small steps that give the illusion of continuous progress. If, for example, you code the step option with a function that displays an alert message after each step of the first example, you'll see how many steps this animation is broken down into.

The queue option of the advanced animate method lets you execute an animation immediately without placing it in the queue. You can also use the methods in the second table in this figure to work with the animations in a queue. But as I said at the start of this topic, you may never find the need for the advanced animate syntax or the methods for working with queues.

The advanced syntax for the animate method

```
animate({properties}, {options})
```

Some of the options for the advanced syntax

Option	Description
duration	A string or number that specifies the duration of the animation.
easing	A string that specifies an easing function.
complete	A callback function that runs when the animation is complete.
step	A function to call after each step that the animation is broken down into.
queue	A Boolean value. If true, the animation will be placed in the queue. If false, the animation will start immediately.
specialEasing	A map of one or more of the properties in the properties map with their corresponding easings.

The methods for working with animation queues

Method	Description
queue([name])	Get the queue for the selected element.
queue([name], newQueue)	Replace the queue for the selected element with a new queue.
queue([name], callback)	Add a new function (callback) to the end of the queue for the selected element.
dequeue([name])	Run the next item in the queue for the selected element.
clearQueue([name])	Remove all items that haven't yet been run from the queue.

An animate method that uses the advanced syntax

```
$("#faqs h1").animate(
    { fontSize: "650%", opacity: 1, left: "+=175" },
    { duration: 2000,
      specialEasing: { fontSize: "easeInExpo", left: "easeOutExpo" },
      complete: function() {
          $("#faqs h2").next().fadeIn(1000).fadeOut(1000); }
    }
);    // end animate
```

How to provide easings by property with the basic syntax

```
$("#faqs h1").animate(
    { fontSize: ["650%", "easeInExpo"],
      opacity: [1, "swing"],
      left: ["+=275", "easeOutExpo"] }, 2000
);    // end animate
```

Description

- The specialEasing option of the advanced syntax of the animate method lets you specify easings by property, as shown by the first example. However, you can also do that with the basic syntax as shown by the second example.

- The name parameter in the methods for working with queues isn't needed for the default queue (fx). It's only needed for custom queues that you create.

Figure 6-10   How to use the advanced animate syntax and the methods for queues

A Carousel application with animation

This chapter ends by presenting a common application called a Carousel application. It makes use of a simple animate method, but the setup for using that method is extensive.

The user interface, HTML, and CSS

Figure 6-11 presents the user interface, HTML, and CSS for the Carousel application. Because carousels are so common, you've most likely used one on more than one website. If you click on the button to the right of the three books in the carousel shown here, the books slide left and three more are shown. If you click on the button to the left of the books, the books slide right to the previous three books.

In the HTML, you can see that three div elements are coded within a div element for the entire carousel. The first of these div elements contains the left button; the second contains all nine of the books that will be used in the carousel; and the third contains the right button.

Within the second div element, you can see a ul element that contains nine li elements. Then, within each li element, there is an img element for each book within an <a> element. That means that the user can click on each book to go to the page for that book. In this example, the values of all of the href attributes are coded as "newpage.html", but these values would refer to the actual pages for the books in a real-world application.

In the critical CSS for this application, you can see that the width of the middle div element (id is "display_panel") is set to 300 pixels, which is the width of three list items. Also, its overflow property is set to hidden, which means that anything that goes beyond 300 pixels (the other books) will be hidden.

Next, the CSS for the ul element (id is "image_list") sets the position property to relative, which means that any settings for the top or left properties will be relative to the normal position of this element. As you'll see in the jQuery for this application, the books that are displayed in the carousel are determined by the value of the left property. The CSS for this element also sets the width to 900 pixels, and the list-style to "none", which removes the bullets from the list items. The left property for this ul element illustrates one of the browser incompatibilities. With IE, this property must be set to 0. With other browsers, 0 is assumed.

Then, the CSS for the list items floats them to the left. This means that the items in the ul element will be displayed horizontally, but the 900 pixel width (100 pixels for each item) will exceed the width of its div container by 600 pixels. Remember, though, that this overflow will be hidden.

The last CSS rule set sets the width of the img elements within the li elements to 95 pixels. That means that there should be 5 pixels to the right of each image within each of the li items.

Since there are nine images in total and each list item is set to a width of 100 pixels, nine images require 900 pixels and that's the width that the ul element has been set to. For this application to work properly, of course, the widths of the div, ul, and li elements have to be properly coordinated.

A Carousel application

The HTML for the application

```html
<main>
    <h1>View our Books</h1>
    <div id="carousel">
        <div id="left_button" class="button_panel">
            <img src="images/left.jpg" alt=""></div>
        <div id="display_panel">
            <ul id="image_list">
                <li><a href="newpage.html">
                    <img src="images/book1.jpg" alt=""></a></li>
                <li><a href="newpage.html">
                    <img src="images/book2.jpg" alt=""></a></li>
                // 5 more li elements that contain images
                <li><a href="newpage.html">
                    <img src="images/book8.jpg" alt=""></a></li>
                <li><a href="newpage.html">
                    <img src="images/book9.jpg" alt=""></a></li>
            </ul>
        </div>
        <div id="right_button" class="button_panel">
            <img src="images/right.jpg" alt=""></div>
    </div>
</main>
```

The critical CSS for the application

```css
#display_panel {
    width: 300px;
    overflow: hidden;
    float: left;
    height: 125px; }
#image_list {
    position: relative;
    left: 0px;                  // required for IE
    width: 900px;
    list-style: none; }
#image_list li {
    float: left;
    width: 100px; }
#image_list li img {
    width: 95px; }
```

Figure 6-11   The HTML and CSS for the Carousel application

The jQuery

If you look at the jQuery code for this application in figure 6-12, you can see that it consists of two event handlers: one for the right button, and one for the left button. You can also see that the last line in each event handler uses the animate method to change the left property of the slider variable to the value of the variable named newLeftProperty. Since the first line of code in the ready event handler sets the slider variable to the ul element, this means that the ul element is moved right or left based on the value in the newLeftProperty variable.

The trick, then, is setting the value of the newLeftProperty variable each time the right or left button is clicked. That's what the rest of the code in each event handler does. As you study this code, keep in mind that the ul element must move to the left to display the images in the li elements, so the left property will either be zero (the starting position) or a negative number.

Now, look at the event handler for the right button. There, the first statement gets the value of the current left property by using the css method. Then, it uses the parseInt method to convert that value to an integer. The first time the button is clicked, for example, the value will be zero.

The if statement that follows sets the value of the newLeftProperty variable that's used by the animate method. If the current value of the left property (which is either 0 or a negative number) minus 300 (which is the width of three list items) is less than or equal to -900, the new left property is set to zero. Then, the animate method will slide the images all the way back to the right so the first three images will be displayed. Otherwise, 300 is subtracted from the new left property so the animate method will move the slider three images to the left.

The click event handler for the left button works similarly. After it gets the value of the current left property, it uses an if statement to set the new left property. This time, if the current property is less than zero, the new left property is increased by 300. This means that the animate method will move the slider three images to the right. Otherwise, the first three images are already displayed and the slider shouldn't be moved. To indicate that, the new left property is set to zero.

The jQuery for the Carousel application

```
$(document).ready(function() {
    var slider = $("#image_list");      // slider = ul element
    var leftProperty, newleftProperty;

    // the click event handler for the right button
    $("#right_button").click(function() {

        // get value of current left property
        leftProperty = parseInt(slider.css("left"));

        // determine new value of left property
        if (leftProperty - 300 <= -900) {
            newLeftProperty = 0; }
        else {
            newLeftProperty = leftProperty - 300; }

        // use the animate method to change the left property
        slider.animate( {left: newLeftProperty}, 1000);

    }); // end click

    // the click event handler for the left button
    $("#left_button").click(function() {

        // get value of current left property
        leftProperty = parseInt(slider.css("left"));

        // determine new value of left property
        if (leftProperty < 0) {
            newLeftProperty = leftProperty + 300;
        }
        else {
            newLeftProperty = 0;
        }

        // use the animate method to change the left property
        slider.animate( {left: newLeftProperty}, 1000);

    }); // end click
});         // end ready
```

Description

- To get the value of the left property of the ul element, the css method is used.
- The value of the left property for the ul element will range from 0 to -600.

Figure 6-12   The jQuery for the Carousel application

Perspective

Now that you've completed this chapter, you should be able to add some of the common animations to your web pages, like a slide show or a carousel. In the next chapter, though, you'll learn how to use jQuery plugins to create these as well as other types of animations. Because plugins are typically easy to use and because they typically work better than code you could write yourself, you should use them whenever possible.

Terms

animation
effect
callback function
properties map
queue
easing

Summary

- jQuery provides methods for *effects*, like fading in and fading out, that let you add *animation* to your web pages.

- The jQuery animate method lets you change the CSS properties for an element over a specific duration. This lets you create interesting animations.

- To get the animation that you want, you often chain one effect after another. This places the effects in a *queue* so the effects are executed in sequence.

- If a user starts an effect for an element several times in quick succession, the effects are placed in a queue for that element. In some cases in which a user is likely to do that, you may want to use the stop or finish method to stop the effects and clear the queue.

- *Easings* refer to the ways that effects and animations are executed over time. Although jQuery provides for only two easings, linear and swing, jQuery UI provides for many more.

Exercise 6-1   Experiment with animation

In this exercise, you'll experiment with effects, animations, and easings.

Review the application

1. Use your text editor to open the HTML, CSS, and JavaScript files in this folder:

   ```
   c:\jquery\exercises\ch06\animation\
   ```

2. Run the application to see how it works. Note how the top-level heading is animated into view from off the page. Then, click on the FAQ headings to see what happens.

Experiment with the effects for the FAQ headings

3. In the jQuery code, change the effects for the FAQ headings so the answers fade in and fade out of view when the headings are clicked.

4. Now, change the effects for the FAQ headings so the answers slide down and slide up when the headings are clicked.

5. Experiment with the durations and effects to see which ones you think are best for usability.

Experiment with the h1 heading

6. Check the CSS for the h1 heading to see that it starts with its left property at minus 175 pixels. Then, check the jQuery code to see that it moves the left property 375 pixels to the right and then 200 pixels to the left, which means the left property ends at zero pixels.

7. Restart the application and note the animation as the h1 heading moves from off the page into its proper location. Then, click the heading to see that the animation is repeated, which moves the heading farther to the right. Click on it again to see that it's repeated, which moves the heading still farther.

8. Restart the application. Then, click on the top-level heading twice in rapid succession. This should run the animations twice in a row, which shows that the animations are queued.

9. Fix the animation for the top-level heading so it always returns to its proper location above the FAQs at the end of the animation. That way, it won't move across the page. To do that, set its ending left property to zero pixels.

Add jQuery UI easings to the application

10. Note that there's a script element for jQuery UI in the HTML for the page. Then, add the easings shown in figure 6-9 to the effects and animations. Does that improve them?

11. After you run the application to see how those easings work, click on the link at the bottom of the page to go to a demonstration of the jQuery UI easings. Note that this opens a new page or tab in your browser. Then, try some of the other easings to see how you like them.

Exercise 6-2 Modify the Slide Show application

This is a simple exercise that has you experiment with the effects that can be used with the slide show in figure 6-3. It uses the second block of jQuery code that's shown in figure 6-4.

1. Use your text editor to open the HTML, CSS, and JavaScript files in this folder:

   `c:\jquery\exercises\ch06\slide_show\`

   Then, run the application to see how it works.

2. Modify the jQuery so the caption and the image slide up and then back down as the show moves from one slide to the next. Then, test to see how you like this.

3. Modify the jQuery so the caption is hidden by the hide method and displayed by the show method, both over an interval of one second. Also, increase the time for displaying and hiding the slide to two seconds, and increase the interval for the timer to five seconds. Then, test these changes.

4. If you're curious, experiment with effects, durations, and easings until you get the slide show to work in a way that you like.

Exercise 6-3 Modify the Carousel application

This is a simple exercise that will test whether you understand the code for the Carousel application in figures 6-11 and 6-12.

1. Use your text editor to open the HTML, CSS, and JavaScript files in this folder:

   `c:\jquery\exercises\ch06\carousel\`

2. The way it is now, nothing happens if you click on the left button when the first three books are displayed. Change this so the last three books are displayed when you click on the left button while the first three books are visible.

3. Modify the jQuery code so the carousel moves one book at a time when you click on one of the buttons instead of three books at a time. Now, what happens when you click on the right button when the last three books are displayed?

4. Modify the CSS and jQuery code so only one book is displayed. Otherwise, the application should work the same way.

7

How to create and use jQuery plugins

One quick way to improve your web development productivity is to use plugins. As you will see, plugins are available for all of the common web development tasks, and many of them are easy to use. Often, the use of plugins can save you many hours of development time, and most plugins are likely to do their tasks even better than your code might have done them.

In chapter 6, for example, you learned how to use a plugin for easings. Now, in this chapter, you'll first learn the skills for using any jQuery plugin. Then, you'll learn how to create your own plugins.

Introduction to plugins

In this introduction, you'll learn how to find and use plugins. A *jQuery plugin* is just a JavaScript application that does one web task or a set of related web tasks. A plugin makes use of the jQuery library, and most plugins can save you many hours of development time.

How to find jQuery plugins

Figure 7-1 starts with a screen capture that shows the results of a Google search for "jquery plugin form validation". Here, you can see the first three items in the search results. Often, doing a search like this is the best way to find what you're looking for. Note, however, that the search entry includes the word *jquery* because there are other types of plugins.

Another way to find the type of plugin that you're looking for is to go to the URLs for the websites in the table in this figure. The first one is for the jQuery Plugin Repository, which is part of the jQuery website, and the second one is for a site that is only for jQuery plugins.

In contrast, the next three websites are repositories for many types of code, including jQuery plugins. As a result, you must search for jQuery plugins to find what you want on these sites.

In most cases, jQuery plugins are free or are available for a small price or donation. Besides that, jQuery plugins can often save you hours of development time and do their jobs better than you would have done them with your own code. For those reasons, it makes sense to look for a plugin whenever you need to add a common function to your website.

A Google search for form validation plugins

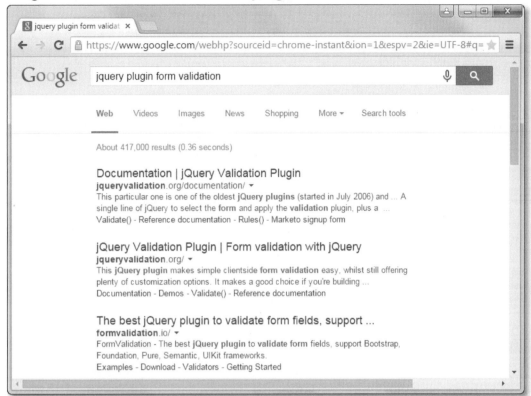

Websites for finding jQuery plugins

Site name	URL
jQuery Plugin Repository	http://plugins.jquery.com
jQuery Plugins	http://jquery-plugins.net
Google Code	http://code.google.com
GitHub	https://github.com
Sourceforge	http://sourceforge.net

Description

- jQuery *plugins* are JavaScript applications that extend the functionality of jQuery. These plugins require the use of the core jQuery library.

- Plugins are available for hundreds of web functions like slide shows, carousels, tabs, menus, text layout, data validation, and mobile application development.

- Some of the websites that provide jQuery plugins are listed above. Often, though, you can find what you're looking for by searching the Internet.

- In general, if you can find a plugin for doing what you want, that's better than writing the jQuery code yourself.

Figure 7-1   How to find jQuery plugins

Some of the most useful plugins

Figure 7-2 summarizes some of the most useful plugins. These are grouped by type of plugin. In a moment, you'll see an example for displaying images using the Lightbox plugin, you'll see an example for creating a slide show using the Malsup jQuery Cycle 2 plugin, and you'll see an example for creating a carousel using the bxSlider plugin. Then, in chapter 8, you'll learn how to validate forms using the jQuery Validation plugin. In section 3, you'll learn how to use the jQuery UI plugin for themes, widgets, interactions, and effects. And in section 5, you'll learn how to use the jQuery Mobile plugin.

Some of the most useful plugins

Plugins for displaying images	
Lightbox	http://lokeshdhakar.com/projects/lightbox2/
Fancybox	http://fancybox.net
ThickBox	http://codylindley.com/thickbox/
ColorBox	http://www.jacklmoore.com/colorbox

Plugins for slide shows, carousels, and galleries	
bxSlider	http://bxslider.com
Malsup jQuery Cycle 2	http://jquery.malsup.com/cycle2
jCarousel	http://sorgalla.com/jcarousel
Galleria	http://galleria.io

Plugins for text layout	
UI Layout	http://layout.jquery-dev.net
Masonry	http://masonry.desandro.com
Columnizer	http://welcome.totheinter.net/columnizer-jquery-plugin
jsColumns	http://code.google.com/p/js-columns
jLayout	http://www.bramstein.com/projects/jlayout/jquery-plugin.html

Plugins for forms	
Malsup jQuery Form	http://jquery.malsup.com/form
Ideal Forms	http://code.google.com/p/idealforms
jQuery Validation	http://jqueryvalidation.org
jqTransform	http://www.dfc-e.com/metiers/multimedia/opensource/jqtransform

Plugins for interface design	
jQuery UI	http://plugins.jquery.com/
Isotope	http://isotope.metafizzy.com
WOW	http://mynameismatthieu.com/WOW/
Wijmo	http://wijmo.com

Plugin for mobile development	
jQuery Mobile	http://www.jquerymobile.com

Description

- The table above lists some of the most useful plugins. But if you need a plugin for other purposes, just search for it. You'll probably find it.

Figure 7-2   Some of the most useful plugins

How to use any plugin

Figure 7-3 shows how to use any plugin after you find the one you want. First, if you haven't already done so, you study the documentation for the plugin so you know what HTML and CSS it requires and what methods and options it provides. Usually, you'll do this as you evaluate the plugin to see if it does what you want and if its documentation tells you everything you need to know.

Second, you usually download the files for the plugin and save them on your web server. This download is often in the form of a zip file, and it will always include at least one JavaScript file. In addition, it may include CSS or image files that are used by the plugin.

The download may also include two versions of the main JavaScript file. If you want to review the code for the file, you can open the full version in your text editor. But the one you should use for your applications is the compressed version, which usually has a name that ends with min.js.

For some plugins, the files are also available from a Content Delivery Network (CDN). If you want to access the files that way, you can record the URLs for the files. Then, you can use those URLs in the link and script elements for the files.

Third, if a plugin requires one or more CSS files, you code the link elements for them in the head element of the HTML. Then, you code the script elements for the JavaScript files for the plugin. Usually, only one JavaScript file is required, but some plugins require more than one.

Fourth, if the download includes a folder for images, you need to make sure the folder has the right structural relationship with the CSS and JavaScript files for the plugin. Otherwise, you may have to adjust the CSS or JavaScript code so it can find the images folder (and you probably don't want to do that).

At this point, you're ready to use the plugin. So, fifth, you code the HTML and CSS for the plugin. In some cases, that's all you need to do because the HTML will include the code for using the plugin. In other cases, though, the sixth step is to code the JavaScript for using the plugin. This code can be in an external file or it can be within the head element of the HTML.

This procedure is illustrated by the example in this figure, which uses the bxSlider plugin. Here, the script elements show that the element for the plugin must come after the element for the jQuery library. That's because all jQuery plugins use the jQuery library. As the first caution in this figure points out, not coding these script elements in this sequence is a common error.

The HTML that follows shows the elements that the plugin requires. In particular, the id attribute for the unordered list is set to "slider" so the jQuery code can select that element when it calls the bxSlider method of the plugin.

This is followed by the jQuery code for using this plugin. Here, the bxSlider method is called as the first statement within the function for the ready method for the document. This method initializes the bxSlider plugin. Then, the method name is followed by a set of braces that contains the code for setting four options for the method.

Before you continue, note the second caution in this figure. That is that some plugins require a specific version of jQuery, which may not be the latest version.

General steps for using a plugin within your web pages

1. Study the documentation for the plugin so you know what HTML and CSS it requires as well as what methods and options it provides.

2. If the plugin file or files are available via a Content Delivery Network (CDN) and you want to access them that way, get the URLs for them. Otherwise, download the file or files for the plugin, and save them in one of the folders of your website.

3. In the head element of the HTML for a page that will use the plugin, code the link elements for any CSS files that are required. Also, code the script elements for the JavaScript files that are required. These script elements must be after the one for the core jQuery library because all jQuery plugins use the core library.

4. If the download for a plugin includes an images folder, make sure the folder has the right structural relationship with both the CSS and JavaScript files for the plugin.

5. Code the HTML and CSS for the page so it is appropriate for the plugin.

6. If necessary, write the jQuery code that uses the methods and options of the plugin.

The script elements for the jQuery library and the bxSlider plugin

```
<!-- the script element for the core jQuery library -->
<script src="http://code.jquery.com/jquery-2.1.4.min.js"></script>
<!-- the script element for the plugin when it has been downloaded -->
<script src="js/jquery.bxSlider.min.js"></script>
```

The HTML used by the bxSlider plugin

```
<ul id="slider">
    <li><img src="images/building_01.jpg" alt="" title="Front"></li>
    <li><img src="images/building_02.jpg" alt="" title="Left side"></li>
    <!-- more li elements -->
</ul>
```

The jQuery for using the bxSlider plugin

```
$(document).ready(function(){
    $("#slider").bxSlider({
        minSlides: 2,
        maxSlides: 2,
        slideWidth: 250,
        slideMargin: 10
    });
});
```

Two cautions

*   Make sure that you include a script element for jQuery and make sure that the script element for the plugin comes after it. Not doing one or the other is a common error.

*   Some plugins won't work with the latest version of jQuery. So if you have any problems with a plugin, check its documentation to see which version of jQuery it requires.

Description

*   Some plugins can be accessed via a CDN, but most must be downloaded and stored on your server.

Figure 7-3   How to use any plugin

How to use three of the most useful plugins

Now, you'll get a close-up view of three of the most useful plugins. This will introduce you to the power of plugins. It will also show you how the procedure in the last figure works with specific plugins.

How to use the Lightbox plugin for images

Figure 7-4 presents the Lightbox plugin. This is a popular plugin that displays a larger version of a thumbnail image when the user clicks on the thumbnail image. This image is displayed in a modal dialog box, which means that it must be closed before the user can continue. The image in this box has a thick white border, and it may have a caption below it. The part of the web page that's outside of the dialog box is darkened. To close the dialog box, the user clicks on the "X" in the bottom right corner.

If images are grouped in sets, this plugin not only displays the dialog box for the thumbnail, it also displays the image number and total number of images below the image, as in "Image 3 of 5". Also, when the mouse hovers over the left or right side of an image, previous and next icons are displayed. Then, if the user clicks on an icon, the display is moved to the previous or next image.

As the link and script elements in this example show, this plugin requires both CSS and JavaScript files. These elements use the names of the downloaded files. Remember, though, that the script element for the plugin must come after the script element for the jQuery library.

The download also includes an img folder that contains the images used by the plugin. Here again, you must maintain the proper relationship between the img folder and the JavaScript and CSS files for this plugin.

Next, this figure shows the HTML for using this plugin. Here, img elements that represent the thumbnail images are coded within <a> elements. To make this work, each <a> element must have an href attribute that identifies the related large image and a data-lightbox attribute that activates the Lightbox plugin.

If you're using the Lightbox plugin with independent images, the value of the data-lightbox attribute should be unique for each <a> element. On the other hand, if you're using this plugin with a set of related images as shown here, the value of this attribute should be the same for all <a> elements. The last attribute shown here, data-title, provides a caption for each image.

Once all of that's done, you're done. Because the data-lightbox attribute activates the plugin and the data-title attribute provides the caption, you don't have to use any jQuery code. The plugin just works!

A Lightbox after the user has clicked on a thumbnail image to start it

The URL for this plugin

```
http://lokeshdhakar.com/projects/lightbox2/
```

The link and script elements for the Lightbox plugin

```
<link href="main.css" rel="stylesheet">
<link href="lightbox.css" rel="stylesheet">
<script src="http://code.jquery.com/jquery-2.1.4.min.js"></script>
<script src="js/lightbox.js"></script>
```

The HTML for the Lightbox plugin

```
<a href="images/building_01.jpg" data-lightbox="vecta" data-title="Front">
    <img src="images/building_01_thumb.jpg" alt=""></a>
<a href="images/building_02.jpg" data-lightbox="vecta" data-title="Left side">
    <img src="images/building_02_thumb.jpg" alt=""></a>
...
```

Description

- The Lightbox plugin can be used to display larger versions of thumbnail images. The Lightbox starts when the user clicks one of the thumbnail images. Then, the rest of the page outside the larger image is darkened and a caption is displayed if specified.

- If the image is one in a set of images, a counter is also displayed. Then, if the mouse pointer moves over the larger image, next or previous icons appear.

- The Lightbox download includes a CSS file, a plugin file, and an img folder that contains an image for loading and images for the close, next, and previous icons.

- The HTML for a Lightbox consists of img elements within <a> elements. The src attributes of the img elements identify the thumbnail images, and the href attributes of the <a> elements identify the larger images.

- The data-lightbox attributes of the <a> elements activate Lightbox. Their values should be unique for independent images but the same for a group of images.

- The data-title attributes of the <a> elements can be used to provide captions.

Figure 7-4   How to use the Lightbox plugin for images

How to use the bxSlider plugin for carousels

Figure 7-5 presents the bxSlider plugin for creating carousels. In the example, this plugin displays two images at a time, it slides from one set of images to the next automatically, it provides captions in the slides, it provides controls below the carousel, and the user can move to the next or previous images by clicking on the right or left icons that are displayed.

If you download the JavaScript file for this plugin, the script element can refer to it as shown in this figure. As part of the download, you also get a CSS file and an images folder that contains the images that can be used with this plugin.

One way to set up the HTML for use with this plugin is shown in this figure. Here, img elements are coded within the li elements of an unordered list. Then, the src attributes of the img elements identify the images that are displayed, and the title attributes provide the captions.

To run the bxSlider plugin, you use the jQuery code in this figure. Within the ready function, the selector selects the ul element that contains the slides and executes the bxSlider method.

If you want to change how the carousel works, you can code one or more options on the bxSlider method. In this example, several options are set. The auto option makes the carousel run automatically, the autoControls option puts the controls below the carousel, the captions option causes the title attributes to be used for captions, the minSlides and maxSlides options set the carousel so two slides are always displayed, and the slideWidth and slideMargin options set the size of the slides and the space between them.

These options show just some of the capabilities of this plugin. To learn more, you can go to the website for this plugin and review its demos and option summaries.

By the way, if you try to run a page that contains a bxSlider plugin from Aptana, you'll see that the plugin doesn't work. Because of that, you'll need to run the page from outside of Aptana.

When you use this plugin, you will often want to change the location of components like the left and right icons, the captions (which I adjusted for this example), and the controls below the carousel. To do that, you can adjust the styles in the CSS file for this plugin.

If, for example, you want to adjust the location of the left and right icons, like moving them outside of the slider, you can modify the CSS for the bx.next and bx.prev classes. You won't find these classes in the HTML, though, because they're added to the DOM by the plugin. Usually, you'll learn a lot by studying the code in the CSS files for plugins and by making adjustments to that code.

Although it isn't necessary and it isn't done in this example, it's a good practice to code the width and height attributes for the img elements and set them to the exact size of the images. That way, the browser can reserve the space for the images and continue rendering the page while the images are being loaded.

A web page that uses the bxSlider plugin for a carousel

The URL for the bxSlider website

```
http://bxslider.com
```

The link and script elements for the bxSlider plugin

```html
<link href="main.css" rel="stylesheet">
<link href="jquery.bxslider.css" rel="stylesheet">
<script src="http://code.jquery.com/jquery-2.1.4.min.js"></script>
<script src="js/jquery.bxSlider.min.js"></script>
```

The HTML for the bxSlider plugin

```html
<ul id="slider">
    <li><img src="images/building_01.jpg" alt="" title="Front"></li>
    <li><img src="images/building_02.jpg" alt="" title="Left side"></li>
    ...
</ul>
```

The jQuery for using some of the bxSlider options

```javascript
$(document).ready(function(){
    $("#slider").bxSlider({
        auto: true,
        autoControls: true,
        captions: true,
        minSlides: 2,
        maxSlides: 2,
        slideWidth: 250,
        slideMargin: 10
    });
});
```

Description

- The bxSlider plugin makes it easy to develop a carousel. The HTML is an unordered list with one list item for each slide that contains images or other HTML.

- The bxSlider website provides excellent examples and option summaries.

- If the slides contain images with title attributes, the captions option will make them captions.

- The bxSlider download consists of a JavaScript file, a CSS file, and an images folder that contains the images that are used by the plugin.

Figure 7-5   How to use the bxSlider plugin for carousels

How to use the Cycle 2 plugin for slide shows

Figure 7-6 shows how to use the Cycle 2 plugin for slide shows. The easiest way to include this plugin in your web pages is to use the URL for the CDN that's shown in this figure. This plugin doesn't require a CSS file or any images.

The HTML for this plugin works with the children of a div element. These children are usually img or div elements. When you use div elements, you can code whatever you want within them, including headings, text, lists, and images. In this example, there is one img element for each slide that's contained within the div element for the slide show. Note that the class attribute for this div element must be set to "cycle-slideshow" to initialize the slide show.

If you don't want to set any options for the slide show, that's all you need. Otherwise, you can set options by coding data-cycle attributes for the main div element. In this example, options are set for the effect (fx) that's used to move from slide to slide, how many milliseconds each slide should be displayed, where the captions should be displayed, and what caption template should be used. Here, the caption option points to the div that has been added after the img elements.

If you go to the Cycle 2 website, you'll find demos that show the many ways that this plugin can be used. You'll also find a complete summary of its options. Incidentally, instead of using the "cycle-slideshow" class to initialize a slide show and setting options using data-cycle attributes, you can call the cycle method of the div element that contains the slides and code the options like you do for the bxSlider plugin. The preferred method, though, is the one shown here.

A web page that uses the Cycle 2 plugin for a slide show

On June 6th, 2012, Vecta Corp. moved into its new 4 story, 35,000 square foot facilty. Below are a few pictures of the new facility.

Slide 2: Left side

The URL for the Cycle 2 website

```
http://jquery.malsup.com/cycle2/
```

The script elements for the Cycle 2 plugin

```html
<script src="http://code.jquery.com/jquery-2.1.4.min.js"></script>
<script src="http://malsup.github.com/jquery.cycle2.js"></script>
```

The HTML for the Cycle 2 plugin

```html
<div class="cycle-slideshow"
        data-cycle-fx="scrollHorz"
        data-cycle-timeout="2000"
        data-cycle-caption="#adv-custom-caption"
        data-cycle-caption-template="Slide {{slideNum}}: {{cycleTitle}}">
    <img src="images/building_01.jpg" alt="" data-cycle-title="Front">
    <img src="images/building_02.jpg" alt="" data-cycle-title="Left side">
    ...
    <!-- empty element for caption -->
    <div id="adv-custom-caption"></div>
</div>
```

Description

- The Cycle 2 plugin treats the children of a div element as the slides. Those children are usually img elements, but they can be div elements that contain both text and images.
- The best way to include this plugin in your web pages is to use the GitHub CDN for it.
- The Cycle 2 website provides excellent demos and summaries that let you enhance a slide show in many ways.
- To set options for a slide show, you can code data-cycle attributes for the div element.
- To provide captions below the slides, you can code data-cycle-title attributes for the img elements, data-cycle-caption attributes for the div element, and an empty div element for the captions below the slides.

Figure 7-6   How to use the Cycle 2 plugin for slide shows

How to create your own plugins

One of the features of jQuery is that it provides an *API* (*Application Programming Interface*) that lets you create your own plugins. Since it sometimes makes sense to do that, the topics that follow present the basic skills. Keep in mind, though, that it takes time to develop your own plugins. So before you start the development of a plugin, you should ask yourself a few questions.

First, have you done a thorough search for a plugin that does what you want to do so you don't have to create your own? Second, is the plugin that you plan to create one that you will use for many web pages? Third, are you sure your plugin will improve the effectiveness and usability of your web pages? If you can answer "yes" to questions like these, it probably does make sense to create the plugin.

The structure of a plugin

The first two examples in figure 7-7 show two ways to structure a plugin. In both examples, the plugin function is wrapped within an *Immediately Invoked Function Expression* (*IIFE*):

```
(function($) {
    // the plugin goes here
})(jQuery);
```

Here, the jQuery library that's coded within parentheses at the end of the IIFE is assigned to the $ sign parameter of the function. That way, the scope of the library is limited to the plugin, and you can continue to use the $ sign in the other jQuery code for an application just as you've learned in previous chapters. If a plugin isn't coded this way, it can cause conflicts with other libraries and plugins that use the $ sign.

Within the IIFE, $.fn refers to the object that contains all of the jQuery object methods. When you create a plugin, you can extend jQuery by adding methods to this object.

The only code that changes from one plugin to another is the method name and the code that implements the plugin. In the function for the plugin, the each method is called for the object that the plugin is applied to, which is referred to by the this keyword. Then, if the object consists of more than one element, the plugin function is applied to each element.

At the end of the plugin function in the first example, the return statement returns the object, again by using the this keyword. This means that the plugin method can be chained with other methods. In the second example, the return statement precedes the this.each method. This gets the same result as the first example, and this is the way professionals usually code this structure.

The example after the two structures presents a simple plugin. Here, the each method contains one alert method that uses the text method to display the text of the this object. If this object consists of only one element, this method displays one alert dialog box. If this object consists of more than one element, this method displays one alert dialog box for each element.

The structure of a plugin

One way to code this structure

```
(function($){
    $.fn.methodName = function() {
        this.each(function() {
            // the code for the plugin
        });
        return this;
    }
})(jQuery);
```

The way most professionals code this structure

```
(function($){
    $.fn.methodName = function() {
        return this.each(function() {
            // the code for the plugin
        });
    }
})(jQuery);
```

A simple Selection plugin that uses this structure

The jQuery for a plugin in a file named jquery.selection.js

```
(function($){
    $.fn.displaySelection = function() {
        return this.each(function() {
            alert("The text for the selection is '" + $(this).text() + "'");
        });
    }
})(jQuery);
```

The script element for this plugin

```
<script src="jquery.selection.js"></script>
```

The jQuery for using this plugin

```
$(document).ready(function(){
    $("#faqs h2").displaySelection();
});
```

Naming conventions for plugin files

```
jquery.pluginName.js
```

The API standards for plugins

- The plugin should support implicit iteration.
- The plugin should preserve chaining by returning the selected object.
- The plugin definitions should end with a semicolon.
- The plugin options should provide reasonable defaults.
- The plugin should be well-documented.

Description

- For many plugins, most of the code will be in the function of the each method.
- When the plugin finishes, the this object should be returned to the calling application.

Figure 7-7   The structure of a plugin

Because this plugin is stored in a file named jquery.selection.js, the script element for using this plugin uses that name in its src attribute. Then, the jQuery for using this plugin makes a selection and calls the displaySelection method of the plugin to operate upon the selection. In this example, the selection is all of the h2 elements in an element with "faqs" as its id attribute. As a result, one alert dialog box will be displayed for each h2 element.

Figure 7-7 also shows the naming conventions for plugin files as well as the API standards for plugins. To support "implicit iteration", you use the each method within the plugin function. To preserve chaining, you return the this object. Beyond that, you should be sure to end all method definitions with a semicolon, and you should provide reasonable defaults if your plugin offers options. Above all, your plugin should be well documented if it's going to be used by others.

How to code a plugin that highlights menu items

Now that you know the structure of a plugin, figure 7-8 shows how to create a plugin that sets CSS styles for the items in a menu that consists of <a> elements within the li elements of an unordered list. This plugin also highlights an item when the mouse enters the item, and it returns the item to its original styles when the mouse leaves the item.

The code for this plugin uses the second structure in the previous figure. Within its each method, the first statement selects the <a> elements within the li elements of the element that the plugin is applied to. It stores these elements in a variable named items.

Then, the plugin uses the jQuery css method to apply six styles to the items in the items variable, which are the <a> elements in the menu. Note here that the css methods are chained to the items object. That's possible because each css method returns the object that it was applied to.

Next, the plugin provides functions for the mouseover and mouseout events of the <a> elements in the items variable. The function for the mouseover event changes the background color and color for the item. The function for the mouseout event returns the background color and color for the item to the original colors.

Because the plugin is stored in a file named jquery.highlight.js, the script element for the plugin reflects this. Then, the jQuery to activate the plugin selects the unordered list by its id and calls the highlightMenu method of the plugin.

A menu that is highlighted by the highlightMenu plugin

The HTML for a menu that can be highlighted by the plugin

```html
<ul id="vecta_menu">
    <li><a href="index.html">Home</a></li>
    <li><a href="aboutus.html">About Us</a></li>
    <!-- the rest of the links for the menu -->
</ul>
```

The highlightMenu plugin in a file named jquery.highlight.js

```javascript
(function($){
    $.fn.highlightMenu = function() {
        return this.each(function() {
            var items = $("li a");
            items.css('font-family', 'arial, helvetica, sans-serif')
                .css('font-weight', 'bold')
                .css('text-decoration', 'none')
                .css('background-color', '#dfe3e6')
                .css('color', '#cc1c0d')
                .css('width', '125px');
            items.mouseover(function() {
                $(this).css('background-color', '#000')
                    .css('color', '#fff');
            });
            items.mouseout(function() {
                $(this).css('background-color', '#dfe3e6')
                    .css('color', '#cc1c0d');
            });
        });
    }
})(jQuery);
```

The script element for the plugin

```html
<script src="jquery.highlight.js"></script>
```

jQuery that uses the highlightMenu plugin

```javascript
$(document).ready(function() {
    $("#vecta_menu").highlightMenu();
});
```

Description

- The code in the highlightMenu plugin sets CSS styles for the links within the selected list items. It also changes two of those styles for the mouseover and mouseout events.

Figure 7-8   A plugin that highlights the items in a menu

How to add options to a plugin

To make a plugin more useful, you usually provide some options for it. To do that, you can use the coding technique that is illustrated in figure 7-9.

To start, you code an options parameter in the function for the plugin method. This is highlighted in the figure. This parameter will receive all of the options that are set by the user in name/value pairs within an object.

As the API standards for plugins in figure 7-7 point out, a plugin should always provide defaults for the options so the users don't have to set the options if they don't want to. To do that, you can use the $.extend method to set up the defaults as shown in this example. Here, a variable named defaults is set to the object that's created by the $.extend method.

The first parameter of the $.extend method consists of name/value pairs that provide the properties for the object that's created, and the second parameter is set to the options that are passed to the plugin, which are also treated as object properties. Then, when this method is executed, the user options are merged with the default options and the user options replace any default options with the same name. The result is that the default variable contains one property for each option that is either the default property or the property that the user set to override the default property.

Within the each method for this plugin, a variable named *o* is created and set to the object for the options. Then, you can refer to these options within the plugin function by using object notation. For instance,

        o.hoverBgColor

refers to the option named hoverBgColor and returns the value of that option. When this is assigned to an <a> element, it sets the background color either to the default or the option that the user set.

This figure also shows the code for using the plugin and setting its options. In this case, the user overrode just two of the options. This, of course, is where the plugin documentation should make it easy to find out what the names of the options are and how they should be coded. Without documentation, the users of this plugin will have to study the plugin code to figure out how to set the options, and untrained users may not be able to do that.

Incidentally, you still need to provide some CSS rule sets for a menu that is highlighted by this plugin. For instance, you need to set the display property for the <a> elements in the menu to "block". You need to set the padding and margins for the list items. And you need to set the list-style property of the list items to "none".

The highlightMenu plugin with options

```
(function($){
    $.fn.highlightMenu = function(options) {
        var defaults = $.extend({
            'bgColor'       : '#000000',
            'color'         : '#ffffff',
            'hoverBgColor'  : '#cccccc',
            'hoverColor'    : '#000000',
            'linkWidth'     : '125px',
        }, options);

        return this.each(function() {
            var items = $("li a");
            var o = defaults;

            items.css('font-family', 'arial, helvetica, sans-serif')
                .css('font-weight', 'bold')
                .css('text-decoration', 'none')
                .css('background-color', o.bgColor)
                .css('color', o.color)
                .css('width', o.linkWidth);

            items.mouseover(function() {
                $(this).css('background-color', o.hoverBgColor)
                    .css('color', o.hoverColor);
            });

            items.mouseout(function() {
                $(this).css('background-color', o.bgColor)
                    .css('color', o.color);
            });
        });
    }
})(jQuery);
```

jQuery that uses the highlightMenu plugin and sets just two of its options

```
$(document).ready(function() {
    $("#vecta_menu").highlightMenu({
        bgColor: '#dfe3e6',
        color: '#cc1c0d'
    });
});
```

Description

- To provide options for a plugin, you code a parameter for the plugin that will receive the options that the user sets. In the example above, this parameter is named "options".

- To set the default options, you use the $.extend method, which creates an object from the name/value pairs in its first parameter. Then, it merges those pairs with the name/value pairs in its second parameter, which are the options set by the user. This replaces the pairs in the first parameter that have the same names, so the user options override the defaults.

- To refer to the options in the object that's created, you use object, dot, property notation.

Figure 7-9   The highlightMenu plugin with options

A web page that uses two plugins

This chapter ends by showing the code for a page that uses two plugins. This illustrates how two or more plugins can be used for a single page.

The user interface

Figure 7-10 presents the user interface for this web page. Here, a slide show is displayed beneath the heading for the page. It uses the Cycle 2 plugin to cycle through the images for three products. However, this slide show pauses if the user hovers the mouse over an image.

Then, in the left column of the page, the highlightMenu plugin is used to highlight the items in the menu. This is the custom plugin that's shown in the previous figure.

The script elements

Figure 7-10 also shows the script elements that this application requires. The first one is for the core jQuery library. The second one is for the Cycle 2 plugin. And the third one is for the highlightMenu plugin.

In this case, the script elements for both of the plugins must come after the script element for the jQuery library. However, it doesn't matter what sequence the script elements for the plugins are in.

The page layout

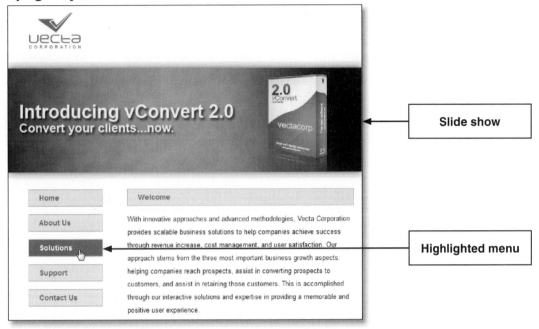

The script elements in the head section of the HTML

```
<!-- script element for the jQuery library -->
<script src="http://code.jquery.com/jquery-2.1.4.min.js"></script>

<!-- script element for the Cycle 2 plugin -->
<script src="http://malsup.github.com/jquery.cycle2.js"></script>

<!-- script element for the custom highlightMenu plugin -->
<script src="js/jquery.highlight.js"></script>
```

Description

- This web page uses two plugins.
- The Cycle 2 plugin cycles through the images for three Vecta Corp products.
- The highlightMenu plugin in figure 7-9 is used to format the menu and highlight any menu item that has the mouse over it.
- The script elements for the plugins must come after the script element for the core jQuery library, but it doesn't matter which one comes first.

Figure 7-10 The user interface and script elements for the Vecta Corp page

The HTML for the elements used by the plugins

Figure 7-11 presents the HTML for the portions of the web page that use the plugins. This starts with the div element that contains the three images for the slide show. This element is followed by the unordered list for the menu that will be highlighted by the highlightMenu plugin.

Notice that the div element for the slide show includes a class attribute that initializes the slide show. In addition, it includes three data-cycle attributes that set options of the plugin. Because of that, no jQuery is required for this plugin. jQuery is required for the highlightMenu plugin, though.

The jQuery for using the highlightMenu plugin

Figure 7-11 also shows the jQuery for using the highlightMenu plugin. Notice that this plugin is called from the event handler for the ready event. As a result, it starts as soon as the page is ready.

Since you already know how to use this plugin, you shouldn't have any trouble understanding the code shown here. The only difference from what you've already seen is that some of the options are set differently.

The HTML for the Cycle 2 and highlightMenu plugins

```
<body>
    ...
    <!-- the slides used by the Cycle 2 plugin -->
    <div class="cycle-slideshow"
            data-cycle-fx="fade"
            data-cycle-speed="1000"
            data-cycle-pause-on-hover="true">
        <img src="images/rotator01.jpg" width="697" height="240"
            alt="vProspect 2.0">
        <img src="images/rotator02.jpg" width="697" height="240"
            alt="vConcert 2.0">
        <img src="images/rotator03.jpg" width="697" height="240"
            alt="vRetain 1.0">
    </div>

    <!-- the menu used by the custom highlightMenu plugin -->
    <nav>
        <ul id="vecta_menu">
            <li><a href="index.html">Home</a></li>
            <li><a href="aboutus.html">About Us</a></li>
            <li><a href="solutions.html">Solutions</a></li>
            <li><a href="support.html">Support</a></li>
            <li><a href="contactus.html">Contact Us</a></li>
        </ul>
    </nav>
    ...
</body>
```

The jQuery that uses the highlightMenu plugin

```
$(document).ready(function() {
    $("#vecta_menu").highlightMenu({
        bgColor: '#dfe3e6',
        color: '#cc1c0d',
        hoverBgColor: '#cc1c0d',
        hoverColor: '#fff',
        linkWidth: '125px'
    });
});
```

Figure 7-11   The HTML and jQuery for the plugins used by the Vecta Corp page

Perspective

Now that you've finished this chapter, you should be able to find and use plugins for common web development functions. This by itself can improve your productivity as you develop web pages, and often the plugin functions will work better than the ones you could write by yourself.

If you need to create a plugin of your own, you should be able to do that too. However, you should only develop your own plugin if the plugin function is clearly needed, isn't already available, and will be reused often.

Terms

plugin
API (Application Programming Interface)
IIFE (Immediately Invoked Function Expression)

Summary

- If you need a common function for a web page, chances are that a *plugin* is already available for it. By using a plugin, you can often save hours of work and do the job even better than you would have done it on your own.

- Perhaps the best way to find a plugin is to search the Internet. However, you can also go to code repositories like Google Code, GitHub, and Sourceforge.

- Some plugins can be accessed from a Content Delivery Network (CDN), but others need to be downloaded and saved on your server. The downloads for some plugins consist of only a single JavaScript file, but some include files like CSS and image files.

- To access a plugin, you code a script element for it in the head element of the HTML document. This script element must come after the script element for the jQuery library, because all jQuery plugins use that library.

- To use some plugins, you initialize them by calling their methods within the ready event handler for a page. Then, if you want to set options to control how a plugin works, you can code the options as part of the method call.

- To use other plugins, you code attributes in the HTML to initialize the plugin and set options.

- Three of the most useful plugins are Lightbox for displaying images, bxSlider for carousels, and Cycle 2 for slide shows.

- When you create a plugin, you use jQuery's *Application Programming Interface* (*API*) for plugins. This API describes the way the plugins should be coded.

- To adhere to the plugin API, you code each plugin within an *Immediately Invoked Function Expression* (*IIFE*) to prevent any conflicts over the use of the $ sign. In most cases, you also use the jQuery each method to operate on each of the selected elements. And when the plugin function is finished, you always return the object for the selected elements so the plugin method can be chained.

Exercise 7-1   Experiment with the Cycle 2 plugin

In this exercise, you'll experiment with the Cycle 2 plugin and the slide show that's in figure 7-6. You'll also review the documentation for this plugin. This will give you a better idea of how you can use plugins.

Review the application

1. Use your text editor to open the HTML file in this folder:

    `c:\jquery\exercises\ch07\cycle2\`

2. Note that the options for using the Cycle 2 plugin are coded as attributes in the HTML for the slide show. Then, run the application to see how it works.

Experiment with the options

3. Change the value of the data-cycle-fx option to "fadeout". Then, add a data-cycle-speed option with a value of "1000". Test the application to see how this changes the way it works.

4. Go to the website for the Cycle 2 plugin, which is at this URL:

    `http://jquery.malsup.com/cycle2/`

    Click on the Demos link on the Home page, then review any of the demos to see the information they present.

5. Go back to the Home page of the website, then click on the API link to learn more about the options you can use with this plugin.

6. If you're interested, try using one or more of these options.

Check out the download

7. Go back to the Home page one more time, and click on the Download button for the production version of the plugin. This goes to a new page or tab that displays the JavaScript for the plugin. Although this isn't the way most downloads work, this is relatively common with plugins.

8. To download the plugin, right-click in the code, select Save As from the menu that's displayed, and save the file in a new folder named "js" in your website.

9. Change the script element for the Cycle 2 plugin so it refers to the file you just downloaded. Then, make sure the application still works.

Exercise 7-2 Experiment with the Selection plugin

This exercise has you experiment with the Selection plugin in figure 7-7 to see how it works and to demonstrate that the standard plugin structure facilitates chaining.

1. Use your text editor to open the HTML file and the two JavaScript files in this folder:

   `c:\jquery\exercises\ch07\selection\`

2. The Selection plugin is in the file named jquery.selection.js, and the jQuery for using that plugin is the first statement within the ready event handler in the file named faqs.js. Note that this statement selects all h2 elements in the "faqs" element before calling the plugin method. If you look at the HTML for this application, you can see that it includes three h2 elements

3. Run the application to see that the text for the three h2 elements are displayed in alert dialog boxes. Then, change the selection to all h1 elements and run the application again to see that the text for the one h1 element is displayed.

4. To prove that the standard plugin structure facilitates chaining, chain the css method that follows to the call to the plugin method in the faqs.js file:

   `css("color", "red")`

   Then, test this change. It should change the color of the h1 element to red after the alert dialog box is displayed.

Exercise 7-3 Create a Reveal plugin

In this exercise, you'll create a relatively simple plugin named Reveal. This plugin will set up click event handlers for the selected elements. Alternate clicks of a selected element will first show and then hide the next sibling element.

1. Use your text editor to open the files in this folder:

   `c:\jquery\exercises\ch07\reveal\`

2. In the jquery.reveal.js file, you can see the standard plugin structure with the method name set to reveal. In the faqs.js file, you can see the jQuery for the FAQs application. But the Reveal plugin should do what this code does. So copy the code for the click event handler of the faqs h2 elements into the each method of the reveal file. Then, change the selector for the faqs h2 elements to *this* so the plugin will work with any elements.

3. In the HTML file, add a statement to the last script element that calls the reveal method for the h2 elements. Since this HTML file already contains a script element for the Reveal plugin, you can now test this application. It should show and hide the answers of the FAQs application.

4. Note, however, that this plugin can be used for any application that works like this. The user just has to change the selection that's used.

8

How to work with forms and data validation

To create dynamic web pages, you use HTML to create forms that let the user enter data. Then, the user can click on a button to submit the data to a web server for processing. Before the data is submitted, though, the data is usually validated by JavaScript in the browser.

In this chapter, you'll learn how to use jQuery to work with forms, and you'll learn how to use JavaScript for data validation in the browser. You'll also learn how to use a validation plugin to validate the data in forms.

Introduction to forms and controls

A *form* contains one or more *controls* such as text boxes and buttons. The controls that accept user entries are also known as *fields*. In the three topics that follow, you'll learn how forms work and how to use the HTML5 features for working with forms.

How forms work

Figure 8-1 shows how to create a form that contains three controls: two text boxes and a button. To start, you code the form element. On the opening tag for this element, you code the action and method attributes. The action attribute specifies the file on the web server that will be used to process the data when the form is submitted. The method attribute specifies the HTTP method that will be used for sending the form to the web server.

In the example in this figure, the form will be submitted to the server using the HTTP "get" method when the user clicks the Join our List button. Then, the data in the form will be processed on the server by the code that's in the file named join.php. That file will use PHP as the scripting language.

When you use the get method, the form data is sent as part of the URL for the HTTP request. That means that the data is visible and the page can be bookmarked. This is illustrated by the URL in this figure. Here, the URL is followed by a question mark and name/value pairs separated by ampersands that present the name attributes and field values. In this case, two values are submitted: the email address and first name entries.

When you use the post method, the form data is packaged as part of an HTTP request and isn't visible in the browser. Because of that, the submission is more secure than it is when you use the "get" method, but the resulting page can't be bookmarked.

Within the opening and closing tags of the form element, you code the controls for the form. In this example, the first two input elements are for text boxes that will receive the user's email address and first name. The third input element has "submit" as the value for its type attribute, which means it is a *submit button*. When it is clicked, the data in the form will automatically be submitted to the server.

If the type attribute of an input element is "reset", the button is a *reset button*. When that type of button is clicked, all of the values in the controls of the form will be reset to their starting HTML values.

When a form is submitted to the server, the data in the form is completely validated on the server before the data is processed. Then, if any of the data isn't valid, the form is sent back to the browser with appropriate error messages so the entries can be corrected. This is referred to as *data validation*.

Usually, the form data is validated by the browser too before it is submitted to the server. Note, however, that the browser validation doesn't have to be as thorough as the server-side validation. If the browser validation catches 80 to 90% of the entry errors, it will save many round trips to the server.

A form in a web browser

Email Address: judy@murach.com
First Name: Judy
Join our List

The HTML for the form

```
<form id="email_form" name="email_form" action="join.php" method="get">
    <label for="email_address">Email Address:</label>
    <input type="text" id="email_address" name="email_address"><br>
    <label for="first_name">First Name:</label>
    <input type="text" id="first_name" name="first_name"><br>
    <label> </label>
    <input type="submit" id="join_list" value="Join our List"><br>
</form>
```

The URL that's sent when the form is submitted with the get method

```
join.php?email_address=judy%40murach.com&first_name=Judy
```

Attributes of the form element

Attribute	Description
name	A name that can be referred to by client-side or server-side code.
action	The URL of the file that will process the data in the form.
method	The HTTP method for submitting the form data. It can be set to either "get" or "post". The default value is "get".

Description

- A *form* contains one or more *controls* (or *fields*) like text boxes, radio buttons, lists, or check boxes that can receive data.

- When you click on a *submit button* for a form (type is "submit"), the form data is sent to the server as part of an HTTP request. When you click on a *reset button* for a form (type is "reset"), the form data is reset to its default values.

- When a form is submitted to the server for processing, the data in the controls is sent along with the HTTP request.

- When you use the get method to submit a form, the URL that requests the file is followed by a question mark and name/value pairs that are separated by ampersands. These pairs contain the name attributes and values of the data that is submitted. When you use the post method, the data is hidden.

- *Data validation* refers to checking the data collected by a form to make sure it is valid, and complete data validation is always done on the server. Then, if any invalid data is detected, the form is returned to the client so the user can correct the entries.

- To save round trips to the server when the data is invalid, some validation is usually done on the client before the data is sent to the server. However, this validation doesn't have to be as thorough as the validation that's done on the server.

Figure 8-1   How forms work

The HTML5 controls for working with forms

In case you aren't familiar with the HTML5 input controls, the first table in figure 8-2 summarizes the ones you'll use most often. When you use these controls, the type attribute indicates what type of data should be entered in the control. Then, in some cases, the browser will validate the data that's entered into the text box that's displayed to be sure it's the right type. In other cases, the browser will display other types of controls to assist users in entering a valid value.

If, for example, you use "email" for the type attribute, all five of the major browsers except Safari (Chrome, IE, Firefox, and Opera) will provide data validation for the email address that's entered into the text box. If you use "number" for the type attribute, all five of the major browsers except IE will implement the control as a text box with up and down arrows that let the user increase or decrease the current value. And if you use "date" as the type attribute, Chrome and Opera will display a popup calendar that lets the user select a date. At the least, these attributes indicate the type of data that the control is for, and that's good for semantic reasons.

HTML5 also provides new attributes for working with controls, and two of the basic attributes are summarized in the second table in this figure. The autofocus attribute moves the focus to the control when the form is loaded. This means that you don't need to use JavaScript to do that. Also, the placeholder attribute can be used to put starting text in a control to help the user enter the data in the correct format. When the user moves the focus to the control, that text is removed.

Some of these controls and attributes are illustrated in the code example in this figure. Here, the type attribute for the input control that accepts an email address is set to "email". In addition, since this is the first input control in the form, the autofocus attribute is included so the control will have the focus when the page is first displayed. In the form below the code example, you can see the error message that's displayed in Chrome when an invalid entry is made in the email field.

Because the third input field in this example is for a telephone number, its type attribute is set to "tel". Although none of the current browsers provide data validation for this type, it's good to use it for semantic reasons. This control also uses the placeholder attribute to indicate the format of the phone number that should be entered. You can see part of this placeholder in the form in this figure.

Common HTML5 controls for input data

Control	Description
email	Gets an email address with validation done by the browser.
url	Gets a URL with validation done by the browser.
tel	Gets a telephone number with no validation done by the browser.
number	When supported, gets a numeric entry with min, max, and step attributes, browser validation, and up and down arrows.
range	When supported, gets a numeric entry with min, max, and step attributes, browser validation, and a slider control.
date	When supported, gets a date entry with min and max attributes and may include a popup calendar or up and down arrows.
time	When supported, gets a time entry with min and max attributes and may include up and down arrows.

The basic HTML5 attributes for working with forms

Attribute	Description
autofocus	A Boolean attribute that tells the browser to set the focus on the field when the page is loaded.
placeholder	A message in the field that is removed when the control receives the focus.

The HTML for a form that uses some of these controls and attributes

```
<form id="email_form" name="email_form" action="join.php" method="get">
    <label for="email_address">Email Address:</label>
    <input type="email" id="email_address" name="email_address" autofocus><br>
    <label for="name">Name:</label>
    <input type="text" id="name" name="name"><br>
    <label for="phone">Phone Number:</label>
    <input type="tel" id="phone" name="phone" placeholder="999-999-9999"><br>
    <label> </label>
    <input type="submit" id="join_list" value="Join our List"><br>
</form>
```

The form in Chrome with an error message for the email address

Description

- Many of the HTML5 input controls provide for basic data validation. You can also use the HTML5 attributes in figure 8-3 for data validation.

- For a complete description of the HTML5 and CSS3 features for working with forms, please refer to *Murach's HTML5 and CSS3*.

Figure 8-2   The HTML5 controls for working with forms

The HTML5 and CSS3 features for data validation

In addition to the HTML5 controls you saw in the last figure, HTML5 and CSS3 provide some features specifically for data validation. These features are presented in figure 8-3.

The table at the top of this figure summarizes the HTML5 attributes for data validation. To start, the required attribute causes the browser to check whether a field is empty before it submits the form for processing. If the field is empty, it displays a message and the form isn't submitted. The browser also highlights all of the other required fields that are empty when the submit button is clicked.

If you code a title attribute for a field, the value of that attribute is displayed when the mouse hovers over the field. It is also displayed at the end of the browser's standard error message for a field.

The pattern attribute provides for data validation through the use of regular expressions. A *regular expression* provides a way to match a user entry against a *pattern* of characters. As a result, regular expressions can be used for validating user entries like credit card numbers, zip codes, dates, or phone numbers. Regular expressions are supported by many programming languages including JavaScript and PHP, and now regular expressions are supported by HTML5. The trick of course is coding the regular expressions that you need, and that can be difficult.

If you want to stop a control from being validated, you can code the novalidate attribute for that control. And if you want to turn the auto-completion feature off for a control, you can set its autocomplete attribute to "off". The *auto-completion feature* is on by default in all modern browsers, which means that a browser will display a list of entry options when the user starts the entry for a field. These options will be based on the entries the user has previously made for fields with similar names.

The code example in this figure illustrates how you can use some of these attributes. This is the same form that was presented in the previous figure except this time, the required attribute is coded for each input field so the user must make an entry. In addition, the auto-completion feature is turned off for the email field, and a pattern and title are specified for the phone field. In the form below this code, you can see the error message that's displayed if the user enters a phone number with an invalid format. It includes the browsers standard error message as well as the text that's specified by the title attribute for this field.

This figure also presents three CSS3 pseudo-classes that you can use to format required, valid, and invalid fields. For instance, you can use the :required pseudo-class to format all required fields, and you can use the :invalid pseudo-class to format all invalid fields.

For simple forms, you may already be able to get by with just HTML5 controls and data validation attributes. For most forms, though, you are going to need JavaScript. One reason for that is the HTML5 features aren't supported by all browsers yet. The other reason is that the HTML5 features don't provide for all of the types of validation that most forms need.

The HTML5 attributes for data validation

Attribute	Description
required	A Boolean attribute that indicates that a value is required for a field.
title	Text that is displayed in a tooltip when the mouse hovers over a field. This text is also displayed after the browser's default error message.
pattern	A regular expression that is used to validate the entry in a field.
novalidate	A Boolean attribute that tells the browser that it shouldn't validate the form or control that it is coded for.
autocomplete	Set this attribute to off to tell the browser to disable auto-completion. This can be coded for a form or a control.

CSS3 pseudo-classes for required, valid, and invalid fields

```
:required :valid :invalid
```

The HTML for a form that uses some of these attributes

```
<form id="email_form" name="email_form" action="join.php" method="get">
    <label for="email_address">Email Address:</label>
    <input type="email" id="email_address" name="email_address"
           required autofocus autocomplete="off"><br>
    <label for="name">Name:</label>
    <input type="text" id="name" name="name" required><br>
    <label for="phone">Phone Number:</label>
    <input type="tel" id="phone" name="phone" required
           pattern="\d{3}[\-]\d[3][\-]\d{4}"
           title="Must be 999-999-9999"><br>
    <label> </label>
    <input type="submit" id="join_list" value="Join our List"><br>
</form>
```

The form in Chrome with an error message for the phone field

Two of the reasons why you need JavaScript for data validation

- The HTML5 input controls and attributes for data validation aren't implemented by all current browsers, and the ones that are may not be implemented the same way.

- HTML5 is limited in the types of validation it can do. For instance, HTML5 can't check whether a field is equal to another one or look up a state code in a table.

Description

- At this writing, Chrome, IE, Firefox, and Opera all support the HTML5 attributes and CSS3 pseudo-classes shown above. Even so, you typically need to use JavaScript and jQuery and maybe even a plugin to do an adequate job of client-side validation.

Figure 8-3   The HTML5 and CSS3 features for data validation

How to use jQuery to work with forms

To make it easier to work with forms, jQuery provides selectors, methods, and event methods that are designed for that purpose. However, as the next two figures show, jQuery doesn't provide specific features for data validation.

The jQuery selectors and methods for forms

The first table in figure 8-4 summarizes the jQuery selectors that you can use with forms. As you can see, these selectors make it easy to select the various types of controls. They also make it easy to select disabled, enabled, checked, and selected controls.

The second table in this figure summarizes the val methods that you are already familiar with. They let you get and set the value in a control. For instance, the first example in this figure gets the entry in the control with "age" as its id. The code also parses this entry into an integer before saving it in the variable named "age".

The third table summarizes the trim method, which is one of the miscellaneous jQuery methods. It is useful because JavaScript doesn't provide its own trim method. In the second example in this figure, you can see how this method is used to trim the entry in the control with "first_name" as its id before the entry is saved in the variable named "firstName". The second statement in this example puts that trimmed entry back into the control.

The third example in this figure shows how to get the value of the checked radio button in a named group. Here the selector starts by selecting all of the input elements with "contact_by" as the name attribute. That includes all the radio buttons in the group, since they all must have the same name. Then, it uses the :checked selector to get the radio button within that group whose checked attribute has a value of true. This works because only one radio button in a named group can be selected. For a radio button, the val method returns the value of the value attribute, so that's what's saved in the variable named radioButton.

The last example shows how to get an array of the selected options in a select list that allows multiple selections. First, an empty array named selectOptions is created. Next, the :selected selector is used to get all of the selected options in a select list with "select_list" as its id. These options are then saved in the selectOptions variable.

Notice in this example that there's a space between the id of the select list and the :selected selector. That's because a select list consists of a select element that contains option elements. So the selector in this example selects all the descendant option elements that are selected. Another way to code this statement would be like this:

```
selectOptions = $("select_list option:selected");
```

In contrast, there's no space before the :checked selector in the third example. That's because a group of radio buttons consists of independent input elements with the same name attribute. So the selector in this example selects the radio button that's checked in the group.

The jQuery selectors for form controls

Selector	Selects
:input	All input, select, textarea, and button elements.
:text	All text boxes: input elements with type equal to "text".
:radio	All radio buttons: input elements with type equal to "radio".
:checkbox	All check boxes: input elements with type equal to "checkbox".
:file	All file upload fields: input elements with type equal to "file".
:password	All password fields: input elements with type equal to "password".
:submit	All submit buttons and button elements: input elements with type equal to "submit" and button elements.
:reset	All reset buttons: input elements with type equal to "reset".
:image	All image buttons: input elements with type equal to "image".
:button	All buttons: button elements and input elements with type equal to "button".
:disabled	All disabled elements: elements that have the disabled attribute.
:enabled	All enabled elements: elements that don't have the disabled attribute.
:checked	All check boxes and radio buttons that are checked.
:selected	All options in select elements that are selected.

The jQuery methods for getting and setting control values

Method	Description
val()	Gets the value of a text box or other form control.
val(*value*)	Sets the value of a text box or other form control.

The jQuery method for trimming an entry

Method	Description
trim()	Removes all spaces at the start and end of the string.

How to get the value of a numeric entry from a text box

```
var age = parseInt($("#age").val());
```

How to trim the value of an entry and put it back into the same text box

```
var firstName = $("#first_name").val().trim();
$("#first_name").val(firstName);
```

How to get the value of the checked radio button in a group

```
var radioButton = $("input[name='contact_by']:checked").val();
```

How to get an array of the selected options from a list

```
var selectOptions = [];
selectOptions = $("#select_list :selected");
```

Description

- jQuery provides special selectors for selecting the controls on a form; the val method for getting and setting the value in a control; and a trim method that can be used to trim a user's entry.

Figure 8-4   The jQuery selectors and methods for forms

The jQuery event methods for forms

The first table in figure 8-5 summarizes the jQuery event methods for working with forms, and you have already been introduced to some of these. For instance, the handler for the focus event method is run when the focus moves to the selected element, and the handler for the change event method is run when the value in the selected element is changed.

The last event method in this table runs when the submit event occurs. That event occurs when the user clicks on a submit button or when the user moves the focus to the submit button and presses the Enter key. But it also occurs when the submit method is used to trigger the event.

The second table in this figure summarizes the jQuery methods for triggering (or starting) events. If, for example, you code the focus method for a text box, the focus is moved to that text box and the focus event is triggered. However, if a handler hasn't been assigned to that event, that event isn't processed. Please note that the names of these triggering methods are the same as the ones for the event methods.

The examples in this figure show how you can use these event methods. In the first example, the change event method is used to create an event handler for the change event of a check box with "contact_me" as its id. Then, the function within this handler checks the value of the check box's attr property to see if the check box is checked. If it is checked, the code turns off the disabled attribute of all of the radio buttons on the form. Otherwise, the code turns on the disabled attribute for all of the radio buttons.

This is useful in an application in which the radio buttons should only be enabled if the check box is checked. If, for example, the user checks the Contact Me box, the radio buttons should be enabled so the user can click the preferred method of contact. Otherwise, the radio buttons should be disabled.

The second example in this figure shows how you can trigger the submit event at the end of an event handler for the click event of an input button with "button" as its type attribute. Here, the function for the event handler starts by validating the code in all of the entries. Then, if all the entries are valid, it uses the submit method to initiate the submit event of the form, and that will send the form to the server. This is the method that you've been using in the Email List application in earlier chapters.

The other way to provide for data validation is to use a submit button instead of a regular button. Then, you can code an event handler for the submit event of the form. Within that handler, you can test all of the entries for validity. If they are all valid, you can end the handler, so the form will be submitted. But if one or more entries are invalid, you can issue the preventDefault method of the event object for the submit event to cancel the submission of the form. You'll see this illustrated in figure 8-7.

The jQuery event methods for forms

Event method	Description
`focus(`*`handler`*`)`	The handler runs when the focus moves to the selected element.
`blur(`*`handler`*`)`	The handler runs when the focus leaves the selected element.
`change(`*`handler`*`)`	The handler runs when the value in the selected element is changed.
`select(`*`handler`*`)`	The handler runs when the user selects text in a text or textarea box.
`submit(`*`handler`*`)`	The handler runs when a submit button is clicked.

The jQuery methods for triggering events

Event method	Description
`focus()`	Moves the focus to the selected element and triggers the focus event.
`blur()`	Removes the focus from the selected element and triggers the blur event.
`change()`	Triggers the change event.
`select()`	Triggers the select event.
`submit()`	Triggers the submit event for a form.

A handler that disables or enables radio buttons when a check box is checked or unchecked

```
$("#contact_me").change(         // the change event for a check box
    function(){
        if ($("#contact_me").attr("checked")) {
            $(":radio").attr("disabled", false) }   // enables radio buttons
        else {
            $(":radio").attr("disabled", true)}     // disables radio buttons
});
```

A handler that triggers the submit event after some data validation

```
$(document).ready(function() {
    $("#join_list").click(      // join_list is a button, not a submit button
        function() {
            // data validation code
            $("#email_form").submit();
        }     // end function
    );        // end click
});           // end ready
```

Description

- You can use event handlers for the focus, blur, change, and select events to process data as the user works with individual controls.

- You can use an event handler for the click event of a regular button, not a submit button, to validate the data in a form. Then, if the data is valid, you can use the submit method to submit the form. That's the way data validation has been done in the Email List applications.

- You can also use an event handler for the submit event of a form to validate data before it is sent to the server. Then, if any of the data is invalid, you must issue the preventDefault method of the event object to cancel the submission of the data to the server.

Figure 8-5   The jQuery event methods for forms

A Validation application that uses JavaScript

To show you how you can use jQuery to work with forms, you will now study a simple Validation application. As you will see, jQuery makes it easy to access the user entries and display error messages. To test the validity of the user entries, though, you need to use JavaScript.

The user interface and HTML

Figure 8-6 presents the user interface and HTML for the Validation application. To use the form, the user enters data into its nine fields and clicks on the Submit button. Or, if the user wants to start over, she can click on the Reset button to return the fields to their original values.

In the HTML for this form, you can see that the id of the form is "member_form" and the Submit button at the bottom of the form is the "submit" type. This means that it will automatically submit the form to the server when it is clicked. As you will see, though, the JavaScript for this form will validate the entries before the form is actually submitted and cancel the submission if any entries are invalid.

You should also note that the HTML for each field consists of just a label and an input element. Unlike the Email List application that you worked with before, those fields aren't followed by span elements. However, span elements will be added by the JavaScript and will be used to display error messages to the right of the user entries.

You might also notice that HTML5 placeholder attributes are used for two of the fields on this form. This attribute is used for the phone number field to show the user the entry formats that should be used. And it's used for the password field to provide an entry hint. Remember, though, that as soon as the focus is moved to a field with a placeholder, the placeholder text disappears.

On the other hand, this HTML doesn't use the HTML5 type attributes for email, phone, and date entries. That way, you don't have to worry about getting some unexpected validation messages from the browser, like a message that indicates an invalid email address. Instead, the JavaScript will have complete control of the validation that's done.

The form for a Validation application

Membership Form

```
┌─ Registration Information ─────────────────────────────────────┐
│  Email Address:  [zak@modulemedia    ]  Must be a valid email address.  │
│       Password:  [•••               ]  Must be 6 or more characters.    │
│  Verify Password:[                  ]  This field is required.          │
└────────────────────────────────────────────────────────────────┘

┌─ Member Information ───────────────────────────────────────────┐
│      First Name:  [Zak            ]                                      │
│      Last Name:   [Ruvalcaba      ]                                      │
│          State:   [CA             ]                                      │
│       ZIP Code:   [94999.9999     ]  Use either 99999 or 99999-9999 format. │
│   Phone Number:   [999-999-9999   ]  This field is required.            │
│     Start Date:   [05/20/2015     ]                                      │
└────────────────────────────────────────────────────────────────┘

┌─ Submit Your Membership ───────────────────────────────────────┐
│                    [  Submit  ]    [  Reset  ]                          │
└────────────────────────────────────────────────────────────────┘
```

The HTML

```html
<form action="register.html" method="get"
    name="member_form" id="member_form">
    <fieldset>
        <legend>Registration Information</legend>
        <label for="email">Email Address:</label>
        <input type="text" id="email" name="email"><br>
        <label for="password">Password:</label>
        <input type="password" id="password" name="password"
            placeholder="At least 6 characters"><br>
        <label for="verify">Verify Password:</label>
        <input type="password" id="verify" name="verify"><br>
    </fieldset>
    <fieldset>
        <legend>Member Information</legend>
        <!-- Four fields are missing here -->
        <label for="phone">Phone Number:</label>
        <input type="text" id="phone" name="phone"
            placeholder="999-999-9999"><br>
        <label for="start_date">Start Date:</label>
        <input type="text" id="start_date" name="start_date"><br>
    </fieldset>
    <fieldset id="buttons">
        <legend>Submit Your Membership</legend>
        <label> </label>
        <input type="submit" id="submit" name="submit" value="Submit">
        <input type="reset" id="reset" name="reset" value="Reset"><br>
    </fieldset>
</form>
```

Figure 8-6   The user interface and HTML for the Validation application

Some of the JavaScript for the application

Figure 8-7 presents some of the JavaScript for this application. This will give you a better idea of how you can use jQuery for data validation, and why you need JavaScript if you want to do a thorough job of data validation.

The first statement in the ready event handler adds a span element after each input control. To do that, the statement uses the :text selector to select all input elements with type equal to "text" and the :password selector to select all input elements with type equal to "password". Then, the after method is used to insert a span element after each of the selected fields. (You'll learn more about this method in the next chapter.) These span elements will be used to display the error messages.

The next block of code uses a Date object and some string handling to set the start_date field to the current date. That way, the user doesn't have to enter a date if the current date is okay. This type of processing is often done to set the controls in a form to the right starting values.

Note here that the fifth and sixth statements in this block use what's called a *conditional operator*. This operator starts by evaluating the conditional expression. Then, if the expression is true, the value of the middle expression is returned. Otherwise, the value of the third expression is returned. In this case, the conditional operator is used to include a "0" before the month and day if either of them is a single digit.

The rest of the code in this figure is the event handler for the submit event of the form. The code in this event handler contains the validation routines for just three of the nine fields, but that should give you a better idea of how jQuery and JavaScript can be used for data validation.

The validation for the email entry assigns a regular expression to a variable named emailPattern. Later, the test method of this regular expression is used in an else if clause to see whether the user's entry matches the pattern. If it doesn't, the jQuery next and text methods are used to display an error message in the span element for the entry that was created by the first statement in the ready event handler.

The validation for the password entry uses the length property of a string to test whether the length of the entry is less than 6. If it is, an error message is displayed.

The validation for the first name entry uses the jQuery trim method to trim the entry before it is tested to see whether it is equal to an empty string. If you don't use the trim method, an entry of one or more spaces won't be equal to an empty string so the entry will be treated as valid.

After the three blocks of code for validating the fields, you can see a final if statement that is true if the isValid variable is false, which means that one or more fields are invalid. In that case, the preventDefault method of the event object is executed. This object is passed as a parameter to the function for the submit event handler. If you don't use the preventDefault method when one or more fields are invalid, the form will be submitted to the server since that's its default action.

If you already know JavaScript, you should understand this code. Otherwise, this shows the need for a basic set of JavaScript skills. Another alternative for data validation, though, is to use a validation plugin like the one that's presented next.

JavaScript validation

```javascript
$(document).ready(function() {
    // add span element after each input element
    $(":text, :password").after("<span>*</span>");

    // put today's date in the start_date text box
    var today = new Date();
    var month = today.getMonth() + 1;     // Add 1 since months start at 0
    var day = today.getDate();
    var year = today.getFullYear();
    var dateText = ((month < 10) ? "0" + month : month) + "/"; // Pad month
    dateText += ((day < 10) ? "0" + day : day) + "/";          // Pad date
    dateText += year;
    $("#start_date").val(dateText);

    $("#member_form").submit(
        function(event) {
            var isValid = true;

            // validate the email entry with a regular expression
            var emailPattern =
                /\b[A-Za-z0-9._%+-]+@[A-Za-z0-9.-]+\.[A-Za-z]{2,4}\b/;
            var email = $("#email").val();
            if (email == "") {
                $("#email").next().text("This field is required.");
                isValid = false;
            } else if ( !emailPattern.test(email) ) {
                $("#email").next().text("Must be a valid email address.");
                isValid = false;
            } else {
                $("#email").next().text(""); }

            // validate the password entry
            var password = $("#password").val();
            if ( password.length < 6) {
                $("#password").next().text("Must be 6 or more characters.");
                isValid = false;
            } else {
                $("#password").next().text(""); }

            // validate the first name entry
            var firstName = $("#first_name").val().trim();
            if (firstName == "") {
                $("#first_name").next().text("This field is required.");
                isValid = false;
            } else {
                $("#first_name").val(firstName);
                $("#first_name").next().text(""); }

            // prevent the submission of the form if any entries are invalid
            if (isValid == false) { event.preventDefault(); }

        }  // end function
    )  // end submit
});  // end ready
```

Figure 8-7   The JavaScript for validating three entries and submitting the form

How to use a plugin for data validation

If you search for validation plugins, you'll see that there are many of them. Some work with certain types of entries and some work with a wide range of entries. One of the most popular of these plugins is presented next.

How to use the validation plugin

Figure 8-8 introduces the validation plugin that was developed by Jörn Zaefferer, a member of the jQuery team and a lead developer of the jQuery UI team. To download this plugin and to get full documentation and more, you can go to URL that's at the start of this figure.

The rest of this figure shows how to use this plugin for the simple form that's shown at the top of the figure. To start, you code a script element for the validation file. This element must come after the script element for jQuery because it uses jQuery.

In the HTML for the form that will be validated by the plugin, you need to use the name attributes for the input fields. These are highlighted in the HTML in this figure. You also need to use a submit button to start the processing of the form.

Then, in the JavaScript, you call the validate method of the form. This is one of the methods in the validation plugin. So, when the submit method of the form is activated, usually by the user clicking on the submit button, the validation plugin intervenes and validates the fields of the form. If any of them are invalid, the plugin cancels the default action of the form and displays the error messages. Otherwise, the form is submitted to the server.

To specify the validation that should take place, you code a rules map as the first parameter of the validate method as shown in this figure. For each field that is going to be validated, you code the value of its name attribute in the HTML. Then, you code a set of braces that contains one or more validation options. For instance, the rules for the field that's named email_address specify that the required option is true and the email option is also true. That way, the validation option will first check this field to make sure it's there, and then check it to make sure the entry is a valid email address. You'll learn about the basic validation options that are available in just a minute.

For each validation option, the validation plugin provides a default error message. If you want to change the default messages, you can code a second parameter for messages as shown in this figure. Here, for example, the first set of message options changes the default message for the required option of the email_address field to "Please supply an email address." It also changes the default message for the email option to "This is not a valid email address."

Another way to use this plugin is to embed attributes for the rules and messages in the HTML instead of coding them as parameters of the validate method. Then, you just call the validate method without any parameters. Although this works okay for simple forms, it's usually better to use the technique that's illustrated in this figure. That separates the validation rules from the HTML so the code is easier to maintain and debug, especially for longer, more complicated forms.

The user interface

Email Address:	zak.modulemedia	This is not a valid email address.
First Name:		Please supply a first name.
	Join our List	

The URL for the validation plugin

http://jqueryvalidation.org

The script elements in the head section of the HTML

```html
<script src="http://code.jquery.com/jquery-2.1.4.js"></script>
<script src="jquery.validate.min.js"></script>
<script src="email_list.js"></script>
```

The form in the body of the HTML

```html
<form id="email_form" name="email_form" action="join.html" method="post">
    <label for="email_address">Email Address:</label>
    <input type="text" id="email_address" name="email_address"><br>
    <label for="first_name">First Name:</label>
    <input type="text" id="first_name" name="first_name"><br>
    <label> </label>
    <input type="submit" id="join_list" value="Join our List"><br>
</form>
```

The JavaScript (email_list.js) that uses the validate method of the plugin

```javascript
$("#email_form").validate({       // use the id attribute to select the form
    rules: {
        email_address: {          // use name attributes to refer to fields
            required: true,
            email: true },
        first_name: {
            required: true }
    },
    messages: {
        email_address: {          // use name attributes to refer to fields
            required: "Please supply an email address.",
            email: "This is not a valid email address." },
        first_name: {
            required: "Please supply a first name." }
    }
});     // end validate
```

Description

- The validation plugin was written and is maintained by Jörn Zaefferer, a member of the jQuery team and a lead developer on the jQuery UI team.

- One way to use this plugin is to run the validate method for the form and specify the validation rules and messages for the entries as parameters, as shown above.

- Another way to use the validate method of this plugin is to embed attributes for the rules and messages in the HTML. For simple forms, this is easier, but it's harder to maintain and debug.

Figure 8-8   How to use the validation plugin

The options and default error messages for the validation plugin

Now that you have a general idea of how to use the validation plugin, figure 8-9 summarizes the basic options that it provides along with their default error messages. As you can see, this plugin validates email addresses, URLs, dates, numbers, digits, and credit card numbers. It can check to make sure that an entry is within a certain range or that the number of characters in an entry is within a certain range. And it can check to make sure one entry is equal to another entry.

Unfortunately, that doesn't provide for every type of entry that a form might require, and it doesn't do every validation the way you might want it to. One way to add to this list is to use the additional-methods file that can be downloaded from the validation website. This file, for example, adds phoneUS and phoneUK options as well as an option for checking file extensions. You'll see this file used in the application at the end of this chapter.

Another option is to write your own methods for this plugin. You can also use some of the customizing options that are presented in the plugin. But the more time you spend going beyond what's readily available, the less valuable the use of this plugin becomes. At some point, then, you're probably better off writing your own data validation code in JavaScript so your forms will work exactly the way you want them to.

Remember, though, that the browser validation doesn't have to be perfect. If it catches most of the errors in a form, that may be good enough. Then, the server validation can finish the job.

This figure also shows how the validation plugin adds error messages to your HTML. To do that, it just adds a label element with the class attribute set to "error" after each input element with the text set to the error message. As a result, you can use CSS to specify the formatting for the messages in the "error" class.

The validation options for the validate method of the plugin

Option	Default message
`required: true`	This field is required.
`email: true`	Please enter a valid email address.
`url: true`	Please enter a valid URL.
`date: true`	Please enter a valid date.
`dateISO: true`	Please enter a valid date (ISO).
`number: true`	Please enter a valid number.
`digits: true`	Please enter only digits.
`creditcard: true`	Please enter a valid credit card number.
`equalTo: "selector"`	Please enter the same value again.
`maxlength: value`	Please enter no more than (value) characters.
`minlength: value`	Please enter at least (value) characters.
`rangelength: [value1, value2]`	Please enter a value between (value1) and (value2) characters long.
`max: value`	Please enter a value less than or equal to (value).
`min: value`	Please enter a value greater than or equal to (value).
`range: [value1, value2]`	Please enter a value between (value1) and (value2).

Examples of options in a validate event handler

```
$("#email_form").validate({
    rules: {
        email_address2: { equalTo: "#email_address1" },
        quantity: { digits: true, max: 100 },
        message: { rangelength: [2, 140] }
    }
}); // end validate
```

How the validation plugin adds an error message for a field

The HTML for a text box

```
<input type="text" id="email_address2" name="email_address2"><br>
```

The label that gets added to the DOM if the email address is invalid

```
<input type="text" id="email_address2" name="email_address2">
<label class="error">Please enter a valid email address.</label><br>
```

Description

- The basic options of the validation plugin are adequate for the client-side validation of many forms. The additional-methods file of this plugin also provides some other options, like the phoneUS and phoneUK options for validating phone numbers and the extension option for validating file extensions.

- When the validate method finds an error, it inserts a label element into the DOM right after the input element that has the invalid data. This label displays the error message, and this label is removed from the DOM when the error is corrected. To format the error messages with CSS, you can select labels that have the class attribute set to "error".

Figure 8-9   The options and default error messages for the validation plugin

A Validation application that uses the validation plugin

To give you a better idea of when and how to use the validation plugin, this chapter ends with a Validation application that uses this plugin.

The user interface

Figure 8-10 presents the user interface for this application. Here, you can see that the interface has a few more fields than the one you saw earlier. That will give you a better indication of the strengths and limitations of the validation plugin.

If you look at the expiration date fields near the bottom of the form, you can see that drop-down lists are used for month and year. That way, the user can't enter a month or year in the wrong format.

If you look at the credit card type field, you can see that it uses another drop-down list. Here again, this means that the user can't enter an invalid credit card type. This shows that using check boxes, radio buttons, lists, and drop-down lists usually eliminates the need for validation.

If you refer to the list of options in the previous figure, though, you can see that the validation plugin doesn't provide for all of the validation that this form requires. In particular, it doesn't have an option for state code, zip code, phone number, and requested start date.

By using the additional-methods file, though, you can provide validation for a US phone number. You'll see how to use this file in the next two figures. Remember that you can also customize the error messages as shown in figure 8-8. But you're still left to decide whether the rest of the validation is adequate for your purposes.

The Validation application

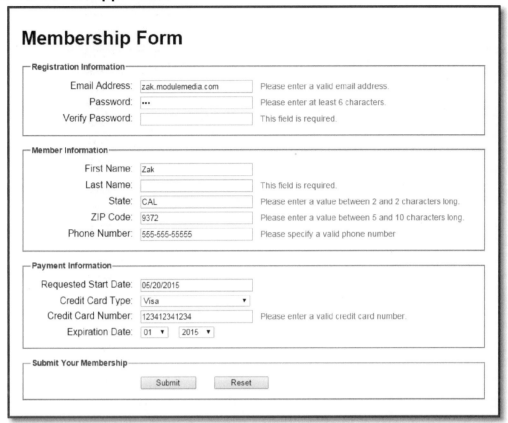

Fields that aren't adequately validated by the basic plugin options

- State code, zip code, phone number, and requested start date

Description

- When the user clicks the Submit button, the validation plugin tests the fields in the form for validity based on the options you have set. Then, it displays any error messages to the right of the invalid fields.

- Using just the basic options of the validation plugin, you can do 80% or more of the validation for a form like this. With the additional-methods file, you can do even more.

- In general, you don't need to validate radio buttons, check boxes, and select lists because they only allow valid entries.

- To avoid the need for validating an entry like a state code, you can replace its text box with a drop-down list that includes only the valid codes.

- To avoid the need for validating date entries, you can use drop-down lists for month, day, and year or a jQuery UI calendar widget (see chapter 10).

Figure 8-10   The Validation application with the validation plugin

The HTML

Figure 8-11 presents the HTML for this form. In the head section, you can see the script element for jQuery, followed by one for the validation plugin and one for the additional-methods file. The last script element is for the file that contains the validation code for this form. This sequence is essential because each file calls methods in the previous file.

In the HTML for the form, name attributes are coded for the individual input fields. That's because the validation plugin uses those names. You can also see that the fields aren't followed by elements that will display the error messages. That's because the validation plugin will add label elements for the messages whenever they're needed.

The form also includes a submit button that's used to submit the form to the server. Before that happens, though, the validation plugin checks the data to be sure it's valid.

The script elements for the validate and additional-methods plugins

```html
<script src="http://code.jquery.com/jquery-2.1.4.min.js"></script>
<script src="jquery.validate.min.js"></script>
<script src="additional-methods.min.js"></script>
<script src="member.js"></script>
```

The form element in the body of the HTML

```html
<form action="register.html" method="get"
    name="member_form" id="member_form">
    <fieldset>
        <legend>Registration Information</legend>
        <label for="email">Email Address:</label>
        <input type="text" name="email" id="email" autofocus><br>
        <label for="password">Password:</label>
        <input type="password" name="password" id="password"
            placeholder="At least 6 characters"><br>
        <label for="verify">Verify Password:</label>
        <input type="password" name="verify" id="verify"><br>
    </fieldset>
    <fieldset>
        <legend>Member Information</legend>
        <!-- Four fields are missing here -->
        <input type="text" name="phone" id="phone"
            placeholder="999-999-9999"><br>
    </fieldset>
    <fieldset>
        <legend>Payment Information</legend>
        <label for="start_date">Requested Start Date:</label>
        <input type="text" name="start_date" id="start_date"
            placeholder="99/99/9999"><br>
        <label for="payment_type">Payment Type:</label>
        <select name="payment_type" id="payment_type">
            <option value="v">Visa</option>
            <option value="m">Master Card</option>
            <option value="x">American Express</option>
        </select><br>
        <label for="card_number">Credit Card Number:</label>
        <input type="text" name="card_number" id="card_number"><br>
        <select name="expiry_month" id="expiry_month">
            <option value="01">01</option>
            <option value="02">02</option>
            <!-- The rest of the option elements for months -->
        </select>
        <select name="expiry_year" id="expiry_year">
            <option value="2015">2015</option>
            <option value="2016">2016</option>
            <!-- The rest of the option elements for years -->
        </select><br>
    </fieldset>
    <fieldset id="buttons">
        <legend>Submit Your Membership</legend>
        <label> </label>
        <input type="submit" id="submit" value="Submit">
        <input type="reset" id="reset" value="Reset"><br>
    </fieldset>
</form>
```

Figure 8-11   The HTML for the Validation application

The CSS

Figure 8-12 starts by showing the CSS for the labels that are used to display the validation error messages. The float property indicates that these labels shouldn't be floated. To understand how this works, you need to remember that the labels that identify the text fields are floated to the left of the text fields. However, you want the error labels to appear to the right of the text fields, and setting the float property to "none" accomplishes that.

The next two properties set the color for the error messages to red and reduce their font size to 87.5% so the long messages will fit into the space provided. Of course, you can set the CSS for these labels any way you want, which lets you control where and how they're displayed.

The jQuery

Figure 8-12 also presents the jQuery for this form. Before the validate method, you can code any setup operations for the form like moving the focus to the first field on the form, setting the starting dates, or loading the options of the drop-down lists.

Then, you code the validate method for the form along with its rules as the first parameter. Here, the phoneUS method is one of the methods in the additional-methods file, and it does a good job of validating a US phone number. Most of the other validation is adequate too, but the validation for the state code and zip code could be improved, especially since the zip code in this application can be either a five- or a nine-digit code.

For most forms, you will also want to provide some custom error messages, as shown in figure 8-8. For instance, you could change the message for the state code from "Please enter a value between 2 and 2 characters long" to something like "Please enter a two-character state code."

The CSS for the error messages of the plugin

```
label.error {
    float: none;
    color: red;
    font-size: 87.5%;
}
```

The jQuery for the Validation application

```
$(document).ready(function() {
    $("#email").focus();

    // other setup processing can go here

    $("#member_form").validate({
        rules: {
            email: {
                required: true,
                email: true
            },
            password: {
                required: true,
                minlength: 6
            },
            verify: {
                required: true,
                equalTo: "#password"
            },
            first_name: {
                required: true
            },
            last_name: {
                required: true
            },
            state: {
                required: true,
                rangelength: [2, 2]
            },
            zip: {
                required: true,
                rangelength: [5, 10]
            },
            phone: {
                required: true,
                phoneUS: true
            },
            start_date: {
                required: true,
                date: true
            },
            card_number: {
                required: true,
                creditcard: true
            }
        }
    });     // end validate
});         // end ready
```

Figure 8-12   The CSS and jQuery for the Validation application

Perspective

At this point, you should be comfortable with the jQuery features for working with forms, and you should understand the differences between writing your own JavaScript code for validation and using a validation plugin. Eventually, you will probably want to learn more about JavaScript so you can write your own data validation code. When that day comes, please remember our JavaScript book.

Terms

form	data validation
control	regular expression
field	pattern
submit button	auto-completion feature
reset button	conditional operator

Summary

- A *form* contains one or more *controls* like text boxes, radio buttons, and check boxes that can receive data. These controls are also referred to as *fields*. When a form is submitted to the server for processing, the data in the controls is sent along with the HTTP request.

- A *submit button* submits the form data to the server when the button is clicked. A *reset button* resets all the data in the form when it is clicked.

- HTML5 introduces some input controls like the email, url, tel, and date controls that are good semantically because they indicate what types of data the controls are for. HTML5 also introduces some attributes for *data validation*, and CSS3 introduces some pseudo-classes for formatting required, valid, and invalid fields.

- When a form is submitted to the server, the server script should provide complete validation of the data in the form and return the form to the client if any errors are found.

- Before a form is submitted to the server, JavaScript should try to catch 80% or more of the entry errors. That will reduce the number of trips to the server and back that are required to process the form.

- jQuery provides some selectors, methods, and event methods for working with forms, but nothing for data validation. So, to validate the entries that a user makes, many developers use JavaScript features like *regular expressions* and string methods that aren't presented in this book.

- Another way to validate the user entries in a form is to use a validation plugin. That usually makes it easier to add validation to a form, but the validation may not be adequate for all forms.

Exercise 8-1 Validate with JavaScript

Since you already know how to validate some types of fields with JavaScript, most of the code for this exercise is provided for you. However, you will make some enhancements to this code. The form that you will be working with looks like this:

Please join our email list

Email Address:	anne@murachcom	Must be a valid email address.
Re-enter Email Address:	anne@murach.com	Must equal first email entry.
First Name:		This field is required.
Last Name:	Boehm	
2-Character State Code:	cal	Use 2-character code.
5-Digit Zip Code:	9999999	Use 99999 format.

[Join our List] [Reset]

1. Use your text editor to open the HTML and JavaScript files in this folder:
   `c:\jquery\exercises\ch08\email_list_javascript\`

2. In the HTML file, note that span elements aren't coded after each input field. In the JavaScript file, then, add a statement that adds an empty span element after each input field. To do this, you need to use a statement similar to the first one in figure 8-7.

3. Review the code in the JavaScript file and note that it contains validation routines for the first five fields. Then, test this form by clicking the Join our List button before you enter any data in this form. Oops! The data is submitted even though no entries have been made.

4. To fix this, you must stop the default action of the submit button. To do that, code the preventDefault method of the event object in the if statement at the end of the file, as in figure 8-7. Remember that the name that you use for the event object must be the same as the name of the parameter that's used for the submit event handler. Now, test again with empty fields. This should display "This field is required." to the right of each field except the zip-code field.

5. Enter four spaces in the first-name field and click the Join our List button again. Note that the error message is removed, which means the four spaces have been accepted as a valid entry.

6. Fix this problem by trimming the first-name entry before it is validated, as in the code for the last-name entry. This trimmed value should also be placed in the text box if the entry is valid. Test this enhancement by first entering just four spaces in this field and then by entering four spaces followed by a first name.

7. Add the code for validating the zip-code field by testing to make sure it consists of five characters. To do this, you can copy and modify the code that's used to validate the state-code field. Now, test this change.

Exercise 8-2   Use the validation plugin

This exercise will give you a chance to use the validation plugin that's presented in figures 8-8 through 8-12. You will use this plugin to validate the data in a form that looks like this:

Please join our email list

Email Address:	anne@murach.com	
Re-enter Email Address:	ann@murach.com	This entry must equal previous entry.
First Name:	Anne	
Last Name:	Boehm	
2-Character State Code:	cal	Please enter a 2-character state code.
5-Digit Zip Code:	123456	Please enter a 5-digit zip code.

Join our List   Reset

1. Use your text editor to open the HTML, CSS, and JavaScript files in this folder:

   `c:\jquery\exercises\ch08\email_list_plugin\`

2. In the HTML file, note the script element for the validation plugin. Note too that the folder for this application includes that plugin file.

3. In the JavaScript file, add the code for using the validation plugin to edit the six fields in the form above. The validation should be as follows:

   All of the fields are required.

   The first two fields should be valid email addresses, and the second email address should be the same as the first.

   The state code should be a two-character code.

   The zip code should be a five-digit number, so it should be tested both for digits and five characters.

4. Test the validation that's done and note that the messages aren't displayed how or where you want them. To fix that, add the CSS code at the top of figure 8-12 to the CSS file. You may also want to add a margin-left property to the rule set that puts some space before the error messages.

5. Test the validation again and note the default messages that are displayed. Then, replace the default messages with the three custom messages that are shown above. You can use figure 8-8 as a guide for doing that.

6. Note that the validation for the state and zip codes could be improved by using JavaScript to do lookups. But remember that all entries will be thoroughly validated by the server-side code. As a result, client-side validation at this level is usually acceptable.

9

How to use the DOM manipulation and traversal methods

In chapter 5, you learned a few of the methods for scripting the DOM. Now, this chapter presents most of the other methods for DOM manipulation and DOM traversal. Once you master these methods, you'll be able to get your DOM scripting applications to work just the way you want them to.

The DOM manipulation methods

In the next four figures, you'll learn how to use the methods for *DOM manipulation*, except the ones for working with styles and positioning. Then, after you review an application that uses DOM manipulation, you'll learn the methods for working with styles and positioning.

The methods for working with attributes

The first table in figure 9-1 presents the methods for working with attributes. You were introduced to the first two methods in chapter 5. These methods get and set the value of the attribute you name. You can also set the value of multiple attributes with a single method by using a map to provide name/value pairs.

For instance, the first attribute example sets the src attribute of an img element with "image" as its id to a value of "book1.jpg". That will change the image that is displayed in the element. In contrast, the second example uses a map to set the values of both the src and alt attributes with a single method. This map, which is coded within braces, is like the properties maps that you used with the animate method in chapter 6.

Finally, you can set the value of a named attribute to the result of a function. If you use a function with the attr method, you should know that two parameters are passed to the function. The first parameter is an index that indicates which element in the set of selected elements is being processed. The second parameter is the old value of the attribute. You should also know that because the function is executed once for each selected element, you can use the this keyword within the function to refer to the current element. This works just like the each method that you learned about in chapter 5.

This is illustrated by the third example, which uses a function as the second parameter to provide the values that the href attributes for the selected <a> elements should be set to. To generate these values, the first statement in the function concatenates the index value of the <a> element plus 1 to the literal "#heading". Because the index values of the elements start with zero, that means that the href values that are returned to the attr method will be "#heading1", "#heading2", and so on.

You can use the last method in this table to remove an attribute from selected elements. To specify the attribute you want to remove, you code its name. This is illustrated by the fourth example, which removes the id attribute from each h2 element within an element that has "faqs" as its id.

The second table in this figure summarizes the methods for working with class attributes, and you were introduced to some of these in chapter 5. As a result, you shouldn't have any trouble using them. Here again, though, you can use a function to supply the values that are required by some of these methods, and these functions receive an index and the old class value.

The first class attribute example shows how you can use the hasClass method to test whether an element has a specific class. The second example shows how you can add a "minus" class to an element. And the third example shows how you can remove a "minus" class.

The methods for working with attributes

Method	Description
attr(*name*)	Gets the value of the named attribute from the first selected element.
attr(*name, value*)	Sets the value of the named attribute for each selected element.
attr(*map*)	Sets the value of multiple attributes specified by the name/value pairs in the attribute map.
attr(*name, function*)	Sets the value of the named attribute to the value returned by the function.
removeAttr(*name*)	Removes the named attribute from each selected element.

The methods for working with class attributes

Method	Description
hasClass(*name*)	Returns true if the named class is present in any selected elements.
addClass(*name*)	Adds the named class to each selected element.
addClass(*function*)	Adds the class specified by the value returned by the function.
removeClass(*name*)	Removes the named class from each selected element.
removeClass(*function*)	Removes the class specified by the value returned by the function.
toggleClass(*name*)	If the named class is present, remove it from each selected element. Otherwise, add it.
toggleClass(*function*)	If the class specified by the value returned by the function is present, remove it. Otherwise, add it.

Attribute examples

Set the value of the src attribute of an image to the value of a variable
```
$("#image").attr("src", "book1.jpg");
```

Use a map to set the values of two attributes
```
$("#image").attr( {"src": "book1.jpg", "alt": "Book 1" } );
```

Use a function to set the value of the href attribute of each <a> element
```
$("aside a").attr("href", function(index) {
    var href = "#heading" + (index + 1);
    return href;
    });
```

Remove the id attribute from all h2 elements within the "faqs" element
```
$("#faqs h2").removeAttr("id");
```

Class attribute examples

Test whether an element has a "closed" value in its class attribute
```
if ($("#faqs").hasClass("closed")) { ... }
```

Add a class to the h2 descendants of the "faqs" element
```
$("#faqs h2").addClass("minus");
```

Remove the "minus" class from the class attribute of the h2 descendants
```
$("#faqs h2").removeClass("minus");
```

Figure 9-1   The methods for working with attributes

The methods for DOM replacement

Figure 9-2 summarizes the methods for DOM replacement, and you should already know how to use the val and text methods to work with the values in a control or the text within an element. Note, however, that like many of the methods you saw in the previous figure, you can use the value returned by a function to specify the value or text.

The examples in this figure show you how to use the other methods for DOM replacement. The first example shows how to use the html method to get the HTML that's within an aside element, and the second shows how to put HTML into an aside element. In this case, an h2 element is placed within the aside element.

The third example uses the replaceWith method to replace all elements with "old" as a class with empty h2 elements. Here, the selector gets the elements that are replaced and the parameter supplies the content that will replace them.

In contrast, the fourth example uses the replaceAll method to get the same result. This time, the h2 element is coded where the selector is normally coded, and the parameter specifies the target elements that will be replaced.

The methods for DOM replacement

Method	Description
`val()`	Gets the value of the first selected form element.
`val(value)`	Sets the value of the selected form elements.
`val(function)`	Sets the value of the selected form elements to the value returned by the function.
`text()`	Gets the combined text contents of all selected elements including their descendants.
`text(textString)`	Sets the contents of each selected element to the specified text.
`text(function)`	Sets the contents of each selected element to the text returned by the function.
`html()`	Gets the HTML contents of the first selected element.
`html(htmlString)`	Sets the HTML contents of each selected element to the specified HTML string.
`html(function)`	Sets the HTML contents of each selected element to the HTML string returned by the function.
`replaceWith(content)`	Replaces each selected element with the specified content. This could be an HTML string, a DOM element, or a jQuery object.
`replaceAll(target)`	Replaces each target element with the selected elements. This is the reverse of how the replaceWith method is coded.

Examples

Display all of the HTML in the aside element
```
alert($("aside").html());
```

Put an h2 element into an aside element
```
$("aside").html("<h2>Table of contents</h2>");
```

Replace all elements that have a class named "old" with an h2 element
```
$(".old").replaceWith("<h2></h2>");
```

Replace all elements that have a class named "old" with an h2 element
```
$("<h2></h2>").replaceAll(".old");
```

Description

- In chapter 5, you learned how to use the val and text methods to get and set values and text. Note, however, that you can also use functions to supply the values and text.

- If you use a function with the val, text, or html method, the function receives two parameters. The first is the index of the current element in the set, and the second is the old value, text, or html of the element.

- The replaceWith and replaceAll methods provide two different ways to replace one set of elements with another set.

Figure 9-2   The methods for DOM replacement

The methods for DOM insertion and cloning

Figure 9-3 summarizes the methods for inserting content into the DOM. For instance, the prepend method inserts content at the start of an element, and the append method inserts content at the end of an element. In contrast, the before method inserts content before an element, and the after method inserts content after an element. The critical distinction is that the prepend and append methods insert content within an element, while the before and after methods insert content before and after an element.

This is illustrated by the first two examples. In the first example, an h2 element is inserted within an aside element. In the second example, an <a> element is inserted after the last <p> element in an article.

The prependTo, appendTo, insertBefore, and insertAfter methods reverse the coding sequence by specifying the target elements in their parameters. This is illustrated by the third example in this figure. Here, all of the <a> elements in an article element are inserted after the h2 elements in an aside element. But note that the <a> elements will be removed from the article element. In other words, the elements are moved, not copied.

If you don't want the <a> elements removed from the article element, you need to clone them before you insert them after the h2 element. This is illustrated by the fourth example. Note that chaining is used in this example. This works because the clone method returns the objects that were just cloned.

The methods for DOM insertion and cloning

Method	Description
prepend(*content*)	Inserts the specified content at the start of each selected element.
prepend(*function*)	Inserts the content returned by the function at the start of each selected element.
prependTo(*target*)	Inserts all of the selected elements at the start of each target element.
append(*content*)	Inserts the specified content at the end of each selected element.
append(*function*)	Inserts the content returned by the function at the end of each selected element.
appendTo(*target*)	Inserts all of the selected elements at the end of each target element.
before(*content*)	Inserts the specified content before each selected element.
before(*function*)	Inserts the content returned by the function before each selected element.
insertBefore(*target*)	Inserts all of the selected elements before each target element.
after(*content*)	Inserts the specified content after each selected element.
after(*function*)	Inserts the content returned by the function after each selected element.
insertAfter(*target*)	Inserts all of the selected elements after each target element.
clone([*withEvents*])	Creates a copy of the selected elements. The parameter is a Boolean that indicates if the event handlers are also copied.

Examples

Insert an h2 element at the end of an aside element
```
$("aside").append("<h2>Table of contents</h2>");
```

Insert an <a> element after the last <p> element in an article
```
$("article p:last").after("<a href='#top'>Back to top</a>");
```

Insert the <a> elements in an article after the h2 elements in an aside
```
("article a").insertAfter($("aside h2"));
```

Clone the <a> elements and insert them after the h2 element in an aside element
```
("article a").clone().insertAfter($("aside h2"));
```

Description

- The prepend and append methods insert the content at the start or end of the selected elements, but within the elements.

- The before and after methods insert the content before or after the selected elements, not within the selected elements.

- If you use a function with the prepend or append method, it receives the index of the current element in the set and the old HTML for the element. If you use a function with the before or after method, it receives just the index of the current element.

- If you want to copy an element before you insert it somewhere else in the document, you need to use the clone method. Otherwise, the element is moved from its old location to its new one.

Figure 9-3   The methods for DOM insertion and cloning

The methods for DOM wrapping and removal

Figure 9-4 presents the methods for wrapping and removing DOM elements. For instance, the first example wraps all <a> elements within <h2> elements, like this:

```
<h2><a id="heading1">The text for the a element</a></h2>
```

The second example wraps just the text of an h1 element with an <a> element, like this:

```
<h1><a id="top">The text for the h1 element</a></h1>
```

The third example removes the first <a> element in an article.

The methods for DOM wrapping and removal

Method	Description
`wrap(element)`	Wraps the specified element around each selected element.
`wrap(function)`	Wraps the element returned by the function around each selected element.
`wrapAll(element)`	Wraps the specified element around all of the selected elements.
`wrapInner(element)`	Wraps the specified element around the content of each selected element.
`wrapInner(function)`	Wraps the element returned by the function around the content of each selected element.
`empty()`	Removes all of the child nodes of each selected element.
`remove([selector])`	Removes the selected elements from the DOM. If a selector is specified, it filters the selected elements.
`unwrap()`	Removes the parent of each selected element.

Examples

Wrap all <a> elements in h2 elements
```
$("a").wrap("<h2></h2>");
```

Wrap the h1 text in an <a> element
```
$("article h1").wrapInner("<a id='top'></a>");
```

Remove the first <a> element in an article
```
$("article a:first").remove();
```

Description

- The DOM elements for wrapping let you wrap elements like <a> elements around other elements or text that you want to treat in a different way.

- If you use a function with the wrap or wrapInner method, it receives a single parameter with the index of the current element in the set.

- The DOM methods for removal and unwrapping let you remove or unwrap elements.

Figure 9-4   The methods for DOM wrapping and removal

The TOC application

If you're wondering how or why you would use the methods that you've just learned, you will now review an application that should give you some ideas.

The user interface and HTML

Figure 9-5 presents the user interface for a TOC (table of contents) application. It provides a series of links in the sidebar for the page that let the user jump to any of the seven topics in the article. It also provides a "Back to top" link after each topic that lets the user return to the top of the page.

In the HTML for this page, you can see that HTML5 main, aside, and article elements are used to structure the page. But note that the aside element is empty. That means that the jQuery will provide all of the content for the aside.

In the article element, you can see that each topic consists of an h2 element followed by one or more paragraphs. But note that the last paragraph in each topic isn't followed by a "Back to top" link. That means that the jQuery will also have to provide for those links.

After the HTML, you can see the effect that the DOM scripting in this application will have on the HTML. Although the HTML isn't actually changed (the DOM is), this shows the changes that have to be made to the DOM.

First, an <a> element has been wrapped around the text in the h1 element. The id in this element is "top", which means that another <a> element can link to it by using "#top" as its href attribute. In other words, the <a> element within the h1 element is a placeholder that other <a> elements can link to. That's the way HTML works, so the jQuery just has to set up the id and href attributes for the <a> elements.

Second, all of the code in the aside element has been generated by the jQuery. That consists of one h2 element followed by one <a> element for each topic in the article. Note that the text for each <a> element is the same as the text for each h2 element in the article. Note too that the href attributes in these <a> elements are "#heading1", "#heading2", and so forth.

Third, an <a> element has been wrapped around the text in each h2 element in the article. Note here that the id attributes in these <a> elements are "heading1", "heading2", and so on. That means that each link in the aside will jump to the corresponding heading in the article when the user clicks on it.

Last, an <a> element has been inserted after the last paragraph for each topic in the article. Each of these has its href attribute set to "#top". That means that clicking on one of these links will jump to the top of the page, because the id for the <a> element within the h1 element is "top".

The user interface for the TOC application

7 reasons why trainers like our books

Table of contents

Modular book organization

Top-down chapter design

Paired-pages format

Performance on the job

More practice in less time

Complete, real-world applications

Complete instructor's materials

Modular book organization

In the first section or two of all our books, we present the core content for the book, which includes a complete subset of usable skills. After the core content, each section of the book is designed as an independent module. This means that these sections don't have to be taught in sequence. As a result, you can customize your courses by assigning just those sections that you want to teach.

Whenever possible, each of the chapters is also designed as an independent module. When this is true, you can assign just those chapters that are right for your courses. This approach also makes the chapters better for on-the-job reference later on.

Back to top

Top-down chapter design

Unlike many competing books and products, most chapters in our books have a unique top-down design that moves from the simple to complex. This

The HTML

```
<body>
    <main>
        <h1>7 reasons why trainers like our books</h1>
        <aside></aside>
        <article>
            <h2>Modular book organization</h2>
            <p>In the first section or two of all our books, ... </p>
            <p>Whenever possible, each of the chapters is also ... </p>
            <h2>Top-down chapter design</h2>
            <p>Unlike many competing books and products, ... </p>
            <!-- The other h2 headings and paragraphs for the article -->
        </article>
    </main>
</body>
```

How the jQuery will modify the DOM

```
<h1><a id="top">7 reasons why trainers like our books</a></h1>
<aside>
    <h2>Table of contents</h2>
    <a href="#heading1">Modular book organization</a>
    <a href="#heading2">Top-down chapter design</a>
    <!-- The rest of the a elements for the headings -->
</aside>
<article>
    <h2><a id="heading1">Modular book organization</a></h2>
    <p>In the first section or two of all our books, ... </p>
    <p>Whenever possible, each of the chapters is also ... </p>
    <a href="#top">Back to top</a>
    <h2><a id="heading2">Top-down chapter design puts</a></h2>
    <p>Unlike many competing books and products, ... </p>
    <a href="#top">Back to top</a>
    <!-- The other h2 headings and paragraphs for the article -->
</article>
```

Figure 9-5   The user interface and HTML for the TOC application

The jQuery

When you develop an application like this, you need to plan what has to be done and what sequence it needs to be done in. This is illustrated by the simple plan at the start of figure 9-6. This plan is reflected by the comments in the jQuery for this application.

First, the jQuery uses an append method to add the "Table of contents" heading to the aside. Second, the jQuery uses a wrapInner method to wrap an <a> element around the text for each h2 element in the article.

Third, the jQuery adds id attributes to those <a> elements. To do that, it uses an each method to process each <a> element within the article. In the function for this each method, the parameter named index will receive the index value for each of the <a> elements, starting with zero. Then, the index plus 1 is concatenated to the word "heading" and stored in a variable named id. Last, the attr method is used to set the id attribute of each <a> element (this) to the value of the id variable. As a result, the id values will be "heading1", "heading2", and so on.

Fourth, all the <a> elements in the article are cloned and inserted after the h2 element in the aside. This creates all of the links that are needed. But fifth, the id attributes of the <a> elements in the aside are removed because they aren't needed. Besides that, the duplicate ids would cause errors.

Sixth, the href attributes that are needed are added to those <a> elements. This time, a function is used as the second parameter in an attr method to set the values of these href attributes. An each method could have been used to get the same result, but this shows that jQuery often provides more than one way to accomplish the same task.

At this point, the links will work, but there's no way for the user to get back to the top of the page other than clicking on the Back button or scrolling. To fix that, the seventh block of code wraps an <a> element around the text in the h1 element with "top" as its id.

Then, the last block of code uses three statements to add "Back to top" links after the last paragraph for each topic. Here, the first statement adds the links before all of the h2 elements. However, that puts a link before the first h2 element, which isn't needed, and it doesn't put a link after the last paragraph, which is needed. To fix that, the second statement removes the first link in the article, and the third statement adds a link after the last paragraph in the article.

This is a useful application because it will work with any article that consists of h2 headings and paragraphs. On the other hand, it only does what can be done by HTML itself. Worse, this application won't work in browsers that don't have JavaScript enabled. What's most important, though, is that this application should give you an early indication of what you can do when you script the DOM with jQuery.

The jQuery plan

- Add the h2 element for the "Table of contents" heading to the aside.
- Wrap the text of the h2 elements in the article with <a> elements.
- Add the correct id attributes to the <a> elements in the article.
- Clone the <a> elements in the article and insert them after the h2 element in the aside.
- Remove the id attributes from the <a> elements in the aside.
- Add the correct href attributes to the <a> elements in the aside.
- Wrap an <a> element with "top" as its id around the text in the h1 element.
- Insert <a> elements that go to the h1 element at the end of each topic.

The jQuery

```
$(document).ready(function() {
    // add an h2 heading to the aside
    $("aside").append("<h2>Table of contents</h2>");

    // wrap the h2 text in the article with <a> tags
    $("article h2").wrapInner("<a></a>");

    // add ids to the new <a> tags
    $("article a").each (function(index) {
        var id = "heading" + (index + 1);
        $(this).attr("id", id);
    });

    // clone the <a> tags in the article and insert them into the aside
    $("article a").clone().insertAfter($("aside h2"));

    // remove the id attributes from the <a> tags in the aside
    $("aside a").removeAttr("id");

    // add the href attributes to the <a> tags in the aside
    $("aside a").attr("href", function(index) {
        var href = "#heading" + (index + 1);
        return href;
    });

    // wrap an <a> tag around the h1 text
    $("h1").wrapInner("<a id='top'></a>");

    // insert "back to top" <a> tags after each topic
    $("article h2").before("<a href='#top'>Back to top</a>");
    $("article a:first").remove();
    $("article p:last").after("<a href='#top'>Back to top</a>");
})
```

Description

- Because the functions of the jQuery methods often overlap, you can code this application in many different ways and still get the same results.

Figure 9-6   The jQuery for the TOC application

The methods for working with styles and positioning

The next two topics present the jQuery methods for working with styles and positioning. Then, you'll see how some of these methods can be used to enhance the TOC application that you just studied.

The methods for working with styles

Figure 9-7 presents the DOM manipulation methods for working with styles. Like the attr method, the css method lets you get and set CSS properties. You can also use a map to set more than one property with a single method, and you can use a function to set the value of a property. The first two examples in this figure show how to set one or more than one property with the css method.

The various height and width methods let you get and set the heights and widths of elements. These methods vary by whether they include margins, padding, and borders in their measurements. For instance, the third example in this figure uses the height method to get the height of an article element, which doesn't include padding, margins, or borders.

The methods for working with styles

Method	Description
css(*name*)	Gets the value of the named property from the first selected element.
css(*name, value*)	Sets the value of the named property for each selected element.
css(*map*)	Sets the values of multiple properties specified by the name/value pairs in the properties map.
css(*name, function*)	Sets the value of the named property to the value returned by the function.
height()	Gets the height of the first selected element. This height doesn't include padding, margins, or borders.
height(*value*)	Sets the height of each selected element.
innerHeight()	Gets the height of the first selected element including padding but not margins or borders.
outerHeight([*includeMargin*])	Gets the height of the first selected element including padding and borders. If the parameter is set to true, it also includes margins.
width()	Gets the width of the first selected element. This width doesn't include padding, margins, or borders.
width(*value*)	Sets the width of each selected element.
innerWidth()	Gets the width of the first selected element including padding but not margins or borders.
outerWidth([*includeMargin*])	Gets the width of the first selected element including padding and borders. If the parameter is set to true, it also includes margins.

Examples

Set the CSS color property for all h2 elements to blue
```
$("h2").css("color", "blue");
```

Use a map to set two CSS properties for all h2 elements
```
$("h2").css( { "color": "blue", "font-size": "150%" } );
```

Get the height of an article element
```
var height = $("article").height();
```

Description

- These methods make it easy to get and set the properties for an element and also to get and set the height and width of an element.

- When you get a height or width value, it is returned as a number and pixels are assumed.

- When you specify a number for a height or width value, pixels are assumed. If you want to include the unit of measurement, enclose the value in quotation marks.

- If you use a function with the css method, it receives a parameter with the index of the current element in the set and a parameter with the old property value.

Figure 9-7   The methods for working with styles

The methods for positioning elements

Figure 9-8 presents the methods for positioning elements. Here, the offset method gets the coordinates for the offset position of an element relative to the document window. In contrast, the position method gets the coordinates relative to the parent element (its containing element). These coordinates are returned in an object with top and left properties that give the distances from the top and left of the document or parent element.

For instance, the first example gets the top coordinate for an article element relative to the document. In contrast, the second example creates a new coordinates object and assigns it to a variable named asideCoordinates like this:

```
var asideCoordinates = new Object();
```

This is the JavaScript way to create a new, general-purpose object. Then, the next two statements assign values to the top and left properties of the object. Last, the offset method is used to set the top and left coordinates for the aside element to the ones in the object.

Similarly, you can use the scroll methods to get and set the top and left positions of the vertical and horizontal scroll bars. For instance, the third example uses the scrollTop method to set the top of the vertical scroll bar for the window to zero. This means that the scroll bar will be at the top of the window.

The methods for positioning elements

Method	Description
`offset()`	Gets the coordinates of the first selected element and returns them in an object with top and left properties. These coordinates are relative to the document.
`offset(coordinates)`	Sets the coordinates of each selected element relative to the document. The parameter is an object with top and left properties.
`position()`	Gets the coordinates of the first selected element and returns them in an object with top and left properties. These coordinates are relative to the parent element.
`scrollTop()`	Gets the position of the vertical scroll bar for the first selected element.
`scrollTop(value)`	Sets the position of the vertical scroll bar for each selected element.
`scrollLeft()`	Gets the position of the horizontal scroll bar for the first selected element.
`scrollLeft(value)`	Sets the position of the horizontal scroll bar for each selected element.

Examples

Get the top offset for an article element
```
var offsetTop = $("article").offset().top;
```

Set the offset coordinates for an aside element
```
var asideCoordinates = new Object();
asideCoordinates.top = 200;
asideCoordinates.left = 100;
$("aside").offset(asideCoordinates);
```

Move the scroll bar for the window to the top
```
$(window).scrollTop(0);
```

Description

- The scroll methods apply to window objects, elements with the overflow CSS property set to scroll, and elements with the overflow property set to auto if the height of the elements are smaller than their contents.

- The scrollTop method returns the number of pixels that are hidden from view above the scrollable area. If the scroll bar is at the top or if the element isn't scrollable, this number is 0.

- The scrollLeft method returns the number of pixels that are hidden from view to the left of the scrollable area. If the scroll bar is all the way to the left or if the element isn't scrollable, this number is 0.

Figure 9-8   The methods for positioning elements

The enhanced TOC application

To show you how these methods can be put into use, figure 9-9 presents an enhanced version of the TOC application. This application works like the earlier application, but with two enhancements.

First, the heading of the selected topic is enlarged and changed to blue when the user clicks on the link for it in the aside so it's easy to tell which heading has been selected. Second, the table of contents moves to the left of the selected heading each time the user clicks a link. That way, the table of contents is always visible, and the users can easily select the next topics that they're interested in. That means that the "Back to top" links aren't needed, although one could be added at the bottom of the TOC.

The jQuery code for these enhancements is in the event handlers for the click event of the <a> elements in the aside. The default action for the click event of each of these links is to jump to the related heading in the article. But this event handler will add to that default action.

The first block of code in this event handler gets the id selector of the h2 heading in the article for the link that was clicked. To do that, it uses the this keyword to refer to the link, and it uses the attr method to get its href attribute. This attribute is then assigned to a variable named "id". If, for example, the third link in the table of contents was clicked, the id selector will be "#heading3".

The second block of code uses that id selector to get the heading in the article. For instance, "#heading3" is a selector that gets the element with "heading3" as its id. Then, the css method is used to set two properties for the selected heading.

The third block of code moves the aside element so it is to the left of the selected heading. The first three statements in this block get the top offset of the selected heading, the height of the aside, and the height of the article. Then, it uses those values to determine what the offset for the table of contents should be.

If the offset for the selected heading plus the height of the aside is less than or equal to the height of the article, the aside is given the same offset as the selected heading. That means that the top of the aside will align with the heading in the article. Otherwise, the offset for the aside is set to the article height minus the aside height, which means the aside will be located at the bottom of the page, but not past the bottom of the page.

The last statement in this block uses the css method to set the top property of the aside to the value specified by that offset. That's what moves the aside up and down on the page.

For this to work, the position property for the body should be set to relative, and the position property for the aside should be set to either relative or absolute. Then, the TOC will be positioned within the aside based on the setting for the CSS top property. However, that location will vary slightly based on whether relative or absolute positioning is used for the aside.

Please note that this application will work the same whether you use the position method or the offset method to get the top offset. Note too that this application will work whether the HTML for the links is generated by jQuery, as in figure 9-6, or whether the links are entered manually into the HTML.

The TOC application with the TOC moving to the selected topic

7 reasons why trainers like our books

Modular book organization

In the first section or two of all our books, we present the core content for the book, which includes a complete subset of usable skills. After the core content, each section of the book is designed as an independent module. This means that these sections don't have to be taught in sequence. As a result, you can customize your courses by assigning just those sections that you want to teach.

Whenever possible, each of the chapters is also designed as an independent module. When this is true, you can assign just those chapters that are right for your courses. This approach also makes the chapters better for on-the-job reference later on.

Table of contents

Modular book organization

Top-down chapter design

Paired-pages format

Performance on the job

More practice in less time

Complete, real-world applications

Complete instructor's materials

Top-down chapter design

Unlike many competing books and products, most chapters in our books have a unique top-down design that moves from the simple to complex. This makes it easier for trainees to learn. It also means that you can present the topics at the start of a chapter to make sure everyone understands the essential details, without presenting all of the topics in a chapter. Then, your trainees can learn the other topics on their own or as they're needed on the job.

Paired-pages format

If you page through one of our books, you'll see that all of the information

The position property for the aside must be either relative or absolute

```
body  { position: relative; }
aside { position: absolute; }
```

The jQuery event handler that has been added to the application

```
// change the CSS for the selected topic and move the TOC
$("aside a").click (function() {
    // get the id selector of the selected h2 element from the <a> tag
    id = $(this).attr("href");

    // change the styles for the selected heading
    $(id).css({ "color": "blue", "font-size": "150%" });

    // move the aside so it is next to the selected heading
    var h2Offset = $(id).offset().top;           // get top offset of the h2
    var asideHeight = $("aside").height();        // get height of aside
    var articleHeight = $("article").height();   // get height of article
    if ((h2Offset + asideHeight) <= articleHeight) {
        asideOffset = h2Offset;}
    else {
        asideOffset = articleHeight - asideHeight; }
    $("aside").css("top", asideOffset);
});
```

Description

- This application changes the color and size of the heading for the selected topic so it's easy to tell which topic has been selected.

- This application also moves the table of contents next to the selected topic so it's easy to select the next topic. Since the TOC moves, "Back to top" links aren't required.

Figure 9-9   The enhanced TOC application

Two event methods used with DOM manipulation

In chapter 5, you were introduced to the on and off event methods that you can use to attach and remove any event. Now, you'll see why these event methods are particularly useful when you manipulate the DOM.

How to use the on and off event methods

Figure 9-10 presents the expanded syntax of the on and off event methods. Here, you can see that in addition to the events and the event handler that you code as parameters of these methods, you can include a selector. This selector is used to filter the elements that will trigger the events.

To understand how the on method works, it helps to compare it to a shortcut method like click. The first example in this figure uses the click method to attach an event handler to the click event of all h2 elements that are subordinate to an element with "accordion" as its id. You've seen event handlers like this throughout this book. The problem with using a shortcut method like this is that the event handler will only be executed for h2 elements that exist in the DOM when the event handler is attached.

In contrast, you can use the on event method to execute an event handler for elements that don't exist in the DOM when the event handler is attached. To do that, you attach the event handler to a parent of the elements that does exist. Then, you code a selector for the descendant elements that you want to trigger the event as a parameter of the on method.

The second example in this figure illustrates how this works. Here, you should notice that the event handler is attached to the click event of the element with "accordion" as its id, not to its descendant h2 elements as in the first example. Then, the first parameter of the on method specifies the event to be handled, and the second parameter is a selector for the descendant h2 elements. This filters the descendants of the selected element so the event will only be triggered for the named elements. Finally, the last parameter is the function that contains the code that will be executed when the event is triggered.

The third example in this figure illustrates that you can use the off method to remove an event handler that's attached using a shortcut method. In this case, it's used to remove the event handler that's attached using the click method in the first example.

The fourth example is similar, but it removes the event handler that's attached in the second example using the on method. To do that, the h2 selector is included as the second parameter of the off method just as it is in the on method.

Notice that no event handler is included in either example that uses the off method. That's because only one event handler has been attached to the click event. If you needed to, though, you could attach two or more handlers to an event. To do that, you'd use named functions instead of anonymous functions. Then, if you needed to remove a single event handler, you could name its function in the handler parameter of the off method.

Two event methods used with DOM manipulation

Event	Description
on(*events*[, *selector*], *handler*)	Attach an event handler to one or more events of the selected elements.
off(*events*[, *selector*][, *handler*])	Remove an event handler from one or more events.

A click event method that handles the click event of an h2 element

```
$("#accordion h2").click(function() {
    // the code for the event handler
});
```

An on event method that handles the click event of an h2 element

```
$("#accordion").on("click", "h2", function() {
    // the code for the event handler
});
```

An off event method that removes the first click event handler above

```
$("#accordion h2").off("click");
```

An off event method that removes the second click event handler above

```
$("#accordion").off("click", "h2");
```

Description

- When you use a shortcut event method like click or mouseover to attach an event handler, the on method is used internally in this format:

    on(*event, handler*)

    An event handler that's attached like this is referred to as *directly bound*.

- When you use a directly bound event handler, the handler is executed whenever an event is triggered on the selected elements. In the first example above, the handler is executed whenever the user clicks an h2 element that has a parent with "accordion" as its id. This works only for elements that exist in the DOM when the event handler is attached.

- The on event method lets you execute an event handler for elements even if they don't exist when the event handler is attached. To do that, you attach the handler to one or more events of a parent element that does exist. Then, you include the selector for the descendant elements that you want to trigger the events in the on method. An event handler that's attached like this is referred to as *delegated*.

- In the second example above, the on method is used to attach a handler to the click event of an element with "accordion" as its id. Because a selector for h2 elements is included in the on method, though, the event will be triggered only when an h2 element is clicked.

- You can use the off event method to remove an event handler that's attached with either a shortcut method or the on event method.

- If you attach two or more named functions to the same event, you can remove a specific function by naming it on the handler parameter of the off method.

Figure 9-10   How to use the on and off event methods

An Employee List application
that uses the on method

To illustrate when you might want to use the on and off methods, figure 9-11 presents an Employee List application that uses the on method. When this application starts, the names of the existing employees are listed at the right side of the page. Then, the user can click on a name to display or hide additional information as shown in the first screen in this figure. This works like the FAQs application that you saw in chapter 5.

The left side of the page contains controls that let the user add a new employee to the list. To do that, the user enters data into the text boxes and text area and clicks the Add Employee button. Then, the user can click on the name of the new employee to display or hide additional information as shown in the second screen in this figure. This works because the on method is used to attach the event handler that's executed when a name is clicked. If the click method had been used instead, the event handler wouldn't be executed for new employees because they don't exist in the DOM when the click event handler is attached to the employee names.

An Employee List application before an employee is added

Add an employee

Name: `Damon Dell`

Position: `VP of Development`

Description:
```
Damon creates learning
materials for Vecta Corp. as
well as consulting for
customers to integrate
vSolutions into their
production pipeline and
business processes.
```
`Add Employee`

Employee list

− Wilbur Wilkes

Founder and CEO

While Wilbur is the founder and CEO of Vecta Corp, he is primarily known for being the pioneer and world leader of creating vSolutions. Wilbur has led the commercialization of vSolution technology and its success as the world's fastest-growing, most advanced technologies in its respective industry.

✦ **Agnes Agnew**

✦ **Mike Masters**

The list after an employee is added

Add an employee

Name:

Position:

Description:

`Add Employee`

Employee list

− Wilbur Wilkes

Founder and CEO

While Wilbur is the founder and CEO of Vecta Corp, he is primarily known for being the pioneer and world leader of creating vSolutions. Wilbur has led the commercialization of vSolution technology and its success as the world's fastest-growing, most advanced technologies in its respective industry.

✦ **Agnes Agnew**

✦ **Mike Masters**

− Damon Dell

VP of Development

Damon creates learning materials for Vecta Corp. as well as consulting for customers to integrate vSolutions into their production pipeline and business processes.

Description

- The employee list in this application works like the FAQs application you saw in chapter 5. When the user clicks on an employee name in the list, additional information is displayed for the employee.

- This application also provides for adding employees to the list. Because the HTML for these employees isn't included in the DOM when the click event handler is attached to the employee names, the on method must be used so the user can click on a new name to display the information for that employee.

Figure 9-11   An Employee List application that uses the on method

The HTML for the application

Figure 9-12 presents the HTML for the Employee List application. Here, you can see that the main element contains the code for the employee list. It includes an h2 element and a div element for each employee. The h2 element contains an <a> element with the employee's name, and the div element contains h3 and <p> elements with the employee's position and description. It's the contents of the div element that are displayed when the user clicks an h2 element.

The aside element contains the controls for adding an employee to the list. Here, a label is used to identify the two text boxes and the text area, and a standard button is used to add the employee.

The jQuery for the application

Figure 9-12 also presents the jQuery for the Employee List application. The event handler for the ready event consists of two additional event handlers. The first one uses the on event method to attach an event handler to the click event of the element with "accordion" as its id. If you look back at the HTML, you'll see that this is the main element that contains the employee list. Because the on method includes a selector for h2 elements, though, this event will only be triggered when one of the h2 elements within the main element is clicked.

The code for this event handler works just like the code for the FAQs application you saw in chapter 5. It uses the toggleClass method to add a class named "minus" to the h2 element that was clicked if it doesn't already contain that class or to remove the class if it does. This determines whether a plus or minus sign is displayed to the left of the heading. Next, an if statement is used to check if the h2 element that was clicked is assigned to the class named "minus". If it isn't, the div element that follows the h2 element is hidden. Otherwise, it's displayed.

The second event handler is for the click event of the Add Employee button. It gets the values of the two text boxes and the text area and formats them as HTML. Then, this HTML is appended to the employee list. Finally, the values of the text boxes and the text area are cleared to prepare for the entry of another employee.

To help you focus on the jQuery for expanding and collapsing the employee information and adding new employees, this code doesn't include any data validation. For this application, though, you would simply need to check that the user enters values in the two text boxes and the text area. To refresh your memory on how to do that, you can refer back to chapter 8.

The HTML for the application

```html
<aside>
    <h2>Add an employee</h2>
    <label for="name">Name:</label>
    <input type="text" id="name" name="name"><br>
    <label for="position">Position:</label>
    <input type="text" id="position" name="position"><br>
    <label for="description">Description:</label>
    <textarea id="description" name="description"></textarea><br>
    <label> </label>
    <input type="button" id="add" name="add" value="Add Employee">
</aside>
<main id="accordion">
    <h1>Employee list</h1>
    <h2><a href="#">Wilbur Wilkes</a></h2>
    <div>
        <h3>Founder and CEO</h3>
        <p> While Wilbur is the founder and CEO of Vecta Corp, he ... </p>
    </div>
    <h2><a href="#">Agnes Agnew</a></h2>
    <div>
        <h3>VP of Accounting</h3>
        <p> With over 14 years of public accounting and business ... </p>
    </div>
    <h2><a href="#">Mike Masters</a></h2>
    <div>
        <h3>VP of Marketing</h3>
        <p> Mike serves as the Vice President of Sales and Marketing ... </p>
    </div>
</main>
```

The jQuery for the application

```javascript
$(document).ready(function() {

    $("#accordion").on("click", "h2", function() {
        $(this).toggleClass("minus");
        if ($(this).attr("class") != "minus") {
            $(this).next().hide();
        }
        else {
            $(this).next().show();
        }
    }); // end click

    $("#add").click(function() {
        var html = "";
        html += "<h2><a href='#'>" + $("#name").val() + "</a></h2>";
        html += "<div><h3>" + $("#position").val() + "</h3>";
        html += "<p>" + $("#description").val() + "</p></div>";
        $("#accordion").append(html);
        $("#name").val("");
        $("#position").val("");
        $("#description").val("");
    }); // end click

}); // end ready
```

Figure 9-12   The HTML and jQuery for the Employee List application

The DOM traversal methods

The next two figures in this chapter present the *DOM traversal* methods. These methods make it easier to get any of the elements in the DOM that you want to work with.

The tree traversal methods

If you study the table in figure 9-13, you can see that jQuery provides a comprehensive set of methods for traversing (traveling through) the DOM tree. Those methods make it relatively easy to select the siblings, children, parents, and ancestors of another element. For instance, the first example selects the first <p> sibling before the element with "last_heading" as its id. The second example selects the parent of the element with "faqs" as its id.

This set of methods includes a find method that lets you get the descendants of the selected elements that match the specified selector. For instance, the third example in this figure uses the find method to get the span elements within the <p> elements within an article element. Often, though, the find method gets a result that could also be done with a normal selector.

The tree traversal methods

Method	Description
siblings([*selector*])	Gets the siblings of each selected element, optionally filtered by a selector.
next([*selector*])	Gets the first sibling that follows each selected element, optionally filtered by a selector.
nextAll([*selector*])	Gets all siblings that follow each selected element, optionally filtered by a selector.
nextUntil(*selector*)	Gets all siblings that follow each selected element, up to but not including the element specified by the selector.
prev([*selector*])	Gets the first sibling that precedes each selected element, optionally filtered by a selector.
prevAll([*selector*])	Gets all siblings that precede each selected element, optionally filtered by a selector.
prevUntil(*selector*)	Gets all siblings that precede each selected element, up to but not including the element specified by the selector.
children([*selector*])	Gets the children of each selected element, optionally filtered by a selector.
parents([*selector*])	Gets the ancestors of each selected element, optionally filtered by a selector.
parentsUntil(*selector*)	Gets the ancestors of each selected element, up to but not including the element specified by the selector.
parent([*selector*])	Gets the parent of each selected element, optionally filtered by a selector.
offsetParent()	Gets the closest ancestor of an element that is positioned.
closest(*selector*[, *context*])	Gets the first element that matches the specified selector, beginning at the current element and going up the DOM tree. If the context parameter is specified, it specifies a DOM element within which the selected element must be found.
find(*selector*)	Gets the descendants of each selected element after it has been filtered by the specified selector.

Examples

Get the previous paragraph sibling of an element
```
var previousParagraph = $("#last_heading").prev("p");
```

Get the parent of an element
```
var parent = $("#faqs").parent();
```

Get all span elements within <p> elements within an article element
```
$("article p").find("span").css("color", "red");
```

Description

- The tree traversal methods help you select the siblings, children, parents, and ancestors of selected elements in the DOM.

Figure 9-13   The tree traversal methods

The filtering methods

To enhance the tree traversal methods, the DOM traversal methods also include filtering methods. These are summarized in the table in figure 9-14. For instance, the first example in this figure shows how to use the filter method to select only the h2 elements that are in the "best" class. And the second example shows how to use the not method to select all <p> elements except the ones in the "first" class.

The third example shows how to use the slice method to select all of the images in the element with "slides" as its id from the second image through the last one. To do that, it uses an index value of 1, which gets the second image since the indexes start with zero.

In many cases, these filtering methods duplicate the results that you can get with normal selectors and with the find method. For instance,

```
$("h2.best")
```

selects the same elements as

```
$("h2").filter(".best")
```

In some cases, though, the filtering methods can get results that you can't get with a normal selector.

The other benefit of the filtering methods is that they facilitate chaining. This is illustrated by the last example in this figure. Here, the methods are coded over several lines, but the methods could be coded in a single line.

In the first line of methods, the first method is used to filter the set of images in the element with "slides" as its id so it contains just the first image. Then, that image is faded out. In the second line, the next method is used to get the first sibling of the first image, which is the second image. Then, that image is faded in.

At that point, the only object in the set is the second image. Because of that, the method that follows in the chain will be executed on that image. For example, if the method that follows is the appendTo method shown in this example, this method will move the second image to the end of the other images. In this case, though, you want to move the first image to the end of the images so it will be displayed again after the last image in the original set of images is displayed. To accomplish that, the end method is executed before the appendTo method. This returns the set of selected elements to it previous state, which is the set that contains just the first image. You'll see how this works in a slide show in the next figure.

The filtering methods

Method	Description
filter(*selector*)	Reduces the set of selected elements to those that match the selector.
filter(*function*)	Reduces the set of selected elements to those that pass the function's test.
not(*selector*)	Removes the elements specified by the selector from the set of selected elements.
not(*elements*)	Removes the specified elements from the set of selected elements.
not(*function*)	Removes the elements that pass the function's test from the set of selected elements.
has(*selector*)	Reduces the set of selected elements to those that have a descendant that matches the selector.
eq(*index*)	Reduces the set of selected elements to the one at the specified index.
first()	Reduces the set of selected elements to the first one in the set.
last()	Reduces the set of selected elements to the last one in the set.
slice(*start*[, *end*])	Reduces the set of selected elements to the those within the range of indexes that are specified by the parameters.
end()	Returns the set of selected elements to its previous state.

Examples

Change a property for the h2 elements that are in the "best" class
```
$("h2").filter(".best").css("color", "red");
```

Change a property for all <p> elements except the ones in the "first" class
```
$("p").not(".first").css("text-indent", "1.5em");
```

Hide all images in the "slides" element except for the one with index 0
```
$("#slides img").slice(1).hide();
```

Work with the images in a set
```
$("#slides img")
    .first().fadeOut(1000)     // fade out first img element in set
    .next().fadeIn(1000)       // fade in the next element in set
    .end()                     // return to first element in set
    .appendTo("#slides");      // append first element to end of set
```

Description

- Many of the filtering methods duplicate functions that can be done with selectors.
- The benefit of using the filtering methods is that they facilitate chaining. In particular, the end method lets you return the object in the chain to the original selection.
- If you use a function with the filter or not method, it receives a parameter with the index of the current element in the set.

Figure 9-14   The filtering methods

A Slide Show application
that uses DOM traversal methods

Figure 9-15 shows how the DOM traversal methods can be used in a slide show. Here, the slides are img elements that are in a div element with "slides" as its id. Then, the jQuery fades these images out and in to create a slide show.

For this code to work, the position property for the images must be set to absolute by the CSS. Otherwise, the image that fades in will appear briefly to the right of the faded out image before it moves to the left. That's because the fadeIn method starts slightly before the fadeOut method is finished.

To show that the jQuery can be written in more ways than one, this figure presents two ways to run the slide show. In the first example, the first statement uses a slice method to hide all of the images except the first one. Next, the first statement in the setInterval function uses the first method to get the first image. Then, that image is faded out and the next image is faded in.

The key to this code is the end method that follows. It returns the chaining object to the first image after the next method has set it to the second image. Then, the appendTo method moves the first image to the end of the images. At that point, there's a new first image and the chain of methods can start again with that image.

In the second example, the images stay where they are in the DOM, and the eq method is used to select the images that are faded in and faded out. For instance, the first method in the setInterval method fades out the image with an index that's equal to the value of the slideIndex variable. Since this variable starts at 0, this application starts by fading out the first image in the "slides" division.

Then, an if statement is used to determine which slide is faded in. If the slideIndex variable is less than the topIndex value for the slides, which is one less than the length of the images, the next image is faded in and the slide index is increased by 1. Otherwise, the image with an index value of zero is faded in and the slide index is set back to 0. In this way, the slide show cycles through as many images as there are in the "slides" division.

A Slide Show application

The HTML

```
<main>
    <h1>Current Books Slide Show</h1>
    <div id="slides">
        <img src="images/book1.jpg" alt="HTML5 and CSS3">
        <img src="images/book2.jpg" alt="PHP and MySQL">
        <!-- more images -->
    </div>
</main>
```

The critical CSS

```
#slides img { position: absolute; }
```

One way to write the jQuery code

```
$(document).ready(function() {
    $("#slides img").slice(1).hide();
    setInterval(function(){
        $("#slides img").first().fadeOut(1000)    // fade out 1st image
        .next().fadeIn(1000)                       // fade in next image
        .end()                                     // return object to 1st image
        .appendTo("#slides");                      // move 1st image to last
    }, 3000);
});
```

Another way to write the jQuery code

```
$(document).ready(function() {
    $("#slides img").slice(1).hide();
    var slideIndex = 0, topIndex = $("#slides img").length - 1;
    setInterval(function(){
        $("#slides img").eq(slideIndex).fadeOut(1000);
        if (slideIndex < topIndex) {
            $("#slides img").eq(slideIndex).next().fadeIn(1000);
            slideIndex++ }
        else {
            $("#slides img").eq(0).fadeIn(1000);
            slideIndex = 0; }
    }, 3000);
});
```

Figure 9-15   A Slide Show application that uses DOM traversal methods

Perspective

As you have seen, the DOM manipulation and traversal methods let you select elements and script the DOM in a variety of ways. The trick of course is using them to get the results that you want. However, if you can plan the scripting operations that need to be done for an application, this chapter provides the methods that you need for doing them.

Terms

DOM manipulation
directly bound event handler
delegated event handler
DOM traversal

Summary

- The *DOM manipulation* methods let you get and set attribute values. They also let you replace, insert, copy, wrap, and remove DOM elements.

- The *DOM traversal* methods let you get the siblings, children, parents, ancestors, and descendants of selected elements. They also let you filter a set of elements so you can get just the elements that you want.

- The on an off event methods are particularly useful with DOM manipulation because they let you attach an event handler to and remove an event handler from objects that don't exist in the DOM.

- The end method facilitates the chaining of methods because it returns the chaining object to the one that was used at the start of the chain.

Exercise 9-1   Modify the TOC application

In this exercise, you'll change the TOC application that's presented in figures 9-5, 9-6, and 9-12. That will force you to use the DOM manipulation and DOM traversal methods. When you're through, the application should look like this:

7 reasons why trainers like our books

Modular book organization

In the first section or two of all our books, we present the core content for the book, which includes a complete subset of usable skills. After the core content, each section of the book is designed as an independent module. This means that these sections don't have to be taught in sequence. As a result, you can customize your courses by assigning just those sections that you want to teach.

Whenever possible, each of the chapters is also designed as an independent module. When this is true, you can assign just those chapters that are right for your courses. This approach also makes the chapters better for on-the-job reference later on.

Table of contents

Modular book organization

Top-down chapter design

Paired-pages format

Performance on the job

More practice in less time

Complete, real-world applications

Complete instructor's materials

Back to top

Top-down chapter design

Unlike many competing books and products, most chapters in our books have a unique top-down design that moves from the simple to complex. This makes it easier for trainees to learn. It also means that you can present the topics at the start of a chapter to make sure everyone understands the essential details, without presenting all of the topics in a chapter. Then, your trainees can learn the other topics on their own or as they're needed on the job.

Paired-pages format

If you page through one of our books, you'll see that all of the information is presented in "paired pages." In each pair, the right page is a figure that contains the syntax, guidelines, and examples, and the left page is text that contains the perspective and extra explanation.

One benefit of this format is that it lets trainees learn at their own pace.

Review the application

1. Use your text editor to open the HTML file in this folder:

    `c:\jquery\exercises\ch09\toc\`

    Note that this file contains the script element that has the JavaScript for this application.

2. Run the application and click on several of the links in the TOC to see how the navigation works. Note that this application doesn't include "Back to top" links after each topic. Note too that when a topic is selected, its h2 heading in the article is enlarged and changed to blue, but the heading isn't reset to its original CSS values when another topic is selected.

Enhance the application

3. The third block of code in the ready event handler adds ids to the <a> elements that have just been added to the article. Comment out this code. Then, right below it, rewrite the code so it uses a function with the attr method instead of an each event method to set the ids. If you have any trouble with this, look at the code three blocks down that uses a function to set the href attributes in the <a> elements of the aside. When you're done, test this change.

4. Add a "Back to top" \<a\> element at the end of the aside. When clicked, this link should go to the first heading in the article. Note that there's space between the other links and the "Back to top" link, and you can get that space by inserting a \<br\> element ahead of the "Back to top" link.

5. Indent all of the paragraphs for each topic except the first one as shown above. To do that, set the text-indent property to 1.5em. If you use a DOM traversal method, you can set the indents with a single statement. Otherwise, it's okay to use two statements to get that result.

6. In the event handler for the click event of the \<a\> elements in the aside, the first block sets the color and font size for the \<a\> element in the article that has just been selected. Right after that, add code that resets all of the other \<a\> elements in the article to the color black and a font size of 120% since those were the starting values in the CSS. (To select all \<a\> elements except the one that's currently selected, try using the not method.)

Section 3

jQuery UI essentials

jQuery UI (User Interface) is a free, open-source, JavaScript library that extends the jQuery library by providing themes, widgets, interactions, and effects. In chapter 10 of this section, you'll get off to a fast start with jQuery UI by learning how to use widgets like accordions, tabs, and sliders to enhance your web pages. Then, in chapter 11, you'll learn how to use jQuery UI's interactions and effects.

The information presented in this section is based on version 1.11.4 of jQuery UI. Keep in mind as you read this section, though, that new versions of jQuery UI become available frequently. When that happens, the jquery UI website is also updated. So don't be surprised if what you see on the website doesn't match what's shown here.

10

Get off to a fast start with jQuery UI themes and widgets

In this chapter, you'll get off to a fast start with jQuery UI by learning how to use its themes and widgets. As you will see, widgets can add useful features to your web pages with a minimum of development time. That's why they're used by many websites. In fact, widgets may be the only jQuery UI components that you will want to use in your web pages.

Introduction to jQuery UI

To get you started with jQuery UI, you'll first learn what it is, where to get it, and what components it contains.

What jQuery UI is and where to get it

jQuery UI (User Interface) is a free, open-source, JavaScript library that extends the use of the jQuery library by providing higher-level features that you can use with a minimum of code. To provide those features, the jQuery UI library uses the jQuery library. In fact, you can think of jQuery UI as the official plugin library for jQuery.

Figure 10-1 shows the home page and the URL for the jQuery UI website. But you can also get to this site by clicking on the UI tab at the top of the jQuery home page. And you can get back to the jQuery home page by clicking on the jQuery tab to the left of the jQuery UI tab.

This figure also summarizes the four types of features that jQuery UI provides. *Themes* provide the formatting for widgets and interactions, and they are implemented by a CSS style sheet that's part of the jQuery UI download. When you build this download as described later in this chapter, you can select from 24 predefined themes that come with jQuery UI. You can also create a custom theme if none of these 24 are right for you.

Widgets are features like accordions, tabs, and date pickers. In this chapter, you'll learn how to use several of the widgets that are currently provided by jQuery UI. In the next chapter, you'll learn how to use interactions and effects.

The jQuery UI website

The URL for jQuery UI

```
http://jqueryui.com/
```

The four types of features provided by jQuery UI

Name	Description
Themes	24 predefined themes as well as a ThemeRoller application that lets you create a custom theme. A theme is implemented by a CSS style sheet.
Widgets	Accordions, tabs, date pickers, and more.
Interactions	Draggable, droppable, resizable, and more.
Effects	Color animations, class transitions, and more.

Description

- *jQuery UI* is a free, open-source, JavaScript library that extends the jQuery library by providing higher-level features. jQuery UI uses jQuery and can be thought of as the official plugin library for jQuery.

- The jQuery UI website can be accessed by the URL above or by clicking on the jQuery UI tab at the top of the home page for the jQuery website.

Figure 10-1   What jQuery UI is and where to get it

The jQuery UI components

Figure 10-2 summarizes the components that are supported by jQuery UI 1.11.4. When you build a jQuery UI download, you decide which of these components you want to use in your web pages. Naturally, the fewer you choose, the smaller the jQuery UI file that has to be loaded into a user's browser.

The core jQuery UI components in the first group in this figure are divided into core, widget, mouse, and position. Core is always required when you use jQuery UI. Widget is required if you use widgets. Mouse is required if you use interactions. And position is required if you use elements that require positioning relative to other elements on a web page.

The next three groups list the widgets, interactions, and effects that jQuery UI currently provides. Of these, the widgets are the ones that get the most use. However, if you aren't going to use some of these widgets, you can exclude them from your download.

Note that this chapter doesn't cover all the widgets that are listed here. Because you use the same basic techniques to work with these widgets that you do to work with the other widgets that you'll see in this chapter, though, you shouldn't have any trouble using them if you ever need to.

Note too that some of these widgets are similar to controls that were introduced with HTML5, and some of them provide enhancements to HTML controls. For example, the SelectMenu widget provides a customizable and themeable version of an HTML select element. And the HTML5 date, progress, range, and number controls provide the basic functions of the Datepicker, Progressbar, Slider, and Spinner widgets, although these controls may not work the same in every browser. So before you use a widget, you should consider whether an HTML control will work just as well.

In contrast to widgets, many websites don't use any of the interactions. If that's the case for your website, you can exclude them from your download. Note, however, that the Dialog widget depends on both the Draggable and Resizable interactions, so you have to include these interactions if you're going to include the Dialog widget.

The power of the jQuery UI interactions is that they can be applied to any HTML element. For instance, you can make the items in an unordered list sortable, or you can make a row within a table selectable. For uses like those, you need to include the interactions in your download. In chapter 11, you'll learn how to use the interactions.

The jQuery UI effects can be used with interactions and widgets. For instance, an effect can be used to control how a new tab is displayed in a Tabs widget. In addition, jQuery UI effects can be used with HTML elements that aren't a part of jQuery UI. In chapter 11, you'll also learn how to use the effects.

jQuery UI components

Core components	
Core	Provides the core functionality. It is required for all interactions and widgets.
Widget	Provides the base functionality for all widgets.
Mouse	Provides the base functionality for all interactions that require the mouse.
Position	Required for all interactions that require the positioning of elements.

Widgets	
Accordion	An accordion.
Autocomplete	A text box that displays a list of suggested items based on the user entries.
Button	A customizable button.
Datepicker	A calendar that can be toggled from a textbox or displayed inline.
Dialog	A modal dialog box that is resizable and draggable.
Menu	A menu that can include submenus.
Progressbar	A status indicator that can be used to display progress or percentage values.
SelectMenu	A list box or drop-down list that's customizable and themeable.
Slider	A slider that can display a range of values.
Spinner	A text box with up and down arrows for increasing or decreasing the number.
Tabs	A set of tabs that reveals a tab's contents when the tab is clicked.
Tooltip	A tooltip that's customizable and themeable.

Interactions	
Draggable	Makes an element on a web page draggable.
Droppable	Defines targets that draggable objects can be dropped within.
Resizable	Makes an element on a web page resizable.
Selectable	Makes an element selectable with a mouse.
Sortable	Makes a list of items sortable.

Effects	
Effects core	Required for all of the effects.
Blind	Creates a blind effect similar to vertical blinds on a window.
Bounce	Bounces an element up and down or side to side.
Clip	Clips the element on and off.
Drop	Moves an element in one direction and hides it at the same time.
Explode	Explodes an element in all directions. Also supports imploding.
Fade	Fades the element in or out.
Fold	Folds an element horizontally and then vertically.
Highlight	Highlights an element's background with a color for a specified length of time.
Puff	Grows and hides or shrinks and shows an element.
Pulsate	Pulsates an element for a certain amount of time by changing the opacity.
Scale	Grows or shrinks an element and its content.
Shake	Shakes an element up and down or side to side for a specified amount of time.
Size	Changes the size of an element to the specified width and height.
Slide	Slides an element in and out of the screen.
Transfer	Transfers an element from one element to another.

Figure 10-2   The jQuery UI components

How to build and use a jQuery UI download

In contrast to a jQuery download, you have to build a jQuery UI download before you download it. That lets you select the components for the download, which lets you keep the download to the minimum size that you need for your web pages.

How to build a download

Figure 10-3 shows the Download Builder page that you get to by clicking on the button or link in the jQuery UI home page. This is the page that lets you select the components that you want in the download. This page includes a components list, a drop-down Theme list, and a Download button.

The Components list includes all of the components in the four groups that are summarized in the previous figure: UI core, Interactions, Widgets, and Effects. To start, all of the components are selected. This results in a JavaScript library that is roughly 200KB in size. Then, to reduce this size, you can deselect (uncheck) the components that you aren't going to use. However, if you try to uncheck a component that is required by another component, a message will be displayed indicating that both components will be removed. For instance, this happens if you try to uncheck the Draggable component without first unchecking the Droppable and Dialog components because these components depend on the Draggable component. Then, you can continue by removing all the dependent components or by canceling the operation.

For many websites, you can uncheck all or most of the interactions and effects. If, for example, you're going to use only a few of the widgets and you're not going to use the Dialog widget, you can uncheck all of the other widgets, the interactions, and the effects.

After you select the components you want, you can select a theme from the 24 that are in the drop-down Theme list or choose No Theme. Or, if you want to create a custom theme, you can click on the "design a custom theme" link, which will direct you to the ThemeRoller page in the next figure. You can also set the scope for the theme. You do this when you want to apply different themes to different areas of a page.

When you're confident that you have everything the way you want it, you can click the Download button, which will download a zipped folder to your computer. Then, you can unzip the folder to use the files it contains in your applications. You'll learn more about this download and how to use it in figure 10-5.

The Download Builder page

How to build your custom jQuery UI library and download your files

1. From the home page, click the Download link in the navigation bar or the Custom Download button. That will take you to the Download Builder page.

2. Select or deselect the interactions, widgets, and effects until the checked boxes identify the components that you want in your download. The fewer you select, the smaller your download will be.

3. If you want to select a theme for the download, use the drop-down list at the bottom of the page. Or, if you want to build a custom theme, click on the link above the drop-down list. That will take you to the ThemeRoller page in the next figure.

4. After you select a theme or design a custom theme and return to the page above, click the Download button to download a zipped folder that contains the jQuery UI files.

Figure 10-3   How to build a download

How to use ThemeRoller to build a custom theme

If you prefer to "roll your own" theme, maybe to match the color scheme used by your website, you can use jQuery UI's ThemeRoller application to do that. The use of this application is summarized in figure 10-4.

Interestingly, the left sidebar on the ThemeRoller page is a Tabs widget that has Roll Your Own, Gallery, and Help tabs. Also, within the Roll Your Own tab, an Accordion widget is used for the eleven categories that you can change. As this accordion shows, you can customize a variety of CSS properties. The best way to find out what's available is to review this page yourself, and you'll get a chance to do that in the exercises at the end of this chapter.

In this example, the Font Settings panel has been opened, and the font weight has been changed to bold. As soon as a setting is changed, the change is reflected in the widgets to the right of the sidebar. In this case, for example, the headings in the accordion have been changed from normal to bold.

If you click on the Gallery tab of the ThemeRoller sidebar, you'll see that the tab shows how the 24 predefined themes look in a Datepicker widget. Next, if you click on the Datepicker widget for a theme, you'll see how that theme is applied to the other widgets that are to the right of the sidebar. Then, if you like a predefined theme, you can click on the Download button that's below that theme to go back to the Download Builder page with that theme selected in the drop-down Theme list.

Another alternative is to click the Edit button that's below a theme. That will send you back to the Roll Your Own tab with all of the properties within each category set to the base properties for that theme. Then, you can make any changes to those settings, and click the Download Theme button to go back to the Download Builder page with Custom Theme selected in the drop-down Theme list.

The ThemeRoller page

How to use ThemeRoller to create a custom theme

- Use the accordion in the left sidebar to customize the properties for any of the items in the list. After you change a setting, you can see its effect in the widgets to the right of the sidebar.

- When you're satisfied with your theme, click the Download Theme button. That will return you to the Download Builder page with Custom Theme selected in the drop-down Theme list.

Description

- jQuery UI has 24 predefined themes that you can select from the Themes list in the Download Builder page. Beyond that, jQuery UI's ThemeRoller lets you create your own custom theme.

- If you want to start a custom theme from one of the predefined themes, click the Gallery tab in the sidebar of the ThemeRoller page. Then, you can click one of the themes to see what it will look like when applied to the widgets, and you can select the theme by clicking its Download button. Or, to edit the theme before downloading it, you can click its Edit button to return to the Roll Your Own tab.

- The accordion in the left sidebar for ThemeRoller lists the customizable properties for a theme. The widgets to the right of the sidebar show how the custom properties will look.

- If you prefer to use your own CSS style sheet instead of a jQuery UI style sheet, you don't have to select a theme from the Download Builder page or use ThemeRoller to build your own theme.

Figure 10-4   How to use ThemeRoller to build a custom theme

How to use the downloaded folders and files

Figure 10-5 shows the folders and files that are included in a typical jQuery download. For widgets, you only need the jquery-ui.min.css file, the jquery-ui.min.js file (the jQuery UI library), and the images in the images folder. The min files are compressed versions of the CSS and jQuery UI files, which are smaller than the uncompressed versions.

A jQuery UI download also includes the jQuery library in the external folder, an index.html file that displays a page that demonstrates the features that your download includes, and uncompressed versions of the CSS and jQuery files. You can use these versions if you want to see the code in these files. And you can use the jQuery library file if you haven't already downloaded jQuery and aren't using a CDN to get the jQuery library.

Last, the download includes structure and theme CSS files. However, all of the rule sets for these files are included in the core CSS file. As a result, you don't need these files unless you want to use only the structure or theme rule sets.

After you download these files, you may want to use your text editor or IDE to open the uncompressed CSS file. Then, you can review the rule sets in this file to get an idea of the classes that are supported. These are the styles that are applied to widgets and interactions, but you can also use these styles to format your own HTML elements.

To include the jQuery UI CSS and JavaScript files in a web page, you use the link and script elements that are shown in this figure. Here, the first link element points to the min version of the CSS file, and the second link element points to the developer's external style sheet. Then, the first script element points to the CDN address for the jQuery library (it doesn't use the downloaded jQuery file). And the second script element points to the min version of the jQuery UI file. But note that the script element for the jQuery UI file must follow the script element for the jQuery file because jQuery UI uses jQuery.

The last script element either points to the developer's external JavaScript file or it contains the JavaScript code. If the code that's needed is short, it is often embedded within the script element in the HTML document. Otherwise, an external JavaScript file can be used.

The link and script elements for jQuery UI in this example assume that the jQuery UI folders and files are stored in the root folder of the website within the top-level folder that's downloaded. But you can organize the downloaded files in the way that you think is best for your applications. You can see this in the downloaded applications for this chapter.

The folders and files in a full jQuery UI download

Name ▲	Date modified	Type	Size
external	5/28/2015 4:15 PM	File folder	
images	5/28/2015 4:15 PM	File folder	
index.html	3/11/2015 8:49 AM	Chrome HTML Do...	31 KB
jquery-ui.css	3/11/2015 8:49 AM	Cascading Style S...	35 KB
jquery-ui.js	3/11/2015 8:49 AM	JScript Script File	460 KB
jquery-ui.min.css	3/11/2015 8:49 AM	Cascading Style S...	30 KB
jquery-ui.min.js	3/11/2015 8:49 AM	JScript Script File	235 KB
jquery-ui.structure.css	3/11/2015 8:49 AM	Cascading Style S...	18 KB
jquery-ui.structure.min.css	3/11/2015 8:49 AM	Cascading Style S...	15 KB
jquery-ui.theme.css	3/11/2015 8:49 AM	Cascading Style S...	18 KB
jquery-ui.theme.min.css	3/11/2015 8:49 AM	Cascading Style S...	14 KB

How to include the downloaded files in your application

```
<!-- the link element for the jQuery UI stylesheet -->
<link rel="stylesheet" href="/jquery-ui-1.11.4/jquery-ui.min.css">

<!-- the link element for the developer's style sheet -->
<link rel="stylesheet" href="main.css">

<!-- the script element for the jQuery library -->
<script src="http://code.jquery.com/jquery-2.1.4.min.js"></script>

<!-- the script element for the jQuery UI library -->
<script src="/jquery-ui-1.11.4/jquery-ui.min.js"></script>

<!-- the script element for your external JavaScript file or your code -->
<script></script>
```

Description

- A jQuery UI download consists of a zip file that contains the CSS files, the images for the theme that has been selected, the jQuery UI files, and an HTML document that demonstrates the components in the download.

- The only folders and files that you have to include in your pages are the images folder and the min (compressed) versions of the first CSS file and the jQuery UI file.

- The external folder in a download includes the jQuery library file.

- The download also includes full and compressed versions of structure and theme CSS files, but you don't need them because the jquery-ui.css and jquery-ui.min.css files include the rule sets in both the structure and theme files.

Figure 10-5   How to use the downloaded folders and files

How to use jQuery UI widgets

The best way to get off to a fast start with jQuery UI is to begin using its widgets. That will show you how you can quickly add features like accordions and tabs to your web pages with a minimum of code. In the topics that follow, you'll learn how to use eight of the widgets that are currently supported by jQuery UI.

How to use any widget

The next seven figures show how to use eight jQuery UI widgets in their basic forms. That may be all the information that you need for using these widgets in your own web pages. All of these widgets, however, provide options, events, and methods that go beyond what these figures present. So, if you want to see how else these widgets can be used, you can review the jQuery UI documentation for the widgets, which is excellent.

For instance, figure 10-6 shows how to use the documentation for the Accordion widget. A good way to start is to click on the names of the examples in the right sidebar to see how the widget can be used. Then, you can click on the View Source link to see the source code that makes the example work. After that, you can review the options, methods, and events for the widget by clicking on the API Documentation link. (These two links aren't shown here.)

After you're comfortable with the way a widget works, you're ready to implement it on a web page, which you do in three stages. First, you code the link and script elements for jQuery UI in the head element of the HTML as shown in the previous figure. Second, you code the required HTML for the widget. Third, you code the jQuery for running the widget. If you've read the plugins chapter, you'll see that this is how any plugin works.

Beyond that, though, you must make sure that the jQuery UI images folder and the jQuery CSS file have the relationship shown in this figure. That is that the jQuery CSS file must be at the same level as the images folder because that's where it looks to get the images that it requires.

In the jQuery example in this figure, you can see the general structure for the jQuery code that's required for a widget. First, the code for using the widget is within the ready event handler. Second, a jQuery selector is used to select the HTML element that's used for the widget. Third, the method for running the widget is called. Fourth, any options for the widget are coded within braces in the parameter for the method. This too is how any plugin works.

The accordion documentation on the jQuery UI website

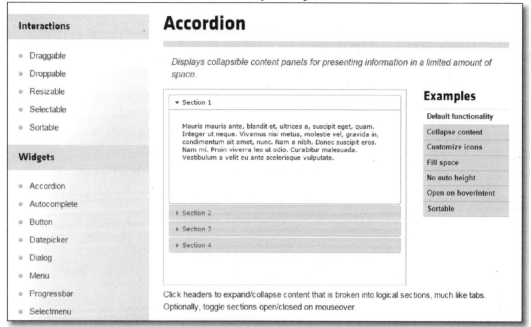

How to use the jQuery UI documentation

- In the left sidebar, click on a widget name to display its documentation.

- In the right sidebar, click on an example name to see a working example, then click on the View Source link to see the code for the example.

- Click the API Documentation link to display information about the widget's options, methods, and events.

The images folder and jquery-ui.min.css relationship that jQuery UI expects

The jQuery for using a widget

```
$(document).ready(function(){
    $("selector").widgetMethod({
        // option settings
    });
});
```

Description

- To use a jQuery UI widget, you code the HTML and jQuery for the widget. In the jQuery, you code a selector, the method to be used, and the options.

- For a widget that requires images, jQuery UI expects the CSS file and the images folder to be at the same level.

Figure 10-6   How to use any widget

How to use the Accordion widget

Figure 10-7 shows how to use an Accordion widget, which consists of two or more headings and the contents for those headings. By default, an accordion starts with the panel for the first heading displayed, and only one panel can be open at a time. Then, when the user clicks on one of the other headings, the contents for that heading are displayed and the contents for the first heading are hidden.

As the HTML in this figure shows, an Accordion widget consists of a top-level div element that contains one h3 element and one div element for each item in the accordion. Although it's not required with jQuery UI versions 1.9 or later, you can also code an <a> element that has an href attribute equal to the hash code (#) around the contents of each h3 element. That makes the accordion more accessible to users who use the keyboard.

In the jQuery for an accordion, you select the top-level div element of the accordion and call the accordion method with or without options. Often, you'll use this method without options because its defaults work the way you want them to.

In the example in this figure, though, two options are coded. The event option changes the event that causes the contents of a heading to be displayed from the "click" to the "mouseover" event, but you could also use other events to activate the accordion. Then, the collapsible option is set to true, which means that all of the panels can be closed at the same time. To close the open panel, you move the mouse over its heading.

Another option that you may want to use is the animated option. This option lets you specify the effect that's used when a panel is opened or closed. Normally, though, using an effect doesn't enhance the usability of the Accordion widget.

Although the basic formatting for an accordion is done by the CSS style sheet for jQuery UI, you can use your own style sheet to format the contents of a panel. In fact, you usually need to do that when the panel consists of several different types of HTML elements.

An Accordion widget

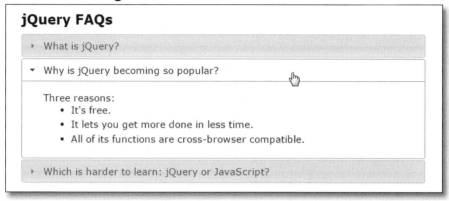

The HTML for the accordion

```
<div id="accordion">
    <h3>What is jQuery?</h3>
    <div>
        <!-- the content for the panel -->
    </div>
    <h3>Why is jQuery becoming so popular?</h3>
    <div>
        <!-- the content for the panel -->
    </div>
    <h3>Which is harder to learn: jQuery or JavaScript?</h3>
    <div>
        <!-- the content for the panel -->
    </div>
</div>
```

The jQuery for the accordion

```
$(document).ready(function(){
    $("#accordion").accordion({
        event: "mouseover",
        collapsible: true
    });
});
```

Description

- The HTML consists of h3 elements that provide the headers for the panels, followed by div elements that contain the contents for the panels. These elements should be within an outer div element that represents the accordion.

- In the jQuery, the accordion method is used to implement the accordion widget for the div element that represents the accordion.

- By default, a panel is opened when its header is clicked, one panel always has to be open, all panels open to the same size, and effects aren't used for opening and closing the panels. To change the defaults, you can use the event, collapsible, heightStyle, and animated options.

- The basic formatting of the accordion is done by the CSS for jQuery UI, but you can use CSS to format the contents within the panels.

Figure 10-7   How to use the Accordion widget

How to use the Tabs widget

Figure 10-8 shows how to use the Tabs widget. This widget has the same general function as an Accordion widget, but it displays the contents of a panel when the related tab is clicked.

As this figure shows, the HTML for a Tabs widget consists of a top-level div element that represents the widget. Then, this element contains an unordered list that contains the headings for the tabs, followed by one div element for each tab that contains the content of the tab. To relate the tab headings to their respective div elements, the href attributes of the <a> elements within the li elements are set to the ids of the div elements.

To activate a Tabs widget with jQuery, you just select the top-level div element and call the tabs method. Usually, you don't need to set any options because the defaults work the way you want them to. However, you can use the event option to change the event for opening a tab from the click event to some other event. You can also use the fx option to add animation to the way the tabs are opened and closed.

Here again, the basic formatting for a Tabs widget is done by the CSS style sheet for jQuery UI. However, you can use your own style sheet to format the contents of a panel. In fact, you usually need to do that when the panel consists of several different types of HTML elements.

A Tabs widget

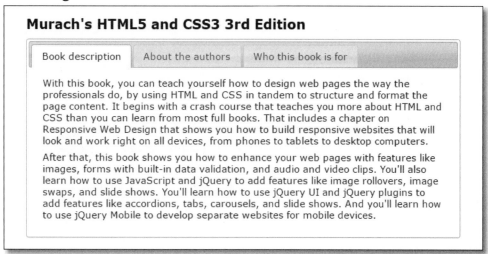

Murach's HTML5 and CSS3 3rd Edition

Book description	About the authors	Who this book is for

With this book, you can teach yourself how to design web pages the way the professionals do, by using HTML and CSS in tandem to structure and format the page content. It begins with a crash course that teaches you more about HTML and CSS than you can learn from most full books. That includes a chapter on Responsive Web Design that shows you how to build responsive websites that will look and work right on all devices, from phones to tablets to desktop computers.

After that, this book shows you how to enhance your web pages with features like images, forms with built-in data validation, and audio and video clips. You'll also learn how to use JavaScript and jQuery to add features like image rollovers, image swaps, and slide shows. You'll learn how to use jQuery UI and jQuery plugins to add features like accordions, tabs, carousels, and slide shows. And you'll learn how to use jQuery Mobile to develop separate websites for mobile devices.

The HTML for the tabs

```html
<div id="tabs">
    <ul>
        <li><a href="#tabs-1">Book description</a></li>
        <li><a href="#tabs-2">About the authors</a></li>
        <li><a href="#tabs-3">Who this book is for</a></li>
    </ul>
    <div id="tabs-1"><!-- the content --></div>
    <div id="tabs-2"><!-- the content --></div>
    <div id="tabs-3"><!-- the content --></div>
</div>
```

The jQuery for the tabs

```javascript
$(document).ready(function(){
    $("#tabs").tabs();
});
```

Description

- The HTML should consist of a div element that contains an unordered list that represents the tabs, followed by div elements that contain the contents for the tabs.
- The heading for each tab should be in an <a> element within an li element of the list. The href attribute for each tab should point to the id of the div element that contains the contents for the tab.
- In the jQuery, the tabs method is used to implement the Tabs widget for the div element that represents the tabs.
- By default, a tab is switched to when its header is clicked, but you can change that by using the event option. You can also use the fx option to add animation to the way tabs are opened and closed.
- The basic formatting of the tabs is done by the CSS for jQuery UI, but you can use CSS to format the contents within the panels.

Figure 10-8   How to use the Tabs widget

How to use the Button and Dialog widgets

Figure 10-9 shows how the Button and Dialog widgets work. The HTML for a Button widget is often an input element of the "button" type, but this widget also works with the "submit", "reset", "radio", and "checkbox" types, and with <a> elements too.

When a Button widget is activated by the jQuery button method, the HTML is converted into a button that uses the jQuery UI theme. Other than that, the button works its normal way. In the example in this figure, the Button widget is coded as an <a> element that contains an img element for a book, and jQuery UI changes its appearance. When the user clicks on it, the dialog box is opened.

In contrast, the HTML for a Dialog widget consists of a div element that contains the contents for the dialog box. The title attribute of this element can be used to specify the heading for the dialog box. And the contents of this element can contain any HTML elements.

When the dialog box is displayed, it is both draggable and resizable. This means that you can drag the box by its title bar, and you can resize the box by dragging any of its sides. You can also close the box by clicking on the "X" icon in the upper right corner.

To display a Dialog widget with jQuery, you use the dialog method. If, for example, you want to display a dialog box right after a page is ready, you select the div element for the dialog box and call the dialog method. If you want the user to have to close the dialog box before continuing, you can also set the *modal* option to true.

Usually, you want to open a dialog box when some event occurs, like the user clicking on a Button widget. Then, you use the jQuery code that's shown in this figure. First, the button method is called to convert the HTML for the button to a Button widget. Then, an event handler for the click event of the button is set up. Within that event handler, the dialog method of the dialog box is called to display the box. Here, the modal option is set to true so the user has to close the dialog box before proceeding. That's why the page behind the dialog box in this figure is dimmed.

You may also need to use some of the other options for a Dialog widget. If, for example, you want to change the height or width of the dialog box, you can set the height or width option. If you don't want the dialog box to be draggable and resizable, you can set those options to false. You can also use the title option to set the title for a dialog box if you don't want to use the title attribute for that purpose.

If you want to add one or more buttons, like an OK button, to a dialog box, you can use the buttons option to do that. If you look at the documentation for this option, you'll see that this is easy to do. The documentation also shows how to code the function for closing the dialog box when a button is clicked.

Incidentally, the Dialog widget is generally considered to be a nice improvement over the JavaScript technique for opening another window and using it as a dialog box. That's especially true because most browsers have built-in features for blocking popup windows.

A Button widget that activates a Dialog widget

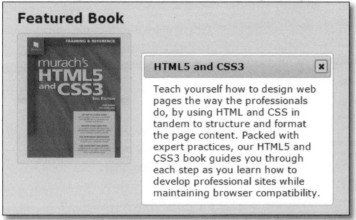

The HTML for the Button and Dialog widgets

```
<a id="book"><img src="images/html5.jpg" alt="HTML5 and CSS3 book"
    width="150" height="188" /></a>
<div id="dialog" title="HTML5 and CSS3" style="display:none;">
    <!-- the content for the dialog box -->
</div>
```

The jQuery for the Button and Dialog widgets

```
$(document).ready(function(){
    $("#book").button();
    $("#book").click(function() {
        $("#dialog").dialog({ modal: true });
    });
});
```

Description

- The HTML for a Button widget can be an input element with any of these type attributes: button, submit, reset, radio, or checkbox. It can also be an <a> element. When activated, jQuery UI styles a Button widget so it looks like a button.

- The HTML for a Dialog widget consists of a div element that contains the contents for the dialog box. The title attribute can provide the heading for the dialog box, but that can also be done by using the title option of the jQuery UI dialog method.

- To prevent the Dialog widget from appearing when the page loads, set its display property to "none". You can do that in a style attribute or in the CSS for the widget.

- In the jQuery, use the button method to activate the Button widget. Then, in the click event handler for the button, use the dialog method to display the Dialog widget.

- jQuery UI provides many options for Dialog widgets. For instance, if the *modal* option is set to true, the box must be closed before the user can proceed. The width option can be used to change the width of the box from its default of 300 pixels. And the buttons option can be used to add buttons to the box that can be used to close the box.

- By default, a dialog box is resizable and draggable, but you can change those options by setting them to false.

Figure 10-9   How to use the Button and Dialog widgets

How to use the Autocomplete widget

Figure 10-10 shows how to use an Autocomplete widget. As the user types one or more characters into the text box for this widget, a list drops down that shows the items that contain those characters. Then, the user can select one of those items by clicking on it or by pressing the down-arrow key to go to an item and the Enter key to select that item. That item then replaces what's typed in the text box.

Note that the items that are displayed in the list don't have to start with the letters you type. In the list shown here, for example, Dreamweaver CC, Web Development, and Web Programming all contain the characters "we", but Dreamweaver CC doesn't start with those letters.

The HTML for this widget consists of a div element that contains an input element. The class attribute of the div element should be set to ui-widget, which is a jQuery UI class that styles the input element and auto-completion list. Note, however, that the input element doesn't contain a type attribute. Instead, jQuery UI will make sure that this element works as a text or search box.

To implement an Autocomplete widget with jQuery, you first define a variable that contains an array of all of the items that can be in the auto-completion list. Notice here that values are assigned to the elements of the array when the array is created. When you use this technique to add values to an array, the length of the array is determined by the number of values that are specified.

Once the array is defined, you select the input element for the widget and call the autocomplete method. The one option for this method that must be set is the "source" option that points to the variable that contains the items array. This figure also mentions some other options that you might want to use for an Autocomplete widget.

If the list for this widget is so long that you want to get it from the server, you can use Ajax and JSON to get the list without making an HTTP request for another web page. You'll learn how to use Ajax and JSON in chapter 12. After that, you can study the documentation for this widget to see how it can work with these technologies.

An Autocomplete widget

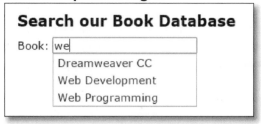

The HTML for the Autocomplete widget

```
<div class="ui-widget">
    <label for="books">Book: </label>
    <input id="books">
</div>
```

The jQuery for the Autocomplete widget

```
$(document).ready(function(){
    var murachBooks =
        ["ADO.NET", "Android", "ASP.NET", "C#", "C++", "CSS",
         "Dreamweaver CC", "HTML5", "Java", "Java Servlets", "JavaScript",
         "jQuery", "MySQL", "Oracle SQL", "PHP", "SQL Server", "VB",
         "Web Development", "Web Programming"];
    $("#books").autocomplete({
        source: murachBooks
    });
});
```

Description

- The HTML for an Autocomplete widget consists of a div element with its class attribute set to "ui-widget". This div element should contain an input element with no type attribute.

- The "ui-widget" class is a jQuery UI class that's used to style the input element and the auto-completion list.

- In the jQuery, define a variable that contains an array of the items for the list in the Autocomplete widget. You can code as many items as you want in this array.

- To activate the Autocomplete widget in the jQuery, use the autocomplete method for the widget and set the source option to the name of the variable that you used for the array.

- You can also code the source option as a callback function. For more information, see the documentation for this widget.

- You can use the delay option to set the number of milliseconds after a character is entered before the Autocomplete widget is activated; the default is 300 milliseconds. You can also use the minLength option to specify the minimum number of characters that must be entered before this widget is activated; the default is 1.

- After you learn how to use Ajax and JSON in chapter 12, you can use the documentation for this widget to learn how to get the items that are displayed by the widget from a web server. If you do that, you usually change the minLength option to 3 or more so the Ajax call isn't done too soon.

Figure 10-10   How to use the Autocomplete widget

How to use the Datepicker widget

Figure 10-11 shows how to use a Datepicker widget that is associated with a text box. Then, when the user clicks in the text box, a calendar is displayed. After the user selects a date, the calendar is hidden and the selected date appears in the text box.

To implement a Datepicker widget, you code a text box in the HTML. Then, you select that text box in the jQuery and call the datepicker method. By default, the calendar looks like the one in this figure with the current date displayed in mm/dd/yyyy format. But many options are available for customizing the date format, language, selectable date ranges, and more.

In the second jQuery example in this figure, three options are set. The first option sets the minimum date to the current date, which is done by assigning a new Date object to the option. The second option sets the maximum date that the widget will accept to 45 days after the current date. And the third option displays a panel beneath the calendar that contains Today and Done buttons. If the user clicks the Today button after moving to another month, the calendar returns to the month that contains the current date. If the user clicks the Done button, the calendar is closed.

A Datepicker widget with no options set

The HTML for the Datepicker widget

```
<label>Arrival date:</label>
<label><input type="text" id="datepicker"></label>
```

The jQuery for the Datepicker widget with no options

```
$(document).ready(function(){
    $("#datepicker").datepicker();
});
```

The jQuery for the Datepicker widget with three options

```
$(document).ready(function(){
    $("#datepicker").datepicker({
        minDate: new Date(),
        maxDate: +45,
        showButtonPanel: true
    });
});
```

Description

- The HTML for a Datepicker widget is a text box.

- The jQuery for a Datepicker widget is a call to the datepicker method.

- By default, the Datepicker widget is displayed when the user moves the focus into the text box, and the current date is highlighted.

- jQuery UI provides many options for the Datepicker widget. For instance, minDate sets the minimum date that the user can select; maxDate sets the maximum date that the user can select; changeMonth and changeYear when set to true provide controls that let the user select the month and year that should be displayed; numberOfMonths sets the number of months that should be displayed; and showButtonPanel displays a bar at the bottom of the widget with Today and Done buttons.

Figure 10-11   How to use the Datepicker widget

How to use the Slider widget

Figure 10-12 shows how to use the Slider widget. This widget lets the user drag the slider to a position that represents a specific value. You can use this widget to limit the values that the user can select to valid values so the entry doesn't have to be validated.

The example in this figure shows how to use a slider in conjunction with a text box that shows the value set by the slider. In this case, the HTML for the Slider widget is preceded by the HTML for the text box.

The HTML for a Slider widget consists of just a div element. Then, the jQuery selects that element and calls the slider method, usually with one or more options. For instance, the example in this figure sets the starting value to 50, the minimum value to 1, and the maximum value to 100. As a result, the user must select a value from 1 to 100 by sliding the slider.

This example also sets the slide option to a function that is called each time the slider is moved by the mouse. This function has two parameters: the first one is for the event object of the slide event, and the second one is for the object that contains the value that has been set by the slider. Within this function, the text box with "employees" as its id is selected, and the val method is used to set its value to the value set by the slider (ui.value). That way, the value in the text box will always be the same as the one selected by the slider.

After the code for the slider method, the ready event handler contains one more statement. That statement selects the text box and sets its value to 50, which is the same as the starting value for the slider. As a result, the text box value and the slider value will be the same from the start.

A Slider widget

Company size: 50

The HTML for the Slider widget

```html
<div id="size">
    <label>Company size: </label>
    <input type="text" id="employees" style="border:0;">
</div>
<div id="slider" style="width:100px;"></div>
```

The jQuery for the Slider widget

```javascript
$(document).ready(function(){
    $("#slider").slider({
        value: 50,
        min: 1,
        max: 100,
        slide: function(event, ui) {
            $("#employees").val(ui.value);
        }
    });
    $("#employees").val(50);
});
```

Description

- The HTML for a slider consists of a div element. To set the size of the slider, you can set the CSS width and height properties. In the HTML above, this is done with a style attribute, but you can also do this in the CSS style sheet.

- In this example, the HTML for the slider is preceded by the HTML for a text box that is used to display the value that's set by the slider.

- In the jQuery for the slider, use the slider method to activate the slider, and use the value, min, and max options to set the starting, minimum, and maximum values for the slider.

- You can also use the slide option to provide a function for the slide event. In the example above, this function sets the value in the text box to the value set by the slider as the slider is moved by the mouse.

- The last line of code in the example above sets the initial value of the text box to 50 so it is the same as the initial value that's set for the slider.

- Other options for the Slider widget let you change the way the slider works. For instance, you can set the orientation option to "vertical" so the slider goes up and down instead of left and right. You can set the range option to true so the slider to provides for a range of values starting with the values that are specified in the values option. And you can set the step option to a numerical value that determines the size of the interval or step that each slider move makes.

Figure 10-12   How to use the Slider widget

How to use the Menu widget

Figure 10-13 shows how to use a Menu widget. This widget makes it easy to create a multi-tier vertical menu with fly-out submenus. In the example in this figure, the menu includes five items and two of those items have submenus.

The HTML for a Menu widget typically consists of a ul element for the main menu, plus a ul element for each submenu. As you can see here, the ul element for each submenu is coded within an li element for the main menu.

The jQuery for a Menu widget selects the ul element for the main menu and calls the menu method. In many cases, you won't need to code any options because the defaults work the way you want them to. In this example, though, the icons option is included. This option changes the icon that's used to indicate a submenu from a right caret (>) to a triangle that points to the right.

In most cases, you'll also want to set the width of the menu since it's set to the width of its container element by default. To do that, you can set the width of the class named "ui-menu" as shown here. This is one of the classes that's defined by the jQuery UI style sheet. Note that this sets the width of the main menu as well as any submenus, so you'll want to be sure that the width you specify will accommodate all the menu items.

A Menu widget

The HTML for the Menu widget

```
<ul id="menu">
    <li><a href="index.html">Home</a></li>
    <li><a href="aboutus.html">About Us</a>
        <ul>
            <li><a href="history.html">Company History</a></li>
            <li><a href="staff.html">Our Staff</a></li>
            <li><a href="headquarters.html">Our Headquarters</a></li>
        </ul>
    </li>
    <li><a href="solutions.html">Solutions</a>
        <ul>
            <li><a href="vProspect.html">vProspect 2.0</a></li>
            <li><a href="vConvert.html">vConvert 2.0</a></li>
            <li><a href="vRetain.html">vRetain 1.0</a></li>
        </ul>
    </li>
    <li><a href="support.html">Support</a></li>
    <li><a href="contactus.html">Contact Us</a></li>
</ul>
```

The CSS for the Menu widget

```
.ui-menu { width: 165px; }
```

The jQuery for activating the Menu widget

```
$(document).ready(function(){
    $( "#menu" ).menu({
        icons: { submenu: "ui-icon-triangle-1-e" }
    });
});
```

Description

- The HTML for a Menu widget typically consists of a ul element for the main menu. It can also include nested ul elements for submenus.

- The default width for a Menu widget is 100% of its container element, but you can change that by setting the width property of the class named "ui-menu".

- If the list items in the main list contain links, those links are underlined. To change that, you can set the text-decoration property of the links to "none".

- In the jQuery, use the menu method to activate the widget.

- To change the icon that's displayed for a submenu, you can use the icons option. The default is a right caret (>).

Figure 10-13   How to use the Menu widget

A web page that uses jQuery UI

This chapter ends by showing the code for a web page that uses five of the jQuery UI widgets. This shows how two or more widgets can be used for a single page.

The user interface

Figure 10-14 presents the user interface for this web page. Here, a Dialog widget is used to give information about the website's support documentation, a Tabs widget is used within a form to get data entered by the user, and a Button widget is used for the Submit Form button.

Beyond that, a Slider widget is used in the Company tab to get the range for the number of employees in the company. Also, a Datepicker widget is used to get a date in the Additional tab. If you run this application on your own computer, you'll get a better feel for how these widgets work.

The link and script elements

Figure 10-14 also shows the link and script elements that this application requires. The first link element is for the jQuery UI CSS style sheet. The second one is for the developer's CSS style sheet.

Similarly, the first script element is for the jQuery library. The second one is for the jQuery UI library. And the third is for the developer's external jQuery file. This of course is the required sequence for these libraries because the developer's jQuery uses both the jQuery and the jQuery UI library, and the jQuery UI library uses the jQuery library.

The page layout

The link and script elements for the web page

```
<!-- jQuery UI style sheet (Includes styles for Smoothness theme) -->
<link rel="stylesheet" href="jquery-ui.min.css">

<!-- normal style sheet used for layout and general formatting -->
<link rel="stylesheet" href="main.css">

<!-- jQuery library -->
<script src="http://code.jquery.com/jquery-2.1.4.min.js"></script>

<!-- jQuery UI library -->
<script src="jquery-ui.min.js"></script>

<!-- The developer's external JavaScript file -->
<script src="vecta_corp.js"></script>
```

Description

- This web page uses three of the jQuery widgets within a form element: a Tabs widget to get data from the user; a Dialog widget to display a help dialog box when the user clicks on the vSupport Documentation link; and a Button widget for the Submit Form button.

- Within the Tabs widget, a Slider widget is used in the Company tab to get the company size range, and a Datepicker widget is used in the Additional tab to get a contact date.

Figure 10-14   The user interface, link, and script elements for the Vecta Corp page

The HTML for the widgets

Figure 10-15 presents the HTML for the portions of the web page that use the widgets. Since you've already seen these widgets in action, you should have no problem understanding this HTML. Note, however, that all five widgets are coded within a form element.

The HTML for the widgets

```
<form id="contactusForm">
    <p>Fill out the form below and a sales representative will contact
        you shortly. For more information on how to fill out this form,
        please review our <a href="#" id="help">vSupport documentation</a>.
    </p>
    <!-- DIALOG WIDGET -->
    <div id="helpdialog" title="vSupport" style="display:none;">
        <p>Our contact form is divided into four sections: ... </p>
    </div>
    <!-- TABS WIDGET -->
    <div id="tabs">
        <ul>
            <li><a href="#tabs-1">Personal</a></li>
            <li><a href="#tabs-2">Company</a></li>
            <li><a href="#tabs-3">Product</a></li>
            <li><a href="#tabs-4">Additional</a></li>
        </ul>
        <div id="tabs-1">
            .
            .
        </div>
        <div id="tabs-2">
            .
            .
            <label>Company Size:</label>
            <input type="text" id="employees" style="border:0;">
            <!-- SLIDER WIDGET -->
            <div id="slider"></div><br>
            .
            .
        </div>
        <div id="tabs-3">
            .
            .
        </div>
        <div id="tabs-4">
            .
            .
            <!-- DATEPICKER WIDGET -->
            <input type="text" id="datepicker"><br>
        </div>
    </div>
    <!-- BUTTON WIDGET -->
    <input type="submit" id="submitbutton" value="Submit Form">
</form>
```

Figure 10-15   The HTML for the widgets of the Vecta Corp page

The jQuery for the widgets

Figure 10-16 shows the jQuery for the widgets. Notice that the methods for all five widgets are called from the event handler for the ready event. Here again, since you already know how to use these widgets, you shouldn't have any trouble understanding the code for using them.

Note, however, that the jQuery code for the dialog box uses the buttons option to add an OK button to the box. Then, the function for this button indicates that the dialog box should be closed when the OK button is clicked.

Also note that the jQuery code for the slider includes range and values options. Because the range option is set to true, the values option can include two values that identify the starting range as 11-50. Then, the user can change that range by dragging the ends of the slider.

The jQuery for the widgets

```
$(document).ready(function(){
    // DIALOG WIDGET
    $("#help").click(function() {
        $("#helpdialog").dialog({
            buttons: {
                OK: function() {
                    $(this).dialog("close");
                }
            }
        });
    });

    // TABS WIDGET
    $("#tabs").tabs();

    //SLIDER WIDGET
    $("#slider").slider({
        min: 1,
        max: 100,
        range: true,
        values: [11, 50],
        slide: function(event, ui) {
            $("#employees").val(ui.values[0] + " - " + ui.values[1]);
        }
    });
    $("#employees").val(11 + " - " + 50);

    //DATEPICKER WIDGET
    $("#datepicker").datepicker();

    // BUTTON WIDGET
    $("#submitbutton").button();
});
```

Figure 10-16   The jQuery for the widgets of the Vecta Corp page

Perspective

Now that you've completed this chapter, you should be able to build a download for jQuery UI that includes a predefined theme or a custom theme. In addition, you should be able to use all of the jQuery UI widgets presented in this chapter. That gets you off to a fast start with jQuery UI because the widgets are the most widely-used jQuery UI components.

Terms

jQuery UI (User Interface)
theme
widget
modal dialog

Summary

- *jQuery UI (User Interface)* is a JavaScript library that extends the jQuery library. Since the jQuery UI library uses the jQuery library, the script element for jQuery UI must come after the script element for jQuery.

- Before you download the jQuery UI library, you can build a custom download that can include a predefined or custom *theme* that is used to style the jQuery UI components that you use. This theme is implemented by a CSS style sheet that is part of the download.

- As you build a jQuery UI download, you can also select the components for the features that you're going to use, including interactions, widgets, and effects. As you would expect, the fewer components you select, the smaller the jQuery UI file that has to be loaded into the user's browser.

- The most widely-used jQuery UI components are the *widgets* that include the Accordion, Tabs, Button, Dialog, Autocomplete, Datepicker, Slider, and Menu widgets.

- To use a widget, you code the prescribed HTML for it. Then, in the jQuery, you select the widget and run its primary method, often with one or more options.

Exercise 10-1   Experiment with the Accordion widget

In this exercise, you'll review the jQuery UI demos and documentation for the Accordion widget. Then, you'll make some minor modifications to the application that uses this widget.

Review the demos and documentation for the widget

1. Go to the jQuery UI website at this URL:

    `http://jqueryui.com/`

    Then, click on the link for the Accordion widget in the left sidebar.

2. Use the accordion at the top of the page to see how it works. Then, click the View Source link below the accordion to display the code that implements it, and review this code. In particular, notice that the accordion method doesn't use any options.

3. Select one or more of the examples to the right of the accordion to see how they change the way the accordion works, and review the jQuery code to see what options are used.

4. Click the API Documentation link and review the options on the page that's displayed.

Review the application

5. Open the HTML file for the accordion application in this folder:

    `c:\jquery\exercises\ch10\accordion\`

    Then, run the application to see how it works.

6. Modify the jQuery code for the accordion so the panels are displayed when the user double-clicks on them rather than when the mouse moves over them. Test this change.

7. Modify the jQuery code so all of the panels are closed when the application starts. To do that, use the active option. Then, test this change.

Exercise 10-2   Experiment with the Datepicker widget

In this exercise, you'll review the jQuery UI demos and documentation for the Datepicker widget. Then, you'll make some modifications to an application that uses this widget.

1. Go to the home page of the jQuery UI website. Then, click on the link for the Datepicker widget in the left sidebar.

2. Try some of the demos for this widget, view the source code to get a better idea of how this widget works, and review the API documentation.

3. Open the HTML file for the datepicker application in this folder:

    `c:\jquery\exercises\ch10\datepicker\`

    Then, run the application to see how it works.

4. Modify the jQuery code so the user can't enter a date before the current date or more than 6 months from the current date. To refer to the current date, you can use a Date object. To refer to 6 months from the current date, you can use the string "+6m". Then, test the application.

5. Modify the jQuery code so the Datepicker widget is displayed when the user clicks the calendar.jpg image that's in the images folder. To learn how to do that, you'll need to review the documentation for the showOn, buttonImage, and buttonImageOnly options. Then, test the application.

Exercise 10-3   Review the pages for building a download

1. Go to the jQuery UI website at this URL:

    `http://jqueryui.com/`

    Then, click the Custom Download button near the upper right corner to display the Download Builder page.

2. Review the components that are available. Then, drop down the list of themes at the bottom of the page to see what's available.

3. Click the "design a custom theme" link above the drop-down list of themes to display the ThemeRoller page. Then, display the Gallery tab in the left sidebar to see that it lists the available themes and shows how each theme looks when applied to a Datepicker widget.

4. Click on the Datepicker widget for one or more of the themes to see what they look like when applied to the other widgets shown in the main part of the page.

5. Click on the Edit button below one of the themes. You will be returned to the Roll Your Own tab, and the properties of the theme you selected will be listed in the Accordion widget.

6. Make any changes you'd like to the properties of the theme to see how they look when applied to the widgets shown on the page. When you're done, click the Download Theme button at the top of the sidebar to return to the Download Builder page.

7. If you want to create a download that uses the custom theme, remove the checkmark from any components that you don't want to include in the download.

8. When you have just the components you want selected, click the Download button and respond to the dialog boxes that are displayed. Then, unzip the download folder and review the files it contains.

11

How to use jQuery UI interactions and effects

In addition to the widgets that you learned about in the previous chapter, a jQuery UI download can include interactions and effects. Although interactions and effects aren't used as widely as widgets, they provide the basis for some interesting jQuery applications. In this chapter, you'll learn how to use them.

How to use interactions

The jQuery UI *interactions* provide behaviors that you can apply to HTML elements. As a result, they provide the basis for some interesting jQuery applications.

Introduction to interactions

Figure 11-1 starts by presenting an example of an interaction. Here, the resizable interaction is applied to a div element that is formatted to look similar to a dialog. Notice in the HTML that a class is assigned to both the div element and the h3 element it contains. These classes are included in the jQuery UI CSS file that's part of a jQuery UI download. As you'll see in the examples of interactions in the figures that follow, classes like these are used frequently with interactions.

To use an interaction, you code jQuery UI methods with or without options just like you do when you use widgets. In this figure, for example, the resizable method is used to make the element with an id of "dialog" resizable. Then, the four options specify the minimum and maximum height and width for the resizable element.

This figure also lists the jQuery UI interactions that you were introduced to in the previous chapter. As you learn about these interactions in the pages that follow, keep in mind that the jQuery UI website provides excellent documentation and demos for them. So, use this chapter to get started with interactions, and use the documentation and demos when you need to expand upon what you've learned.

An element that uses the resizable interaction

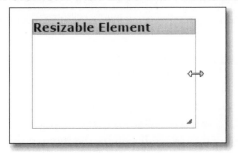

The HTML for the element

```
<div id="dialog" class="ui-widget-content">
    <h3 class="ui-widget-header">Resizable Element</h3>
</div>
```

The jQuery for the interaction

```
$(document).ready(function() {
    $("#dialog").resizable({
        maxHeight: 250,
        maxWidth: 350,
        minHeight: 150,
        minWidth: 200
    });
});
```

The five jQuery UI interactions

- Draggable
- Droppable
- Resizable
- Selectable
- Sortable

Description

- jQuery UI *interactions* can be used to provide interactivity that would be difficult to code with JavaScript.
- Like widgets, interactions have options that control how they work.
- Interactions rely on classes within the CSS for jQuery UI more so than widgets do.
- The documentation and demos for interactions on the jQuery UI website is excellent.

Figure 11-1   Introduction to the jQuery UI interactions

How to use the draggable and droppable interactions

Figure 11-2 shows how to use the draggable and droppable interactions. Here, the user can drag any of the three products at the top of the page and drop it onto the shopping cart at the bottom of the page.

Any HTML element can be defined as draggable or droppable. In the example in this figure, the draggables are defined as div elements and the droppable is defined as a ul element within a div element. In this case, the three div elements that define draggable objects contain images. In contrast, the ul element that defines the droppable area is empty when the application starts.

The jQuery that implements the draggable and droppable interactions starts by selecting the first three div elements and calling the draggable method. This method includes the cursor option, which identifies the cursor that should be displayed as an element is dragged. You can see this cursor over the element that's being dragged in the web page.

Next, the jQuery selects the ul element within the fourth div element and calls the droppable method. This method includes a drop event with a callback function that indicates what happens when an element enters the drop area. Notice that this function receives two parameters: event and ui. Although the event parameter isn't used here, the ui parameter is used to get the draggable object. Then, the children of that draggable object (the img element) is added as the HTML content of an li element. Finally, the appendTo method is used to add the li element to the droppable object (this).

In most cases, you'll use the draggable and droppable interactions together as shown here. Although you can use the draggable interaction without the droppable interaction, it usually doesn't make sense to let a user drag an element without providing a place to drop it.

A draggable element as it's being dragged onto a droppable element

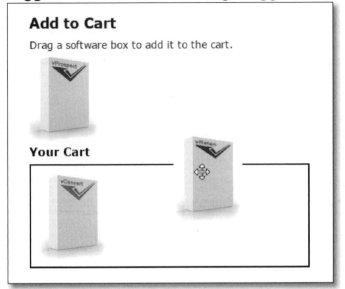

The HTML for the draggable and droppable elements

```
<div id="vprospect"><img src="images/vprospect.png"></div>
<div id="vconvert"><img src="images/vconvert.png"></div>
<div id="vretain"><img src="images/vretain.png"></div>

<div id="cart"><ul></ul></div>
```

The jQuery for the interactions

```
$(document).ready(function() {
    $("#vprospect, #vconvert, #vretain").draggable({ cursor: "move" });
    $("#cart ul").droppable({
        drop: function(event, ui) {
            $("<li></li>").html(ui.draggable.children()).appendTo(this);
        }
    });
});
```

Description

- The draggable and droppable interactions can be used with any HTML element. A droppable element defines the area where a draggable element can be dropped.

- In the jQuery, the draggable method is used to make an element draggable, and the droppable method is used to make an element the target of a draggable element.

- jQuery UI provides a variety of options for the draggable method, many of which control how and where an element can be dragged.

- jQuery UI also provides options for the droppable method. For example, the accept option identifies the elements that a droppable object will accept, and the tolerance option indicates when a draggable object is considered to be over a droppable object.

- To control what happens when a draggable object is dropped, you can code a callback function for the drop event of the droppable object.

Figure 11-2 How to use the draggable and droppable interactions

How to use the resizable interaction

Figure 11-3 shows how to use the resizable interaction. Here, the interaction is applied to a text area so it can be enlarged to make room for the user to enter more text. However, the resizable interaction can be used with any HTML element.

The HTML for the text area consists of just an opening tag with an id and a closing tag. Then, the jQuery selects the text area by its id and calls the resizable method. In this example, the handles option is included on this method to indicate which directions the area can be enlarged. Here, "se" stands for southeast, which refers to the bottom right corner.

When you provide for resizing an element by dragging a corner, stripes appear near that corner. Often, though, those stripes aren't inside the corner as shown here. To fix that, you can override the properties of the class that's assigned to the element based on the value of the handles option. In the CSS in this figure, for example, the bottom and right properties of the ui-resizable-se class are specified.

Before I go on, you should realize that some browsers automatically provide for resizing a text area by dragging its bottom right corner. Other browsers, however, especially older ones, don't provide for this feature. Because of that, it's best to use the resizable interaction whenever you want the user to be able to enlarge a text area by dragging it. Keep in mind, though, that a vertical scroll bar is added to a text area if more text is entered than can be displayed at one time. In most cases, that's sufficient.

A text area that can be resized

Questions / Comments:

We are a small publishing company that has been in business for 40 years. We are looking for new ways to grow our customer base, particularly in the college market.

The HTML for the text area

```
<p>Questions / Comments:</p>
<textarea id="questions"></textarea>
```

The jQuery for the interaction

```
$(document).ready(function() {
    $("#questions").resizable({
        handles: "se"
    });
});
```

The CSS for the interaction

```
.ui-resizable-se {
    bottom: 13px;
    right: -3px;
}
```

Description

- The resizable interaction can be used with any HTML element. To enable the resizable interaction, you use the jQuery resizable method.

- By default, you can drag the bottom right corner or the right or bottom side of an element to resize it. To change this default, you use the handles option. The values you code for this option refer to directions. For example, "se" stands for southeast, which refers to the bottom right corner.

- If an element can be resized by dragging a corner, stripes appear near the corner of the element. If the stripes don't appear where you want them, you can move them by overriding properties of the appropriate jQuery UI CSS class.

- To restrict the size of an element, you can use the minWidth, minHeight, maxWidth, and maxHeight options. You can also use the containment option to restrict the bounds of the element.

Figure 11-3   How to use the resizable interaction

How to use the selectable interaction

Figure 11-4 shows how to use the selectable interaction, which is often used to provide a more visual means of selecting one or more options. In this case, the selectable interaction is used to select one or more of three products represented by images.

In the HTML in this figure, you can see that the selectable elements are coded as items within a list. Note, however, that any HTML element or group of elements can be selectable. For example, div elements are often used with the selectable interaction.

The jQuery for this example starts by selecting the list element that contains the selectable elements and calling the selectable method. Within this method, a callback function is coded for the stop event, which occurs when the interaction ends. In this case, the selectable interaction ends each time a product is selected. That's because the only way to select multiple images is to hold down the Ctrl key and then click on them. In contrast, if you're working with elements that contain text, you can select multiple elements by dragging around them. Then, the selectable interaction ends when you release the mouse button.

The callback function for the stop event starts by selecting the span element that is coded within the <p> element that follows the selectable list. Then, it clears the text from the span element since the code that follows will process all of the selected elements. Next, it selects all elements that have been assigned to the ui-selected class. Because this class is automatically assigned to an element when it's selected, this includes all selected elements. Then, the each method is called on each selected element. The callback function for this method uses the append method to add the id of the selected element (this), followed by a space, to the span element.

Because no properties are defined by default for the ui-selected class, a selected element doesn't appear any differently than elements that aren't selected. To change that, you can include CSS for this class. In this example, this class adds a background color to the selected elements.

Two selected elements in a list of selectable elements

Product(s) selected: vConvert vRetain

The HTML for the list of selectable elements

```
Select the products that you're interested in:<br>
<ol id="solutions">
    <li id="vProspect"><img src="images/logo_vprospect.gif"></li>
    <li id="vConvert"><img src="images/logo_vconvert.gif"></li>
    <li id="vRetain"><img src="images/logo_vretain.gif"></li>
</ol>
<p>Product(s) selected: ><span id="selected"></span></p>
```

The jQuery for the interaction

```
$(document).ready(function() {
    $("#solutions").selectable({
        stop: function() {
            $("#selected").text("");
            $(".ui-selected").each(function() {
                $("#selected").append(this.id + " ");
            });
        }
    });
});
```

The CSS for the interaction

```
.ui-selected {
    background-color: #dfe3e6;
}
```

Description

- The selectable interaction can be used to make any HTML element or group of elements selectable. To enable the selectable interaction, you use the selectable method. Then, you can select one or more elements using standard techniques.

- Although it's common to define selectable elements as list items, you can also use other elements such as div elements.

- By default, all of the elements within a selectable object are selectable. To change that, you can use the filter option to identify the selectable elements.

- When an element is selected, the ui-selected class is automatically assigned to it. To control how an element is displayed when it's selected, you can set properties of this class.

- To perform an operation when a selectable interaction ends, you can code a callback function for the stop event of the element. Within this function, you can refer to each selected element using the .ui-selected class.

Figure 11-4　How to use the selectable interaction

How to use the sortable interaction

Figure 11-5 shows how to use the sortable interaction to provide for sorting a group of HTML elements. When an element is sortable, the user can drag it from one location to another. As you can see in this figure, when an element is positioned between two other sortable elements, a placeholder appears. Then, the user can drop the element onto that placeholder to change the sort sequence.

In most cases, you'll use the sortable interaction with an unordered list as shown in this figure. However, you can use this interaction with any group of HTML elements.

Notice in the HTML shown here that the ui-state-default class is assigned to each line item in the sortable list. This class provides the default appearance shown in this figure. Of course, you can override this class to change the appearance.

In the jQuery for the sortable interaction, you select the element that contains the sortable items. Then, you call the sortable method on this element. In this example, the placeholder option is included on this method. This option assigns the ui-state-highlight class to the placeholder that appears as a sortable element is dragged.

By default, the ui-state-highlight class changes the border around the placeholder to a light yellow and the background color of the placeholder to an even lighter yellow. In this figure, though, you can see that the height property has been added to this class. The value of this property will cause the placeholder to be about the same height as the sortable elements.

A sortable list as one of the items is dragged downward

The HTML for the sortable list

```
<ul id="vsupport">
    <li class="ui-state-default">Blog / How-To Articles</li>
    <li class="ui-state-default">Discussion Forum</li>
    <li class="ui-state-default">Knowledge Base</li>
    <li class="ui-state-default">Phone Support</li>
    <li class="ui-state-default">Wiki Support</li>
</ul>
```

The jQuery for the interaction

```
$(document).ready(function() {
    $("#vsupport").sortable({
        placeholder: "ui-state-highlight"
    });
});
```

The CSS for the interaction

```
.ui-state-highlight {
    height: 1.5em;
}
```

Description

- The sortable interaction can be used to make a group of HTML elements sortable. To enable the sortable interaction, you use the sortable method.

- Although it's common to define sortable elements as list items, you can also use other elements such as div elements.

- To move an element, just drag it to a new location within the list. When the element is positioned between two other sortable elements, a placeholder appears and you can drop the element on that placeholder.

- To stylize the elements in a sortable list, you can assign the ui-state-default class to the sortable elements. To stylize the placeholder for a list, you can assign the ui-state-highlight class to the placeholder option of the sortable method.

Figure 11-5   How to use the sortable interaction

How to use effects

In the topics that follow, you'll learn the basic skills for using the many effects that jQuery UI provides.

Introduction to effects

Figure 11-6 presents the jQuery UI *effects*. The table at the top of this figure lists the effects that are included in the effects core component. These effects extend the effects provided by jQuery. For example, jQuery UI extends the animate method to provide for animating color transitions.

This figure also lists the 15 individual effects that jQuery UI provides. You can apply these effects to widgets and interactions as well as other HTML components.

To use these effects, you must include the jQuery UI core effects component in your download. In addition, you must include the specific component for an effect. To use the blind effect, for example, you must include the "Blind Effect" component.

Here again, the jQuery UI website provides excellent documentation and demos. So, use this chapter to get started with effects, and use the documentation and demos when you need to expand upon what you've learned.

As you learned in chapter 6, when you use one of the basic jQuery effects, you can apply a jQuery UI *easing* to it. If you would like to see a full list and demonstrations of these easings, you can go to the URL in this figure.

jQuery UI core effects

Effect	Description
Color transitions	Provides for animating background color, border colors, text color, and outline color.
Class transitions	Provides for animations while a class is being added, deleted, or changed.
Easing	Provides easing effects to animated elements.
Visibility transitions	Provides for applying an individual effect to an element while showing, hiding, or toggling the element.

jQuery UI individual effects

blind	fade	scale
bounce	fold	shake
clip	highlight	size
drop	puff	slide
explode	pulsate	transfer

The URL for demonstrations of the easings on the jQuery UI website

`http://jqueryui.com/easing`

Description

- The jQuery UI core effects component extends jQuery functionality by providing color transitions, class transitions, easing, and visibility transitions.

- The jQuery UI library includes 15 individual effects that you can apply to widgets, interactions, and even your own non-jQuery UI HTML elements. Each of these effects requires the core effects component as well as an individual effect component.

- The documentation and demos for effects on the jQuery UI website are excellent.

- In figure 6-9 of chapter 6, you learned how to use *easings* with effects and animations. For a full list and demonstrations of all the jQuery UI easings, you can go to the URL shown above.

Figure 11-6   Introduction to the jQuery UI effects

How to use individual effects

To use the individual effects, you call the effect method shown in figure 11-7. In the syntax for this method, you can see that the only required parameter is the name of the effect. In addition to this parameter, though, you can code one or more options, a duration, and a callback function.

In the example in this figure, the highlight and pulsate effects are applied to the sortable list you saw in figure 11-5. If you refer back to that figure, you'll see that the HTML for the list in this figure is identical. However, two events have been added to the sortable method in the jQuery.

The first event, start, is triggered when the sorting interaction starts. That happens when the user starts to drag a sortable element. Then, the callback function for this event calls the effect method of the element that's being dragged and causes it to pulsate for one and one half seconds. That's why this element appears to be dimmed in the web page in this figure.

One option is also coded for this effect. This option, times, controls the number of times that the element pulsates. The default is five, but the option in this example changes it to three.

Notice here that the callback function for the start method accepts two parameters: event and ui. Although the event parameter isn't used in this example, the item property of the ui parameter is used to identify the element that's currently being dragged. You'll use this parameter often to refer to the current item in a group of items.

The second event, update, is triggered when the user stops dragging a sortable element and its position changes in the list. The callback function for this event accepts event and ui parameters just like the callback function for the start event. Then, the item property of the ui parameter is used to select the element that was dragged to a new position, and the effect method is called to apply the highlight effect to that element using the specified color for two seconds.

The syntax for the effect method

```
effect(effect[, {options}][, duration][, callback])
```

A sortable list that uses highlight and pulsate effects

The HTML for the sortable list

```
<ul id="vsupport">
    <li class="ui-state-default">Blog / How-To Articles</li>
    <li class="ui-state-default">Discussion Forum</li>
    <li class="ui-state-default">Knowledge Base</li>
    <li class="ui-state-default">Phone Support</li>
    <li class="ui-state-default">Wiki Support</li>
</ul>
```

The jQuery for the effects

```
$(document).ready(function() {
    $("#vsupport").sortable({
        placeholder: "ui-state-highlight",
        start: function(event, ui) {
            $(ui.item).effect("pulsate", { times: 3 }, 1500);
        }
        update: function(event, ui) {
            $(ui.item).effect("highlight", { color: "#7fffd4" }, 2000);
        }
    });
});
```

Description

- You can use the jQuery UI effect method to apply an individual effect to one or more elements. The only argument that's required by this method is the name of the effect.

- If you code a callback function as a parameter of the effect method, the function is called after the effect is executed.

- If you code the effect method within a callback function, the function should accept event and ui parameters. The event parameter contains information about the original browser event, and the ui parameter contains information about the selected item.

- You can also use some of the individual effects with the show, hide, and toggle methods. For more information, see figure 11-10.

Figure 11-7   How to use individual effects

How to use color transitions

Figure 11-8 shows how to use *color transitions* to animate a change from one color to another. To do that, you use the animate method that you learned about in chapter 6. Then, you include the color properties in the properties map, and you include a duration that indicates how long it takes the colors to change. This makes for a smoother transition from one color to another.

The example in this figure uses a text area to illustrate how color transitions work. Here, the user can click on a link to increase the size of the text area. When that happens, the background color and text color of the text area also change.

The jQuery for this example contains an event handler for the click event of the link. Within this event handler, the animate method is called on the text area. Then, the properties map for this method includes the four properties that change the width, height, background color, and text color. Finally, the duration parameter is coded so the transition takes place over a period of one second.

A text area that grows and changes color when a link is clicked

Customer Experience Survey

Please help us improve our service by sending us your comments:

```
If you run out of room as you type, you can click the link below to
make this box larger. As the box increases in size, the background
color and the color of any text that it contains will change.
```

Increase text area

The HTML for the text area and link

```html
<textarea id="comments" style="width:350px;height:125px;"></textarea><br>
<a href="#" id="grow_textarea">Increase text area</a>
```

The jQuery for the transition

```javascript
$(document).ready(function() {
    $("#grow_textarea").click(function() {
        $("#comments").animate({
            width: 500,
            height: 200,
            backgroundColor: "#ededed",
            color: "green"
        }, 1000 );
    });
});
```

Color properties that can be animated

color	borderRightColor
backgroundColor	borderTopColor
borderBottomColor	outlineColor
borderLeftColor	

Description

- The animate method has been extended by jQuery UI to support *color transitions*.
- To use color transitions, you include the color properties in the properties map for the animate method.
- You can identify the color for a color transition using standard CSS or CSS3 color specifications.
- Please refer to chapter 6 for more information on coding the animate method.

Figure 11-8   How to use color transitions

How to use class transitions

Figure 11-9 shows how to use *class transitions*. Class transitions provide for changing the class that's assigned to one or more elements over a specified period of time so the change is gradual. You can use class transitions with the jQuery addClass, removeClass, and toggleClass methods that you learned about in chapter 7. You can also use them with the switchClass method, which is part of the jQuery UI core effects component.

The example in this figure shows how you can use a class transition to change the font size for a paragraph of text. To change the font size, the user can click the Medium, Large, or X-Large button on the page. Then, the event handler for the click event of the button that's clicked is executed.

You can see these event handlers in the jQuery code in this figure. For each handler, a function named setSize is called with a value that indicates the name of the class that should be assigned to the paragraph. These classes are defined in the CSS as shown here.

The setSize function starts by calling the jQuery removeClass method to remove any classes that are currently assigned to the paragraph. Then, this function calls the jQuery UI addClass method to add the class with the name that was passed to the function. This change takes place over a period of one second.

The syntax of the methods for class transitions

```
addClass(className[, duration])
removeClass(className[, duration])
toggleClass(className[, duration])
switchClass(removeName, addName[, duration])
```

Text before and after its size is changed

The HTML for the class transition

```
Change text size:
<input type="button" id="button1" value="Medium">
<input type="button" id="button2" value="Large">
<input type="button" id="button3" value="X-Large">
<h2>Welcome</h2>
<p id="p1">... INSERT CONTENT HERE ...</p>
```

The jQuery for the class transitions

```
$(document).ready(function() {
    $("#button1").click(function() { setSize("medium"); });
    $("#button2").click(function() { setSize("large"); });
    $("#button3").click(function() { setSize("x_large"); });

    function setSize(size) {
        $("#p1").removeClass();    // jQuery method to remove all classes
        $("#p1").addClass(size, 1000);
    }
});
```

The CSS for the classes

```
.medium {font-size: 100%;}
.large {font-size: 120%;}
.x_large {font-size: 150%;}
```

Description

- jQuery UI provides for animating the transition between two classes over a specified duration. The animation can be applied to any properties that contain numeric values.

- *Class transitions* can be applied using the addClass, removeClass, toggleClass, and switchClass methods.

Figure 11-9   How to use class transitions

How to use visibility transitions

Figure 11-10 shows how to use *visibility transitions* to apply individual effects to an element as it's displayed or hidden. You can use these transitions with the show, hide, and toggle methods that you learned about in chapter 6. You can see the syntax for using these methods with visibility transitions at the top of this figure. Except for the method name, this syntax is the same as the syntax of the effect method you saw in figure 11-7.

To illustrate how visibility transitions work, the example in this figure presents a menu that has a submenu that can be displayed or hidden. Here, the main menu is implemented as an unordered list, and each list item contains an <a> element. Then, the third list item is followed by a div element that contains a submenu that consists of three <a> elements.

The jQuery for this example contains an event handler for the click event of the menu item that contains the submenu. Within this event handler, the div element that contains the submenu is selected, and the toggle method is called for it. If the submenu is hidden when this method is called, it causes the submenu to be displayed. If the submenu is displayed, it causes it to be hidden.

Two parameters are coded on the toggle method. The first one is for the effect that will be used to display and hide the submenu. In this case, the blind effect is used, which causes the submenu to be lowered and raised like vertical blinds. The second parameter is for the duration of the effect, which in this case is half a second.

The syntax of the methods for visibility transitions

```
{show|hide|toggle}(effect[, {options}][, duration][, callback])
```

A visibility transition that's used to show and hide a submenu

The HTML for a menu with an item that contains a submenu

```html
<ul>
    <li><a href="index.html">Home</a></li>
    <li><a href="aboutus.html">About Us</a></li>
    <li><a href="#" id="solutions">Solutions</a></li>
    <div id="solutions_menu">
        <a href="solutions.html#vprospect">vProspect 2.0</a>
        <a href="solutions.html#vconvert">vConvert 2.0</a>
        <a href="solutions.html#vretain">vRetain 1.0</a>
    </div>
    <li><a href="support.html">Support</a></li>
    <li><a href="contactus.html">Contact Us</a></li>
</ul>
```

The jQuery for the visibility transition

```javascript
$(document).ready(function() {
    $("#solutions").click(function() {
        $("#solutions_menu").toggle("blind", 500);
    });
});
```

Description

- jQuery UI provides for applying individual effects to elements using the show, hide, and toggle methods.
- All of the individual effects shown in figure 11-6 except for bounce, highlight, pulsate, shake, size, and transfer can be applied with these methods.

Figure 11-10   How to use visibility transitions

Perspective

With the information in this chapter, you should now be able to use any of the jQuery UI components. That includes the widgets you learned about in the last chapter, as well as the interactions and effects you learned about in this chapter. Keep in mind, though, that the interactions and effects have many more options and events than what's presented here. So you may need to do some additional research to get them to work exactly the way you want them to.

Terms

interaction	color transition
effect	class transition
easing	visibility transition

Summary

- The jQuery UI *interactions* provide for enhancing the usability of HTML elements. The five interactions include draggable, droppable, resizable, selectable, and sortable.

- To use an interaction, you select the element you want to apply it to and then call its method, often with one or more options and events.

- In many cases, you use classes in the jQuery UI download to format an element during different stages of an interaction.

- *Effects* can be divided into two categories: the effects that are included in the jQuery UI core effects component, and the individual effects that are implemented as separate components.

- To use the individual effects, you call the effect method on the element you want to apply the effect to. This method names the effect and can also include options, a duration, and a callback function that's called after the effect is executed.

- The jQuery UI core effects include color transitions, class transitions, visibility transitions, and easing.

- To implement a *color transition*, you include color properties in the properties map for the animate method, along with a duration parameter.

- To implement a *class transition*, you use extensions of the jQuery addClass, removeClass, and toggleClass methods or the jQuery UI switchClass method. With all four methods, you can provide a duration parameter.

- To implement a *visibility transition*, you use extensions of the jQuery show, hide, or toggle method, and you specify the effect for the transition in the first parameter.

Exercise 11-1 Use the sortable interaction

In this exercise, you'll experiment with a sortable list like the one in figure 11-5. Then, you'll add some options and events to the sortable method for this list. As you do this exercise, you may need to or want to refer to the documentation and demos on the jQuery UI website.

Review the application

1. Use your text editor to open the HTML file in this folder:

    `c:\jquery\exercises\ch11\sortable\`

2. Run the application. Then, try to drag one of the items outside the list including below the last item to see what happens.

Add three more options to the sortable method

3. Add the containment option to the sortable method with either "parent" or the id of the element that contains the list items ("#vsupport") as its value. Then, run the application and notice that you can't drag an item to the right or left of the list, below the last item in the list, or above the first item in the list.

4. Comment out the containment option. Then, add the items option to indicate that all of the items in the list are sortable except for the last item. To do that, add a class named "sortable" to all of the list items in the HTML except the last one, and use this class (.sortable) as the value of the items option. Run the application to see that you can no longer drag the last item.

5. Add the revert option to the sortable method, and set its value to true. Then, run the application, drag an item to a new location, and notice that the item glides into its new location instead of snapping there.

Add two events to the sortable method

6. Add a start event to the sortable method with a callback function that accepts the event and ui parameters like the start event in figure 11-7. Within this function, use the removeClass method to remove the ui-state-default class from the item that's currently being dragged. To refer to this item, use the item property of the ui parameter. Then, use the addClass method to add the ui-state-active class to the item.

7. Run the application and drag an item to a new location. Notice that as you start dragging, the appearance of the item changes. However, the appearance doesn't change back when you drop it in its new location.

8. To fix that, add a stop event to the sortable method. The callback function for this event should work like the function for the start event, except it should remove the ui-state-active class and add the ui-state-default class. Run the application one more time to see that an item returns to its original appearance when it's dropped in a new location.

Exercise 11-2   Use transitions

In this exercise, you'll enhance an application that uses jQuery effects and animations by adding jQuery UI color and visibility transitions.

Review the application

1. Use your text editor to open the HTML file in this folder:

    `c:\jquery\exercises\ch11\animation\`

2. Run the application, and notice the jQuery animation that's done for the "jQuery FAQs" heading. Then, click on one of the subheadings to display the answer for the question, and click on the heading again to hide it.

Enhance the animation for the heading

3. Using figure 11-8 as a guide, add color animations to the heading. In the first animation, change the background color from its starting value of white to blue and the text color from its starting value of blue to red. In the second animation, reverse those color changes.

Enhance the effects for the subheadings

4. Using figure 11-10 as a guide, change the slideUp and slideDown methods in the callback function for the click event of the h2 headings to hide and show methods with visibility transitions. For the show method, use the jQuery UI bounce effect over 500 milliseconds. For the hide method, use the jQuery UI puff effect over 1500 milliseconds.

5. Go to this URL to review the effects that jQuery UI provides:

    `http://jqueryui.com/effect/`

    Then, try two of the other effects in this application.

Section 4

Ajax, JSON, and APIs

The three chapters in this section show you how to use Ajax, how to use JSON data, how to use Ajax with the APIs (Application Programming Interfaces) for two popular websites, and how to use three of the many HTML5 APIs. These are important skills for developing modern websites.

In chapter 12, you'll learn how to use Ajax to load HTML, XML, and JSON data from a web server without loading a new web page. This chapter also shows you how to use Ajax with the feed API for Flickr to retrieve photos and information about them. This is a typical use of Ajax.

Then, in chapter 13, you'll learn how to use the API for Google Maps so you can include maps and driving directions in your websites. When you complete these chapters, you'll be able to apply what you have learned as you explore the APIs for other websites.

To add to these skills, chapter 14 presents some of the most useful HTML5 APIs. That includes Geolocation, which lets you get the global position associated with a browser or mobile device; Web Storage, which is storage that can be processed by JavaScript on the browser; and Web Workers, which allows for multi-threading within a JavaScript application.

12

How to use Ajax, JSON, and Flickr

This chapter shows you how to use Ajax to update a web page with HTML, XML, or JSON data without loading a new web page into the browser. Since Ajax is commonly used to get data from popular websites, this chapter also shows how to use Ajax with the API for getting feeds from Flickr.

Introduction to Ajax

The four topics that follow introduce you to Ajax, the types of data that are commonly used with Ajax, and the XMLHttpRequest object that is the basis for Ajax.

How Ajax works

Ajax is the acronym for *Asynchronous JavaScript and XML*. As shown in figure 12-1, Google's Auto Suggest feature is a typical Ajax application. As you type the start of a search entry, Google uses Ajax to get the terms and links of items that match the characters that you have typed so far. Ajax does this without refreshing the page so the user doesn't experience any delays. This is sometimes called a "partial page refresh."

To make this work, all modern browsers provide an *XMLHttpRequest object* (or *XHR object*) that is used to send an Ajax request to the web server and to receive the returned data from the server. In addition, JavaScript is used in the browser to issue the request, parse the returned data, and modify the DOM so the page reflects the returned data. In many cases, a request will include data that tells the server what data to return.

On the web server, an application program or script that's written in a language like PHP or ASP.NET is commonly used to return the data that is requested. Often, these programs or scripts are written before the JavaScript developers use them so they know how their requests must be coded. Otherwise, the JavaScript developers and the server-side developers need to coordinate so the Ajax requests can be processed by the server scripts.

The two diagrams in this figure show how a normal HTTP request is made and processed as well as how an Ajax request is made and processed. The main difference is that the server returns an entire page for a normal HTTP request so the page has to be loaded into the browser. In contrast, an Ajax request sends an XMLHttpRequest object to get data and the server returns only the data. In addition, JavaScript is used to send the request, process the returned data, and script the DOM with the new data. As a result, the web page doesn't have to be reloaded.

Because this Ajax technology is so powerful, it is commonly used by websites like Facebook and Google Maps. When you post a comment to a friend's Facebook page, for example, the comment just appears. And when you drag within a Google Map, the map is automatically adjusted. In neither case is the page reloaded.

Beyond that, websites like YouTube, Twitter, and Flickr provide *Application Programming Interfaces* (*APIs*) that show how to use Ajax to get data from their sites. This means that you can get data from these sites to enhance your own web pages. Since this is a skill that every modern web developer should have, this chapter shows you how to use the API for Flickr. Then, in the next chapter, you'll learn how to use the API for Google Maps.

Google's Auto Suggest is an Ajax application

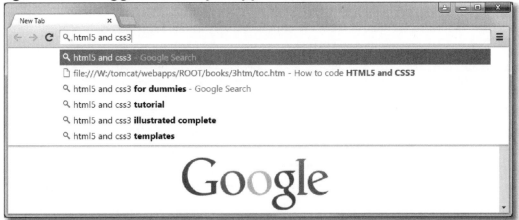

How a normal HTTP request is processed

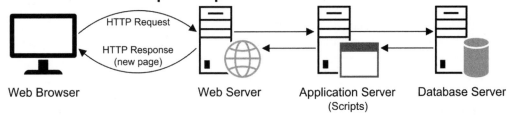

How an Ajax XMLHttpRequest is processed

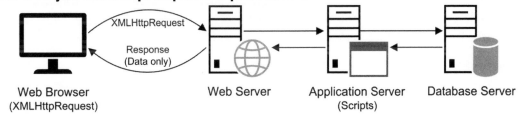

Description

- *Ajax* stands for *Asynchronous JavaScript and XML*. Unlike normal HTTP requests, Ajax lets you receive data from a web server without reloading the page. This is sometimes known as a "partial page refresh."

- As the Ajax name implies, JavaScript is essential to the use of Ajax because JavaScript not only sends the requests but also processes the responses and updates the DOM with the new data.

- To send an Ajax request, JavaScript uses a browser object known as an *XMLHttpRequest* (*XHR*) *object*. This object can include data that tells the application server what data is being requested.

- An XHR object is often processed by a program or script on the application server. Then, the JavaScript programmer must coordinate the Ajax requests with the application scripts.

- Today, websites like Google's Blogger, YouTube, Twitter, and Flickr provide *APIs* (*Application Programming Interfaces*) that let you use Ajax to get data from their sites.

Figure 12-1   How Ajax works

Common data formats for Ajax

Figure 12-2 presents the three common data formats for Ajax applications. The easiest one to use is HTML, which you're already familiar with. When you use Ajax to load HTML data into a web page, you don't have to parse the data because it already includes the HTML tags for the data. In contrast, you do have to parse the data when you work with XML or JSON data.

Ajax was originally designed to be used with *XML (eXtensible Markup Language)*, which is why XML is part of the Ajax name. XML is an open-standard, device-independent format for exchanging data across the Internet, and its syntax and document tree mimic that of HTML. The downside to XML is that it's relatively difficult to use JavaScript and jQuery to parse the data in XML files.

Today, *JSON (JavaScript Object Notation)* is the most popular format for working with Ajax. JSON, pronounced "Jason" is easy to understand, and most server-side languages already provide functions for JSON encoding. PHP for example, has the json_encode() function, and ASP.NET has the DataContractJsonSerializer class.

JSON is based on a subset of the JavaScript programming language, and it uses conventions that are familiar to programmers of C-style languages like C, C++, Java, and JavaScript. Since its structure is a hierarchy of name/value pairs that are returned as an object, it is relatively easy to parse the JSON data with JavaScript and jQuery.

Although HTML, XML, and JSON are the three most popular data formats for working with Ajax, they aren't the only ones that are supported. In fact, you can also use plain text, YAML, and CSV files with Ajax.

The common data formats for Ajax

Format	Description	File extension
HTML	Hypertext Markup Language	html
XML	eXtensible Markup Language	xml
JSON	JavaScript Object Notation	json is often used

XML data

```
<?xml version="1.0" encoding="utf-8"?>
<management>
    <teammember>
        <name>Agnes</name>
        <title>Vice President of Accounting</title>
        <bio>With over 14 years of public accounting ... </bio>
    </teammember>
    <teammember>
        <name>Wilbur</name>
        <title>Founder and CEO</title>
        <bio>While Wilbur is the founder and CEO ... </bio>
    </teammember>
</management>
```

JSON data

```
{"teammembers":[
    {
        "name":"Agnes",
        "title":"Vice President of Accounting",
        "bio":"With over 14 years of public accounting... "
    },
    {
        "name":"Wilbur",
        "title":"Founder and CEO",
        "bio":"While Wilbur is the founder and CEO ... "
    }
]}
```

Description

- The common data formats for working with Ajax are HTML, XML, and JSON.

- *XML* (*eXtensible Markup Language*) is an open-standard, device-independent format that must be parsed by JavaScript or jQuery in the browser.

- *JSON* (*JavaScript Object Notation*) is the most popular format for Ajax applications. In general, JSON files are smaller and faster than XML files. They are also easier to parse since JSON data is returned as JavaScript objects.

- Most server-side languages have methods that can be used to encode JSON data on the server. PHP 5.0 and later, for instance, has the json_encode() method, and ASP.NET 3.0 and later has the DataContractJsonSerializer class.

- For more information on JSON APIs that are built into your favorite programming language, you can visit www.json.org.

Figure 12-2   Common data formats for Ajax

The members of the XMLHttpRequest object

Figure 12-3 presents all of the *members* (methods, properties, and events) of the XMLHttpRequest object. This object is behind every Ajax request, no matter what type of data is being requested. You'll see how the members of this object are used in the application in the next figure.

The two methods that are used with every request are the open and send methods. The open method is used to open a connection for a request. As you can see in the parameters for the open method, this method specifies whether the request is a GET or POST request and it provides the URL for the request. In a production application, the URL is for the script or program on the application server that will process the request. When you're testing an application, though, the URL is typically for a file that contains test data.

After the open method is issued, the send method is used to send the request. If necessary, this method can include a data parameter that sends data to the server along with the request. This data is typically used to filter the data that's returned.

As you can see in the list of properties, the readyState property indicates the state of the request, the status and statusText properties provide the status code and status message that's returned by the server, and the responseText and responseXML properties provide the returned data in plain or XML format.

The last member in this figure is the onreadystatechange event that can be used for an event handler that processes the returned data. You'll see how this works in the next figure.

Incidentally, the GET and POST methods are the same ones that are used for an HTML form. When you use the GET method, the data is sent to the web server as part of the URL, but the total amount of data that can be sent is limited. When you use the POST method, the data that is sent is hidden and unlimited.

Members of the XMLHttpRequest object

Method	Description
abort()	Cancels the current request.
getAllResponseHeaders()	Returns a string that contains the names and values of all response headers.
getResponseHeader(*name*)	Returns the value of a specific response header.
open(*method,url*[,*async*] [,*user*][,*pass*])	Opens a connection for a request. The parameters let you set the method to GET or POST, set the URL for the request, set asynchronous mode to true or false, and supply a username and password if authentication is required. When asynchronous mode is used, the application continues while the request is being processed.
send([*data*])	Starts the request. This method can include data that gets sent with the request. This method must be called after a request connection has been opened.
setRequestHeader(*name,value*)	Specifies a name and value for a request header.
Property	**Description**
readyState	A numeric value that indicates the state of the current request: 0 is UNSENT, 1 is OPENED, 2 is HEADERS_RECEIVED, 3 is LOADING, and 4 is DONE.
responseText	The content that's returned from the server in plain text format.
responseXml	The content that's returned from the server in XML format.
status	The status code returned from the server in numeric format. Common values include 200 for success and 404 for not found.
statusText	The status message returned from the server in text format.
Event	**Description**
onreadystatechange	An event that occurs when the state of the request changes.

Description

- The table above shows the *members* (methods, properties, and events) that can be used with the XMLHttpRequest object.

Figure 12-3   The members of the XMLHttpRequest object

How to use the XMLHttpRequest object

Figure 12-4 shows how you can use the XMLHttpRequest object to get XML data from the web server without refreshing the web page. Here, the first example shows a portion of the XML file, but you can assume that this file includes all of the team members with full data in the bio fields. Then, the second example shows the div element that will receive the data returned by the XHR object.

The third example shows the JavaScript code for using an XHR object to send an Ajax request and receive the returned data. This is coded within the event handler for the ready event. The first statement in this JavaScript code uses the *new* keyword to create a new XHR object. This is followed by an event handler for the onreadystatechange event. The first statement in this handler is an if statement that tests whether the readyState property is 4 and the status property is 200, which means that the request has finished and was successful. If that's true, the if statement parses the returned data. Otherwise, it does nothing.

To parse the data, the first statement in the handler saves the responseXML property of the XHR object in a variable named xmlDoc. Then, the next statement uses the JavaScript getElementsByTagName method to store the data for each team member in an array variable named team. Next, it sets a variable named html to an empty string. This is the variable that the for loop that follows will fill with the formatted data for the team members.

In the for loop, one statement is executed for each team member in the team array. This statement uses the getElementsByTagName method to get the name, title, and bio data for each team member in the array. It also concatenates this data to the html variable along with br elements that provide the spacing between the data items. When the for loop finishes, the first statement after it uses the innerHTML property to save the data in the html variable as the HTML contents of the div element with "team" as its id. That will display the data as shown in the web page at the top of this figure.

At this point, though, the Ajax request hasn't been sent. The code has just set up the event handler for after it has been sent. To send the request, the open method that follows the event handler opens the connection for the request. It sets the method for the request to GET, provides the URL for the XML data, and sets asynchronous to true. In this case, the URL parameter is a relative URL that shows that the team.xml file is in the same folder as the file that contains the JavaScript.

Then, the send method sends the request. Once that's done, the onreadystatechange event will occur, and the event handler will parse the returned data if the request was successful.

With the exception of the ready event method, this example uses JavaScript instead of jQuery. This should give you some idea of how the XHR object has been traditionally used. Please note, however, that jQuery could be used for this application. In fact, with the advent of jQuery, Ajax programming has become much easier. Just keep in mind that the XHR object is used with every Ajax request, whether or not jQuery is used to issue the request.

A web page that uses the XHR object and JavaScript to load XML data

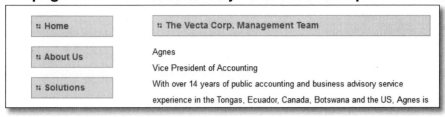

The XML file (team.xml)

```xml
<?xml version="1.0" encoding="utf-8"?>
<management>
    <teammember>
        <name>Agnes</name>
        <title>Vice President of Accounting</title>
        <bio>With over 14 years of public accounting ... </bio>
    </teammember>
    ...
</management>
```

The HTML div element that receives the data

```html
<div id="team"></div>
```

The JavaScript for getting and parsing the data

```javascript
$(document).ready(function() {
    var xhr = new XMLHttpRequest();
    xhr.onreadystatechange = function() {
        if (xhr.readyState == 4 && xhr.status == 200) {
            xmlDoc = xhr.responseXML;
            var team = xmlDoc.getElementsByTagName("teammember");
            var html = "";
            for (i = 0; i < team.length; i++) {
                html +=
                    xmlDoc.getElementsByTagName("name")[i]
                        .childNodes[0].nodeValue + "<br>" +
                    xmlDoc.getElementsByTagName("title")[i]
                        .childNodes[0].nodeValue + "<br>" +
                    xmlDoc.getElementsByTagName("bio")[i]
                        .childNodes[0].nodeValue + "<br><br>";
            }
            document.getElementById("team").innerHTML = html;
        }
    }
    xhr.open("GET", "team.xml", true);
    xhr.send();
});
```

Description

- This application uses the XHR object to load all of the team members in the file named team.xml on the web server and display them in the div element with "team" as its id.

- The event handler for the onreadystatechange event parses the data returned by the method if the readyState property is 4 and the status property is 200.

Figure 12-4   How to use the XMLHttpRequest object

How to use the jQuery shorthand methods for Ajax

Now that you understand how Ajax works and how you use JavaScript with Ajax programming, you're ready to learn about the jQuery shorthand methods that make Ajax programming easier.

The jQuery shorthand methods for working with Ajax

Figure 12-5 summarizes the jQuery methods for working with Ajax. Here, the load method is used to get HTML data. The $.get and $.post methods are commonly used to get XML data, which is the default data type for these methods. And the $.getJSON method is used to get JSON data.

The examples show how these methods work. The first example uses the load method to load the HTML from a file named solutions.html. The second example uses the $.get method to load XML data. And the third example uses the getJSON method to load JSON data.

In the second example, the $.get method is coded with three parameters. The first parameter is the URL for a PHP script that will process the Ajax request. The second parameter passes data to the request in the form of a string. This data will be used by the PHP script to determine what data is returned. The third parameter names the function that will be called if the request is successful.

In the third example, the URL parameter for the $.getJSON method is for a JSON file. This method doesn't have a data parameter, and its success parameter consists of an embedded function that will be called if the request is successful.

The $.each method is also included in this figure. This method is commonly used for processing the data that's returned by an Ajax request. You'll see how this works in figure 12-8.

The shorthand methods for working with Ajax

Method	Description
load(*url*[,*data*][,*success*])	Load HTML data.
$.get(*url*[,*data*][,*success*[,*dataType*]])	Load data with a GET request.
$.post(*url*[,*data*][,*success*[,*dataType*]])	Load data with a POST request.
$.getJSON(*url*[,*data*][,*success*])	Load JSON data with a GET request.

The parameters for the shorthand methods

Parameter	Description
url	The string for the URL where the request is sent.
data	A map or string that is sent to the server with the request, usually to filter the data that is returned.
success	A callback function that is executed if the request is successful.
dataType	A string that specifies the type of data (html, xml, json, script, or text). The default is XML.

The $.each method for processing the data that's returned

Method	Description
$.each(*collection*, *callback*)	The collection parameter is an object or array. The callback parameter is a function that's done for each item in the collection.

A load method

```
$("#solution").load("solutions.html");
```

A $.get method that includes data and calls a success function

```
$.get("getmanager.php", "name=agnes", showManager);
```

A $.getJSON method with an embedded success function

```
$.getJSON("team.json", function(data){
    // the statements for the success function
}
```

Description

- jQuery includes several shorthand methods that let you request and receive HTML, XML, or JSON data.

- All of the shorthand methods let you include data that will be used by the web server to filter the results of the request so only the right results are returned. You can send this data as a query string (as in the second example above) or as a map (see figure 12-9).

- The only difference between the $.get and $.post methods is the method that is used for the request (GET or POST). These are the same methods that you specify when you set up an HTML form.

- The $.each method is an expanded form of the each method that can be used to process the items in the returned data (see figure 12-8).

Figure 12-5   The jQuery shorthand methods for working with Ajax

How to use the load method to load HTML data

Figure 12-6 shows how to use the load method to load HTML data with an Ajax request. For this example, three section elements are coded within a file named solutions.html. The ids for these elements are "vprospect", "vconvert", and "vretain", which refer to three products. Then, one of these section elements is loaded when the user clicks on the link for the product in the page shown here.

You can see how this works in the jQuery for this application. It consists of the event handlers for the click events of the three links. In the load methods for these links, the URL not only consists of the name of the HTML file but also a reference to the section element for that link. For instance, #vconvert in the code that follows

```
$("#solution").load("solutions.html #vconvert");
```

gets the HTML for the section element with vconvert as its id.

The one benefit of using HTML data with Ajax requests is that the data is already within HTML elements that can be formatted by the CSS for the page. In other words, you don't have to parse the data that is returned by the request. In contrast, you do need to parse the XML or JSON data that is returned, as you will see in the next two figures.

By the way, you should know that if you test the load method with the Firefox or Safari browsers, it should work even if the HTML files are on your file server. If you're using Chrome, IE, or Opera, though, the HTML files need to be on a web server.

A web page that loads HTML elements when one of the links is clicked

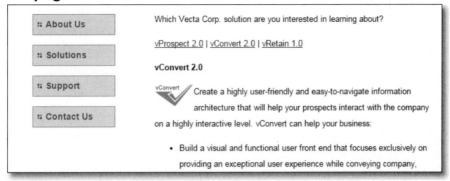

The HTML for the user Interface

```
<p>Which Vecta Corp. solution are you interested in learning about?</p>
<a id="vprospect" href="#">vProspect 2.0</a> |
<a id="vconvert" href="#">vConvert 2.0</a> |
<a id="vretain" href="#">vRetain 1.0</a><br>
<div id="solution"></div>
```

The start of the second section element in the solutions.html file

```
<section id="vconvert">
    <p><strong>vConvert 2.0</strong></p>
    <p><img src="images/logo_vconvert.gif" width="63" height="36" >
        Create a highly user-friendly and easy-to-navigate information ...
    </p>
    <ul>
        <li>Build a visual and functional user front end that ... </li>
        <li>Cause the desired emotional response in a user to ...</li>
        ...
    </ul>
</section>
```

The jQuery that loads the data when a link is clicked

```
$(document).ready(function() {
    $("#vprospect").click(function() {
        $("#solution").load("solutions.html #vprospect");
    });
    $("#vconvert").click(function() {
        $("#solution").load("solutions.html #vconvert");
    });
    $("#vretain").click(function() {
        $("#solution").load("solutions.html #vretain");
    });
});
```

Description

- The load function can only load content from files on the same server as the page making the call.

- During testing, you'll be able to load files from the file system in Firefox and Safari, but Chrome, IE, and Opera require all of the files to be on an actual web server.

Figure 12-6   How to use the load method to load HTML data

How to use the $.get or $.post method to load XML data

The example in figure 12-7 shows how to use the $.get method to load XML data from a web server. Remember, though, that the $.post method works the same way, except the POST method is used to send the request.

The first parameter in the $.get method in this example gives the URL for the XML file that will be loaded by the request. Here again, this URL is relative to the file that contains the jQuery code. Then, the second parameter is the function that will be used to process the returned data. The parameter for this function is the data that's returned by the request.

Within this function, the first statement sets the value of the HTML div element that will receive the processed data to an empty string. Then, to process the returned data, it issues the find method for the data that's returned to find the children of the XML item named "management". Those children are the items named "teammember", and the each method is chained to the children so it can be used to process each of the team members.

The first statement in the each method sets a new variable named xmlDoc to the value of the this keyword, which is the team member that's being processed. Then, the next statement appends the data for that team member to the div element that will receive the processed data. Within the parameter for the append method, three find methods get the data for the "name", "title", and "bio" items in the returned data, and the text method gets the text for those items.

To keep this application simple, the formatting for the data that's returned is limited. Specifically, the name field is parsed into an h3 element, and br elements are added after the title and bio fields to add spacing after these fields.

To test the use of the $.get and $.post methods, the files named in the URL have to be on a web server, not a file server. Specifically, the XML file must be in the same domain as the web page that's making the request. This is required because of the *cross-domain security policy* that is used by most browsers.

A web page that loads XML data

The XML file (team.xml)

```
<management>
    <teammember>
        <name>Agnes</name>
        <title>Vice President of Accounting</title>
        <bio>With over 14 years of public accounting ... </bio>
    </teammember>
    ...
</management>
```

The HTML div element that receives the data

```
<div id="team"></div>
```

The jQuery

```
$(document).ready(function(){
    $.get("team.xml", function(data){
        $("#team").html("");
        $(data).find("management").children().each(function() {
            var xmlDoc = $(this);
            $("#team").append("<h3>" +
                xmlDoc.find("name").text() + "</h3>" +
                xmlDoc.find("title").text() + "<br>" +
                xmlDoc.find("bio").text() + "<br>");
        });
    });
});
```

Description

- The $.get and $.post methods work the same except for the method that's used to send the data in the XHR request.

- You can use the jQuery find method to get the data in an XML file. Here, the first find method starts a chain that gets the children (team members) of the management data that's returned, and the other three find methods get the name, title, and bio fields for each team member.

Figure 12-7   How to use the $.get or $.post method to load XML data

How to use the $.getJSON method
to load JSON data

Figure 12-8 shows how to use the $.getJSON and $.each methods to load JSON data. In the $.getJSON method, the first parameter provides the URL for the JSON file with json as its extension. Then, the second parameter is the function that processes the JSON data if the request is successful. Note that the parameter in this function, data, is an object that will receive the data for the request.

Within the success function, the first $.each method processes each collection of items in the returned object. In this case, the object contains a single collection of team members. The first parameter for this function is the object returned by the request. Then, the second parameter is a function that processes each item in the collection using another $.each method. Here, each item is a team member.

The first parameter of the second $.each method is the this keyword, which refers to the current team member. Then, because the data for each team member consists of key/value pairs, the function for the second parameter accepts a key and a value. Within this function, the name, title, and bio items are appended to the div element with "team" as its id.

To refer to the value of each data item in the inner loop, this example uses object notation like this:

```
value.name
```

This refers to the name item in the object for the current item in the inner loop. If, for example, this inner loop is being executed for the second team member, the data for value.name is Damon, and the data for value.title is Director of Development. This shows how much easier it is to parse JSON data than XML data.

In general, to test the use of the $.getJSON method, the file named in the URL has to be on a web server, not a file server. It must also be in the same domain as the web page that's making the request. However, a simple application like this one where the URL points to a JSON file instead of a file for processing the request and returning JSON can be tested on your file server or computer.

A web page that loads JSON data

The JSON file (team.json)

```
{"teammembers":[
    {
        "name":"Agnes",
        "title":"Vice President of Accounting",
        "bio":"With over 14 years of public accounting... "
    },
    {
        "name":"Damon",
        "title":"Director of Development",
        "bio":"Damon is the Director of Development for ... "
    }
]}
```

The HTML div element that receives the data

```
<div id="team"></div>
```

The jQuery

```
$(document).ready(function(){
    $.getJSON("team.json", function(data){
        $.each(data, function() {
            $.each(this, function(key, value) {
                $("#team").append(
                    "Name: " + value.name + "<br>" +
                    "Title: " + value.title + "<br>" +
                    "Bio: " + value.bio + "<br><br>"
                );
            });
        });
    });
});
```

Description

- To process the returned JSON data, you can use nested $.each methods. The function in the first method will process each collection in the returned data (in this case, a single collection of team members).

- The function in the second $.each method will process each item (team member) in the collection. It will have two parameters that represent the key and value of each item. Then, you can use object notation to get the fields in the returned data.

Figure 12-8   How to use the $.getJSON method to load JSON data

How to send data with an Ajax request

Figure 12-9 shows how to send data with an Ajax request. To do that, you use the data parameter of a shortcut method to supply either a string or a map that contains the data. In this figure, the first example uses a string to send one name/value pair that asks for a "name" data item that has a value of "wilbur". The second example uses a map (or object literal) that's coded within braces to send the same name/value pair.

The $.get methods in both of these examples also include a third parameter that names the function that is called if the request is successful. Then, you code this function after the $.get method. This function has one parameter that receives the data returned by the Ajax request. Of course, you can also code the function as a parameter the way it's done in the other examples in this chapter.

In some Ajax applications, forms are used to get the data that should be sent with a request. In that case, you can use the helper methods in this figure to package the data that's sent with the request. The serialize method collects the entries for a form as a string. The serializeArray method collects the entries for a form as an array of name/value pairs.

The next example in this figure shows how the serialize method works with a request for data. Here, the first statement in the ready event handler uses the serialize method to encode the form entries as a string and save that string in a variable named "formData". This is followed by a $.get method that uses the formData variable as its data parameter.

Whenever you send data with an Ajax request, you have to coordinate the data that you send with your request with the way the script on the server is written. For instance, you can tell from the first two examples that the PHP script in the file named getmanager.php accepts a data item named name, but what other data items can you send with a request?

Two ways to send data with an Ajax request

A $.get method that uses a string for the data parameter

```
$(document).ready(function() {
    $.get("getmanager.php", "name=wilbur", showManager);
    function showManager(data) {
        // process data
    }
});
```

A $.get method that uses a map for the data parameter

```
$(document).ready(function() {
    $.get("getmanager.php", {name:wilbur}, showManager);
    function showManager(data) {
        // process data
    }
});
```

The helper methods for working with Ajax

Function	Description
`serialize()`	Encode a set of form elements as a string that can be used for the data parameter of an Ajax request.
`serializeArray()`	Encode a set of form elements as an array of name/value pairs that can be used for the data parameter of an Ajax request.

The HTML for a form

```
<form id="contactForm">
    <!-- the controls for the form -->
</form>
```

jQuery that uses the serialize method

```
$(document).ready(function() {
    var formData = $("#contactForm").serialize();
    $.get("processcontact.php", formData, processReturnedData);
    function processReturnedData(data) {
        // the statements for the success function
    }
});
```

Description

- When you send data with an Ajax request, the URL is for a server-side script such as a PHP file. Then, the script is responsible for returning the data in XML or JSON format.

- The data parameter in a jQuery shortcut method is a name/value pair that can be set either as a query string or a map (object literal).

- The jQuery helper functions for Ajax make it easy to package form data before sending it to the server.

Figure 12-9   How to send data with an Ajax request

How to use the $.ajax method for working with Ajax

Although you can use the shorthand methods for many Ajax applications, the $.ajax method provides more options for making Ajax requests. You'll learn about this method next.

The syntax of the $.ajax method

Figure 12-10 presents the syntax of the $.ajax method, including some but not all of the options for this method. Besides a function that is executed when the request is successful, this method has options for functions that are done before the request is sent, when the request finishes, after the data is returned but before it is passed to the success function, and when an error occurs. These functions give you more control over the way the method works.

Note in this summary that all four of these functions can have parameters. One of these parameters is jqXHR, which refers to the jQuery XHR object (or *jqXHR object*). This object is a superset of the standard XHR object that includes the properties of the XMLHttpRequest object. This means that you can use the properties in figure 12-3 with this object.

In the beforeSend function, you can use the settings parameter to set properties in the jqXHR object before it is sent with the request. In the complete, error, and success functions, the jqXHR object is passed to the function. The status parameter in these functions returns a string that represents the status of the request. And the error parameter in an error function returns the text portion of the HTTP status.

The jsonp option is used to provide the name of a JSONP parameter that gets passed to the server. *JSONP*, or "JSON with padding", lets you request data from a server in a different domain, which is typically prohibited by web browsers due to their cross-domain security policies. JSONP does this by using a callback function that puts a script element in the DOM that tricks the browser into thinking that the file is actually on the client. JSONP is often used by the APIs for websites.

Other options for the $.ajax method let you provide a password and username if they are needed for authentication. They also let you determine whether the returned data can be cached by the browser and how long a request can last before it times out as a failed request.

The syntax of the $.ajax method

```
$.ajax({ options })
```

Some of the options for the $.ajax method

Option	Description
url	The string for the URL where the request is sent.
beforeSend(*jqXHR, settings*)	A function that is executed before the request is sent. It can pass two parameters: the jqXHR object and a map of the settings for this object.
cache	A Boolean value that determines if the browser can cache the response.
complete(*jqXHR, status*)	A function that is executed when the request finishes. It can receive two parameters: the jqXHR object and a string that represents the status of the request.
data	A map or string that is sent to the server with the request, usually to filter the data that is returned.
dataType	A string that specifies the type of data (html, xml, json, script, or text).
error(*jqXHR, status, error*)	A function that is executed if the request fails. It can receive three parameters: the jqXHR object, a string that represents the type of error, and an exception object that receives the text portion of the HTTP status.
jsonp	A string containing the name of the JSONP parameter to be passed to the server. Defaults to "callback".
password	A string that contains a password that will be used to respond to an HTTP authentication challenge.
success(*data, status, jqXHR*)	A function that is executed if the request is successful. It can receive three parameters: the data that is returned, a string that describes the status, and the jqXHR object.
timeout	The number of milliseconds after which the request will time out in failure.
type	A string that specifies the GET or POST method.
username	A string that contains a user name that will be used to respond to an HTTP authentication challenge.

Description

- The $.ajax method provides options that give you more control over the way the Ajax request works, such as providing a function for handling errors.
- The *jqXHR object* is jQuery's superset of the standard XMLHttpRequest object that provides the properties of that object.
- *JSONP*, or "JSON with padding", is a complement to JSON data that lets you request data from a server in a different domain, which is typically prohibited by web browsers due to their cross-domain security policies.

Figure 12-10   The syntax of the $.ajax method

How to use the $.ajax method to load data

When successful, the application in figure 12-11 is like the one in figure 12-7. However, the $.ajax method sets the timeout option to 10000 milliseconds so it will time out with an error after 10 seconds. In addition, it provides two functions besides the function for successful completion.

In the beforeSend option, you can see the function that is executed before the Ajax request is sent. It just displays "Loading ..." in the div element that will receive the requested data, as shown in this figure. Of course, you could make this more interesting by displaying an animated gif like a progress indicator or a spinning wheel.

In the error option, you can see the function that is executed if an error occurs. This function is coded with three parameters: "xhr" for the jqXHR object, "status" for the string that describes the type of error that occurred, and "error" for the text portion of the HTTP status. Within the function, an alert method is used to display the status of the request (xhr.status), a hyphen, and then the text portion of the HTTP status (error). If, for example, a 404 error occurs, an alert dialog box like the one in this figure will be displayed. This, of course, is a common error when the URL that's specified can't be found.

In the success option, you can see the function for processing the data that's returned. This function has a parameter named "data" that will receive the data returned by the request. Then, the code within this function is the same as the code in the function for the $.get method in figure 12-7. The first statement uses the html method to set the data in the div element with "team" as its id to an empty string. In this case, that replaces the "Loading..." message that was displayed while the request was being processed. The rest of the code uses the find method to find the "management" data in the XML file, uses the children method to get the children (team members) within the management data, and uses the each method to process the data for each child.

A web page with a loading message and an alert dialog box for an error

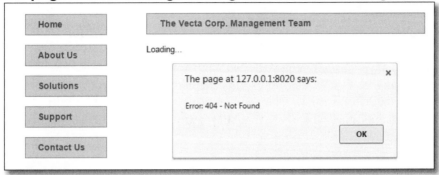

The XML file

```
<management>
    <teammember>
        <name>Agnes</name>
        <title>Vice President of Accounting</title>
        <bio>With over 14 years of public accounting ... </bio>
    </teammember>
    ...
</management>
```

The HTML div element that receives the data

```
<div id="team"></div>
```

The jQuery

```
$(document).ready(function() {
    $.ajax({
        type: "get",
        url: "team.xml",
        beforeSend: function() {$("#team").html("Loading...");},
        timeout: 10000,
        error: function(xhr, status, error) {
            alert("Error: " + xhr.status + " - " + error);
        },
        dataType: "xml",
        success: function(data) {
            $("#team").html("");
            $(data).find("management").children().each(function() {
                var xmlDoc = $(this);
                $("#team").append("<h3>" +
                    xmlDoc.find("name").text() + "</h3>" +
                    xmlDoc.find("title").text() + "<br>" +
                    xmlDoc.find("bio").text() + "<br>");
            });
        }
    });
});
```

Description

- When successful, this application works like the one in figure 12-7. However, it also provides a timeout value and two functions besides the one for successful completion of the request.

Figure 12-11   How to use the $.ajax method to load data

How to use Ajax with Flickr

Once you know how to use Ajax, you have the skills that you need for getting data from popular websites like YouTube, Twitter, and Flickr. In fact, you can get data from any website that provides an API for that.

To give you an idea of how this works, this chapter will now show you how to use Ajax with the API for Flickr. The goal here is not so much to show you how to use Flickr, but rather how to use the API for any website that lets you retrieve data using a URL.

How to use the feed API for Flickr

Flickr is a website that lets you store photos on it for free. This means that you can access your photos anywhere you are as long as you can connect to this website. Since you can also store a description for each photo that includes a thumbnail image and text within HTML tags, this site can also be used as a simple Content Management System (CMS).

The first table in figure 12-12 lists the feeds that Flickr provides. The feed you'll use most often is the public photos & videos feed, and that's the one you'll learn about in the rest of this chapter. This feed allows unauthenticated, public access to any Flickr photos. To see the documentation for this feed, you can go to the URL at the top of this figure.

To retrieve data from the public photo feed, you start with the base URL shown in this figure. Then, you add one or more of the query parameters shown in the second table. To retrieve photos only for a specific user, for instance, you can include the id parameter as illustrated in the first example in this figure. To retrieve photos based on one or more tags that have been added to the photos, you can use the tags parameter. For instance, the first example retrieves all photos with the tag "vectacorp", and the second example retrieves all photos with the tags "waterfall" and "yosemite".

Note that both of these examples also include the jsoncallback parameter. This parameter is required when the format parameter is set to "json", as it is in the examples throughout this chapter. This will cause JSONP to be used as a complement to JSON. As you learned earlier in this chapter, this lets you request data from a server in a different domain, which is typically prohibited by web browsers due to their cross-domain security policies.

Incidentally, the default format for a Flickr feed is the Atom Syndication Format, which is an XML language and a W3 standard. Another common format that Flickr supports is RSS. In this chapter, though, JSON is used for all of the web feeds.

The URL for the Flickr public feed documentation

`www.flickr.com/services/feeds/docs/photos_public/`

Flickr feeds

Feed	Description
Public photos & video	Returns public content matching specified criteria.
Friends photostream	Returns public content from the contacts, friends, and family of a specified user.
Public favorites from a user	Returns public favorites for a specified user.
Group discussions	Returns recent discussions from a specified group.
Group pools	Returns items recently added to the pool of a specified group.
Forum discussions	Returns recent topics from the Flickr forum.
Recent activity	Returns recent activity for a specified user.
Recent comments	Returns recent comments by a specified user.

The base URL for retrieving a public photo stream

`http://api.flickr.com/services/feeds/photos_public.gne`

Common query parameters for the public photos feed

Parameter	Description
`id`	A user id.
`ids`	A comma-delimited list of user ids.
`tags`	A comma-delimited list of tags that identify the photos.
`tagmode`	Controls whether the returned items must match all of the tags specified or any of the tags specified. The default is all.
`format`	The format of the returned feed. Atom 1.0 is the default.
`lang`	The display language of the feed. The default is English.
`jsoncallback`	Optional unless the return format is set to JSON. Then, this parameter must be coded as jsoncallback=?

A URL that gets a JSON feed for a specific user id (in one line)

`http://api.flickr.com/services/feeds/photos_public.gne?`
`id=82407828@N07&format=json&jsoncallback=?&tags=vectacorp`

A URL that gets a JSON feed for all users (in one line)

`http://api.flickr.com/services/feeds/photos_public.gne?`
`&format=json&jsoncallback=?&tags=waterfall,yosemite`

Description

- Flickr is a website that lets you store your photos on it for free. That means you can access your photos wherever you are.

- Flickr provides a number of feeds that you can retrieve photos and related information from. In this chapter, you'll learn how to retrieve photos from the public photos & video feed. To do that, you use a URL with one or more query parameters as shown above.

Figure 12-12   How to use the feed API for Flickr

How to display Flickr data on a page

The table in figure 12-13 summarizes the Flickr data items that are returned from a photo feed. Here, the items data item represents the collection of returned items. You can use this item as the first parameter for the $.each method to process each item. Then, within the callback function for the $.each method, you can use the other data items in this table.

The example in this figure illustrates how this works. To start, the parameters of the URL are set so photos of waterfalls in Yosemite taken by all users will be returned in JSON format. Then, the $.getJSON method is used to get the data from the public photo feed. Within the callback function for this method, the first statement declares a variable named html that will be used to store the HTML for the photos.

Next, a $.each method is used to process each returned item. The callback function for this method formats the HTML for each item. In this case, the HTML includes the title of the photo as the content of an h2 element. It also includes the URL for the photo (media.m) as the value of the src attribute of an img element. This is followed by an empty <p> element to add space between the items.

After all of the items are processed, the last statement in the callback function for the $.getJSON method uses the html method to set the HTML contents of an element with an id of "photos" to the value of the html variable. This causes the data for the photo feed to be displayed on the page.

Although it isn't used in this example, you should realize that the description data item is formatted as HTML in <p> elements. Because of that, you don't have to add the HTML like you do when you use the other data items. In addition, you should realize that the first <p> element contains the name of the user who posted the photo, along with a link to that user's page on Flickr. If the same user posted each photo, you'll probably want to remove this paragraph. You'll see how to do that in figure 12-15.

Data items returned by a photo feed

Data item	Description
items	The collection of returned items.
title	The title of the photo.
link	The URL for the Flickr page for the photo.
media.m	The URL for the photo.
date_taken	The date the photo was taken.
description	Descriptive text for a photo, plus a thumbnail image in an <a> element that links to the full photo on the Flickr site. This data is formatted with HTML tags so it's ready for display.
published	The date and time the photo was uploaded to Flickr.
author	The author's username and email.
author_id	The author's id.
tags	The filtering tags for a photo.

jQuery code that gets the titles and photos from a photo feed

```
var url = "http://api.flickr.com/services/feeds/photos_public.gne?" +
    "format=json&jsoncallback=?&tags=waterfall,yosemite";

$.getJSON(url, function(data){
    var html = "";
    $.each(data.items, function(i, item){
        html += "<h2>" + item.title + "</h2>";
        html += "<img src=" + item.media.m + ">";
        html += "<p></p>";
    });

    $("#photos").html(html);
});
```

Description

- You can use the $.getJSON method that you learned about earlier in this chapter to get data from a Flickr feed. The data that's returned includes the items listed above.

- You can use the $.each method with a callback function to process each item in the collection of items that's returned.

- The description data item consists of two or three <p> elements. The first <p> element contains a link to the user who posted the photo. If the same user posted each photo, you'll probably want to remove this paragraph. You can do that using JavaScript as shown in figure 12-15.

- The second <p> element in the description data item contains a thumbnail image within an <a> element that links to the image on the Flickr site.

- The third <p> element in the description data item is optional and can contain descriptive text.

Figure 12-13   How to display Flickr data on a page

How to review the feed from a website

In some cases, it may be helpful to see the JSON data that's returned from a website. That can help you identify the data items that you can use in your application in case they're not included in the documentation for the API or they're difficult to find in the documentation. That can also help you review the value of the data items so you can be sure that the correct data is displayed on a web page.

Figure 12-14 shows an easy way to display the data from a feed. Here, the URL for the Flickr feed that was shown in figure 12-13 has been copied and pasted into the address bar of a browser. Then, when the Enter key was pressed, the JSON data that will be returned to the application is displayed.

If you review this data, you can see that it's easy to tell what data items the feed contains. For instance, this example shows all of the data items for the first two items with the specified tags. Note that all of these items are contained within a data item named items. You saw how this item is used in the previous figure.

The Flickr feed for the URL in figure 12-13

Description

- To review a feed from the Flickr website, you can type or paste the URL for the feed into the address bar of your browser. Then, when you press the Enter key, you can see the contents of the JSON feed in the browser window.

- The JSON feed identifies the data items that you can use in your application. This is particularly important when you use Flickr because these items aren't identified in the documentation.

- You may also want to use this technique when the documentation for an API is difficult to understand. This can often save you time because you can tell exactly what data the application is going to get.

Figure 12-14   How to review the feed from a website

How to display descriptions for a Flickr photo feed

Figure 12-15 shows how to display the descriptions for the photos in a Flickr feed. In the example at the top of this figure, you can see the description for the first photo in the feed. Here, the description starts with a thumbnail image of the full image. This thumbnail is followed by text that describes the photo.

In the jQuery code for this application, you can see the parameters that are used for the URL. These parameters retrieve photos posted by a specific user that have a specific tag. The $.getJSON and $.each methods that follow are similar to the ones you saw in the previous figure. In this case, though, the description data item is used instead of the media.m data item.

Because the description data item is already formatted as HTML, it's just assigned to the html variable. To understand how this works, this figure presents the description for the first item in the JSON feed. As described in figure 12-13, the first paragraph includes a link to the user who posted the photo. Because this information isn't needed in this example, the last line of the jQuery code in the callback function for the $.each method replaces this paragraph with an empty string. To do that, it uses the replace method of a String object, which replaces the string in the first parameter with the string in the second parameter.

To get this replacement to work right, the first parameter in the replace method must exactly match the data in the description. To make sure it does, you can paste the URL for the feed into the address bar of your browser and open the feed as described in the previous figure. Then, you can copy and paste the HTML that you want to replace. Note that this will only work if the HTML is the same for each item. In this case, this works because all of the photos were posted by the same user.

The next paragraph in the description contains an img element for a thumbnail image coded within an <a> element. The href attribute for this <a> element is set to the URL of the full image on the Flickr site. That way, if the user clicks on the thumbnail, the Flickr page for this photo will be displayed. Finally, the third paragraph contains the descriptive text for the photo.

A web page that displays titles and descriptions for a photo feed

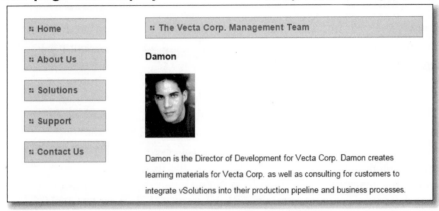

The HMTL element that will receive the data from the feed

```
<div id="team"></div>
```

The jQuery that retrieves and displays the data

```
$(document).ready(function(){
    var url = "http://api.flickr.com/services/feeds/photos_public.gne?
            id=82407828@N07&format=json&jsoncallback=?&tags=vectacorp";

    $.getJSON(url, function(data) {
        var html = "";
        $.each(data.items, function(i, item){
            html += "<h3>" + item.title + "</h3>";
            html += item.description;
            // Remove the first paragraph of the description
            html = html.replace(
                    "<p><a href=\"http://www.flickr.com/people/82407828@N07/\">
                    zakruvalcaba</a> posted a photo:</p>", "");
        });
        $("#team").html(html);
    });
});
```

The description for the first item in the JSON feed

```
<p><a href="http://www.flickr.com/people/82407828@N07/">
    zakruvalcaba</a> posted a photo:</p>
<p><a href="http://www.flickr.com/photos/82407828@N07/7550727736/"
        title="Damon"><img src="http://..." alt="Damon" /></a></p>
<p>Damon is the Director of Development for Vecta Corp. ....</p>"
```

Description

- This application uses the description data item to display the photo as well as the descriptive text. Because the description is formatted with HTML tags, it's not necessary to do that in the jQuery code.

- Because the thumbnail image in the description is within an <a> element, clicking on it goes to the full image on the Flickr site.

Figure 12-15   How to display descriptions for a Flickr photo feed

How to search for photos by tags

So far, you've seen examples that retrieve photos from Flickr that were posted by a specific user, that had specific tags, or that did both. Now, figure 12-16 shows how you can retrieve photos that have been posted by anyone and that have one or more tags entered by the user. Here, the results are shown after the user enters the tags "yacht" and "racing" and clicks on the Search button.

The HTML for this web page includes two input elements. The first one is for the text box where the user enters the tags for the search. The second one is for the Search button that causes the photos to be retrieved. This HTML also includes a div element that will receive the data from the feed.

The jQuery for this application starts by defining a variable named search-Term that will hold the tags entered by the user. Then, the click event handler for the Search button starts by setting this variable to an empty string. Next, it uses an if statement to determine if the user entered a value in the text box. If not, an alert method is used to display a dialog box that tells the user that one or more tags must be entered. If so, the searchTerm variable is set to the value that was entered. Then, that variable is used as the value of the tags parameter in the URL for the query that will be sent to Flickr.

The rest of the code is similar to what you've seen in previous figures. It uses the $.getJSON method to get the data from Flickr. Then, within the $.each method, it gets the title, image, and tags for each photo and formats it as HTML. Finally, it sets the HTML for the div element so it contains that data.

A web page that searches for photos by tags

The HTML that gets the tags and receives the data from the feed

```
Search by tags: <input type="text" size="30" id="search">
<input type="button" value="Search" id="btnSearch">
<h1>Flickr Results</h1>
<div id="photos"></div>
```

The jQuery

```
$(document).ready(function(){
    var searchTerm;
    $("#btnSearch").click(function() {
        searchTerm = "";
        if ($("#search").val() == "") {
            alert("You must enter one or more tags!"); }
        else {
            searchTerm = $("#search").val();

            var url =
              "http://api.flickr.com/services/feeds/photos_public.gne?" +
              "format=json&jsoncallback=?&tags=" + searchTerm + "&tagmode=all";

            $.getJSON(url, function(data){
                var html = "";
                $.each(data.items, function(i, item){
                    html += "<h2>" + item.title + "</h2>";
                    html += "<img src=" + item.media.m + ">";
                    html += "<p><b>Tags: </b>" + item.tags + "</p>";
                });
                $('#photos').html(html);
            });
        }
    });
});
```

Figure 12-16   How to search for photos by tags

Perspective

Now that you've completed this chapter, you should be able to use jQuery to make Ajax requests that return HTML, XML, and JSON data from your server. You should also be able to use Ajax to get data from Flickr.

In the next chapter, you'll learn how to use the API for Google Maps, which is a complicated API. After that, our hope is that you'll have the confidence to dig into the API for any website and figure out how to use it to do what you want.

Terms

Ajax (Asynchronous JavaScript
   and XML)
XMLHttpRequest (XHR) object
API (Application Programming
   Interface)
XML (eXtensible Markup Language)

JSON (JavaScript Object Notation)
member
cross-domain security policy
jqXHR object
JSONP

Summary

- *Ajax*, which standards for *Asynchronous JavaScript and XML*, lets you get data from a web server without refreshing the page. This means that a page can display new information based on the user's actions without the normal delays.

- To make an Ajax request possible, modern browsers provide an *XMLHttpRequest (XHR) object*. This object is used to make the request as well as receive the returned the data. An enhanced version of this object called the *jqXHR object* is used with Ajax requests that are done with jQuery.

- When you use Ajax, you use JavaScript (or jQuery) to make the request, process the returned data, and update the DOM so the data is displayed on the web page.

- The three common data formats for Ajax are HTML, *XML (eXtensible Markup Language)*, and *JSON (JavaScript Object Notation)*. Because JSON makes it easier to parse the returned data, it has become the most popular format for working with Ajax.

- To make Ajax programming easier, jQuery provides shorthand methods like the $.get and $.getJSON methods, the $.ajax method, the $.each method, and two serialize methods for packaging form data so it can be used with an Ajax request.

- Many Ajax requests are processed on the web server by programs or scripts in languages like PHP or ASP.NET. Then, the web developers have to coordinate their Ajax requests with the programs or scripts that process the requests.

- *JSONP*, or "Jason with Padding", lets you get JSON data from a server in a different domain. This gets around the *cross-domain security policy* that most browsers have.

- Many popular websites such as Blogger, YouTube, Twitter, and Flickr provide *APIs* (*Application Programming Interfaces*) that let you use Ajax to get data from their sites.

- Two ways to prepare for using a website like Flickr are studying the API documentation and reviewing the JSON feed for a site in your browser.

- To retrieve JSON data from Flickr, you must use JSONP. To do that, you set the jsoncallback query parameter to a question mark (?).

Exercise 12-1   Enhance a Flickr application

In this exercise, you'll enhance a Flickr application so it includes additional information. When you're done, the web page should look like this:

Yosemite waterfalls

Cherry Creek

2015-06-10T07:06:56-08:00

Fluid Light Images posted a photo:

This is a scene from our second night's camp on my recent Cherry Creek kayak expedition. It was a lot of work to get here and not many humans have seen this spot but I would say that the effort is worth it!

Lush green landscape of Yosemite Valley

2014-04-26T19:58:04-08:00

Speaking Lens posted a photo:

Lush green meadows and trees at the backdrop of Upper Yosemite fall. It was a windy and cloudy day during late spring. Felt like wind was trying to help trees meet waterfall.

My obsession for Yosemite National Park makes me post it's photos again and again.

Review the Flickr application

1. Use your text editor to open the HTML file in this folder:
    `c:\jquery\exercises\ch12\flickr\`

2. Review the URL that's used to retrieve the data from Flickr, and notice that it includes two tags but no id.

3. Run the application to see that it displays the title and photo for each item that's returned. Point to any photo to see that it's not linked to the Flickr website.

Add additional information

4. Replace the last statement in the callback function for the $.each method with a statement that adds the description data item to the html variable. Then, run the application to see that each photo is followed by a link to the author's Flickr page, a duplicate photo, and descriptive text (if there is any).

5. Click on any of the duplicate photos to see that it displays the photo on the Flickr website. Then, close the new tab or web page for the photo.

6. Use figure 12-14 as a guide to display the JSON feed that's returned to the application. Review this information for the first few items, paying particularly close attention to the HTML in the description data item.

7. Replace the statement in the jQuery code that adds an img element for the media.m data item to the html variable with a statement that adds a <p> element for the date_taken data item.

8. Improve the formatting for the data that's displayed. At the least, add some space below the paragraphs. Note, however, that you have no control over how the person who posted the photo entered the descriptive text. For example, the second description above includes several br elements that start new lines within the descriptive text.

13

How to use the API for Google Maps

In the last chapter, you learned how to use the API for Flickr to get content from that site for your own web pages. Now, you'll learn how to use the API for Google Maps so you can add a map to your website and provide driving directions between two points on the map.

Introduction to Google Maps

You've probably used more than one Google map by now, either on the Google Maps website or on another website. If so, you know how easy they are to use. You may have also used Google Maps to get directions from one point to another.

The good news is that you can add Google maps to your own website, either for free or for a small fee. At this writing, for example, Google Maps allows 25,000 free map requests per day before it starts charging a small fee. That means that you can use your website to show your customers your location on a Google map and even provide driving directions from your customers' locations to yours.

Introduction to the Google Maps API

In figure 13-1, you can learn how to get started with the Google Maps API. To start, you can use the documentation to learn about the API. When you display this documentation, you'll see that it is extensive. That of course is because this API provides so many capabilities, but that also makes this API difficult to comprehend and use.

For instance, the screen in this figure shows the start of the Contents for the API Reference. But that Contents scrolls down for many pages, and it's hard to figure out how to get started with it. A better way to get started with this documentation is to use the guides and samples that are available by clicking the Guides and Samples links at the top of the page. Then, you can come back to the reference when you need more specific information.

In this chapter, though, you'll learn how to use this API to develop some of the most useful map applications. If you refer to the API reference as you read this chapter, you'll realize that this chapter has done its best to simplify what you need to know. You'll also realize that this chapter presents just a small fraction of the classes and methods that this API provides. Later, if you want to use Google Maps for other applications, you'll have to dig into this documentation on your own.

If you're going to use the Google Maps API for your own website or a website that you're developing (not for a school project), you should get an API key. This figure directs you to information on the Google website that steps you through the procedure for getting an API key. Once you have a key, you'll be able to monitor your application's usage of this API. This also provides a way for Google to contact you if your application exceeds the maximum number of free requests that Google allows.

The URL for the Google Maps API reference

`developers.google.com/maps/documentation/javascript/reference`

The web page for the start of the API reference

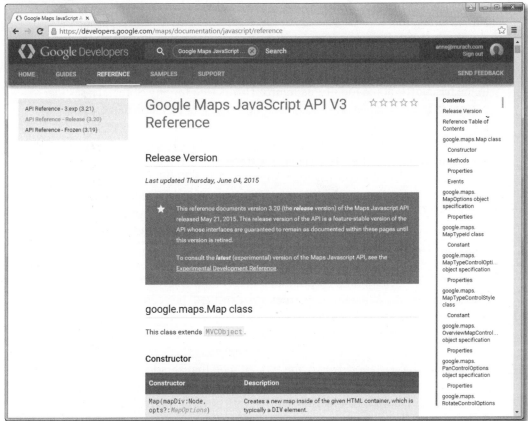

How to get a key for the Google Maps API

- If you're going to publish your website to a web server, you'll want to get an API key for the Google Maps API. This allows both you and Google to monitor your application's usage of the API.

- To get an API key, you can follow the procedure at this URL:
  `developers.google.com/console/help/new/?hl=en_US#api-keys`

- When you go to the Google Developers Console as directed in step 1 of this procedure, you may need to create a Google account or log in before continuing. Also, when you create the key as described in step 5, you want to create a browser key since the application that contains the map will run in a browser.

Description

- The Google Maps API reference documents the many classes provided by this API and is extensive. The documentation also includes useful guides and samples.

- Google Maps allows up to 25,000 free requests per day before charging a small fee.

Figure 13-1   Introduction to the Google Maps API

The classes for adding a Google map to a web page

The Google Maps API consists of *classes* that provide the methods and properties that you need for adding Google maps to your web pages. For instance, the first table in figure 13-2 summarizes three of the classes that you use for adding a map to a web page.

Because the documentation is so extensive for the Google Maps classes, it's sometimes useful to use a URL to go to the documentation for a class. For instance, you can go to the documentation for the LatLng class by adding #LatLng to the base URL at the top of this figure. This is true for any of the classes that are presented in this chapter. Just add the pound sign and the class name to the base URL in the address bar.

To use many of the classes in the Google Maps API, you use a *constructor* to create an *object* from the class. That constructor may require one or more parameters. For instance, the constructor for the Map class in the first table requires two parameters. The first one identifies the DOM object for the HTML element that will receive the map. The second one provides one or more options for the map. When this constructor is executed, it creates a Map object, and the map for that object is displayed in the HTML element of the page.

Similarly, the constructor for the LatLng class requires two parameters. The first one is for the latitude of a point in a map, and the second one is for the longitude of that point. When this constructor is executed, it creates a LatLng object that can be used to mark the center of a map.

The MapTypeId class in the first table is a different type of class that isn't used to create objects. Instead, it provides *constants* that can be used with other classes. These constants identify the type of map that should be displayed.

The second table in this figure summarizes the three required options for the second parameter of the constructor for a Map object. Then, the example that follows shows how the three options and classes are used to add a map to a web page. First, a variable named mapOptions is created that contains three options. The zoom option is set to 8, which is a good starting value for most maps. The center option is set to a LatLng object that's created using the LatLng constructor. And the mapTypeId option is set to the ROADMAP constant in the MapTypeId class.

The next statement uses the constructor for the Map class to create a Map object. The first parameter in this constructor starts with a selector for the HTML element that has its id attribute set to "map". Note, however, that this is followed by a get(0) method. This is a jQuery method that gets the DOM object for that element, which is required by the Map constructor. The second parameter is the mapOptions variable that was created by the first statement.

When the Map constructor is executed, it uses the Google Maps API to create the specified map and display it in the HTML element that's specified by the first parameter. In this example, the map is also stored in a variable named "map", but that isn't necessary unless you need to refer to it later.

Notice that all three of the classes that are used in this example are referred to through the google.maps *namespace*. This namespace contains all of the classes for the Google Maps API, and you'll see it used throughout this chapter. Note too

The base URL for the Google Maps API reference

developers.google.com/maps/documentation/javascript/reference

The placeholders for the classes below

#Map

#MapTypeId

#LatLng

The classes for adding a map to a web page

Class/Constructor	Description
`Map(element, options)`	This constructor creates a Map object. The first parameter specifies the DOM object for the HTML element that receives the map. The second parameter provides options for the map.
`LatLng(latitude, longitude)`	This constructor creates a LatLng object based on its latitude and longitude parameters.
`MapTypeId`	This class provides constants for the four map types: ROADMAP, HYBRID, SATELLITE, and TERRAIN.

The required options for the Map constructor

Option	Setting
`zoom`	A number that provides the initial zoom level.
`center`	A new LatLng object that identifies the center of the map.
`mapTypeId`	A MapTypeId constant that specifies the map type.

How to use the three classes to create a map object

```
var mapOptions = {
    zoom: 8,
    center: new google.maps.LatLng(33.4936111, -117.1475),
    mapTypeId: google.maps.MapTypeId.ROADMAP
};
var map = new google.maps.Map($("#map").get(0), mapOptions);
```

Description

- A *constructor* for a *class* creates a new *object* from that class. For instance, the constructor for the Map class creates a Map object. Then, the methods of the class can be called from the Map object. The new keyword must be used with any constructor.

- The constructor for a Map object can include many options in its second parameter, but only the three in the table above are required.

- For the zoom option, you can experiment with the values until you get the map the way you want it, but a value of 8 is a good place to start your experimentation.

- To provide the value for the center option, the new keyword is used with the LatLng constructor.

- To provide the value for the mapTypeId option, one of the *constants* in the MapTypeId class is used.

- To create a Map object, you use a jQuery selector to identify the HTML element that will receive the map. Then, you use the get(0) method to get the DOM object for that element.

Figure 13-2 The classes for adding a Google map to a web page

that the constructors for both the LatLng and Map classes are preceded by the new keyword. This is required when you use a constructor to create a new object.

The script element for the Google Maps API

Figure 13-3 shows how to use the classes of the previous figure to add a map to a web page. But note first the script element that refers to the Google Maps API. This is required for every application for this chapter, although it isn't shown in the other figures, and it can be coded before or after the one for jQuery because the Google Maps API doesn't use jQuery.

Note that the URL for this API includes a key parameter that you can use to specify your API key. Although it isn't indicated here, you should know that when you include a key, you shouldn't embed it directly in your code. Instead, you should keep it secure by storing it in a file or environment variable outside of your application. For information on getting an API key, see figure 13-1.

How to add a Google map to a web page

Figure 13-3 also shows the HTML for the div element that will receive the map in this example, along with the jQuery for displaying the map in that element. Here, the jQuery code is the same as in the previous figure. First, a variable with the three required map options is created. Then, the Map constructor is used to create the map with those options and display it in the div element. Here again, you don't need to store the Map object in a variable unless you're going to need to refer to that map later on in your code.

In this example, the LatLng constructor for the center option is coded with actual latitude and longitude values, which represent Temecula, California. You can do that if you happen to know the values that you want to use. However, you can also use geocoding to get those values as shown in the next two figures.

Once you add a Google map to a web page, it works just like a map on the Google Maps website. As a result, the user can use the controls to zoom in or out of the map or to move the map up, down, right, or left. The user can also drag the map up, down, right, or left. To reveal different portions of the map based on the user's actions, Google Maps uses Ajax.

A web page that displays a Google map

The script element for the Google Maps API (on one line)

```
<script src="https://maps.googleapis.com/maps/api/js?key=your_api_key
&sensor=false"></script>
```

The HTML for the div element that will receive the map

```
<div id="map"></div>
```

The jQuery

```
$(document).ready(function(){
    var mapOptions = {
        zoom: 8,
        center: new google.maps.LatLng(33.4936111, -117.1475),
        mapTypeId: google.maps.MapTypeId.ROADMAP
    };
    var map = new google.maps.Map($("#map").get(0), mapOptions);
});
```

Description

- To use the Google Maps API for a web page, you must always include a script element like the one above. Although the API key is optional, Google recommends you include it.

- When you use the Map constructor to create a Google map, the map is displayed in the HTML element that is identified by the first parameter of the constructor. To get the DOM object for this element, you use the jQuery get method with a parameter of zero.

- In this example, the LatLng method is used with actual values for the latitude and longitude parameters. Often, though, you'll use geocoding to get those parameter values, as shown in the next two figures.

- When you add a Google map to a web page on your site, the users can use the controls on the map and drag the map horizontally and vertically just as they would with a map at the maps.google.com website.

Figure 13-3   How to add a Google map to a web page

How to display markers on a map

In the topics that follow, you'll learn how to add markers to a map. As part of that, you'll learn how to use geocoding to get the latitude and longitude for an address.

The classes and methods for geocoding and markers

Figure 13-4 presents the classes and methods that you need for geocoding and for adding a marker to a map. *Geocoding* refers to the conversion of an address into a location that consists of the latitude and longitude for the location, and vice versa. That's what the Geocoder class and its geocode method do.

As the second table in this figure shows, the geocode method has two parameters. The first one is for the request, which is a GeocoderRequest object. This object can have several properties, including the two properties in the third table in this figure. If the conversion is from an address to a location, the address property should be used. If the conversion is from a location to an address, the location property should be used.

The second parameter of the geocode method is a callback function that receives the results of the request in the form of a GeocoderResult object. This object contains several properties including those in the fourth table in this figure.

This method is illustrated by the first example in this figure. Here, the first parameter is a request object that consists of an address (4340 N Knoll, Fresno, CA), so the conversion will be to a LatLng object for the location of that address. Note here that you don't use a constructor to create the GeocoderRequest object. Instead, you use an *object literal* like the one shown here that specifies the address or location.

The second parameter of the geocode method is a callback function that receives the result object as its parameter. In this case, that parameter is referred to as results.

The alert statement within the callback function shows how to get the location from the result object. To get the formatted_address property of the object, this code is used:

```
results[0].formatted_address
```

Here, the index refers to the first item in the object, which can be an array. Then, to get the location property of the object, this code is used:

```
results[0].geometry.location
```

Note that both properties are available in the result object, even though the address was part of the request. Note too that the lat method is used to get the latitude of the location, and that the lng method could be used to get its longitude.

The next example in this figure shows how to use the constructor for the Marker class. Although this constructor can be coded with many options, only the position and map options are required. Here, the position option is coded as a new LatLng object, and the map option is coded with the name of the variable that the map is stored in. When this constructor is executed, the marker is added to the map.

The classes for geocoding and markers

Class constructor	Description
`Geocoder()`	This constructor creates a Geocoder object that provides methods that communicate with Google servers and return geocodes.
`Marker(options)`	This constructor creates a Marker object that marks a position on a map. Two of the commonly-used options are position, which gives the location of the marker as a LatLng object, and map, which identifies the map for the marker.

One of the methods of the Geocoder class

Method	Description
`geocode(request, callback)`	Sends a GeocoderRequest object to Google servers that contains an address or a location and returns a GeocoderResult object that contains the results in an array.

Two of the properties of the GeocoderRequest object

Property	Description
`address`	The address of the request as a string.
`location`	The location of the request as a LatLng object.

Three of the properties of the GeocoderResult object

Property	Description
`address_components`	The components of the address. From this property, you can use long_name and short_name to get those properties.
`formatted_address`	The formatted address as a string.
`geometry.location`	The location of the request as a LatLng object. From this property, you can use the lat() and lng() methods to get the latitude and longitude of the location.

How to use the geocode method

```
var geocoder = new google.maps.Geocoder();
geocoder.geocode({address: "4340 N Knoll, Fresno, CA"}, function(results) {
    alert("Latitude for " + results[0].formatted_address + " is " +
        results[0].geometry.location.lat());
});
```

How to create a Marker object

```
var marker = new google.maps.Marker({
    position: new google.maps.LatLng(36.799793, -119.858135),
    map: map});         // assuming the Map object is in a variable named map
```

Description

- *Geocoding* refers to the conversion of addresses into locations, and vice versa. This conversion is done by the geocode method of the Geocoder class.
- To add a marker to a map, you create a Marker object.

Figure 13-4   The classes and methods for geocoding and markers

How to create an address list that displays markers

Figure 13-5 shows how to use the constructors and methods that you just learned about to add a marker to a web page. Here, a marker is added when a user clicks on one of the city links in the right sidebar. In fact, this application will add a marker for each link that's clicked, which is how three markers are shown on the map.

The HTML for this map consists of a div element for the map and a ul element for the city links. A style sheet is used to float both of these elements so they appear as shown.

In the jQuery for this application, you can see that the first statement in the ready event handler creates a Geocoder object named geocoder. This is followed by the statements that create the map. These are the same statements that you saw in figure 13-3.

Then, the Geocoder object is used by the click event method that creates event handlers for each of the links. Within the function for this method, the first statement uses the this keyword and the text method to get the address from a link and store it in a variable named "address". This is typical jQuery code that you learned in section 2.

Next, the geocode method of the Geocoder object is used to get the location of the address for the link and return the results in its callback function. Then, within that callback function, a Marker object is created using the location that's returned by the geocode method for the position option and the map that has been created for the map option. Later, when the user clicks on a city link and the Marker object is created, it is added to the map.

A marker is added to the map when the user clicks on an address link

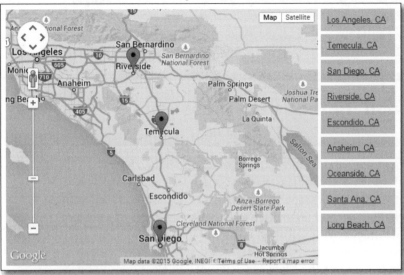

The HTML for the map and links

```
<div id="map"></div>
<ul id="links">
    <li><a href="#">Los Angeles, CA</a></li>
    <li><a href="#">Temecula, CA</a></li>
    <!-- the li elements for other cities -->
</ul>
```

The jQuery

```
$(document).ready(function(){
    var geocoder = new google.maps.Geocoder();
    var myLatLng = new google.maps.LatLng(33.4936111, -117.1475);
    var mapOptions = {zoom: 8, center: myLatLng,
                    mapTypeId: google.maps.MapTypeId.ROADMAP};
    var map = new google.maps.Map($("#map").get(0), mapOptions);

    $("#links a").click(function() {
        var address = $(this).text();   // gets address from <a> element
        geocoder.geocode({address: address}, function(results) {
            new google.maps.Marker({
                position: results[0].geometry.location,
                map: map
            });
        });
    });
});
```

Description

- In the click event handler for the address links, the geocode method converts the address to a location and passes a result object to its callback function.

- Within the callback function, the Marker constructor uses the results object to get the position for the marker. When the Marker object is created, it is added to the map.

Figure 13-5   How to create an address list that displays markers on a map

How to display messages on a map

Now, you'll learn how to display messages for the markers on a map. To do that, you're going to learn how to use three more classes and several new methods.

The classes and methods for messages and markers

Figure 13-6 presents three more classes, several methods for those classes, and two methods of the Marker class. In brief, the InfoWindow class provides methods that let you add a message to a marker. The OverlayView class provides three methods that let you add an overlay to a map in the form of a custom message. And the MapCanvasProjection class provides a method that lets you position a custom message.

You might note here that the MapCanvasProjection class doesn't have a constructor. Instead, a MapCanvasProjection object is created by the getProjection method of the OverlayView class. This is another way that objects can be created from a class.

The last table in this figure presents two of the methods of the Marker class that was introduced in the last two figures. The getPosition method gets the latitude and longitude coordinates of a marker that's on a map, which can be used to position a message. The setMap method puts a marker on a map, or, if its parameter is set to null, it removes the marker from the map.

You'll see all of these classes and methods illustrated in the three figures that follow. As you study the applications for these figures, you can refer back to the tables in this figure.

The classes for adding messages to markers

Class/Constructor	Description
InfoWindow(*options*)	This constructor creates an object that works as a message balloon for a marker. Its content option provides the content for the balloon, and the content can be coded with plain text or HTML.
OverlayView()	This constructor creates an object that can be used to overlay objects on the map.
MapCanvasProjection	An object is created from this class when the getProjection method of an OverlayView object is called.

One method of the InfoWindow class

Method	Description
open(*map, marker*)	Opens the message balloon for the map and marker.

Three methods of the OverlayView class

Method	Description
draw()	Draws or updates the overlay.
setMap(*map*)	Adds the overlay to the map.
getProjection()	Returns a MapCanvasProjection object for the overlay.

One method of the MapCanvasProjection class

Method	Description
fromLatLngToContainerPixel(*markerPosition*)	Returns the pixel coordinates for a marker's position.

Two methods of the Marker class

Method	Description
getPosition()	Gets the latitude and longitude coordinates of the marker.
setMap(*map*)	Renders the marker on the specified map. If the parameter is null, it removes the marker from the map.

Description

- You'll see these classes and methods in action in the three figures that follow.

Figure 13-6   The classes and methods for messages and markers

How to add messages to markers

Figure 13-7 shows how to add a message to a marker by using the InfoWindow class. Here again, a marker is added to the map when the user clicks on a city link. But this time, a message is also added. Also, when one marker is added to the map, the previous one is removed.

In the jQuery code for this application, the first statement in the ready event handler declares a variable named marker. That way, it will be available when the click event method is executed. Then, the next four statements create the Geocoder object and the map, just as in figure 13-5.

In the click event handler, the first statement is the same as before, but the second statement tests to see whether the variable named marker contains a value. If it does, the setMap method for the marker is set to null, which removes the marker from the map. The first time the if statement is executed, of course, the marker will be null, so the setMap method won't be executed.

Next, in the callback function for the geocode method, the marker is created just as in figure 13-5. This is followed by a statement that creates an InfoWindow object that specifies the content for this object. Note here that this content can include HTML elements. The last statement in this function uses the open method of the InfoWindow object to specify that the window (or message balloon) should be opened for the map and marker that's specified by the parameters.

A marker and message are added when the user clicks on a link

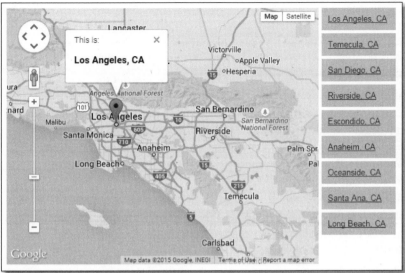

The jQuery

```
$(document).ready(function(){
    var marker;
    var geocoder = new google.maps.Geocoder();
    var myLatLng = new google.maps.LatLng(33.4936111, -117.1475);
    var mapOptions = {zoom: 8, center: myLatLng,
        mapTypeId: google.maps.MapTypeId.ROADMAP};
    var map = new google.maps.Map($("#map").get(0), mapOptions);

    $("#links a").click(function() {
        var address = $(this).text();    // gets address from <a> element
        if (marker) { marker.setMap(null); }    // deletes current marker
        geocoder.geocode({address: address}, function(results) {
            marker = new google.maps.Marker({
                position: results[0].geometry.location,
                map: map
            });
            // adds message balloon
            var infoWindow = new google.maps.InfoWindow({
                content: "This is: <h3>" + address + "</h3>"}
            );
            infoWindow.open(map, marker);
        });
    });
});
```

Description

- As in figure 13-5, this application adds a marker to the map when the user clicks on an address link. This time, though, an InfoWindow object is used to add a message at the location of the marker, and only one marker can be displayed at a time.

- The HTML for this application is the same as in figure 13-5.

Figure 13-7   How to add messages to markers

How to add custom messages to markers

Figure 13-8 shows how to add custom messages to markers by using the OverlayView and MapCanvasProjection classes and another of the Marker methods. Here, the message balloon is actually an HTML div element with its id attribute set to "message". This div element is styled by a separate style sheet. The style attribute is included in the code that's shown here, though, so you can see that the display property is set to none when the page is first displayed.

In the jQuery code, the first five statements are the same as in the previous figure. The start of the click event handler for the address links is also the same as in the previous figure. But after the marker is set in the function for the geocode method, the code changes.

Still in the function for the geocode method, an OverlayView object is created. Then, its draw method is executed, and the function for this method starts by creating a point variable that is going to contain the location of the marker for the link in pixels. This variable will be used later on to position the custom message.

To get the location of this point, the getProjection method of the OverlayView object creates a MapCanvasProjection object for the overlay. Then, the fromLatLngToContainerPixel method of the MapCanvasProjection object is used to get the location of the marker in pixels. The parameter for this method is the position for the marker, which is returned by the getPosition method of the marker for the link. (You may be wondering who dreams this stuff up, but that's the way you get the location value that you want.)

Once that value is calculated, the rest is easy. Still in the function for the draw method of the overlay object, the html method is used to add the contents of the message to the HTML div element with "message" as its id. Then, the show method is used to show this div element, and the css method that's chained to the show method places the message near the marker by setting its top and left properties relative to the value in the point variable, which represents the y and x coordinates in pixels.

At this point, though, the message hasn't been displayed in the web page. To do that, the last statement in the function for the geocode method issues the setMap method for the overlay object. Then, the message is displayed over the map that's specified by the parameter.

In this example, the content for the message balloon contains some HTML, including an <a> element that links to the Google Maps website. This URL includes a daddr parameter for the address of the marker. This is simply intended to show that you can get creative with the content for a message balloon.

A web page that displays a custom message for a marker

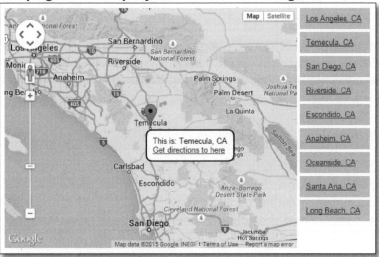

The HTML for the message balloon

```
<div id="message" style="display:none;"></div>
```

The jQuery

```
$(document).ready(function(){
    // same first five statements as in the previous figure
    $("#links a").click(function() {
        var address = $(this).text();
        if (marker) { marker.setMap(null); }
        geocoder.geocode({address: address}, function(results) {
            marker = new google.maps.Marker({
                position: results[0].geometry.location, map: map
            });
            var overlay = new google.maps.OverlayView();
            overlay.draw = function() {
                var point =
                    overlay.getProjection().fromLatLngToContainerPixel(
                        marker.getPosition());
                $("#message").html(
                    "This is: " + address +
                    "<br><a href=http://maps.google.com/maps?daddr=" +
                    address + ">Get directions to here</a>");
                $("#message").show().css({
                    top: point.y + 10,
                    left: point.x
                });
            };
            overlay.setMap(map);
        });
    });
});
```

Description

- After OverlayView and Marker methods get the position of the marker in pixels, the html and css methods create and position the HTML, which is styled by a style sheet.

Figure 13-8   How to add custom messages to markers

How to add Flickr images to messages

Figure 13-9 shows how a message balloon for a marker can be enhanced by an image that's retrieved from the Flickr website. This combines skills that you learned in the last chapter with the skills you're learning now. The application in this figure is like the one in the last figure except that it displays a Flickr image in the message balloon for a city.

The jQuery code for this application is just like the code for the application in the previous figure until you get to the comment in the middle of the click event handler. After that, the first statement creates a URL for Flickr that uses the address of a link to get a related photo. Then, the second statement uses the $.getJSON method and the $.each method to get the image for the address and store it in the HTML div element for the message.

This is followed by the chained show and css methods that are like the ones in the previous figure. Here again, the function for the geocode method ends by issuing the setMap method of the overlay object to display the message.

A web page that displays a Flickr image for the location

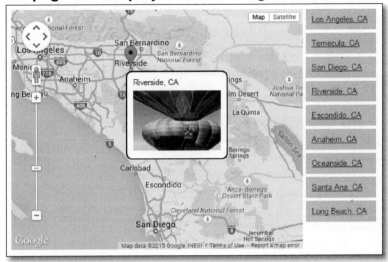

The code for setting up the click event handlers for the links

```
$("#links a").click(function() {
    var address = $(this).text();
    if (marker) { marker.setMap(null); }
    geocoder.geocode({address: address}, function(results) {
        marker = new google.maps.Marker({
            position: results[0].geometry.location, map: map
        });
        var overlay = new google.maps.OverlayView();
        overlay.draw = function() {
            var point =
                overlay.getProjection().fromLatLngToContainerPixel(
                    marker.getPosition());
            // the changed code for this application follows
            var url =
                // the url that follows has to be coded in a single line
                "http://api.flickr.com/services/feeds/photos_public.gne?
                format=json&jsoncallback=?&tags=" + address;
            $.getJSON(url, function(data) {
                $.each(data.items, function(i, item){
                    $("#message").html(address + "<br><img src=" +
                        item.media.m + " width=150 height=100>");
                });
            });
            $("#message").show().css({
                top: point.y + 10, left: point.x
            });
        };
        overlay.setMap(map);
    });
});
```

Description

- This is like the application in the previous figure except that it gets an image from Flickr using Ajax and JSON and then puts the image in the HTML for the message.

Figure 13-9   How to add Flickr images to messages

How to display driving directions on a web page

If you use a Google Map to show your users the location of your company, you may also want to provide driving directions to that location. In the next two figures, you'll learn how to do that.

The classes and methods for directions and listeners

The first three tables in figure 13-10 summarize the classes and methods that you need for providing driving directions. In brief, you use the DirectionsService class and one of its methods to get the directions. Then, you use the DirectionsRenderer class and three of its methods to display the directions.

The first example in this figure shows how to use these classes and methods. This assumes that the DirectionsService and DirectionsRenderer objects have already been created. Then, a variable is set up for the three required properties of a request. Like the GeocoderRequest object that's used with the geocode method that you saw earlier in this chapter, this variable is for an object literal that defines a DirectionsRequest object. Here, the origin property of this object is set to the position of a marker, the destination property is set to the position of another marker, and the travelMode property is set to the DRIVING constant of the TravelMode class.

This is followed by a statement that uses the route method of a DirectionsService object to get the directions. In the callback function for this method, the setDirections method of the DirectionsRenderer object is used to display the results. The parameter for this method is the result object that's returned by the request.

The last table in this figure summarizes three methods of the event namespace that you can use to provide event handlers for the events of the Google Maps API classes. In the terminology of this API and many programming languages, a *listener* listens for an event and directs it to the event handler for that event. When you use the listener methods, you don't have to first create an object because the event namespace is always available to a Google Maps application.

To add a listener to an application, you use the addListener method, which has three parameters: the object for the event, the event, and the event handler. This is illustrated by the example after this table. Here, the addListener method is used to listen for the click event of a marker. When that event occurs, an event object is passed to the event handler, which is then executed. One of the properties of this event object, the latLng property, can be used to get the location of the click on the map.

Once you create a listener, you can use the trigger method to trigger its event. Also, if you save the listener for an event handler in a variable, you can use the removeListener method to remove it later on. You'll see this illustrated in the application in the next figure.

The classes for retrieving and displaying driving directions

Class/Constructor	Description
`DirectionsService()`	This constructor creates an object that can be used to retrieve driving directions from the Google server.
`DirectionsRenderer()`	This constructor creates an object that can be used to render driving directions.
`TravelMode`	This class provides contants for four travel modes: DRIVING, BICYCLING, TRANSIT, and WALKING.

One method of the DirectionsService class

Method	Description
`route(request, callback)`	Issues a directions request. Its first parameter is a DirectionsRequest object that has three required properties: origin (starting location), destination, and travel mode. This method returns a DirectionsResult object and a DirectionsStatus object.

Three methods of the DirectionsRenderer class

Method	Description
`setMap(map)`	Specifies the map for which directions will be rendered.
`setPanel(panel)`	Specifies the HTML div element that will receive the directions.
`setDirections(result)`	Renders the result of a directions request in a div element.

A typical directions request

```
var request = {
    origin: marker1.getPosition(),
    destination: marker2.getPosition(),
    travelMode: google.maps.TravelMode.DRIVING
};
directionsService.route(request, function(result, status) {
    directionsRenderer.setDirections(result);
});
```

Three methods of the event namespace for using event handlers

Method	Description
`addListener(object, event, handler)`	Registers an event handler for an object and event. It returns an event object that has properties related to the event.
`removeListener(listener)`	Removes the specified listener.
`trigger(object, event)`	Fires the specified event for the specified object.

How to use the addListener method to register an event handler

```
google.maps.event.addListener(marker, "click", function(event) {
    // code for the event handler
});
```

Figure 13-10   The classes and methods for directions and listeners

How to display driving directions with a map

Figure 13-11 presents an application that provides driving directions on a web page. Here, the directions are displayed to the right of the map after the user clicks on two points in the map, and the positioning of the map and the directions is done by a style sheet.

To start, the ready event for this application creates a new DirectionsService object and stores it in a variable named directionsService. Then, because this application works with two different markers, it declares an array named markers that will be used to store the markers. Finally, after the map is added to the web page, a listener is created for the click event of the map.

To create the listener, the first parameter of the addListener method is set to the variable named "map", which contains the Map object. The second parameter is set to "click", which is the event that will be listened for. Then, in the function (event handler) for this listener, a new marker is created when the user clicks on the map. This function uses the latLng property of the event object that's passed to the event handler to set the position for the marker. After that, the marker is added to the end of the array.

Next, an if statement tests whether the number of markers in the array is greater than one. If it is, the user has already clicked on two points in the map so two markers have been created. Then, the statements for the if clause are executed. Otherwise, nothing else is done by the event handler.

If the statements in the if clause are executed, the first statement removes the listener. That way, the user can't add a third marker to the map. This is followed by a statement that creates a new DirectionsRenderer object and stores it in a variable named directionsRenderer. Then, the setMap method of this object sets its map to the map that has been created, and the setPanel method sets its display panel to the div element with "directions" as its id attribute. Note here that the get(0) method has to be chained to the selector so the setPanel method receives the DOM object for the div element.

The next statement creates a variable named "request" that will be used as the request object in the statement that follows. Its origin property is set to the position of the first marker. Its destination property is set to the position of the second marker. And its travelMode property is set to the DRIVING constant of the TravelMode class. To get the positions for the two markers, the getPosition method of the Marker objects is used.

At this point, both the DirectionsService and DirectionsRenderer objects are ready to get the directions and display them. Then, the last statement in the if clause of the listener calls the route method of the DirectionsService object with the request variable as its first parameter. This method also returns the result and status and passes them to its callback function.

Within the callback function, the if statement checks the status object to see if the request was successful. This uses yet another class named DirectionsStatus with the OK constant. If it is successful, the setDirections method of the DirectionsRenderer object displays the result in the "directions" div element.

A web page that displays the driving directions between two points

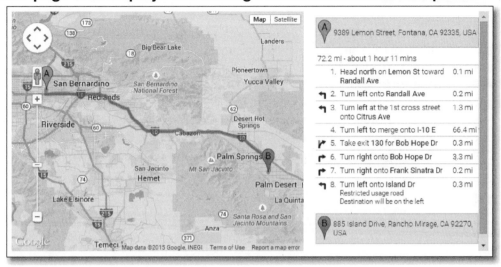

The HTML for the map and the directions panel

```
<div id="map"></div>
<div id="directions"></div>
```

The jQuery

```
$(document).ready(function(){
    var directionsService = new google.maps.DirectionsService();
    var markers = [];
    var myLatLng = new google.maps.LatLng(33.4936111, -117.1475);
    var mapOptions = {zoom: 8, center: myLatLng, mapTypeId:
        google.maps.MapTypeId.ROADMAP};
    var map = new google.maps.Map($("#map").get(0), mapOptions);

    var listener =
            google.maps.event.addListener(map, "click", function(event) {
        var marker =
            new google.maps.Marker({position: event.latLng, map: map});
        markers[markers.length] = marker;
        if (markers.length > 1) {
            google.maps.event.removeListener(listener);
            var directionsRenderer = new google.maps.DirectionsRenderer();
            directionsRenderer.setMap(map);
            directionsRenderer.setPanel($("#directions").get(0));
            var request = { origin: markers[0].getPosition(),
                destination: markers[1].getPosition(),
                travelMode: google.maps.TravelMode.DRIVING };
            directionsService.route(request, function(result, status) {
                if (status == google.maps.DirectionsStatus.OK) {
                    directionsRenderer.setDirections(result); }
            });
        }
    });
});
```

Figure 13-11   How to display driving directions with a map

Perspective

If you've been referring to the documentation for the Google Maps API as you've read this chapter, you know that the documentation is both extensive and complicated. That's why the goal of this chapter has been to get you started with some of the basic classes and methods and some of the common map applications.

With this start, we hope you'll be able to develop variations of the chapter applications on your own. We also hope you'll be able to explore the Maps documentation and figure out how to develop other types of map applications.

Terms

constructor	namespace
class	geocoding
object	object literal
constant	listener

Summary

- The Google Maps API consists primarily of *classes* that provide *constructors* that are used to create *objects* from the classes. Then, the objects can be used to call the methods for developing map applications.

- Some of the classes in the Google Maps API aren't used to create objects. Instead, they provide *constants* that can be used to provide values.

- All of the classes of the Google Maps API are stored in the google.maps *namespace* and must be referred to through that namespace.

- When you use the constructor for a Map object, you must provide zoom, center, and mapTypeId options. You must also provide the DOM object that represents the div element that the map should be displayed in. When the Map object is created, it is automatically displayed in the div element.

- *Geocoding* refers to the process of converting an address to a location, or vice versa. To do that, you use a Geocoder object and its geocode method.

- Some objects that are used only as method parameters, such as the GeocoderRequest and DirectionsRequest objects, are coded as object literals. An *object literal* simply specifies the properties for the object.

- When you use the constructor of the Marker class to create a marker object, you must provide the position of the marker and the name of the map. Then, when the Marker object is created, a marker is automatically added to the map.

- To provide message balloons for the markers on a map, you can use the objects and methods of the InfoWindow, OverlayView, MapCanvasProjection, and Marker classes.

- A *listener* is used to listen for a specific event on a specific object and run an event handler when that event occurs.

- To display the directions between two points on a map, you can use the objects and methods of the DirectionsService and DirectionsRenderer classes.

Exercise 13-1   Enhance a map application

In this exercise, you'll review some of the Google Maps documentation, and you'll enhance a map application so it shows your home town with a marker and a custom message, and then provides directions from your home town to any spot that's clicked on the map.

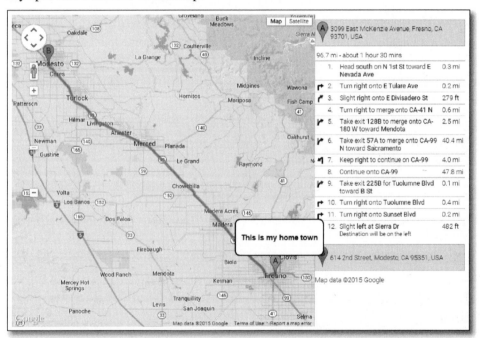

Review the Google Map application and the Google Maps API

1. Use your text editor to open the HTML file in this folder:

   `c:\jquery\exercises\ch13\map\`

   Then, run this application to see that all it does is display a map.

2. Go to the start of the documentation for the Google Maps API by using this URL:

   `developers.google.com/maps/documentation/javascript/reference`

   This presents a list of the many classes that you can click on to review the documentation for a class.

3. Try drilling down into the links for the Map class. To start, click the google.maps.Map link in the Contents list. Note in the constructor for this class that the second parameter has a link to MapOptions. Next, click on that link to see the properties for that parameter, including the required zoom, center, and mapTypeId properties. Then, click on the LatLng link for the center property to see the methods that you can use with a LatLng object. This should give you some idea of how difficult it can be to work with this API.

Enhance the map

4. At the start of the ready method for the map application, use geocoding to get the location of your home town. Then, make the enhancements that follow by placing the code within the callback function for the geocode method.

5. To start, store the location that's returned by the request in a variable named myLatLng. Then, move the code that displays the map so it's executed within the callback function for the geocode method, and change the center option of the map to the myLatLng variable. When you test this change, your home town should be the center of the map that's displayed.

6. Using figure 13-5 as a guide, add a marker for your home town to the map.

7. Using figure 13-8 as a guide, add a custom message above the marker that says: "This is my home town!" This message should be placed within an h3 element. When the message is displayed, the style sheet that's provided for this application will format the message appropriately.

Provide directions for getting to another location

8. Using figure 13-11 as a guide and still coding in the callback function for the geocode method, code a listener that adds a marker to the map when the user clicks on the map. Then, remove the listener.

9. Again using figure 13-11 as a guide, display directions that show how to get from your home town to the point where the user clicked. The style sheet that's provided for this application will display the directions to the right of the map.

If you have the time, do more experimentation. That's the best way to learn.

14

How to use the HTML5 APIs

In this chapter, you'll learn about some of the new APIs that were introduced with HTML5. These APIs provide for a wide variety of functions, and you can start using some of them right away. You'll learn how to use three of the most popular APIs in this chapter: Geolocation, Web Storage, and Web Workers. Once you learn how to use these APIs, you'll have a better idea of how to use the other HTML APIs.

An introduction to the HTML5 APIs

Before you learn the skills for working with any of the APIs, you'll want to have an idea of what some of these APIs can do. You'll also want to know how to get more information about these APIs. That's what you'll learn in the two topics that follow.

Common HTML5 APIs

The table in figure 14-1 summarizes some of the HTML5 APIs that are supported by all modern browsers. Although not all of these APIs have been approved by the World Wide Web Consortium (W3C), they have been thoroughly tested and are ready for use. Other APIs that are only supported on a limited number of browsers are also available. Still others are either in the proposal stage or are waiting for further testing.

In this chapter, you'll learn how to use three of the HTML5 APIs that you interact with using JavaScript. To start, you'll learn how to use the Geolocation API to get information about a user's position. Then, you'll learn how to use the Web Storage API to store data between page requests and even between browser sessions. Finally, you'll learn how to use the Web Workers API to run processes in the background while other processes are running in the foreground. To learn more about these or any of the APIs listed in this figure, you can refer to the websites listed in the next figure.

Some of the HTML5 APIs that are supported by all modern browsers

API	Description
Canvas	Provides for creating graphs, game graphics, art, and other types of visual imagery.
classList	Provides for retrieving and applying CSS classes to elements on a web page.
Constraint	Provides for natively validating forms and form objects within the browser without the need for JavaScript code.
Drag and Drop	Provides for dragging elements on a web page and dropping them into a predefined target area within the same web page.
Geolocation	Allows the browser to determine the latitude, longitude, altitude, heading, and more of the user browsing a geolocation-enabled site.
Page Visibility	Provides for detecting whether a page is the active tab or window so the application can react accordingly.
Server-Sent Events	Similar to the WebSocket API but limited to one-way communication from the server to the client.
Web Storage	Replaces cookies as a simple method for persisting data between page requests.
Web Notifications	Provides for an application displaying notifications to the user that appear outside of the browser window. Icons, text, links, and more can be added to the notifications.
Web Workers	Provides for multi-threaded execution within a JavaScript application. The main thread runs in the foreground while other threads run in the background.
WebGL	Provides for creating interactive 2D and 3D graphics within a web browser without the need for plugins.
WebSocket	Provides for two-way communication between client-side and server-side applications. Useful for web-based chat applications, real-time, turn-based games, social media applications that inform users of updates to their feed, and more.
Vibration	Consists of a single method that sends a request to the user's device (smartphone, tablet, etc.) to initiate a vibration.

Description

- HTML5 includes a number of APIs that perform a wide range of functions. You interact with most of these APIs using JavaScript.
- The APIs listed above are some of the ones that are supported by all modern browsers, even though they may not have been approved by the W3C (World Wide Web Consortium).
- Other APIs are either in the proposal stage, are waiting for further testing, or are only supported on a limited number of browsers.

Figure 14-1   Common HTML5 APIs

How to get information about an HTML5 API

Figure 14-2 provides some useful sources of information on the HTML5 APIs. The platform.html5.org website, for example, lists all of the HTML5 APIs by category. It also provides a direct link to the specification for each API on its respective website. It indicates whether an API is ready for use or should be used with caution. And it indicates what browsers support the API. At the least, you can use this site to decide whether to use an API.

One website that has particularly good information about how to use the APIs is the Mozilla Developer Network. At the top of this figure, for example, you can see the beginning of the documentation for the Geolocation API that's available on this site. This documentation is well-organized, easy to read, and provides helpful examples.

Another way to find information about an API is to search the Internet. When I searched for "geolocation api", for example, the list included the web page that's shown here. This is often easier than drilling down through the sites listed in this figure to find the information you need.

Documentation for the Geolocation API on the Mozilla Developer Network

Using geolocation

The **geolocation API** allows the user to provide their location to web applications if they so desire. For privacy reasons, the user is asked for permission to report location information.

The geolocation object

The geolocation API is published through the `navigator.geolocation` object.

If the object exists, geolocation services are available. You can test for the presence of geolocation thusly:

```
1 if ("geolocation" in navigator) {
2   /* geolocation is available */
3 } else {
4   /* geolocation IS NOT available */
5 }
```

Note: On Firefox 24 and older versions, `"geolocation" in navigator` always returned `true` even if the API was disabled. This has been fixed with Firefox 25 to comply with the spec. (⊜ bug 884921).

Getting the current position

To obtain the user's current location, you can call the `getCurrentPosition()` method. This initiates an asynchronous request to detect the user's position, and queries the positioning hardware to get up-to-date information. When the position is determined, the defined callback function is executed. You can optionally provide a second callback function to be executed if an error occurs. A third, optional, parameter is an options object where you can set the maximum age of the position returned, the time to wait for a request, and if you want high accuracy for the position.

Sources of information about the HTML5 APIs

Source	URL
The Web Platform	platform.html5.org
WHATWG	whatwg.org
Mozilla Developer Network	developer.mozilla.org/en-US/docs/Web/Guide/HTML/HTML5
W3C	www.w3.org/TR/html5 or dev.w3.org/html5/spec
HTML5 Demos and Examples	html5demos.com
w3schools	www.w3schools.com/html

Description

- You can find documentation for the HTML5 APIs at any of the sources listed above.
- You can also find information on a specific API by searching the Internet for that API.

Figure 14-2   How to get information about an HTML5 API

How to use the Geolocation API

One of the most exciting new HTML5 features is the Geolocation feature. This feature lets you get the global position associated with a browser or mobile device. You do that by using the new *Geolocation API*.

How Geolocation works

Figure 14-3 shows how Geolocation works. Here, you can see the HTML for a button that when clicked will display the user's latitude and longitude as well as the accuracy of those coordinates in a dialog box. To make this work, an event handler is attached to the click event of the button.

The code within the event handler calls the getCurrentPosition method of the navigator.geolocation object that provides access to the API. At that point, most browsers will display a dialog box that asks whether the user wants to allow the use of this feature. This is provided for security reasons, and execution will continue only if the user gives permission.

If the user gives permission, the getCurrentPosition method is executed and the position object that it returns is passed to the method's callback function. Within that function, the coords property of the position object can be used to get an object with the properties that are listed in the table in this figure. In this example, three of these properties are displayed in the dialog box: latitude, longitude, and accuracy.

The position that is returned by the getCurrentPosition method is based on network signals such as IP addresses, cell phone IDs, cell tower triangulation, and the GPS coordinates for devices that have GPS capabilities. As a result, the position that's derived is an approximation, not an accurate set of coordinates. For instance, the accuracy property in the first dialog box in this figure shows that the position could be off by as much as 4,156 meters.

For a device that has a GPS capability, though, the result should be much more accurate. For instance, the second dialog box in this figure was displayed by an iPhone. Its accuracy property shows that coordinates for the position are within 65 meters of the actual location.

In most cases, you'll use just the latitude, longitude, and accuracy properties as shown here. That's because few devices today include altimeters, so the altitude and altitudeAccuracy properties usually return null. Similarly, since the heading and speed properties imply the use of multiple readings and GPS data, these properties usually return null as well.

Properties of the coordinates object that defines a location

Property	Description
latitude	The latitude in decimal degrees.
longitude	The longitude in decimal degrees.
accuracy	The accuracy level in meters for the latitude and longitude coordinates.
altitude	The height of the position in meters above the mean sea level.
altitudeAccuracy	The accuracy level in meters for the altitude position.
heading	The direction of travel in degrees from true north.
speed	The current ground speed in meters per second.

The HTML for the button that initiates the Geolocation functionality

```
<button>Get Location</button>
```

jQuery code that uses the Geolocation API

```
$(document).ready(function () {
    $("button").click(function (event) {
        navigator.geolocation.getCurrentPosition(function (position) {
            alert("Latitude: " + position.coords.latitude + "\n" +
            "Longitude: " + position.coords.longitude + "\n" +
            "Accuracy: " + position.coords.accuracy);
        });
    });
});
```

Dialog boxes that give the location for a computer and an iPhone

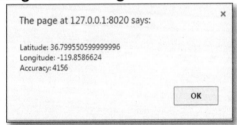

Description

- The Geolocation API lets you get the global position associated with a browser or mobile device. This API is supported by all modern desktop and mobile browsers.

- When the getCurrentPosition method is called, most browsers display a dialog box (not shown) that lets the user decide whether or not to allow the use of this feature.

- The position object that's returned by the getCurrentPosition method is passed to the method's callback function. Then, you can use the coords property to get a coordinates object, and you can use the properties of that object to display position information.

- The latitude, longitude, and accuracy values are based on network signals such as IP addresses, cell phone IDs, cell tower triangulation, and GPS coordinates.

- Since few devices today have altimeters, the altitude and altitudeAccuracy properties usually return null. Also, since the heading and speed properties imply the use of multiple readings and GPS data, these properties usually return null.

Figure 14-3   How Geolocation works

How to show a user's position on a Google map

Figure 14-4 shows how to use the Geolocation API and the Google Maps API to display the user's position on a Google map. Here again, the getCurrentPosition method of the navigator.geolocation object is called and the resulting position object is passed to the callback function.

This time, though, the callback function builds a URL that starts by referring to the Google Maps API. This URL includes several parameters including the position coordinates twice. The first time, the coordinates are used to get the map for the current position. The second time, the coordinates are used to place a red marker at the current position.

After this URL value has been stored in the variable named "url", jQuery is used to set the src attribute for the img element in the HTML to the value in the url variable. This means that the map that is retrieved will be stored in that img element.

Here again, the map will reflect the accuracy or inaccuracy of the getCurrentPosition method. If you're using a device without GPS, your location on the map may be several miles from where you are. But if you're using a device with GPS, your location on the map should be close to where you are.

A web page with a Google Map that shows the user's location

The HTML for the element that receives the map

```
<img src="">
```

The jQuery that shows the user's location on a Google map

```
$(document).ready(function () {
    navigator.geolocation.getCurrentPosition(function (position) {
        var url =
            "http://maps.google.com/maps/api/staticmap?sensor=false" +
            "&center=" + position.coords.latitude + "," +
            position.coords.longitude +
            "&zoom=14&size=300x400&markers=color:red|" +
            position.coords.latitude + "," +
            position.coords.longitude;

        $("img").attr("src", url);
    });
});
```

Description

- The callback function for the getCurrentPosition method constructs a
  Google-proprietary URL that centers the map and adds a marker using the latitude
  and longitude coordinates.

- After the URL is constructed, it's assigned to the src attribute of an img element.
  This gets the map and displays it in that element.

Figure 14-4   How to show a user's position on a Google map

How to handle Geolocation errors

When you use the Geolocation feature, several types of errors can occur. If the user won't allow the page to get the browser's location, that's one type of error. If the Geolocation service in the browser can't get the user's position or if the browser doesn't support the service, that's another type of error. If the service times out before it gets the user's position, that's a third type. Beyond that, other types of errors can occur like too much network traffic interfering with the service.

When an error occurs, you usually want to display an appropriate message or handle it in some other user-friendly way. To do that, you can use a JavaScript function like the one in figure 14-5.

To provide for error handling, the getCurrentPosition method requires two parameters. The first parameter is a function that is called if there aren't any errors. In this figure, that function is named getLocation. Notice that this function receives a position object just like the anonymous functions you saw in the last two figures. In contrast, the second parameter is a function that is called if there are errors. In this example, that function is named errorHandling, and an error object is passed to this function.

In the errorHandling function, a *switch statement* is used to handle three of the error codes that might be stored in the code property of the error object. This is a JavaScript statement that lets you test whether the expression that's coded within the parentheses that follow the *switch* keyword is equal to one of several values. Here, the code property of the error object is tested to see if it's equal to the errors named PERMISSION_DENIED, POSITION_UNAVAILABLE, or TIMEOUT. For each of these codes, an appropriate message is displayed. But if the error code isn't one of these, an "Unknown error" message is displayed.

JavaScript that handles Geolocation errors

```javascript
$(document).ready(function () {
    navigator.geolocation.getCurrentPosition(getLocation, errorHandling);

    function getLocation(position) {
        var url =
            "http://maps.google.com/maps/api/staticmap?sensor=false" +
            "&center=" + position.coords.latitude + "," +
            position.coords.longitude +
            "&zoom=14&size=300x400&markers=color:red|" +
            position.coords.latitude + "," +
            position.coords.longitude;

        $("img").attr("src", url);
    }

    function errorHandling(error) {
        switch(error.code) {
            case error.PERMISSION_DENIED:
                alert("Not sharing your location.");
                break;
            case error.POSITION_UNAVAILABLE:
                alert("Couldn't detect position.");
                break;
            case error.TIMEOUT:
                alert("Position retrieval timed out.");
                break;
            default:
                alert("Unknown error.");
                break;
        }
    }
});
```

The message box that's displayed when permission is denied

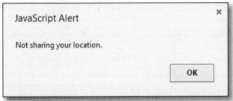

Description

- When you use the Geolocation feature, it won't work if (1) the user won't share his location, (2) the Geolocation service in the browser is unable to detect the user's position, or (3) the retrieval of the position times out.

- To handle Geolocation errors, you can code the getCurrentPosition method so it accepts two parameters. The first parameter is the name of a function that receives the position, and the second is a function that handles the error. The second function is executed if an error occurs.

- In the error-handling function, PERMISSION_DENIED, POSITION_UNAVAILABLE, and TIMEOUT are possible values for the code property of the error object.

Figure 14-5   How to handle Geolocation errors

How to use the Web Storage API

In the past, you had to use cookies to store data on the user's system. But that meant that the data had to be processed by server-side code. That also meant that the data was passed to the browser with every HTTP request. Beyond that, the storage in a cookie is limited to about 4,000 bytes.

But now, HTML5 offers web storage that can be processed by JavaScript on the browser. Then, the data isn't passed to the server with every HTTP request. In addition, web storage can be used to store approximately 5MB of data.

How to use local storage

Figure 14-6 shows how to use the new localStorage object. This object provides for *local storage*, which is storage that persists between browser sessions. Then, you can use the setItem, getItem, and removeItem methods of the localStorage object to add, retrieve, or delete items that have been stored in this object.

The setItem method requires two parameters that provide the name of an item and the value for the item. For instance, you can use code like this to add items named "email" and "phone" that store the email address and phone number for a user:

```
localStorage.setItem("email", "gmm@yahoo.com");
localStorage.setItem("phone", "555-555-1212");
```

Then, you can use the getItem method with the item name as the parameter to retrieve the data for the phone item with a statement like this:

```
var phone = localStorage.getItem("phone");
```

To simplify, you can use the shortcut syntax in this figure. For instance, you can use this code to save the email and phone items:

```
localStorage.email = "gmm@yahoo.com";
localStorage.phone = "555-555-1212";
```

And this code to retrieve the items:

```
var phone = localStorage.phone;
```

The shortcut syntax is used in the example in this figure. Here, an if statement tests to see whether the "hits" item in local storage exists. If it does, it adds 1 to the number in that name/value pair. If it doesn't, it creates a new item named "hits" and saves a value of 1 in it. After that, the value of the "hits" item is included in the content of the <p> element with an id of "hits".

How to use session storage

This figure also shows how to use the sessionStorage object to provide *session storage*. This works the same way that local storage works, but the storage is removed when the browser session ends.

The syntax for working with local or session storage

```
localStorage.saveItem("itemname", "value")   // saves the data in the item
localStorage.getItem("itemname")             // gets the data in the item
localStorage.removeItem("itemname")          // removes the item
localStorage.clear()                         // removes all items

sessionStorage.saveItem("itemname", "value") // saves the data in the item
sessionStorage.getItem("itemname")           // gets the data in the item
sessionStorage.removeItem("itemname")        // removes the item
sessionStorage.clear()                       // removes all items
```

The shortcut syntax for getting or saving an item

```
localStorage.itemname            // saves or gets the data in the item
sessionStorage.itemname          // saves or gets the data in the item
```

JavaScript that uses local storage for a hit counter

```
<script>
    $(document).ready(function () {
        if (localStorage.hits) {
            localStorage.hits = parseInt(localStorage.hits) + 1;
        } else {
            localStorage.hits = 1;
        }
        $("#hits").html("You have visited this page " +
                        localStorage.hits + " time(s).");
    });
</script>
```

The HTML for the element that receives the content

```
<p id="hits"></p>
```

Content that indicates the current value of the hits field in local storage

You have visited this page 5 time(s).

Description

- Web storage is an HTML5 feature that lets the web page use JavaScript to store data in name/value pairs.

- One type of web storage is *local storage*, which is retained indefinitely. The other type of web storage is *session storage*. It works just like local storage, except that session storage is lost when the user closes the browser for the website.

- Unlike cookies, web storage is meant to be accessed by client-side code and it is not passed to the server. If the server-side code needs to access the data, use cookies, not web storage.

- Although the storage limit for cookies is 4K, the HTML5 specification recommends a limit of 5MB for web storage. This limit is supported by every browser except Internet Explorer, which sets its limit at 10MB.

- To refer to web storage from JavaScript, you use the localStorage or sessionStorage object.

Figure 14-6   How to use the Web Storage API

How to use the Web Workers API

In the topics that follow, you'll learn how the *Web Workers API* brings the concept of *multi-threading* to client-side programming. Although this concept has existed in computer programming for many years, it wasn't until now that it was available in JavaScript.

How the Web Workers API works

Multi-threading refers to the ability to execute multiple processes, or *threads*, at the same time. Your computer's operating system is one example of an application that runs multiple threads simultaneously. In this case, each application that's currently running on your computer is using separate memory and processing threads to execute a variety of operations.

Multi-threading can also be useful within JavaScript applications. Suppose, for example, that you need to load a large file but you want the user to be able to interact with the application while that's happening. To do that, you can use a web worker to load the data in a background thread. You'll see an application that accomplishes that in the next figure. But first, you need to learn some basic skills for using the Web Workers API.

Figure 14-7 presents the four members of this API that you're most likely to use. To start, you use the Worker constructor to create a web worker from the JavaScript file you specify and to execute the code in that web worker. Then, you use the onmessage event to listen for messages that are sent back from the web worker. These messages are sent using the postMessage method. You can also use the terminate method to end the execution of the web worker.

The code in this figure shows how to use a simple web worker to count seconds. First, you can see the HTML for a page that includes an output element where the seconds will be displayed, along with two buttons. When the user clicks the first button, the web worker will be created and executed. When the user clicks the second button, the web worker will be terminated.

Within the web worker named count.js, the setInterval method is used to add one to a counter every second. In addition, the function for this method uses the postMessage method to send a message with the number of seconds.

The jQuery code for the page starts by declaring a variable named worker that will hold the web worker. Then, within the click event handler for the Start button, the html method is used to set the contents of the element with "result" as its id to an empty string. That way, if the web worker is started and stopped, the value that's displayed will be cleared if the web worker is started again.

Next, a new web worker is created from the count.js file and assigned to the worker variable. This also starts the execution of the web worker. Then, a function is assigned to the onmessage event of the worker. This function includes a parameter name *e* that receives an object that contains the data that's passed by the postMessage method of the web worker. The data method of that object is then displayed in the output element with "result" as its id.

Finally, an event handler is attached to the click event of the Stop button. This event handler simply terminates the worker so it stops counting seconds.

Common members of the Web Workers API

Member	Type	Description
Worker(*url*)	Constructor	Creates and executes a web worker at the specified URL.
postMessage(*object*)	Method	Sends a message in the form of a JavaScript object.
terminate()	Method	Terminates the web worker even if it's in the middle of an operation.
onmessage	Event	Used to listen for messages sent by a web worker via the postMessage method.

The HTML for the body of the page

```
<body>
    <p>Elapsed time (in seconds): <output id="result"></output></p>
    <button id="start">Start Worker</button>
    <button id="stop">Stop Worker</button>
</body>
```

A web worker (count.js) that increments a number every second

```
var i = 0;

setInterval(
    function() {
        i++;
        postMessage(i);
    },
    1000
);
```

The jQuery that uses the web worker

```
$(document).ready(function() {
    var worker;
    $("#start").click(function() {
        $("#result").html("");
        // create and execute the web worker
        worker = new Worker("count.js");
        // listen for a message sent by the web worker
        worker.onmessage = function(e) {
            $("#result").html(e.data);
        };
    });
    // terminate the web worker
    $("#stop").click(function() {
        worker.terminate();
    });
});
```

Description

- The *Web Workers API* can be used to implement *multi-threading* in JavaScript applications. With multi-threading, one process runs in the foreground while others run simultaneously in the background.

Figure 14-7   How the Web Workers API works

How to use a web worker
to retrieve data using Ajax

Now that you understand the basic skills for using the Web Workers API, you're ready to see an example of a web worker that uses Ajax to retrieve data from a file. The application that uses this web worker is shown in figure 14-8. It uses the same JSON file that you saw in chapter 12 to display information for a company's management team.

The idea here is that because it may take some time to retrieve the data in this file, this process is done in the background using a web worker. In contrast, the rest of the user interface is displayed almost immediately. That way, a user can click on a button in the navigation list to go to another page even if the data hasn't been displayed yet. This is particularly useful for large files that contain thousands of records.

This figure starts by showing the div element where the data from the JSON file will be displayed. Then, it shows the code for the web worker, which is named getJSON.js. This web worker contains a function that's executed when the onmessage event is fired, which happens when the web worker receives a message from the calling application. Note that this function contains a parameter named *e* that receives the message.

The function for the web worker starts by creating an XHR object and assigning it to a variable named xhr. Then, it creates an event handler for the onreadystatechange event of that object. This event will be fired when the state of the request changes. Then, the readyState property is tested to see if it's equal to 4, which means the request is done, and the status property is tested to see if it's equal to 200, which means the request was successful.

If both of these conditions are true, the responseText property is used to get the results. Then, the JSON.parse method is used to convert this text to a JavaScript object. Finally, the postMessage method of the Web Worker API is used to send the object to the onmessage event handler in the calling application.

The two statements that follow the event handler for the onreadystatechange event open the connection for the request and send the request. Here, the open method indicates that the GET method will be used, the data will be retrieved from the file at the URL that was passed to the web worker, and asynchronous processing will be used.

Notice in this code that JavaScript is used rather than jQuery. That's because web workers don't support jQuery without the help of specialized third-party plugins. So you can't use the jQuery shorthand methods like $.getJSON to retrieve data using Ajax.

The jQuery code for the page that uses the web worker starts by creating a new instance of the Worker object. Then, it uses the postMessage method to pass the URL of the file to the web worker. In this case, that's the team.json file in the data folder of the application. Next, the onmessage event handler listens for messages that are posted by the web worker. In contrast to the web worker in the previous figure, this web worker will post just one message when all of the data has been retrieved from the JSON file. Then, nested $.each methods are used to process and display the data using the same technique you learned in chapter 12.

An application that uses a Web Worker to retrieve data using Ajax

The HTML div element that receives the data

```
<div id="team"></div>
```

The JavaScript for the web worker (getJSON.js)

```javascript
onmessage = function(e) {
    var xhr = new XMLHttpRequest();
    xhr.onreadystatechange = function() {
        if (xhr.readyState == 4 && xhr.status == 200) {
            var result = xhr.responseText;
            var object = JSON.parse(result);
            postMessage(object);
        }
    }
    xhr.open("GET", e.data, true);
    xhr.send("");
}
```

The jQuery that uses the web worker

```javascript
$(document).ready(function(){
    var worker = new Worker("getJSON.js");
    worker.postMessage("data/team.json");
    worker.onmessage = function(e) {
        $.each(e.data, function() {
            $.each(this, function(key, value) {
                $("#team").append("<b>" + value.name + "</b>" +
                    "<br>" + value.title +
                    "<br>" + value.bio + "<br><br>");
            });
        });
    };
});
```

Description

- You can use Ajax within a web worker to retrieve data in the background while other functions are being performed in the foreground.

- You can pass data to a web worker using the postMessage method. Then, the web worker must include an onmessage function to listen for the message.

- Because you can't use jQuery within a web worker, you have to use JavaScript to work with Ajax from a web worker.

Figure 14-8   How to use a web worker to retrieve data using Ajax

An application that uses a web worker and web storage

This chapter ends by presenting an application that uses both the Web Workers and Web Storage APIs. That should give you a better idea of how these APIs can be used in a real-world application.

The user interface

Figure 14-9 presents the user interface for this application, which we call the Murach Books application. The Categories page of this application includes a list of book categories. When the user clicks on one of these categories, the Books page is displayed with a list of the books in that category. And when the user clicks on a book, the Book page is displayed with an image and the details for that book.

Although you can't tell here, the image at the top of the Categories page is just one image in a slide show. This slide show, along with the categories data, are loaded in the foreground. In contrast, the book data is loaded in the background. That way, the user can interact with the slide show or select a category while the book data is loading.

The Categories, Books, and Book pages of the Murach Books application

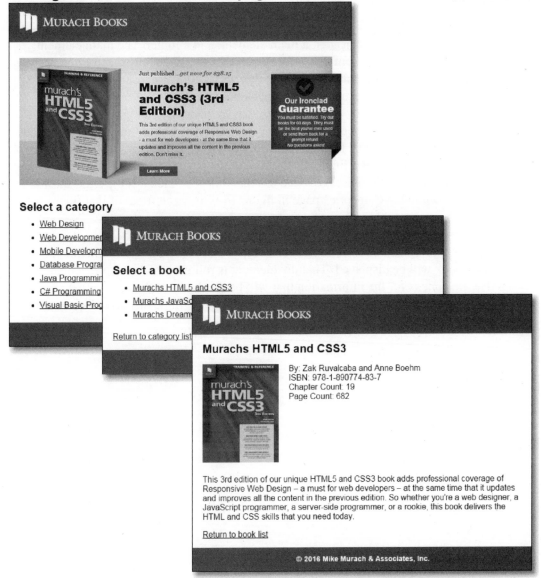

Description

- The Categories page uses Ajax to retrieve categories from a JSON file. These categories are then displayed along with a slide show. This processing is done in the foreground.

- A web worker is used to retrieve book data from a JSON file in the background. This data is saved in session storage so it's available when it's needed by the application.

- When the user clicks on a category, the id for that category is saved in session storage, and the Books page is displayed with the titles of the books in that category.

- When the user clicks on a book title, the id for that book is saved in session storage, and the Book page is displayed with the details for that book.

Figure 14-9   The user interface for the Murach Books application

The HTML

Figure 14-10 shows the HTML for the three pages of this application. Here, all three pages include a header, a main element, and a footer. The main element for the Categories page contains a div element for the slideshow. In addition, it contains an h1 element and a ul element that will display the list of categories. These categories will be retrieved from a JSON file.

The HTML for the Books page is similar. In this case, though, the ul element will display the books in the selected category. These books will also be retrieved from a JSON file, but that process will be done by a web worker. This page also includes a link at the bottom of the page that the user can click to return to the Categories page. Note too that this page includes the slide show that's shown in the Categories page in figure 14-9. It was left out of that figure so all three pages could be shown.

The HTML for the Book page is slightly more complicated because it displays more detailed information. It includes a div element where the image for a book will be displayed. That div element is followed by two <p> elements. The first one is for the information that will be displayed to the right of the image, and the second one is for the description that will be displayed below the image.

The HTML for the Categories page (index.html)

```
<header><a href="index.html"><img src="images/logo.jpg"></a></header>

<main>
    <div class="cycle-slideshow"
        data-cycle-fx="scrollHorz"
        data-cycle-timeout="4000"
        data-cycle-speed="400">
        <div class="cycle-prev"></div>
        <div class="cycle-next"></div>
        <img src="images/image1.png" alt="">
        <img src="images/image2.png" alt="">
        <img src="images/image3.png" alt="">
        <img src="images/image4.png" alt="">
    </div>

    <h1>Select a category</h1>
    <ul id="categories"></ul>
</main>

<footer><p>&copy; 2016 Mike Murach &amp; Associates, Inc.</p></footer>
```

The HTML for the Books page (books.html)

```
<header><a href="index.html"><img src="images/logo.jpg"></a></header>

<main>
    <div class="cycle-slideshow" ... </div>

    <h1>Select a book</h1>
    <ul id="books"></ul>
    <p></p>
    <p><a href="index.html">Return to category list</a></p>
</main>

<footer><p>&copy; 2016 Mike Murach &amp; Associates, Inc.</p></footer>
```

The HTML for the Book page (book.html)

```
<header><a href="index.html"><img src="images/logo.jpg"></a></header>

<main>
    <div class="cycle-slideshow" ... </div>

    <h1></h1>
    <div id="image"></div>
    <p id="details"></p>
    <p id="description"></p>
    <p></p>
    <p><a href="books.html">Return to book list</a></p>
</main>

<footer><p>&copy; 2016 Mike Murach &amp; Associates, Inc.</p></footer>
```

Figure 14-10   The HTML for the Murach Books application

The JSON data

Figure 14-11 shows the two JSON files used by this application. The first file, categories.json, contains the data that's displayed in the list on the Categories page. The second file, books.json, contains the data that will be displayed on the Books and Book pages.

The categoryid in both of these files is used to determine which books are displayed on the Books page when the user selects a category from the Categories page. To accomplish that, the id of the category that's clicked is stored in session storage. Then, when the Books page is displayed, this value is retrieved from session storage and only the books with that categoryid are displayed.

A similar technique is used to determine which book is displayed on the Book page. In this case, though, only the bookid in the books file is used. When the user selects a book from the list on the Books page, the id of that book is stored in session storage. Then, the Book page can retrieve this id from session storage and get the data for the book with that id.

The JSON file that contains the categories data (categories.json)

```
{"categories":[
    {"categoryid":"1","category":"Web Design"},
    {"categoryid":"2","category":"Web Development"},
    {"categoryid":"3","category":"Mobile Development"},
    {"categoryid":"4","category":"Database Programming"},
    {"categoryid":"5","category":"Java Programming"},
    {"categoryid":"6","category":"C# Programming"},
    {"categoryid":"7","category":"Visual Basic Programming"}
]}
```

The JSON file that contains the books data (books.json)

```
{"books":[
    {
        "bookid":"1",
        "title":"Murach's HTML5 and CSS3",
        "author":"Zak Ruvalcaba and Anne Boehm",
        "isbn":"978-1-890774-83-7",
        "chapter_count":"19",
        "page_count":"682",
        "description":"This 3rd edition of our unique HTML and CSS ... ",
        "categoryid":"1",
        "image":"html5-and-css3.jpg"
    },
    .
    .
    .
    {
        "bookid":"21",
        "title":"Murach's ASP.NET 4.5 Web Programming with VB 2012",
        "author":"Mary Delamater and Anne Boehm",
        "isbn":"978-1-890774-76-9",
        "chapter_count":"24",
        "page_count":"822",
        "description":"If you know how to create Windows applications ... ",
        "categoryid":"7",
        "image":"asp_with_vb.jpg"
    }
]}
```

Description

- The two JSON files used by this application are stored within the data folder of the application. Because of that, they are static files and can be saved in web storage.

- If a file is stored outside of the application and it can change as the application is executed, it shouldn't be saved in web storage. Instead, it should be retrieved each time it's used.

- The books.json file includes the name of an image for each book. These images are stored within the images folder of the application, but it's common to store them outside of the application.

Figure 14-11   The JSON data

The jQuery code

Figure 14-12 presents the jQuery code for the three pages of this application. In part one of this figure, you can see the code for the Categories page. It starts by creating a web worker from a file named getJSON.js, which is the same web worker that you saw in figure 14-8. Then, it uses the postMessage method to pass the URL of the JSON file to be retrieved to the web worker. When the web worker posts the data that's retrieved, the statement in the event handler for the onmessage event stores the data in session storage. But first, it uses the JSON.stringify method to convert the data to a string.

While the web worker is retrieving the book data in the background, processing continues in the foreground. First, the $.getJSON method is used to retrieve the data from the categories.json file. For each category in this file, an li element is appended to the element with "categories" as its id, which is the ul element for the categories list. Each li element contains an <a> element with its href attribute set to the books.html page so that page will be displayed if a category is clicked. In addition, the id of each <a> element is set to the categoryid value so it can be used to identify a category when it's clicked, and the content is set to the category value.

The code for this page ends with the event handler for the click event of an <a> element in the categories list. Notice here that the on method is used to attach the event handler instead of the click method. That way, the event handler is attached to the <a> elements that are added when the category data is retrieved from the JSON file.

Within the event handler, the first statement uses the this keyword to get the value of the id attribute of the <a> element that was clicked, which is the value of the categoryid. Then, this value is stored in session storage so it can be accessed from the books page that's displayed next.

The jQuery code for the Categories page   **Page 1**

```javascript
$(document).ready(function(){
    // create a web worker to retrieve JSON data in the background
    var worker = new Worker("getJSON.js");
    worker.postMessage("data/books.json");
    worker.onmessage = function(e) {
        // store the JSON data in session storage for later use
        sessionStorage.books = JSON.stringify(e.data);
    };

    // get JSON data from the categories.js file in the foreground
    $.getJSON("data/categories.json", function(data) {
        $("#categories").html("");
        $.each(data, function() {
            $.each(this, function(key, value) {
                $("#categories").append(
                    '<li><a href="books.html" id="' +
                    value.categoryid + '">' +
                    value.category + '</a></li>');
            });
        });
    });

    // handle the click event of a category
    $("#categories").on("click", "a", function() {
        // retrieve the selected category id and save it in session storage
        var categoryID = $(this).attr("id");
        sessionStorage.categoryID = categoryID;
    });
});
```

Description

- When the application starts, a new web worker is created and executed and the returned JSON data is stored in session storage. This happens while the slide show and categories are loaded in the foreground.

- The code for the web worker is identical to the code in figure 14-8, so it's not repeated here.

- The $.getJSON() method is used to retrieve the categories from the categories.json file. Then, each category is displayed within a link whose id is set to the categoryid value.

- When the user clicks on the link for a category, the categoryid value is saved in session storage and the Books page is displayed.

Figure 14-12   The jQuery code for the Murach Books application (part 1 of 2)

Part 2 of figure 14-12 shows the code for both the Books and Book pages. The code for the Books page starts by retrieving the categoryid from session storage and storing it in a variable named categoryID. This is the id of the category that was selected on the Categories page. Then, it retrieves the books data from session storage, uses the JSON.parse method to convert the string back to a JSON object, and stores the data in a variable named data.

Next, the nested $.each loops iterate through the books data to identify all of the books in the category specified by the categoryID variable. To do that, an if statement is used to check if the categoryid of the book is equal to the categoryID variable. If it is, an li element is appended to the element with "books" as its id, which is the ul element for the books list. The content of each li element is an <a> element whose href attribute is set to book.html. That way, the book page will be displayed if any of the list items are clicked. Then, the id attribute of each book is set to the bookid value and the content is set to the title value.

This page ends with an event handler for the click event of the <a> elements in the list. Like the event handler for the Categories page, the on method is used to attach the event handler to the click event. This event handler gets the bookid from the id attribute of the <a> element. Then, it stores that id in session storage so it can be accessed by the Book page.

The code for the Book page is similar, except that it doesn't include an event handler. It starts by retrieving the bookid and books data from session storage. Then, it iterates through the books and locates the one with the specified bookid. When it finds that book, it creates the html to be added to the page and sets the contents of the appropriate elements.

The jQuery code for the Books page   **Page 2**

```
$(document).ready(function(){
    // retrieve the category id and book data from session storage
    var categoryID = sessionStorage.categoryID;
    var data = JSON.parse(sessionStorage.books)
    // loop through the data and display the book titles
    $.each(data, function() {
        $.each(this, function(key, value) {
            if (value.categoryid == categoryID) {
                $("#books").append(
                    '<li><a href="book.html" id="' +
                    value.bookid + '">' +
                    value.title + '</a></li>');
            }
        });
    });

    // handle the click event of a book
    $("#books").on("click", "a", function() {
        // retrieve the selected book id and save it in session storage
        var bookID = $(this).attr("id");
        sessionStorage.bookID = bookID;
    });
});
```

The jQuery code for the Book page

```
$(document).ready(function(){
    // retrieve the book id and book data from session storage
    var bookID = sessionStorage.bookID;
    var data = JSON.parse(sessionStorage.books)
    // loop through the data and display the book details
    $.each(data, function() {
        $.each(this, function(key, value) {
            if (value.bookid == bookID) {
                $("h1").html(value.title);
                $("#image").html("<img src=images/" + value.image + ">");
                $("#details").html(
                    "By: " + value.author + "<br>" +
                    "ISBN: " + value.isbn + "<br>" +
                    "Chapter Count: " + value.chapter_count + "<br>" +
                    "Page Count: " + value.page_count);
                $("#description").html(value.description);
            }
        });
    });
});
```

Description

- The jQuery for the Books page starts by retrieving the categoryid and book data that have been saved in session storage. Then, the book title for each book with that categoryid is displayed in a link whose id is set to the bookid. If the user clicks on the link for a book, the id for that book is saved in session storage and the Book page is displayed.

- The jQuery for the Book page starts by retrieving the bookid and book data that have been saved in session storage. Then, the data for the book with that id is displayed.

Figure 14-12   The jQuery code for the Murach Books application (part 2 of 2)

Perspective

This chapter has presented the basic skills for using three of the HTML5 APIs. It has also introduced you to all of the APIs that are currently supported by all of the modern browsers, and it has shown you where to get more information about these APIs. With that information, you should be able to research and use any of these APIs.

Terms

Geolocation API	Web Workers API
Web Storage API	multi-threading
local storage	thread
session storage	

Summary

- The *Geolocation API* lets you use JavaScript to get the latitude and longitude for a browser. You can use this feature with the Google Maps API to show the location of the user on a Google map.

- The API for *Web Storage* provides for both *local storage, which persists between browser sessions,* and *session storage, which is removed when the session ends.* To work with web storage, you use JavaScript to store and retrieve the data from name/value pairs in the localStorage and sessionStorage objects.

- The *Web Workers API* allows a developer to create client-side applications that make use of *multi-threading*. Multi-threading provides for executing one or more threads in the background using web workers while the main thread is executing in the foreground.

Exercise 14-1   Use Geolocation and web storage

In this exercise, you'll add error handling to code that uses Geolocation and Google Maps to display a map with your current location. You'll also use local storage and session storage to count the number of times the page has been visited. When you're done, the page should look like this:

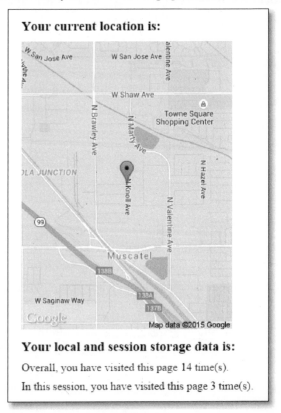

Your current location is:

Your local and session storage data is:

Overall, you have visited this page 14 time(s).

In this session, you have visited this page 3 time(s).

Open and review the HTML file for this page

1. Use your text editor to open the index.html file in this folder:

    ```
    C:\jquery\exercises\ch14\geolocation
    ```

2. Review the code in this page to see that it contains JavaScript that displays a map with your current location. It also contains <p> elements where you can display the value of local and session storage.

Add error handling to the Geolocation code

3. Using figure 14-5 as a guide, add error handling to the JavaScript code that displays the map. To do that, add a function that handles errors. Then, move the code that creates the map to another function. Finally, modify the getCurrentPosition method so it uses these functions.

4. Run the application to be sure that the map is still displayed properly.

Add local and session storage

5. Using figure 14-6 as a guide, use local storage and session storage to keep a count of the number of times the page is displayed.

6. Run the application. When you do that for the first time, both counters should indicate that the page has been displayed 1 time.

7. Click the Refresh or Reload button in your browser to see that both counters are increased by 1. Then, close the browser and run the application again. This time, the counter for local storage should indicate that the page has been displayed one more time than it was the last time the application was run. In contrast, the counter for session storage should be reset to 1.

Exercise 14-2   Use a web worker

In this exercise, you'll use a web worker to calculate the factorial of a number that's entered by the user. When you're done, the page should look like this:

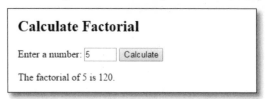

Open and review the HTML file for this page

1. Use your text editor to open the index.html file in this folder:

    `C:\jquery\exercises\ch14\web_worker`

2. Review the code in this page and run the application to see how it works.

Use a web worker to calculate the factorial

3. Use your text editor to open the calculateFactorial.js file that's in the same folder as the index.html file. This file contains a function that's assigned to the onmessage event.

4. Move the statement that declares the factorial variable and the for statement that follows it from the HTML file to the onmessage function in the web worker. Then, modify the for statement so the counter is initialized to the data that's contain in the *e* parameter that's passed to the function.

5. Add a statement to the web worker that posts the calculated factorial back to the calling application.

6. Declare a variable that will store the web worker at the beginning of the ready event handler in the HTML file.

7. Add three statements to the event handler for the click event of the Calculate button that create a web worker from the calculateFactorial.js file, pass the number entered by the user to the web worker, and listen for the message that's passed back from the web worker. These statements should be placed after the statement that clears the content from the <p> element with the id "results".

8. Move the statement that sets the content of the <p> element so it's executed when a message is received from the web worker. Then, modify this statement so it uses the data value of that message for the factorial.

Section 5

jQuery Mobile

jQuery Mobile is a JavaScript library that extends the jQuery library. jQuery Mobile makes it easier than ever to build websites with native interfaces for mobile devices.

In chapter 15 of this section, you'll get off to a fast start with jQuery Mobile by learning the basic jQuery Mobile skills. Then, chapter 16 presents the rest of the skills that you need for getting the most from jQuery Mobile. When you complete these two chapters, you'll be ready to use jQuery Mobile to develop mobile websites at a professional level.

15

Get off to a fast start with jQuery Mobile

In this chapter, you'll learn how to build websites with native interfaces for mobile devices. To do that, you'll use a jQuery library called jQuery Mobile.

How to work with mobile devices

Many different types of mobile devices are in use today, and these devices are frequently used to access websites. Because the screens on these devices are much smaller than standard computer screens, a website that's designed to be used on the desktop can be difficult to work with on a mobile device. To accommodate mobile users, then, web developers typically provide web pages that are designed for mobile devices.

How to provide pages for mobile devices

Today, many companies provide full versions of their websites as well as mobile versions. This is illustrated in the Home pages in figure 15-1. One is for the full version of a site; the other is for the mobile version. In this chapter and the next, you'll learn how to develop a separate version of a website for mobile users using jQuery Mobile. Then, when a user accesses the full version of the site, they're redirected to the mobile version.

To detect mobile devices and redirect them to the mobile versions of the sites, the full versions of the sites use either client-side or server-side code. For instance, JavaScript or jQuery can be used to do that in the browser, and a scripting language like PHP can be used to do that on the web server. You'll learn more about this in the next figure.

When you use this technique, one common convention for the mobile site name is to precede the domain name for the main site with m. For instance, the name for the mobile version of vectacorp.com will be m.vectacorp.com. A second convention is to store the mobile site in a subdirectory of the main site as in vectacorp.com/mobile.

Although jQuery Mobile makes it easy to create a mobile version of a website, you should know that the preferred way to provide web pages for mobile devices today is to use *Responsive Web Design*. Websites that are developed using Responsive Web Design are designed to adapt gracefully to the size of the screen on which the site is being displayed. To develop a responsive design, you use a fluid layout, scalable images, and CSS3 media queries.

When you develop a *fluid layout*, you use percentages to specify the widths of the page and its main structural elements. That way, the widths will change as the screen size changes. *Scalable images* are similar in that their sizes change as the widths of the elements that contain them change.

Media queries are the most important aspect of a responsive design because they let you change the appearance of a page based on conditions, such as the width of the screen. For example, you'll typically change a page that has a multi-column layout when displayed on the desktop to a single column when displayed on a mobile phone. To learn how to code media queries, you can refer to the URL shown in this figure. For more information about the original theory and practice of Responsive Web Design, you can refer to this article by Ethan Marcotte in the May 2010 issue of *A List Apart Magazine*:

`http://alistapart.com/article/responsive-web-design`

The Home pages for a full website and the mobile version of the site

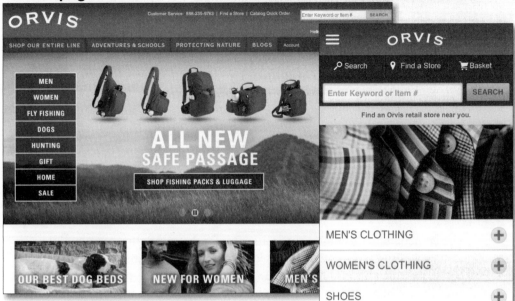

Two ways to provide web pages for a mobile device

- Use *Responsive Web Design* so the pages of a website will work on devices of all sizes, including mobile devices.

- Develop a separate mobile version of the website that the user is redirected to when the browser for a mobile device tries to open the web page for the main site.

Two ways to redirect a user to the mobile version of the site

- Use JavaScript or JQuery to detect mobile devices and redirect them to the mobile version of the site.

- Use a server-side scripting language such as PHP to detect mobile devices and redirect them to the mobile version of the site.

How to use Responsive Web Design

- Use percentages to specify the widths of a page and its main structural elements so the widths change as the screen size changes. This can be referred to as a *fluid layout*.

- Use *scalable images* so the sizes of the images change along with the widths of the elements that contain them.

- Use *media queries* to detect the size of the screen. For more information, go to:
  `http://www.w3.org/TR/css3-mediaqueries/`

Description

- Today, Responsive Web Design is the preferred way to provide web pages for mobile devices. But converting a large, established website to Responsive Web Design is likely to be so time-consuming and expensive that it's impractical.

Figure 15-1   How to provide pages for mobile devices

How to use a JavaScript plugin to redirect mobile browsers to a mobile website

Because there are so many different types of mobile devices and mobile browsers, it would be difficult to code and maintain a JavaScript application that redirects mobile browsers to the mobile version of a website. So when you need to do that, a good way to get started is to look for a plugin that does what you want.

One website that provides scripts for detecting browsers is the Detect Mobile Browsers site shown in figure 15-2. It provides scripts for clients and servers that detect mobile browsers and redirect them to the mobile versions of the sites. As you can see, it provides these scripts in many different languages, including ASP.NET, JSP, PHP, and Python for servers as well as JavaScript and jQuery for browsers.

The procedure in this figure shows how to use the JavaScript version of the application. In brief, you download the JavaScript file, which has a txt extension. Next, you use your editor to modify the URL at the end of the file so it points to your mobile website, rename the file so it has a js instead of a txt extension, and deploy the file to your web server. Then, you code a script element that includes this file in any web page that you want redirected to the mobile site when a mobile browser is detected.

The home page for Detect Mobile Browsers

The URL for Detect Mobile Browsers

```
http://www.detectmobilebrowser.com
```

The end of the code in the downloaded file (detectmobilebrowser.js.txt)

```
...||window.opera,'http://detectmobilebrowser.com/mobile');
```

The end of the code after the URL has been edited

```
...||window.opera,'http://www.vectacorp.com/mobile');
```

The script element for any page that wants to redirect to a mobile site

```
<script src="detectmobilebrowser.js"></script>
```

How to use the JavaScript plugin for mobile browser detection

1. Go to the URL above. Then, click on the JavaScript button under the Download Scripts heading to download a file named detectmobilebrowser.js.txt.

2. Open the file in your text editor, and move the cursor to the end of the JavaScript code, which will include a URL like the one above. Then, change this URL to the path of the mobile site that you want the user redirected to.

3. Save your work, close the file, and rename the file so the .txt extension is removed. Then, deploy the file to your web server.

4. In any web page that you want to redirect to the mobile website, code a script element that refers to the file that you've just deployed.

Description

- The Detect Mobile Browsers website offers many server-side and client-side scripts that will redirect a mobile device from the full version of a site to the mobile version.

- After you modify the URL in the JavaScript plugin so it points to the correct mobile page, you need to provide a script element for it on every page that you want redirected.

Figure 15-2   How to use a JavaScript plugin to redirect users to a mobile website

How to set the viewport properties

When you develop a website for mobile devices, you can use a special meta element that lets you configure a device's *viewport*. This meta element is presented in figure 15-3.

To start, you should know that the viewport on a mobile device works differently from the viewport on a computer screen. On a computer screen, the viewport is the visible area of the web page. However, the user can change the size of the viewport by changing the size of the browser window.

In contrast, the viewport on a mobile device can be larger or smaller than the visible area. In this figure, for example, you can see that the first web page is displayed without a meta element so the entire width of the page is visible. Some mobile browsers reduce a page like this automatically if no meta element is included. In contrast, other mobile browsers don't reduce the page at all, so it extends beyond the visible area of the screen.

The second web page in this figure shows how this same page looks with the viewport set to the width of the device and the scale set to .5. You might want to do this for the pages of a full website to make them easier to work with on a mobile device.

To configure the viewport, you use a meta element with the name attribute set to "viewport". Then, for the content attribute, you can specify any of the properties that are summarized in this figure to set the dimensions and scaling of the web page within the mobile device.

In practice, if the pages you're designing are for mobile devices, you can use a viewport meta element like the first example in this figure. This causes the page to be displayed at its full size so jQuery Mobile has complete control of the formatting. You'll see that illustrated in the application at the end of this chapter.

However, if you're trying to set the viewport for a full website, that may take some experimentation. For example, the second viewport meta element in this figure sets the width of the viewport to the width of the device and the scale to .5. That's illustrated by the page on the right at the top of this figure. This enlarges the page so its content is easier to read. Then, the user can zoom in or out as necessary to interact with the page.

Beyond that, you can experiment with the content properties until you get something that works for your full website. But a better solution is to develop a mobile version of your website, and jQuery Mobile makes that easier than ever.

A web page on an iPhone before and after scaling

No viewport meta element

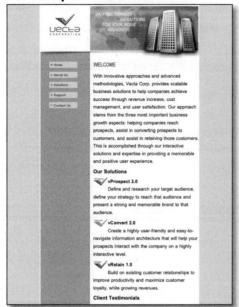

width=device-width, initial-scale=.5

Basic settings for a mobile website

```
<meta name="viewport" content="width=device-width, initial-scale=1">
```

Typical settings for the pages of a full website

```
<meta name="viewport" content="width=device-width, initial-scale=.5">
```

Content properties for viewport metadata

Property	Description
width	The width of the viewport in pixels. You can also use the device-width keyword to indicate that the viewport should be as wide as the screen.
height	The height of the viewport in pixels. You can also use the device-height keyword to indicate that the viewport should be as tall as the screen.
initial-scale	A number that indicates the initial zoom factor that's used to display the page.
minimum-scale	A number that indicates the minimum zoom factor for the page.
maximum-scale	A number that indicates the maximum zoom factor for the page.
user-scalable	Indicates whether the user can zoom in and out of the viewport. Possible values are yes and no.

Description

- The *viewport* on a mobile device determines the content that's displayed on the page. It can be larger or smaller than the visible area of the screen.

Figure 15-3   How to set the viewport properties

Guidelines for designing mobile web pages

If you create web pages specifically for mobile devices, you should follow some general guidelines so it's easy for users to work with those pages. Figure 15-4 presents these guidelines.

In general, you want to simplify the layout and content of your pages. This is illustrated by the two pages in this figure. The first shows the home page for the mobile version of a large website. This page consists primarily of links to the major types of products that the site offers. The second page shows a product list after the user has drilled down into the site. If you review the full version of this site, you'll get a better idea of just how much the full version has been simplified.

Guidelines for testing mobile web pages

Figure 15-4 also presents some guidelines for testing mobile web pages. Because there are so many different mobile devices, it's important to test a mobile web page on as many devices and in as many browsers as possible. Although the best way to test a mobile web page is to deploy the page on a web server and then display it on a variety of devices, that may not be practical. So instead, you may want to use a web-based tool such as ProtoFluid that lets you view a web page in the screen sizes used by many different devices.

Another option is to use the device emulators and browser simulators that are available for many of the most popular mobile devices and browsers. To do that, you typically need to download the required emulator or simulator from the manufacturer's website so you can run it on your desktop. In a few cases, though, you can run the emulator or simulator online. But before you can do that, you need to deploy the website to a server so it can be accessed online.

A simpler way to test a mobile design is to use the developer tools that are provided by most modern browsers. In chapter 4, for example, you learned how to use Chrome's developer tools to find errors. But you can also use these tools to display a page in various screen sizes.

To access these tools in Chrome, you display a page in the browser and then press F12. Then, you can click the Toggle Device Mode icon in the toolbar (the one that looks like a mobile phone) to simulate the page in the last device you selected. To use a different device, you can select it from the drop-down list at the top of the page. Or, you can drag the edges of the screen to create a custom size.

Two pages from the mobile website for www.orvis.com

The Home page

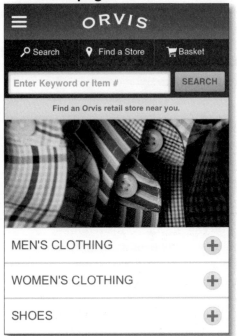

A product list

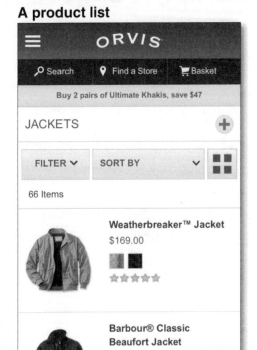

Guidelines for designing mobile web pages

- Keep your layout simple so the focus is on the content. One-column layouts typically work best.
- Include only essential content.
- Keep images small and to a minimum.
- Avoid using Flash. Most mobile devices, including the iPhone, don't support it.
- Include only the essential navigation in the header of the page. The other navigation should be part of the content for the page.
- Make links and other elements large enough that the user can easily manipulate them.
- Use relative measurements so the page looks good regardless of the scale.

Guidelines for testing mobile web pages

- Test all pages on as many different mobile devices and in as many different mobile browsers as possible.
- The best way to test mobile web pages is to deploy them to your web server and test them on the devices themselves.
- When you can't test your pages on the devices themselves, you can use web-based tools such as ProtoFluid, device emulators and browser simulators, or the developer tools that come with Chrome, Firefox, and IE.

Figure 15-4   Guidelines for designing and testing mobile web pages

How to get started with jQuery Mobile

Throughout this book, you have learned how to use jQuery and jQuery UI to enhance your web pages. Now, in this chapter, you'll learn how to use the jQuery Mobile library to develop mobile websites. Although there are other ways to develop mobile websites, we think jQuery Mobile sets a standard that other development methods are going to have a hard time beating.

What jQuery Mobile is and where to get it

As figure 15-5 summarizes, *jQuery Mobile* is a free, open-source, cross-platform, JavaScript library that you can use for developing mobile websites. This library lets you create pages that look and feel like the pages of a native mobile application.

To include jQuery Mobile in your pages, you can download the required JavaScript and CSS files from the jQuery Mobile website, deploy them to your web server, and then include them in your mobile web pages. Or, you can use a Content Delivery Network as we've done with the latest version of jQuery throughout the book.

The jQuery Mobile website (www.jquerymobile.com)

The two jQuery libraries that you need

- jQuery (the core library)
- jQuery Mobile

Description

- jQuery Mobile is a free, open-source, JavaScript library that makes it easier to develop websites for mobile devices. It is used in combination with the core jQuery library.

- jQuery Mobile lets you store multiple pages in a single HTML file; create dialogs, buttons, and navigation bars; format your pages without coding your own CSS; lay out pages with two columns, collapsible content blocks, and accordions; and much more.

- jQuery Mobile is supported by most devices including iPhone iOS, Android, BlackBerry, Windows Phone, Palm WebOS, and Symbian.

- The jQuery Mobile website features all of the documentation, sample code, and downloads that you need for beginning your work with mobile devices.

- To download jQuery Mobile, go to its website (www.jquerymobile.com). However, you won't need to do that if you include it from a CDN (see figure 15-6).

Figure 15-5   What jQuery Mobile is and where to get it

How to include jQuery Mobile in your web pages

To use jQuery Mobile, you need to include the three files listed at the top of figure 15-6 in your web pages: the jQuery file, the jQuery Mobile file, and the jQuery Mobile CSS style sheet. As this figure shows, there are two ways to do that.

The first way to include the three files is illustrated by the first example in this figure. Here, the link element for the CSS file and the script elements for the jQuery and jQuery Mobile files use a Content Delivery Network. At this writing, Microsoft and jQuery are the only CDNs that you can use for getting the jQuery Mobile library, and this example uses the jQuery CDN.

The benefit to using a CDN is that you don't have to manage the jQuery and jQuery Mobile versions on your server as new ones become available. Instead, you just have to change the version numbers in the link and script elements for these files.

The second way is to download the three files and deploy them on your system or web server. To do that, you download the compressed zip files, extract the files from the zip files, and copy the files to your web server. Then, for each web page that uses jQuery Mobile, you code one link element that includes the CSS file and two script elements that include the jQuery and jQuery Mobile files.

This is illustrated by the second example in this figure. Here, the JavaScript file for the jQuery library is included from a CDN as it has been throughout this book, but the CSS and JavaScript files for the jQuery Mobile library have been downloaded and made available from the web server. Notice that the names for the current versions of these files have been retained. Although you can change those names once they're on your server, keeping the downloaded names makes it easy to tell which versions of the files you're using.

No matter which method you use, you must code the script element for jQuery Mobile after the one for jQuery. That's because jQuery Mobile uses the jQuery library.

The three files that you need to include for jQuery Mobile applications

- The jQuery JavaScript file
- The jQuery Mobile JavaScript file
- The jQuery Mobile CSS style sheet

Two ways to include the jQuery files

- Include the files from a Content Delivery Network (CDN) like Microsoft or jQuery.
- Download and deploy the files on your web server. Then, include them from the server.

How to include the jQuery Mobile files from a Content Delivery Network

```
<!-- include the jQuery Mobile stylesheet -->
<link rel="stylesheet"
    href="http://code.jquery.com/mobile/1.4.5/jquery.mobile-1.4.5.min.css">

<!-- include the jQuery and jQuery Mobile JavaScript files -->
<script src="http://code.jquery.com/jquery-2.1.4.min.js"></script>
<script
    src="http://code.jquery.com/mobile/1.4.5/jquery.mobile-1.4.5.min.js">
</script>
```

How to include the jQuery Mobile files when they're on your web server

```
<!-- include the jQuery Mobile stylesheet -->
<link rel="stylesheet" href="jquery.mobile-1.4.5.min.css">

<!-- include the jQuery and jQuery Mobile JavaScript files -->
<script src="http://code.jquery.com/jquery-2.1.4.min.js"></script>
<script src="jquery.mobile-1.4.5.min.js"></script>
```

Description

- To use jQuery, you need to include the three files shown above. The first two are the JavaScript files for jQuery and jQuery Mobile. The third is the CSS file for the jQuery Mobile style sheet.
- jQuery Mobile is continually being improved and enhanced, so check the website often for the latest version.
- At this writing, only Microsoft and jQuery provide Content Delivery Networks (CDNs) that can be used to access the jQuery Mobile files.
- The jQuery and jQuery Mobile filenames always include the version number. At this writing, the latest stable version of jQuery Mobile is 1.4.5.
- If you download and deploy the jQuery files to your system, you can change the filenames so they're simpler. But that way, you can lose track of what versions you're using and when you need to upgrade to newer versions.

Figure 15-6   How to include jQuery Mobile in your web pages

How to create one web page with jQuery Mobile

To give you an idea of how jQuery Mobile works, figure 15-7 shows how to create one web page with it. In the HTML for a page, you use data-role attributes to identify the page, header, and footer components. In contrast, you use the role attribute with a value of "main" to identify the component that will contain the main content for the page. You also assign the class named ui-content to this component.

Note that the technique you use to identify the content component is new in jQuery Mobile 1.4. Previously, you identified this component by coding a data-role attribute with the value "content". Although you can still use the data-role attribute like this, it has been deprecated and will be dropped in version 1.5 of jQuery Mobile. So you should use the role attribute and ui-content class instead.

To define the text that's displayed within the header, you use an h1 element. Similarly, to define the text for the footer, you use an h4 element. In the page that's shown here, you can see how jQuery Mobile automatically formats the header, content, and footer components. Here the text for both the header and footer is centered in bold, dark gray type against a light gray background, while the text for the content is dark gray against an extra light gray background. This is the default styling that's done by jQuery Mobile, and it's similar to the styling for a native iPhone application.

Of course, you can code the HTML for whatever content you need within the header, footer, and content components. You'll see this illustrated in the examples that follow. However, this simple example should give you some idea of how easy it is to code and format a single web page.

A web page that uses jQuery Mobile

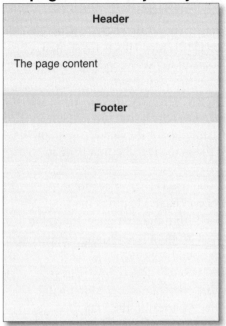

The HTML for the mobile web page

```
<div data-role="page">
    <header data-role="header">
        <h1>Header</h1>
    </header>

    <section class="ui-content" role="main">
        <p>The page content</p>
    </section>

    <footer data-role="footer">
        <h4>Footer</h4>
    </footer>
</div>
```

Description

- The HTML for a typical web page that uses jQuery Mobile will contain div, header, section, and footer elements.

- The data-role attribute is used to identify three parts of a mobile web page: the page itself, the header, and the footer.

- The text that's displayed in the header should be coded within an h1 element. The text that's displayed in the footer should be coded within an h4 element.

- The role attribute with a value "main" is used to identify the section element that contains the main content for the page. This section should also be assigned to the ui-content class. You can code whatever elements you need within this section.

- The style sheet for jQuery Mobile formats the web page based on the values in the data-role, role, and class attributes.

Figure 15-7   How to create one web page with jQuery Mobile

How to code multiple pages in a single HTML file

In contrast to the way you develop the web pages for a full website, jQuery Mobile lets you create multiple pages in a single HTML file. This is illustrated by figure 15-8. Here, you can see two pages of a site along with the HTML for these pages. What's surprising is that both pages are coded within a single HTML file.

For each page, you code one div element with a unique id for each. Then, within each of those div elements, you code the contents for the header, content, and footer of each page. Later, when the HTML file is loaded, the first page in the body of the file is displayed.

To link between the pages in an HTML file, you use HTML placeholders. Here, the id attribute in the div element for the second page identifies the element as a placeholder. Then, to display that page from the first page, the value of the href attribute for the <a> element for the first product is set to the value of the id attribute for the placeholder, preceded by a pound sign (#).

Although this example shows only two pages, you can code many pages within a single HTML file. Remember, though, that all of the pages along with their images are loaded with the single HTML file. As a result, the load time will become excessive if you store too many pages in a single file. When that happens, you can divide your pages into more than one HTML file.

Keep in mind too that because all the pages of a multi-page file are loaded at once, the ids used throughout all the pages must be unique. Even if pages are coded in separate files, though, the ids must be unique across the pages. That's because when the user displays another page, jQuery Mobile adds that page to the DOM instead of replacing the current page.

Two web pages that use jQuery Mobile

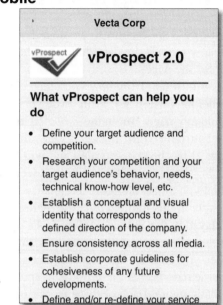

The HTML for the two pages in the body of one HTML file

```
<div data-role="page" id="solutions">
    <header data-role="header"><h1>Vecta Corp</h1></header>
    <section class="ui-content" role="main">
        <h2>Our Solutions</h2>
        <p>Vecta Corp provides scalable business solutions ... </p>
        <h3>vProspect 2.0</h3>
        <img src="images/logo_vprospect.gif" width="84" height="48">
        <p>Define and research your target audience, define ...
            <a href="#vprospect">Read more...</a></p>
        <!-- the rest of the section -->
    </section>
    <footer data-role="footer"><h4>&copy; 2016</h4></footer>
</div>
<div data-role="page" id="vprospect">
    <header data-role="header"><h1>Vecta Corp</h1></header>
    <section class="ui-content" role="main">
        <img src="images/logo_vprospect.gif" width="84" height="48">
        <h2>vProspect 2.0</h2>
        <h3>What vProspect can help you do</h3>
        <ul>
            <!-- the list items -->
        </ul>
    </section>
</div>
```

Description

- When you use jQuery Mobile, you don't have to develop a separate HTML file for each page. Instead, within the body element of a single HTML file, you code one div element for each page with its data-role attribute set to "page".

- For each div element, you set the id attribute to a placeholder value that can be referred to by the href attributes in the <a> elements of other pages.

Figure 15-8   How to code multiple pages in a single HTML file

How to use dialogs and transitions

Figure 15-9 shows how to create a *dialog* that opens when a link is tapped. To do that, you code the data-dialog attribute with a value of "true" on the div element for the page.

This is different from how you created a dialog with versions of jQuery Mobile before version 1.4. With those versions, you coded the dialog just as you would any page. But in the <a> element that goes to that page, you coded a data-rel attribute with "dialog" as its value. Although you can still use this technique, it has been deprecated and will be dropped in version 1.5 of jQuery Mobile. So you shouldn't use it in new web pages you develop.

When you create a dialog, the jQuery Mobile CSS file formats it as shown in the example in this figure. Here, the dialog doesn't occupy the entire screen, and it's displayed with rounded corners and a drop shadow. In addition, it has an "X" in the header that the user must tap to return to the previous page.

When you code an <a> element that goes to another page or dialog, you can also use the data-transition attribute to specify one of the nine *transitions* that are listed in this figure. Each of these transitions is meant to mimic an effect that a mobile device like an iPhone uses.

Incidentally, the transitions work even if the pages are stored in separate files. That's because jQuery Mobile automatically creates an Ajax request for a page that's in a different file than the one for the current page. Then, the next page is added to the DOM, and the transition works as if both pages were in the same file. This is sometimes referred to as "Hijax." If you want to stop this default behavior, you can set the <a> element's data-ajax attribute to "false". Then, the transition will work the way it does for a standard web page.

A page and a dialog that have the same HTML

The web page

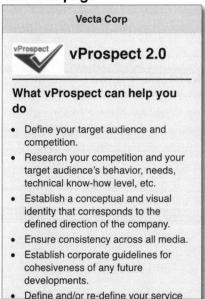

The dialog

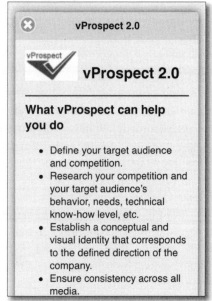

The transitions that can be used

```
slide          slidefade       pop
slideup        fade            turn
slidedown      flip            flow
```

HTML that causes the page to open as a dialog

```
<div data-role="page" id="vprospect" data-dialog="true">
```

HTML that opens the page with the "pop" transition

```
<a href="#vprospect" data-transition="pop">
```

Description

- To display a page as a dialog, you include the data-dialog attribute with the value "true" on the div element for the page. To close the dialog, the user taps the X in the header of the dialog.

- To specify the way a page or a dialog is opened, you can use the data-transition attribute with one of the values listed above. If a device doesn't support the transition that you specify, the attribute is ignored.

- The styling for a dialog is done by the jQuery Mobile CSS file.

Figure 15-9   How to use dialogs and transitions

How to create buttons

Figure 15-10 shows how to use buttons to navigate from one page to another. To do that, you just set the data-role attribute for an <a> element to "button", and jQuery Mobile does the rest.

However, you can also set some other attributes for buttons. If, for example, you want two or more buttons to appear side by side, like the first two buttons in this figure, you can set the data-inline attribute to "true".

If you want to add one of the 22 icons that are provided by jQuery Mobile to a button, you also code the data-icon attribute. For instance, the third button in this example uses the "delete" icon, and the fourth button uses the "home" icon. All of these icons look like the icons that you might see within a native mobile application. Incidentally, these icons are not separate files that the page must access. Instead, they are provided by the jQuery Mobile library.

If you want to group two or more buttons horizontally, like the Yes, No, and Maybe buttons in this figure, you can code the <a> elements for the buttons within a div element that has "controlgroup" as its data-role attribute and "horizontal" as its data-type attribute. Or, to group the buttons vertically, you can change the data-type attribute to "vertical".

If you set the data-rel attribute for a button to "back" and the href attribute to the pound symbol (#), the button will return to the page that called it. In other words, the button works like a Back button. This is illustrated by the last button in the content for the page.

The last two buttons show how buttons appear in the footer for a page. Notice in the code for these buttons that, even though the data-inline attribute isn't set to "true", the buttons appear side by side. That's because this is the default for buttons in a footer. Also notice that the class attribute for the footer is set to "ui-bar". That causes jQuery Mobile to put a little more space around the contents of the footer.

A mobile web page that displays buttons

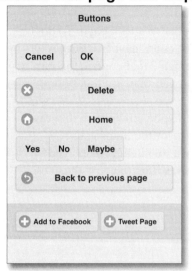

The icons that are provided by jQuery Mobile

```
delete       arrow-l       arrow-r       arrow-u       arrow-d       search
plus         minus         check         gear          refresh       forward
back         grid          star          alert         info          home
carat-l      carat-r       carat-t       carat-b
```

The HTML for the buttons in the main content

```html
<!-- For inline buttons, set the data-inline attribute to true -->
<a href="#" data-role="button" data-inline="true">Cancel</a>
<a href="#" data-role="button" data-inline="true">OK</a>
<!-- To add an icon to a button, use the data-icon attribute -->
<a href="#" data-role="button" data-icon="delete">Delete</a>
<a href="#" data-role="button" data-icon="home">Home</a>
<!-- To group buttons, use a div element with the attributes that follow -->
<div data-role="controlgroup" data-type="horizontal">
    <a href="#" data-role="button">Yes</a>
    <a href="#" data-role="button">No</a>
    <a href="#" data-role="button">Maybe</a>
</div>
<!-- To code a Back button, set the data-rel attribute to back -->
<a href="#" data-role="button" data-rel="back" data-icon="back">
    Back to previous page</a>
```

The HTML for the buttons in the footer

```html
<footer data-role="footer" class="ui-bar">
    <a href="http://www.facebook.com" data-role="button"
        data-icon="plus">Add to Facebook</a>
    <a href="http://www.twitter.com" data-role="button"
        data-icon="plus">Tweet Page</a>
</footer>
```

Description

- To add a button to a web page, you code an <a> element with its data-role attribute set to "button".

Figure 15-10   How to create buttons

How to create a navigation bar

Figure 15-11 shows how you can add a navigation bar to a web page. To do that, you code a div element with its data-role attribute set to "navbar". Within this element, you code a ul element that contains li elements that contain the <a> elements for the items in the navigation bar. Note, however, that you don't code the data-role attribute for the <a> elements.

By default, all of the items in a navigation bar are displayed with a light gray background and dark gray type. If you want to make one of the items active, though, you can assign the ui-btn-active class to it. Then, the item is displayed with an attractive blue background and white type. This is illustrated by the "Solutions" item shown here.

A mobile web page with a navigation bar

The HTML for the navigation bar

```
<header data-role="header">
    <h1>Vecta Corp</h1>
    <div data-role="navbar">
        <ul>
            <li><a href="#home" data-icon="home">Home</a></li>
            <li><a href="#solutions" class="ui-btn-active"
                data-icon="star">Solutions</a></li>
            <li><a href="#contactus" data-icon="grid">Contact Us</a></li>
        </ul>
    </div>
</header>
```

How to code the HTML for a navigation bar

- Code a div element within the header element. Then, set the data-role attribute for the div element to "navbar".

- Within the div element, code a ul element that contains one li element for each item.

- Within each li element, code an <a> element with an href attribute that refers to the placeholder for the page that the link should go to. Then, set the data-icon attribute to the icon of your choosing.

- For the active item in the navigation bar, set the class attribute to "ui-btn-active". Then, this item will be displayed with a blue background and a white font by default.

Description

- A navigation bar is a type of jQuery Mobile toolbar. The other types of toolbars are the header bar and footer bar that you learned about in figure 15-7.

- Navigation bars are commonly coded within the header for a web page as shown above.

Figure 15-11   How to create a navigation bar

How to format content with jQuery Mobile

As you've already seen, jQuery Mobile automatically formats the components of a web page based on its own style sheet. Now, you'll learn more about that, as well as how to adjust the default styling that jQuery Mobile uses.

How to work with the default styles

Figure 15-12 shows the default styles that jQuery Mobile uses for common HTML elements. For all of its styles, jQuery Mobile relies on the browser's rendering engine so its own styling is minimal. This keeps load times fast and minimizes the overhead that excessive CSS would impose on a page.

In general, jQuery Mobile's styling works the way you want it to. For instance, the dark gray type on the light gray background is consistent with the formatting for native mobile applications.

To fine tune that styling, though, you often need to provide your own CSS style sheet. For instance, the spacing before and after HTML elements may not be the way you want it. Or, you may want to add top or bottom borders to elements. Then, you can use the border, margin, and padding properties in your own style sheet to get this formatting the way you want it.

The default styles for common HTML elements

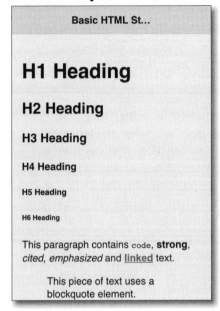

Basic HTML St...

H1 Heading

H2 Heading

H3 Heading

H4 Heading

H5 Heading

H6 Heading

This paragraph contains code, **strong**, *cited*, *emphasized* and <u>linked</u> text.

> This piece of text uses a blockquote element.

- Unordered list item 1
- Unordered list item 2
- Unordered list item 3

1. Ordered list item 1
2. Ordered list item 2
3. Ordered list item 3

Description term 1
  Description text 1
Description term 2
  Description text 2

The example below shows how jQuery Mobile handles tables:

Sales by Book

Book	Author	Sales
PHP	J. Murach	$372,381
HTML5	A. Boehm	$243,762
Dreamweaver	Z. Ruvalcaba	$52,447
Total Sales		$821,590

Description

- By default, jQuery Mobile automatically applies styles to the HTML elements for a page. These styles are not only attractive, but also mimic a browser's native styles.
- By default, jQuery Mobile applies a small amount of padding to the left, right, top, and bottom of each mobile page.
- By default, links are slightly larger than normal text. This makes it easier for the user to tap the links.
- By default, links are underlined with blue as the font color.
- To get the formatting for a page the way you want it, especially for borders and spacing before and after an element, you often need to use your own style sheet.

Figure 15-12   The default styles that jQuery Mobile uses

How to apply themes to HTML elements

The styles that jQuery Mobile uses are provided by its default *theme*, which is meant to mimic the appearance of a native mobile application. This theme includes some global settings, such as the font family, as well as two *swatches*: swatch a and swatch b. These swatches control the color schemes that are used by various elements. Figure 15-13 shows how these theme swatches work.

By default, jQuery Mobile uses swatch "a", which is the swatch you've seen so far in this chapter. You can use one of two techniques to change an element so it uses swatch "b". First, you can code a data-theme attribute with the swatch letter as its value. You can see this in the HTML for the second header in this figure. Here, the data-theme attribute applies swatch "b" to the header and swatch "a" to the items in the navigation bar. That's why the header appears with white type on a dark gray background.

Before I go on, you should realize that when you apply a swatch to an element, it's inherited by any child elements. For instance, because swatch "b" is coded for the header in the second example, the items in the navigation bar inherit that swatch. To use swatch "a" for those items, then, you must code the data-theme attribute for them.

The other way to apply swatches is to set the class attribute for an element to a class name that indicates a swatch. This is illustrated by the second example after the code for the second header. Here, the class attribute is used to apply both the "ui-bar" and "ui-bar-b" classes to a div element. As a result, jQuery Mobile first applies its default styling for a bar to the element and then applies swatch "b" to that styling.

You may be interested to know that versions of jQuery Mobile prior to 1.4 provided five different swatches. Even though these swatches have been simplified and reduced to two basic swatches, you should know that you can modify these swatches and create additional swatches. To do that, you use the ThemeRoller application as described next.

Two headers and navigation bars that illustrate the use of theme swatches

Header "a", bar "b"

Header "b", bar "a"

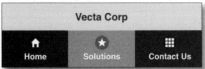

The HTML for the second header and navigation bar

```
<header data-role="header" data-theme="b">
    <h1>Vecta Corp</h1>
    <div data-role="navbar">
        <ul>
            <li><a href="#home" data-icon="home"
                    data-theme="a">Home</a></li>
            <li><a href="#solutions" data-icon="star"
                    data-theme="a" class="ui-btn-active">Solutions</a></li>
            <li><a href="#contactus" data-icon="grid"
                    data-theme="a">Contact Us</a></li>
        </ul>
    </div>
</header>
```

Two ways to apply a swatch

By using a data-theme attribute

```
<li><a href="#home" class="ui-btn-active"
        data-icon="home" data-theme="b">Home</a></li>
```

By using a class attribute that indicates the swatch

```
<div class="ui-bar ui-bar-b">...</div>
```

The URL for a page that illustrates the two swatches

```
http://demos.jquerymobile.com/1.4.5/theme-default/
```

Description

- jQuery Mobile includes a default *theme* that consists of global settings, including the font and the corner radius of buttons and boxes, and swatches.

- The two *swatches* that come with the default theme define different color combinations for various elements. In general, swatch "a" (the default) provides a light gray background with a dark gray font, and swatch "b" provides a dark gray background with a white font.

- If you specify a swatch for an element, that swatch is inherited by any child elements. If that's not what you want, you can specify a different swatch for the child elements as shown above for the second header and navigation bar.

Figure 15-13   How to apply themes to HTML elements

How to use ThemeRoller to roll your own theme

In addition to changing the theme swatches that are applied, you can "roll your own" theme. To do that, you can use jQuery Mobile's ThemeRoller application, which is summarized in figure 15-14. This application lets you set custom properties for the jQuery Mobile elements as a whole as well as set the properties for swatches a, b, and c.

To change the color for a component of a swatch, you just drag it from the color palette at the top of the page to the component. If, for example, you want to change the swatch A color for a link to a darker blue, you drag the color to the link that's shown for that swatch. You can also use the collapsible panels for a tab in the left sidebar to adjust other properties. When you've made all of the changes that you want to make, you download the CSS file for the theme that you've created as described in this figure and deploy it to your web server.

To use your own theme for the pages in an HTML file, you add a link element to the file that refers to the downloaded CSS file. Note, however, that this link element must come after the one for the jQuery Mobile CSS file. Once that's done, the custom styles that you've created will override the default styles.

As a practical matter, you may decide that you don't need to roll your own theme for your website. That's because the default styles do a good job of simulating native user interfaces. If you want to improve on that, though, the ThemeRoller is available to you.

Roll your own theme with ThemeRoller

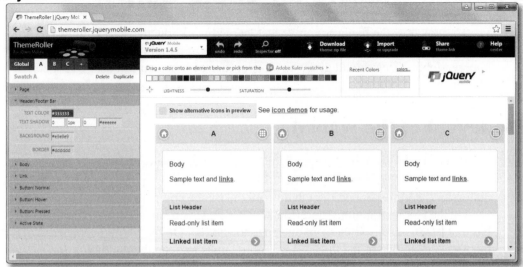

The URL for ThemeRoller

jquerymobile.com/themeroller/

How to roll your own theme

1. Adjust the global properties or the properties for a swatch by using the collapsible panels for a tab and by dragging colors from the color palette to specific elements.

2. When you're satisfied with your theme, click the "Download theme zip file" button in the navigation bar at the top of the page.

3. In the Download Theme dialog box, enter a name for your theme. Then, click the Download Zip button to download a zip file that contains the CSS file for the theme.

4. Extract and deploy the CSS file on your web server.

How to use your own theme

- Add a link element that refers to the CSS file to each HTML file that uses the theme. This link element must come after the one for the jQuery Mobile CSS file.

Description

- ThemeRoller lets you create your own custom themes based on the default jQuery Mobile theme.

- You can choose the colors for a swatch from ThemeRoller's color library or from Adobe's Kuler swatches.

- The collapsible panels in the Global tab of the sidebar let you adjust the font, the active state of an element, the corner radius of a box, the icons used, and box shadows.

- The collapsible panels in tabs A, B, and C let you customize the colors of the header and footer bar, the content body, and the normal, hover, and pressed states of buttons.

- If you click on the last tab (the one with the plus sign), another swatch is added.

Figure 15-14   How to use ThemeRoller to roll your own theme

A mobile website for Vecta Corp

To show how the features you've just learned work together in a complete website, this chapter ends by presenting four pages of a mobile site that uses jQuery Mobile. This should give you a better idea of how you can use jQuery Mobile to build your own sites.

The layout of the website

Figure 15-15 presents four pages of the mobile version of the Vecta Corp website. That includes the Home, Solutions, and Contact Us pages, as well as the dialog for the vProspect product that is offered by the company.

On the Home, Solutions, and Contact Us pages, you can see the navigation bar that lets the user switch from one page to another. On the Solutions page, the user can tap one of the three "Read more" links to open the dialog for that product. Then, the user must tap the "X" in the header for the product dialog to close the dialog and return to the Solutions page.

On the Contact Us page, you can see a phone number, a mailing address, and an email address. If the user taps on the phone number, the user's device will try to call that number. If the user taps on the email address, the user's device will try to start an email to that address. And if the user taps the Back button at the bottom of the Contact Us page, the previous page is displayed.

The page layouts for a simple mobile website that uses jQuery Mobile

The Home page

The Solutions page

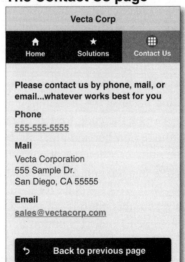

The vProspect dialog

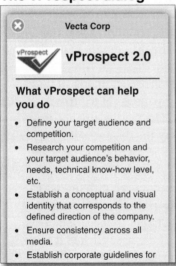

The Contact Us page

Description

- When the user taps a button or a link for another page, the page is opened.
- When the user taps the phone number on the Contact Us page, the device's phone feature will try to call the number.
- When the user taps the email address on the Contact Us page, the device's email feature will try to start an email for that address.
- When the user taps the button at the bottom of the Contact Us page, the previous page is reopened.

Figure 15-15   A mobile website for Vecta Corp

The HTML for the mobile website

Figure 15-16 presents the HTML for this website in three parts. Since this HTML uses the features that you've just learned, you should understand it without any help. In case you're interested, though, here are a few highlights.

In the head section in part 1, the viewport metadata specifies a width equal to the device width and an initial scale and maximum scale of 1. This should work for all mobile devices, including iPhones and Android devices.

The head section also includes the link elements for the jQuery Mobile CSS file and the developer's CSS file. These link elements are followed by the script elements for jQuery and jQuery Mobile, both of which point to the files in a Content Delivery Network.

In the body section in part 1, you can see the HTML for the Home page of the site. Since this page is first in the file, it is the one that will be displayed when the HTML file is loaded. Like any jQuery Mobile web page, it uses data-role attributes to identify the page, header, and footer components and the role attribute and ui-content class to identify the content component.

In part 2 of this figure, you can see the code for the Solutions page. To go from this page to the dialogs for the three products, each product description ends with a "Read more" link. To add a little fun, three different transitions are used to go to and from the dialogs: slideup, slidedown, and flip. If you run this application on your computer, you'll be able to see the differences in these transitions.

In part 3 of this figure, you can see the code for the vProspect dialog. It will open as a dialog because the data-dialog attribute for the page is set to "true".

You can also see the code for the Contact Us page. Here, <a> elements are used for the phone number and email address. That's why the device will try to call the phone number when the phone number is tapped and will try to start an email message when the email address is tapped.

This page ends with the code for a button that has its data-rel attribute set to "back". As a result, this button will return to the previous page. If, for example, the user clicked the Contact Us button in the Home page to get to the Contact Us page, this button will return the user to the Home page. If the user clicked it from the Solutions page, it will return the user to the Solutions page.

The style sheet for the mobile website

The developer's style sheet for this application uses simple CSS to apply top borders, margins, and padding to some of the elements in the HTML. If you look at the way the Solutions page is displayed in figure 15-15, for example, you can tell that the styles in the developer's style sheet have been used to provide top borders to the h3 elements. They have also been used to set the margins and padding for the elements. Otherwise, this formatting wouldn't be satisfactory. If you want to review this style sheet, you can review the file in the downloaded application.

The HTML for the head section and the Home page

```html
<head>
    <meta charset="utf-8">
    <meta name="viewport" content="width=device-width,
        initial-scale=1, maximum-scale=1">
    <title>Vecta Corp. Mobile</title>
    <!-- style sheets -->
    <link rel="stylesheet"
        href="http://code.jquery.com/mobile/1.4.5/jquery.mobile-1.4.5.min.css">
    <link rel="stylesheet" href="main.css">
    <!-- JavaScript files -->
    <script src="http://code.jquery.com/jquery-2.1.4.min.js"></script>
    <script
        src="http://code.jquery.com/mobile/1.4.5/jquery.mobile-1.4.5.min.js">
    </script>
</head>

<body>
<div data-role="page" id="home">
    <header data-role="header">
        <h1>Vecta Corp</h1>
        <div data-role="navbar">
            <ul>
                <li><a href="#home" data-icon="home"
                        class="ui-btn-active" data-theme="b">Home</a></li>
                <li><a href="#solutions" data-icon="star"
                        data-theme="b">Solutions</a></li>
                <li><a href="#contactus" data-icon="grid"
                        data-theme="b">Contact Us</a></li>
            </ul>
        </div>
    </header>
    <section class="ui-content" role="main">
        <h2>Why people choose Vecta</h2>
        <p>Vecta Corp provides software packages that help companies increase
            sales in three ways:</p>
        <ul>
            <li>Finding prosects</li>
            <li>Converting prospects to customers</li>
            <li>Retaining customers</li>
        </ul>
        <p>To find out more, go to <a href="#solutions">Solutions</a>.</p>

        <h3>What our clients say</h3>
        <q>Throughout the years we have worked with Vecta Corp, we have always
            been amazed at their level of dedication and professionalism.</q>
        <cite>Zak Ruvalcaba, CEO<br>Module Media, Inc.</cite>
        <q>Incredible results from an incredible effort by the Vecta Corp.
            team! We are very pleased with the business benefits we have
            received by working with them.</q>
        <cite>Robin Banks, CEO<br>Profits Financial, Inc.</cite>
    </section>
    <footer data-role="footer"><h4>&copy; 2016</h4></footer>
</div>
```

Figure 15-16   The HTML for the Vecta Corp mobile site (part 1 of 3)

The HTML for the Solutions page

```
<div data-role="page" id="solutions">
    <header data-role="header">
        <h1>Vecta Corp</h1>
        <div data-role="navbar">
        <ul>
            <li><a href="#home" data-icon="home"
                data-theme="b">Home</a></li>
            <li><a href="#solutions" data-icon="star" class="ui-btn-active"
                data-theme="b">Solutions</a></li>
            <li><a href="#contactus" data-icon="grid"
                data-theme="b">Contact Us</a></li>
        </ul>
        </div>
    </header>

    <section class="ui-content" role="main">
        <h2>Our Solutions</h2>
        <p>Vecta Corp provides scalable business solutions to help companies
            achieve success through revenue increase, cost management, and user
            satisfaction.</p>

        <h3>vProspect 2.0</h3>
        <img src="images/logo_vprospect.gif" width="84" height="48">
        <p>Define and research your target audience, define your strategy to
            reach that audience and present a strong and memorable brand to
            that audience.
            <a href="#vprospect" data-transition="slideup">Read more...</a></p>

        <h3>vConvert 2.0</h3>
        <img src="images/logo_vconvert.gif" width="84" height="48">
        <p>Create a highly user-friendly and easy-to-navigate information
            architecture that will help your prospects interact with the
            company on a highly interactive level.
            <a href="#vconvert" data-transition="slidedown">
                Read more...</a></p>

        <h3>vRetain 1.0</h3>
        <img src="images/logo_vretain.gif" width="84" height="48">
        <p>Build on existing customer relationships to improve productivity
            and maximize customer loyalty, while growing revenues.
            <a href="#vretain" data-transition="flip">Read more...</a></p>
    </section>
    <footer data-role="footer">
        <h4>&copy; 2016</h4>
    </footer>
</div>
```

Figure 15-16   The HTML for the Vecta Corp mobile site (part 2 of 3)

The HTML for the vProspect and the Contact Us pages

```
<div data-role="page" id="vprospect" data-dialog="true">
    <header data-role="header">
        <h1>Vecta Corp</h1>
    </header>
    <section class="ui-content" role="main">
        <img src="images/logo_vprospect.gif" width="84" height="48">
        <h2>vProspect 2.0</h2>
        <h3>What vProspect can help you do</h3>
        <ul>
            <li>Define your target audience and competition.</li>
            <li>Research your competition and your target audience&rsquo;s
                behavior, needs, technical know-how level, etc.</li>
            <li>Establish a conceptual and visual identity that corresponds to
                the defined direction of the company.</li>
            <li>Ensure consistency across all media.</li>
            <li>Establish corporate guidelines for cohesiveness of any future
                developments.</li>
            <li>Define and/or re-define your service and/or product
                offerings.</li>
            <li>Define expansion plans and strategies.</li>
            <li>Implement Search Engine Optimization of all Online
                materials.</li>
        </ul>
    </section>
</div>

<div data-role="page" id="contactus">
    <header data-role="header">
        <h1>Vecta Corp</h1>
        <div data-role="navbar">
        <ul>
            <li><a href="#home" data-icon="home" data-theme="b">Home</a></li>
            <li><a href="#solutions" data-icon="star" data-theme="b">
                Solutions</a></li>
            <li><a href="#contactus" data-icon="grid" class="ui-btn-active"
                data-theme="b">Contact Us</a></li>
        </ul>
        </div>
    </header>
    <section class="ui-content" role="main">
        <h4>Please contact us by phone, mail, or email...whatever works best
            for you</h4>
        <h4>Phone</h4><p><a href="tel:555-555-5555">555-555-5555</a></p>
        <h4>Mail</h4>
        <p>Vecta Corporation<br>555 Sample Dr.<br>San Diego, CA 55555</p>
        <h4>Email</h4>
            <p><a href="mailto:sales@vectacorp.com">sales@vectacorp.com</a>
            </p><br>
        <a href"#" data-role="button" data-rel="back" data-icon="back"
            data-theme="b">Back to previous page</a>
    </section>
    <footer data-role="footer"><h4>&copy; 2016</h4></footer>
</div>
</body>
```

Figure 15-16   The HTML for the Vecta Corp mobile site (part 3 of 3)

Perspective

Now that you have completed this chapter, you should be able to build simple websites with jQuery Mobile. You should also realize that jQuery Mobile has made the task of building a mobile website much easier. In the next chapter, you'll learn how to use many of the other features that jQuery Mobile offers.

Terms

Responsive Web Design	jQuery Mobile
fluid layout	dialog
scalable image	transition
media query	theme
viewport	swatch

Summary

- One way to provide web pages for mobile devices is to build a separate website for those devices. Then, you can use client-side or server-side code to detect mobile devices and redirect them from your full website to your mobile website.

- Another way to provide web pages for mobile devices is to use *Responsive Web Design*. This involves using a *fluid layout*, *scalable images*, and *media queries*.

- The *viewport* on a mobile device determines the content that's displayed. To control how that works, you can code a viewport meta element in the head section of a page.

- *jQuery Mobile* is a JavaScript library that's designed for developing mobile websites. jQuery Mobile uses the core jQuery library along with its own CSS file.

- To include the jQuery Mobile and jQuery libraries in a web page, you code script elements in the head section. Because jQuery Mobile uses jQuery, the script element for jQuery Mobile must be coded after the one for jQuery.

- jQuery Mobile lets you code the HTML for many mobile pages in a single HTML file. jQuery Mobile also supports the use of dialogs, transitions, buttons, navigation bars, and more.

- By default, jQuery Mobile uses a *theme* that provides formatting that relies on a browser's native rendering engine. jQuery Mobile also provides two *swatches* that you can use to adjust the default formatting without using CSS style sheets of your own.

- If you want to roll your own theme, jQuery Mobile's ThemeRoller application lets you do that.

Exercise 15-1   Experiment with the mobile website

In this exercise, you'll first test the mobile version of the Vecta Corp website that's presented in this chapter. Then, you'll make some simple modifications to it.

Open and test the mobile website for Vecta Corp

1. Use your text editor to open the HTML page in this folder:

   `c:\jquery\exercises\ch15\vectacorp\`

2. Test this page and the navigation from one page to another within the site. The easiest way to do that is to run the page in Chrome, press F12 to display the developer tools, click the Toggle Device Mode icon, and then choose a mobile device like iPhone 6. Then, you can use your mouse to "tap" on a link. As you go from page to page, remember that all of the pages come from one HTML file. Also, notice the differences in the transitions that are used when you display the dialogs for the three products.

3. From the Home page, click on the Contact Us button in the navigation bar. Then, click on the Back button in the Contact Us page, and note that you return to the Home page. Next, do the same starting from the Solutions page, and note that you are returned to the Solutions page.

Modify the way the pages work and test these changes

4. Modify the code for the button at the bottom of the Contact Us page so it always returns to the Solutions page, no matter how the user got there.

5. Change the vProspect page so it is opened as a page, not as a dialog. When you test this, compare the product page with one of the product dialogs to see the differences in the formatting.

6. Add a button at the bottom of the Solutions page that goes to the Contact Us page. Use theme swatch "b" for this button so it looks like the Back button on the Contact Us page.

7. Create a new page that has "aboutus" as its id. This page should have the same navigation bar as the other pages, but its contents should contain just one heading that says: "About Us". Then, in the Home page, change the paragraph and link that goes to the Solutions page so it goes to the About Us page and reads like this:

   To find out more about us, go to <u>About Us</u>.

8. Temporarily delete or comment out the link for the developer's style sheet. Then, run the website to see the default formatting. This demonstrates the need for a developer's style sheet. Now, restore the link to the style sheet, and run the application again.

9. Add a data-theme attribute to the header of the Home page that changes the default theme to "b", and change the theme for the buttons in the navigation bar on the Home page from "b" to "a". Test the change to see what you think of the results. Then, change the themes back the way they were.

16

How to enhance a jQuery Mobile website

In the last chapter, you were introduced to jQuery Mobile. Now, you'll learn how to enhance your mobile pages with content formatting, list views, and form controls.

How to use the jQuery Mobile documentation

This chapter and the last chapter are designed to get you started fast with jQuery Mobile by showing you the common ways that its components are used. Keep in mind, however, that these chapters don't present everything there is to know about jQuery Mobile. For that, there's the jQuery Mobile website, and the three topics that follow present a few highlights.

The demos for jQuery Mobile

One of the best ways to start learning about jQuery Mobile is to study the many demos that are provided for its components. In figure 16-1, for example, you can see that the home page for the demos includes a list of the jQuery components by category. Then, you can click on the links in the categories to see examples of how to use the components. You learned how to use pages, transitions, buttons, icons, and navigation bars in chapter 15, and you'll learn how to use grids, list views, collapsible content blocks, collapsible sets, and form controls in this chapter. If you need more information about any of these components, you'll find it here.

The data attributes of jQuery Mobile

As you use the components of jQuery Mobile, it's often hard to keep track of what data attributes are available. That's when the Data Attribute Reference in the API section of the documentation can be useful. To display this reference, go to the API documentation, click the Reference link at the left side of the page, and then click the Data Attributes link.

In this figure, the portion of the reference that applies to buttons is shown. It neatly summarizes the attributes that can be used with buttons. You learned about some of this attributes in figure 15-10 of the last chapter, but this shows that there are a few more. For instance, the data-iconpos attribute lets you specify the position of an icon, and the data-mini attribute when set to true produces a smaller version of the button. In the same way, this reference can be useful when you're working with other components.

The events, methods, and properties of jQuery Mobile

When you use jQuery Mobile, you can use its events, methods, and properties whenever they are needed. For example, you can use the changePage method to display one page from another. However, one of the strengths of jQuery Mobile is that it uses these events, methods, and properties automatically, so you don't typically need to code them yourself. For that reason, the two chapters in this book don't show you how to use them. If you're interested, though, you can refer to the API section of the documentation.

The URL for the jQuery Mobile website

`http://jquerymobile.com`

The components by category on the home page for the demos

The data attribute reference for buttons

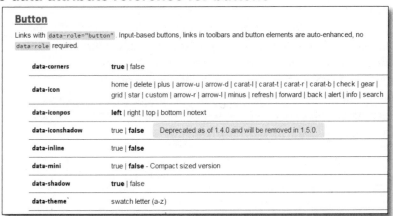

Description

- This chapter and the last chapter are designed to get you started fast with jQuery Mobile by showing you the common ways that its components are used.

- The jQuery Mobile documentation, which is excellent, presents all the ways that its components can be used, including the use of its data attributes.

- To get started, you can go to the jQuery Mobile website shown above, click the Demos link, and then click the link for the current release of jQuery Mobile to display information and demos of the various components.

- If you need additional information, you can click the API Documentation link from the home page of the jQuery Mobile site and then use the available links, categories, and search to get the information you need.

Figure 16-1   How to use the jQuery Mobile documentation

How to use jQuery Mobile to format content

jQuery Mobile provides for formatting content using grids, collapsible content blocks, and collapsible sets. You'll learn how to use these components in the three topics that follow.

How to lay out content in grids

Figure 16-2 shows how to lay out content in grids that consist of rows and columns. In this example, the grid consists of just two columns, but jQuery Mobile provides for up to five columns. In most cases, though, you'll limit the columns to what you can see on a page at one time.

To create columns and rows, you use jQuery Mobile classes that indicate the number of columns and identify the content for each column. In this figure, for example, you can see that all the columns are coded within a section element with the ui-grid-a class. This class is used to format the content into two columns. Then, the content of the first column is coded within a div element with the ui-block-a class, and the content of the second column is coded within a div element with the ui-block-b class.

If you need to extend this code to create additional columns, you can do that by using additional classes. For a three-column grid, for example, you set the class for the section to ui-grid-b. For a four-column grid, you set this class to ui-grid-c. And for a five-column grid, you set this class to ui-grid-d.

After that, you just add the div elements for the additional columns. Then, the third column uses the ui-block-c class, the fourth column uses the ui-block-d class, and the fifth column uses the ui-block-e class.

A mobile web page with a grid that has two columns

The HTML for the two columns

```
<section class="ui-grid-a">
    <div class="ui-block-a">
        <img src="images/agnes.gif" alt="Agnes">
        <h4><a href="#agnes">Agnes Agnew</a></h4>
        <p>VP of Accounting</p>
        <!-- the code for the other speakers in the first column -->
    </div>
    <div class="ui-block-b">
        <img src="images/mike.gif" alt="Mike">
        <h4><a href="#mike">Mike Masters</a></h4>
        <p>VP of Marketing</p>
        <!-- the code for the other speakers in the second column -->
    </div>
</section>
```

How to code the HTML for two columns

- Code a section (or div) element for the two-column area, and set its class to "ui-grid-a".

- Within this section, code one div element for each column, and set the class for these elements to "ui-block-a" and "ui-block-b".

- In the div elements for the columns, code the content for the columns.

Description

- jQuery Mobile lets you lay out content in grids that consist of columns and rows.

- The ui-block-a and ui-block-b classes are formatted by jQuery Mobile so they float left. As a result, the div elements in the example above are displayed in two columns.

- To lay out a page with three columns, set the class for the top-level section or div element to "ui-grid-b" and set the class for the third column to "ui-block-c". This can continue for up to five columns.

Figure 16-2   How to lay out content in grids

How to use collapsible content blocks

Figure 16-3 shows how to use content blocks that collapse so just a heading is displayed. This is similar to how the jQuery UI accordion works, except that more than one content block can be displayed at the same time.

To create *collapsible content blocks*, you code a div element for each block and set its data-role attribute to "collapsible". Then, by default, all of the blocks will be collapsed when the page is first displayed as shown in the first web page in this figure. If that's not what you want, you can set the data-collapsed attribute for one or more blocks to "false". In the code in this figure, this attribute has been added to the second content block. The result is shown in the second web page.

Note that the text that's displayed in the button for a content block is the content of the header element that's coded at the beginning of the block. In this figure, an h3 element is used for the header, but you can use any header element from h1 through h6. The element you use doesn't affect how the text is displayed.

A mobile web page with collapsible content blocks

With all blocks collapsed

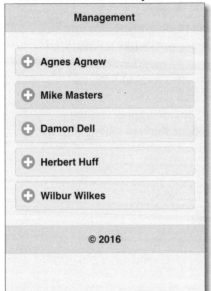

With the second block expanded

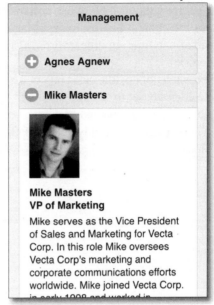

The HTML for the collapsible content blocks

```
<div data-role="collapsible">
    <h3>Agnes Agnew</h3>
    <img src="images/agnes.gif" alt="Agnes">
    <h4>Agnes Agnew<br>VP of Accounting</h4>
    <p>With over 14 years of public accounting and business...</p>
</div>
<div data-role="collapsible" data-collapsed="false">
    <h3>Mike Masters</h3>
    <img src="images/mike.gif" alt="Mike">
    <h4>Mike Masters<br>VP of Marketing</h4>
    <p>Mike serves as the Vice President of Sales and Marketing...</p>
</div>
<!-- the div elements for the other content blocks -->
```

How to code the HTML for collapsible content blocks

- Code a div element for each content block with the data-role attribute set to "collapsible".

- By default, each content block will be collapsed when the page is first displayed. To expand a content block, add the data-collapsed attribute with its value set to "false".

- Within each div element, code a header element (h1 through h6) with the text that will be displayed when a block is collapsed, followed by the HTML for the content.

Description

- More than one *collapsible content block* can be expanded at the same time.

- jQuery Mobile automatically adds the plus and minus icons for the content blocks. You can change these icons using the data-collapsed-icon and data-expanded-icon attributes.

Figure 16-3   How to use collapsible content blocks

How to use collapsible sets

Figure 16-4 shows how to use collapsible sets. *Collapsible sets* are similar to collapsible content blocks, except that the content of only one block can be displayed at one time. In other words, a collapsible set works like a jQuery UI accordion.

To create a collapsible set, you code a section or div element with its data-role attribute set to "collapsible-set". Then, within this element, you code collapsible content blocks like the ones you saw in the last figure. The only difference is that you can only set the data-collapsed attribute to "false" for one of the blocks.

A mobile web page with a collapsible set

With all blocks collapsed

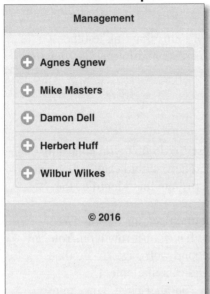

With the first block expanded

The HTML for the collapsible set

```
<section data-role="collapsibleset">
    <div data-role="collapsible" data-collapsed="false">
        <h3>Agnes Agnew</h3>
        <img src="images/agnes.gif" alt="Agnes">
        <h4>Agnes Agnew<br>VP of Accounting</h4>
        <p>With over 14 years of public accounting and...</p>
        <a href="mailto:agnes@vectacorp.com" data-role="button"
            class="ui-bar">Email Agnes</a>
    </div>
    <!-- the div elements for the other content blocks -->
</section>
```

How to code the HTML for a collapsible set

- Code a section (or div) element for the collapsible set, and set its data-role attribute to "collapsibleset".
- Code the content blocks within the set the same way you code collapsible content blocks (see figure 16-3).

Description

- In contrast to collapsible content blocks, only one block in a *collapsible set* can be expanded at the same time. This works just like a jQuery UI accordion.
- jQuery Mobile automatically adds the plus and minus icons for the content blocks. You can change these icons using the data-collapsed-icon and data-expanded-icon attributes.

Figure 16-4   How to use collapsible sets

How to use jQuery Mobile for list views

In jQuery Mobile, a *list view* consists of a list of items that link to other pages. In the topics that follow, you'll learn how to create and format list views so they work the way you want them to.

How to use basic lists

Figure 16-5 shows you how to create a basic list. To do that, you code a ul element and set its data-role attribute to "listview". Then, within each li element for the list, you code an <a> element with an href attribute that identifies the page to be displayed when the list item is tapped.

The first web page in this figure shows the default appearance for a list. Here, the content of each link is displayed along with a right-arrow icon. You can also number the items in the list as shown in the second web page. To do that, you code the li elements within an ol element instead of a ul element.

Note that because each element in a list displays another page, you can use any of the six transitions you learned about in the last chapter to display that page. To do that, you just code the data-transition attribute on the <a> element. If you want the page to slide into view, for example, you can set this attribute to "slide".

Mobile web pages with a list view

A basic list

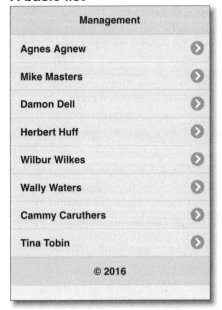

A numbered list

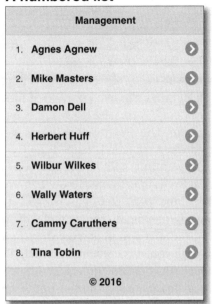

The HTML for the first list view

```
<ul data-role="listview">
    <li><a href="#agnes">Agnes Agnew</a></li>
    <li><a href="#mike">Mike Masters</a></li>
    <li><a href="#damon">Damon Dell</a></li>
    <li><a href="#herbert">Herbert Huff</a></li>
    <li><a href="#wilbur">Wilbur Wilkes</a></li>
    <li><a href="#wally">Wally Waters</a></li>
    <li><a href="#cammy">Cammy Caruthers</a></li>
    <li><a href="#tina">Tina Tobin</a></li>
</ul>
```

How to code the HTML for a basic list

- Code a ul element with its data-role attribute set to "listview".
- Within the ul element, code one li element for each item in your list.
- Within each li element, code an <a> element that links to another page. This element can contain any content you want.
- To create a numbered list, change the ul element to an ol element.

Description

- *List views* are used to display lists of items that link to other pages when tapped.
- jQuery Mobile automatically adds a right-arrow icon to the right side of each list item. You can change this icon using the data-icon attribute.

Figure 16-5   How to use basic lists

How to use split button lists and inset lists

In most cases, you'll want the items in a list to display the same page no matter where the user taps on them. Occasionally, though, you may want to provide list items that can link to two different pages. To do that, you can use *split button lists* as shown in figure 16-6.

In the web pages at the top of this figure, you can see that the list items have two distinct areas: the main portion of the list item and the icon at the right side of the list item. To create a list like this, you code a second <a> element within each list item. The href attribute of this element should indicate the page that's displayed when the icon is tapped.

When you use a split button list, you can also change the icon that's displayed for each list item. To do that, you code the data-split-icon attribute with one of the icon values you learned about in the last chapter. In the second list shown in this figure, for example, the indicator has been changed to a gear.

This example also illustrates an *inset list*. This type of list is typically used when a page contains content other than the list. As you can see, an inset list is formatted with rounded corners, and it is inset from the left and right sides of the screen. To create an inset list, you simply set the data-inset attribute of the ul element to "true".

In the examples in this figure, it's clear that more information about a manager will be displayed when the user taps the main portion of a list item. But how does the user know what will happen when the indicator is tapped? The answer is that the user won't know unless the indicator makes it clear. To indicate that an email will be started, for example, the indicator should be an envelope. Fortunately, you can create custom icons like this for use in your applications. To learn how to do that, you can refer to the documentation for button icons. Then, you can apply this technique to the items in a list.

Mobile web pages with a split button list

With the defaults

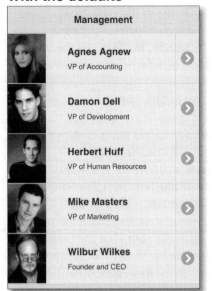

With an inset list and special icon

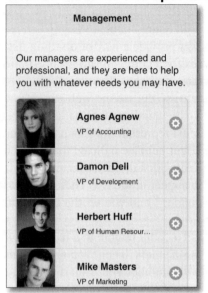

The HTML for the first list

```html
<ul data-role="listview">
    <li>
        <a href="#agnes">
            <img src="images/agnes.gif" alt="Agnes">
            <h3>Agnes Agnew</h3>
            <p>VP of Accounting</p>
        </a>
        <a href="mailto:agnes@vectacorp.com" title="Send Email">
            Send Email</a>
    </li>
    <!-- the li elements for the other items -->
</ul>
```

The ul element for the second list

```html
<ul data-role="listview" data-split-icon="gear" data-inset="true">
```

How to code the HTML for a split button list

- Code the list just as you would a basic list (see figure 16-5).

- Add a second <a> element for each list item that links to a page other than the page that the first <a> element for the item links to. This element should include a title attribute that can be used for accessibility.

- To change the icon, add the data-split-icon attribute to the ul element with its value set to the name of the icon you want to use. See figure 15-10 for a list of the icons.

- To create an inset list, add the data-inset attribute with a value of "true".

Description

- *Split button lists* let you divide each list item into two tappable areas.

- *Inset lists* are typically used when a page has content other than the list.

Figure 16-6   How to use split button lists and inset lists

How to use list dividers and count bubbles

Figure 16-7 shows how to add two additional elements to list views: list dividers and count bubbles. As you can see in the first web page in this figure, *list dividers* provide a way of dividing list items into groups. In this case, the employees for a company are grouped into executives, managers, and other employees.

In contrast, the second web page shows that *count bubbles* provide a way of displaying the number of items in a list item that represents a group. In this case, the list items represent the groups of executives, managers, and other employees, and the count bubbles indicate the number of employees in each group.

To create a list divider, you simply add an li element wherever you want the divider to appear in the list. Then, you set the data-role attribute for this element to "list-divider", and you set the content to what you want displayed in the divider.

To add a count bubble to a list item, you add a span element after the content for the <a> element. Then, you set the class for this element to ui-li-count, and you code the number you want displayed for the content of this element.

Mobile web pages with list dividers and count bubbles

With list dividers

With count bubbles

The HTML for the first list

```
<ul data-role="listview">
    <li data-role="list-divider">Executives</li>
    <li><a href="#agnes">Agnes Agnew</a></li>
    <li><a href="#mike">Mike Masters</a></li>
    <li><a href="#damon">Damon Dell</a></li>
    <li><a href="#herbert">Herbert Huff</a></li>
    <li><a href="#wilbur">Wilbur Wilkes</a></li>
    <li data-role="list-divider">Managers</li>
    <li><a href="#wally">Wally Waters</a></li>
    <li><a href="#cammy">Cammy Caruthers</a></li>
    <li><a href="#tina">Tina Tobin</a></li>
    <!-- the li elements for the other items -->
</ul>
```

The HTML for the second list

```
<ul data-role="listview">
    <li><a href="#emps">Executives<span class="ui-li-count">368</span>
    </a></li>
    <li><a href="#mgrs">Managers<span class="ui-li-count">25</span>
    </a></li>
    <li><a href="#execs">Other Employees<span class="ui-li-count">5</span>
    </a></li>
</ul>
```

How to code the HTML for a list divider

- Add an li element with its data-role attribute set to list-divider.

How to code the HTML for a count bubble

- Code a numeric value within a span element and set the class attribute of the span element to ui-li-count.

Figure 16-7   How to use list dividers and count bubbles

How to use jQuery Mobile for forms

In addition to the jQuery Mobile components you've already learned about, you can use jQuery Mobile to create forms with controls like the ones you saw in chapter 8. In fact, all of the jQuery Mobile form controls are enhanced versions of the standard HTML form controls. So if you know how to code these controls, you won't have any trouble coding the jQuery Mobile controls.

How to use text fields and text areas

Figure 16-8 shows you how to use the text field and text area controls. These controls are similar except that a text area control can accept multiple lines of text.

To create a text field, you code an input element with its type attribute set to any valid HTML5 value. In this figure, for example, the type attribute of the first two fields is set to "text", the type attribute of the third field is set to "tel", and the type attribute of the fourth field is set to "email". jQuery Mobile can use these values to determine if there's a special keypad that can make data entry more efficient. When the user taps on the text field that has the type "tel", for example, the numeric keypad is displayed as shown in the second web page in this figure.

In addition to the type attribute, you should include id and name attributes on the input element. Then, you can precede this element with a label element that identifies the text field. This element should include a for attribute that has the same value as the text field's id attribute.

To create a text area, you code a textarea element with id and name attributes. In addition, you code a label element with a for attribute just like you do for a text field.

By default, the labels for text fields and text areas are displayed above the controls as shown in the web pages in this figure. In most cases, that's what you want. If you want to display the labels to the left of the controls, though, you can do that by wrapping the labels and controls in a div element that has its class attribute set to "ui-field-contain".

Note that the ui-field-contain class is new with jQuery Mobile version 1.4. Previously, you displayed the labels to the left of the controls by setting the data-role attribute of the div element to "fieldcontain". This value has been deprecated in jQuery Mobile 1.4, though, and it will be removed in jQuery Mobile 1.5. So you should use the ui-field-contain class instead.

A mobile web page with text fields and a text area

With text fields and a text area

Contact Us

Name:

Company Name:

Phone:

Email:

Questions/Comments:

With a keypad for numeric input

Company Name:

Phone:

|

Email:

Questions/Comments:

‹ ›		Done
1	**2** ABC	**3** DEF
4 GHI	**5** JKL	**6** MNO
7 PQRS	**8** TUV	**9** WXYZ
+*#	**0**	⌫

The HTML for the text fields and text area

```
<label for="name">Name:</label>
<input type="text" name="name" id="name">
<label for="companyname">Company Name:</label>
<input type="text" name="companyname" id="companyname">
<label for="phone">Phone:</label>
<input type="tel" name="phone" id="phone">
<label for="email">Email:</label>
<input type="email" name="email" id="email">
<label for="questions">Questions/Comments:</label>
<textarea name="questions" id="questions"></textarea>
```

How to code the HTML for a text field or text area

- For a text field, code an input element, set the type to a valid HTML5 value, and include id and name attributes.
- For a text area, code a textarea element with id and name attributes.
- Code a label element before the text field or text area to identify the control. Include a for attribute with its value set to the value of the control's id attribute.

Description

- By default, a label is displayed above its associated control. To display it to the left of the control, wrap the label and control in a div element with its class attribute set to "ui-field-contain".
- You can set the type attribute of a text field to any HTML5 value, including text, password, tel, email, number, and url.
- When the user taps on a field with certain input types, a special keypad is displayed that makes data entry more efficient for that type.

Figure 16-8 How to use text fields and text areas

How to use sliders and switches

Figure 16-9 shows how to use sliders and switches. A slider provides for selecting a value from a range of values. In contrast, a switch provides for selecting a binary on/off or true/false value.

To create a slider, you code an input element with its type attribute set to "range". Then, you set minimum and maximum values for the slider by using the min and max attributes. You can set the starting value for the slider by using the value attribute. And you can set the amount that the value is increased or decreased when the handle is moved by using the step attribute. It's also common to highlight the portion of the slider bar to the left of the handle as shown in this figure. To do that, you set the data-highlight attribute to "true".

Notice that the current value of the slider in this figure is displayed in a text field to the left of the slider. jQuery Mobile automatically adds this field for you so you can tell the exact value of the slider.

Switches are commonly used on mobile web pages because they provide an easy way for a user to select from one of two options. To create a switch, you code a select element with its data-role attribute set to "flipswitch". Then, within the select element, you code two option elements that represent the binary values for the switch. Note that you can code any values you want for these options. Since a switch represents a binary value, though, you'll typically use true/false, on/off, or yes/no values as shown in this figure.

A mobile web page with a slider and a switch

The HTML for the slider and switch

```
<label for="size">Company Size:</label>
<input type="range" name="size" id="size" min="10" max="500" value="300"
    step="10" data-highlight="true"><br>
<label for="currentinstall">Currently installed vSolutions?</label>
<select name="currentinstall" id="currentinstall" data-role="flipswitch">
    <option value="No">No</option>
    <option value="Yes">Yes</option>
</select>
```

How to code the HTML for a slider

- Code a label element with a for attribute that identifies the slider.

- Code an input element with its type attribute set to "range". Set the min, max, and value attributes to identify the minimum, maximum, and initial values. You can also include the step attribute to set the increment or decrement value.

- To highlight the slider bar to the left of the handle, set the data-highlight attribute to a value of "true".

How to code the HTML for a flip switch

- Code a label element with a for attribute that identifies the switch.

- Code a select element and set its data-role attribute to a value of "flipswitch".

- Code two option elements within the select element that represent the "on" and "off" states for the switch.

Description

- jQuery Mobile automatically converts an input element with a type of "range" to a slider and displays the current value in a text field to the left of the slider.

- A switch is used for binary input and can have only one of two values.

Figure 16-9   How to use sliders and flip switches

How to use radio buttons and check boxes

Figure 16-10 shows you how to use radio buttons and check boxes. The difference between these two types of controls is that check boxes work independently of each other, but radio buttons are set up so the user can select only one radio button from a group of buttons. In this figure, for example, the user can select only one of the three radio buttons, but any number of the check boxes.

To create a group of radio buttons, you start by coding a fieldset element with its data-role attribute set to "controlgroup". Then, within this element, you code a legend element that identifies the group. After this element, you code an input element for each radio button, and you set its type attribute to "radio". You must also set the name attribute for each radio button in a group to the same value.

Finally, you code a label element that identifies the radio button. You can do that in one of two ways. First, you can code a label element after the input element for the radio button and then set the for attribute of the label to the same value as the id attribute of the radio button. Second, you can wrap the input element in a label element. In that case, you can omit the for attribute.

You use a similar technique to code a group of check boxes. The only difference is that you set the type attribute for each input element to "checkbox". Remember, though, that you don't have to code check boxes in a group since they're independent of one another. If check boxes aren't related to one another, then, you can omit the fieldset and legend elements and just code the individual check boxes and labels.

By default, radio buttons and check boxes are displayed vertically as shown in the first web page in this figure. If you want to, though, you can display them horizontally instead. In the second web page in this figure, for example, the radio buttons are displayed horizontally. This takes up less space on the page and it can make the buttons easier to tap. To display a group of radio buttons or check boxes horizontally, you simply set the data-type attribute of the fieldset element to "horizontal".

Mobile web pages with check boxes and radio buttons

With vertical controls

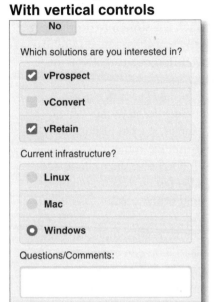

With horizontal radio buttons

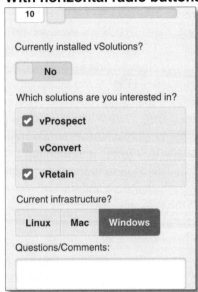

The HTML for the check boxes and radio buttons on the second page

```
<fieldset data-role="controlgroup">
    <legend>Which solutions are you interested in?</legend>
    <input type="checkbox" name="vprospect" id="vprospect">
    <label for="vprospect">vProspect</label>
    <!-- add more inputs/labels here -->
</fieldset>
<fieldset data-role="controlgroup" data-type="horizontal">
    <legend>Current infrastructure?</legend>
    <input type="radio" name="infrastructure" id="linux">
    <label for="linux">Linux</label>
    <input type="radio" name="infrastructure" id="mac">
    <label for="mac">Mac</label>
    <!-- add more inputs/labels here -->
</fieldset>
```

How to code the HTML for a group of radio buttons or check boxes

- Code a fieldset element with its data-role attribute set to "controlgroup". To display the controls within the group horizontally, set the data-type attribute to "horizontal".

- Within the fieldset element, code a legend element that contains the text that describes the group.

- Code an input element with its type attribute set to "radio" for each radio button or "checkbox" for each check box. Be sure to code the same name for each radio button.

- Code a label element for each control with a for attribute that identifies the control. Or, code the input element within the label element.

Description

- Because check boxes are independent of one another, you don't need to code them within a fieldset element. It's common to group related controls, though.

Figure 16-10   How to use radio buttons and check boxes

How to use select menus

Figure 16-11 shows how to use select menus, which are similar to drop-down lists. In fact, the HTML for a basic select menu like the one shown here is almost identical to the HTML for a drop-down list. The only difference is that you must include a label element that identifies the select menu.

Although the HTML for a select menu is similar to the HTML for a drop-down list, it's displayed quite differently. This is illustrated in the web page in this figure. Here, when the user taps a select menu, the list of items is displayed by the phone's roulette. Then, the user can spin the roulette or tap an item in the list to select it, and then tap the Done button to close the roulette and display the selected item in the menu. The user can also tap the less than icon to display the selected item and move to the previous field or the greater than icon to display the selected item and move to the next field.

You can also group two or more related select menus. For example, suppose you want the user to select a month, day, and year. Then, you can create three select menus and group them so they're described by a single text value.

In the second web page in this figure, for example, you can see a group of two select menus. The first one lets the user select a month, and the second one lets the user select a year. To create a group of menus like this, you wrap the menus in a div element with its class attribute set to "ui-field-contain", followed by a fieldset element with its data-role attribute set to "controlgroup". Then, before the first select menu, you code a legend element with the text for the group.

As noted earlier, the ui-field-contain class is new in jQuery Mobile 1.4. It replaces the data-role attribute with a value of "fieldcontain", which is deprecated in version 1.4 and will be removed in version 1.5.

By default, the menus in a group of select menus are displayed vertically with the identifying text to the left of the first menu. When you display menus this way, you usually add an option element at the beginning of each list that identifies the contents of that list. For example, you might add options of "Month" and "Year" to the select menus shown in this figure. In most cases, though, you'll display groups of menus horizontally as shown here. To do that, you set the data-type attribute of the fieldset element to "horizontal".

Mobile web pages with select menus

A single menu

A group of menus

The HTML for the first select menu

```
<label for="hearaboutus">How did you hear about us?</label>
<select name="hearaboutus" id="hearaboutus">
    <option value="magazine">Magazine Ad</option>
    <option value="radio">Radio Ad</option>
    <option value="tv">TV Ad</option>
    <option value="word">Word of Mouth</option>
</select>
```

How to code the HTML for a select menu

- Code a label element with a for attribute that identifies the select element.
- Code a select element with name and id attributes.
- Within the select element, code an option element for each menu item. Include a value attribute with an appropriate value.

How to group select menus

- Code a div element with its class attribute set to "ui-field-contain".
- Within the div element, code a fieldset element with its data-role attribute set to "controlgroup". To create a horizontal group, set the data-type attribute to "horizontal".
- Within the fieldset element, code a legend element with the text you want to display for the group.
- Code the individual select menus as shown above. If necessary, code an additional option element at the beginning of each list with the text to be displayed on the menu.

Description

- When a select menu is tapped, the mobile browser will display the phone's roulette with the list of menu items.

Figure 16-11   How to use select menus

How to submit a mobile form

Figure 16-12 shows you how to submit a jQuery Mobile form. As you can see, this works much the same way that it does for any form. That is, you wrap the controls in a form element and you include an input element with its type attribute set to "submit". Then, when the user taps the submit button, the form is submitted to the server and the script that's identified by the action attribute of the form element is performed.

By default, a jQuery Mobile form is submitted using Ajax. Although using Ajax results in a smoother transition to the resulting page, the added complexity of using Ajax isn't usually worth it. In most cases, then, you'll use a standard HTTP request. To do that, you set the data-ajax attribute of the form element to "false".

Although you haven't seen it in this chapter, you should know that you can include HTML code in your forms that performs client-side validation. For example, you can use the HTML5 required attribute to indicate that the user must enter a value into a field. You can also use regular expressions to indicate the pattern that an entry must match. This provides an easy way to validate the data on a form without using client-side or server-side scripting languages.

A mobile web page that submits a form to a server-side script

The HTML for the form and submit button

```
<form action="../scripts/mobile.asp" method="post" data-ajax="false">
    <!-- mobile form elements go here -->

    <input type="submit" value="Submit Form">
</form>
```

Description

- You can use a standard HTML form element for your mobile web pages.

- To submit a form, you can use an input element with its type attribute set to "submit".

- By default, jQuery Mobile *submits* a form using an Ajax request. Unless you need to use Ajax, you should use a standard HTTP request instead. To do that, set the data-ajax attribute of the form element to "false".

Figure 16-12   How to submit a mobile form

An enhanced mobile website for Vecta Corp

Now that you've learned how to use the other features of jQuery Mobile, you're ready to see a website that uses these features. This website is an enhanced version of the Vecta Corp website that you saw at the end of the last chapter.

The layout of the website

Figure 16-13 presents four pages from the enhanced Vecta Corp mobile website. The pages that aren't shown here are similar to the pages that were shown in the last chapter.

The first change to this website is that the Solutions page has been updated to use a list view. Then, instead of displaying a dialog when a solution is selected, another page is displayed. In this figure, you can see the page for vProspect. Notice that the header of this page includes a Back button that the user can tap to return to the Solutions page.

The second change is that the Contact Us page has been updated to use a form. You saw many of the elements of this page earlier in this chapter.

Finally, an About Us page has been added to the website. This page uses a collapsible set to display information about the executives at Vecta Corp. To display this page, the user can tap the fourth button that's been added to the navigation menu.

The page layouts for an enhanced mobile website that uses jQuery Mobile

The Solutions page

The vProspect page

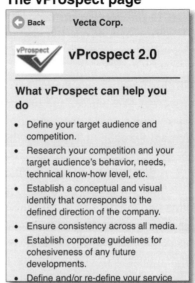

The Contact Us page

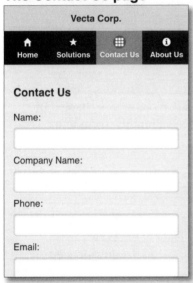

The About Us page

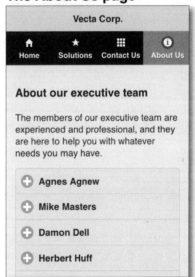

Description

- The Solutions page for this website has been updated to use a basic list view. When the user taps on one of the solutions in this list, the page for that solution is displayed.

- The header in the page for each solution includes a Back button that returns to the Solutions page.

- The Contact Us page has been updated to include form elements that can be submitted to the server and processed by a server-side script.

- The About Us page includes a collapsible set with information about the members of the executive team. This page has been added to the navigation bar.

Figure 16-13   An enhanced mobile website for Vecta Corp

The HTML

Figure 16-14 presents the primary HTML for this website in three parts. Since you've already seen code like this throughout this chapter, you should be able to understand it on your own. In case you're interested, though, here are a few highlights.

Part 1 of this figure shows the HTML for the Solutions page. Within the content section, you can see the list view that's used to format the three solutions. Here, you can see that each list item includes a link to another page. The <a> element for each link includes the image and text that are displayed for that item.

In part 2 of this figure, you can see the code for the vProspect page. Here, the header element for the page contains the <a> element that defines the Back button. Notice that the data-icon attribute for this element is set to "arrow-1" so a left arrow is displayed on the button, and the data-rel attribute is set to "back" so the previous page is displayed when the user taps this button. Because this page can only be displayed from the Solutions page, this button always returns to that page. Finally, the data-transition attribute for the <a> element is set to "slide" so the Solutions page will slide back into view.

Part 2 also shows the code for the About Us page. Here, you can see the section that defines the collapsible set, along with the first content block within that set. When the content block is collapsed, just the employee name is displayed. When the content block is expanded, all of the content, including a link that can be used to send an email, is displayed.

In part 3 of this figure, you can see the content for the Contact Us page. This page includes all of the form elements you learned about in this chapter. In addition, it includes a submit button that you can use to submit the form to the server.

The style sheet

The developer's style sheet for this application uses simple CSS to apply top borders, margins, and padding to some of the elements in the HTML. If you want to review this style sheet, you can review the file in the downloaded application.

The HTML for the Solutions page

```
<div data-role="page" id="solutions">
    <header data-role="header">
        <h1>Vecta Corp.</h1>
        <div data-role="navbar">
            <ul>
                <li><a href="#home" data-icon="home" data-theme="b"
                        data-transition="slide">Home</a></li>
                <li><a href="#solutions" data-icon="star"
                        class="ui-btn-active" data-theme="b"
                        data-transition="slide">Solutions</a></li>
                <li><a href="#contactus" data-icon="grid" data-theme="b"
                        data-transition="slide">Contact Us</a></li>
                <li><a href="#aboutus" data-icon="info" data-theme="b"
                        data-transition="slide">About Us</a></li>
            </ul>
        </div>
    </header>

    <section class="ui-content" role="main">
        <ul data-role="listview">
            <li>
                <a href="#vprospect">
                <img src="images/logo_vprospect.gif" alt="vProspect 2.0">
                <h3>vProspect 2.0</h3>
                <p>Define your target audience</p>
                </a>
            </li>
            <li>
                <a href="#vconvert">
                <img src="images/logo_vconvert.gif" alt="vConvert 2.0">
                <h3>vConvert 2.0</h3>
                <p>Our conversion framework</p>
                </a>
            </li>
            <li>
                <a href="#vretain">
                <img src="images/logo_vretain.gif" alt="vRetain 1.0">
                <h3>vRetain 1.0</h3>
                <p>Maximize customer loyalty</p>
                </a>
            </li>
        </ul>
    </section>

    <footer data-role="footer">
        <h4>&copy; 2016</h4>
    </footer>
</div>
```

Figure 16-14   The HTML for the mobile website (part 1 of 3)

The HTML for the vProspect and About Us pages

```
<div data-role="page" id="vprospect">
    <header data-role="header">
        <a href="#" data-role="button" data-icon="arrow-l" data-rel="back"
           data-transition="slide">Back</a>
        <h1>Vecta Corp.</h1>
    </header>

    <section class="ui-content" role="main">
        <img src="images/logo_vprospect.gif" width="84" height="48">
        <h2>vProspect 2.0</h2>
        <h3>What vProspect can help you do</h3>
        <ul>
            <li>Define your target audience and competition.</li>
            <li>Research your competition and your target audience&rsquo;s
            behavior, needs, technical know-how level, etc.</li>
            <li>Establish a conceptual and visual identity that corresponds
            to the defined direction of the company.</li>
            <li>Ensure consistency across all media.</li>
            <li>Establish corporate guidelines for cohesiveness of any future
            developments.</li>
            <li>Define and/or re-define your service and/or product
            offerings.</li>
            <li>Define expansion plans and strategies.</li>
            <li>Implement search engine optimization of all online
            materials.</li>
        </ul>
    </section>
</div>
```

The HTML for the About Us page

```
<div data-role="page" id="aboutus">
        <!-- header goes here -->

        <section class="ui-content" role="main">
            <h3>About our executive team</h3>
            <p>The members of our executive team are experienced ... </p>
            <section id="team" data-role="collapsibleset">
                <div data-role="collapsible">
                    <h3>Agnes Agnew</h3>
                    <img src="images/agnes.gif" alt="Agnes">
                    <h4>Agnes Agnew<br>VP of Accounting</h4>
                    <p>With over 14 years of public accounting and ... </p>
                    <a href="mailto:agnes@vectacorp.com" data-role="button"
                        class="ui-bar">Email Agnes</a>
                </div>
                <!-- the other content blocks go here -->
            </section>
        </section>

        <footer data-role="footer">
        <h4>&copy; 2016</h4>
    </footer>
</div>
```

Figure 16-14   The HTML for the mobile website (part 2 of 3)

The HTML for the Contact Us page

```
<div data-role="page" id="contactus">
    <!-- header goes here -->
    <section class="ui-content" role="main"><h3>Contact Us</h3>
        <form action="mobile.asp" method="post" data-ajax="false">
            <label for="name">Name:</label>
            <input type="text" name="name" id="name">
            <label for="companyname">Company Name:</label>
            <input type="text" name="companyname" id="companyname">
            <label for="phone">Phone:</label>
            <input type="tel" name="phone" id="phone">
            <label for="email">Email:</label>
            <input type="email" name="email" id="email">
            <label for="size">Company Size:</label>
            <input type="range" name="size" id="size" min="10" max="500"
                value="10" step="10" data-highlight="true"><br>
            <label for="currentinstall">Currently installed
                vSolutions?</label>
            <select name="currentinstall" id="currentinstall"
                    data-role="flipswitch">
                <option value="No">No</option>
                <option value="Yes">Yes</option>
            </select>
            <fieldset data-role="controlgroup">
                <legend>Which solutions are you interested in?</legend>
                <input type="checkbox" name="vprospect" id="vprospect">
                <label for="vprospect">vProspect</label>
                <input type="checkbox" name="vconvert" id="vconvert">
                <label for="vconvert">vConvert</label>
                <input type="checkbox" name="vretain" id="vretain">
                <label for="vretain">vRetain</label>
            </fieldset>
            <fieldset data-role="controlgroup" data-type="horizontal">
                <legend>Current infrastructure?</legend>
                <input type="radio" name="linux" id="linux">
                <label for="linux">Linux</label>
                <input type="radio" name="mac" id="mac">
                <label for="mac">Mac</label>
                <input type="radio" name="windows" id="windows">
                <label for="windows">Windows</label>
            </fieldset>
            <label for="hearaboutus" class="select">
                    How did you hear about us?</label>
            <select name="hearaboutus" id="hearaboutus">
                <option value="magazine">Magazine Ad</option>
                <option value="radio">Radio Ad</option>
                <option value="tv">TV Ad</option>
                <option value="word">Word of Mouth</option>
            </select>
            <label for="questions">Questions/Comments:</label>
            <textarea name="questions" id="questions"></textarea><br>
            <input type="submit" value="Submit Form">
        </form>
    </section>
    <!-- footer goes here -->
</div>
```

Figure 16-14   The HTML for the mobile website (part 3 of 3)

Perspective

Now that you've completed this chapter, you should be able to use jQuery Mobile to develop a mobile version of your website that is a nice complement to the full version of your site. Keep in mind, though, that you can also include jQuery features in a jQuery Mobile website. Together, the jQuery and jQuery Mobile libraries let you bring powerful features to mobile websites.

Terms

collapsible content block	inset list
collapsible set	list divider
list view	count bubble
split button list	

Summary

- The jQuery Mobile documentation is an excellent reference for the components and data attributes that jQuery Mobile provides.

- With jQuery Mobile, you can lay out content in grids that consist of rows and columns.

- You can save space on a page by using *collapsible content blocks* and *collapsible sets*. The difference between the two is that you can display the content for more than one collapsible content block, but you can display the content for only one content block in a collapsible set.

- You can use a *list view* to display a list of items that let you link to other pages. *Split button lists* let you link to one page when the list item is tapped and to another page when the icon is tapped. *Inset lists* can be used when a page contains other content.

- You can add *list dividers* to a list to divide the list items into groups, and you can include *count bubbles* to indicate the number of items in a group when the list items represent groups.

- jQuery Mobile provides many standard form controls for user input, including text fields, text areas, radio buttons, and check boxes. These controls work like their HTML counterparts but are optimized for mobile devices.

- jQuery Mobile also provides for sliders, which work like HTML5 range controls, switches, which can have one of two binary values, and select menus, which work like HTML drop-down lists.

- To submit a mobile form, you code the form controls within a standard form element and you include a submit button.

Exercise 16-1   Review the jQuery Mobile documentation

In this exercise, you'll display the jQuery Mobile website and review some of the documentation it contains.

Review the components for jQuery Mobile

1. Go to the website for jQuery Mobile at this URL:

    `http://jquerymobile.com`

2. Click on the Demos link near the top of the page, and then click on the link for the latest stable version of jQuery Mobile in the page that's displayed.

3. Scroll down the page to see the list of components in the left sidebar and the categories of components in the main portion of the page.

4. Click on the Grids link in the CSS Framework category. Then, review the documentation that's displayed.

5. If you want to, click on ListView Widget in the left sidebar to see its subentries. Then, click on ListView and review its documentation.

6. Return to the Home page for jQuery Mobile. The easiest way to do that is to reenter the URL above into the address bar.

Review the information in the Data Attribute Reference

7. Click on the API Documentation link near the top of the page. Then, click on the Reference link in the left sidebar of the page that's displayed, and click on the Data Attributes link in the next page that's displayed.

8. Scroll through the documentation to see that it lists the data attributes for each type of jQuery Mobile component.

9. Click the header for the slider to see that it takes you to the documentation for that component.

10. Continue experimenting until you're familiar with how the documentation is organized.

Exercise 16-2   Experiment with the mobile website

In this exercise, you'll first test the mobile version of the Vecta Corp website that's presented in this chapter. Then, you'll make some modifications to it.

Open and test the mobile website for Vecta Corp

1. Use your text editor to open the HTML page in this folder:

    `c:\jquery\exercises\ch16\vectacorp\`

2. Test this page and the navigation from one page to another within the site. In particular, use the list items in the list on the Solutions page to display information on the individual solutions, click the Back button in the header of a solution to return to the Solutions page, and click the About Us button in the navigation bar to display the About Us page.

3. Click the Contact Us button in the navigation bar of the Home, Solutions, or About Us page to display the Contact Us page. Then, complete the form and click the Submit button to see what happens.

Change the switch on the Contact Us page to two radio buttons

4. Replace the switch on the Contact Us page with a group of two horizontal radio buttons. Then, test this change to be sure it works.

5. Change the code you just entered so the input element for each radio button is contained within the label element, and delete the for attribute for the label. Then, test this again.

Change the Solutions page so it uses collapsible content blocks

6. Change the li elements in the list view on this page to div elements that have a data-role attribute set to "collapsible", and delete the ul element for the list view.

7. Delete the <a> element from the div elements you just added, but leave its content. Then, move the img element inside the h3 element before the text that element contains.

8. Test this web page to see how it works. When you click one of the content blocks, the paragraph for that block should be displayed. Note that you can display all three of the content blocks at once. Also note that although the formatting for the headings could be improved, they're good enough for now.

9. Replace the <p> element in each content block with the h3 and ul elements from the page for the associated solution. Now when you click on one of the content blocks, all the text that was previously included on a separate page should be displayed.

10. Notice that each content block now starts with two h3 elements. Change the first h3 element in each block to an h2 element and test the page again. Because jQuery mobile always styles the headers the same way, their appearance won't change.

Appendix A

How to set up your computer for this book

This appendix shows how to install the software that we recommend for editing and testing the web pages and applications for this book. That includes Aptana Studio 3 as the text editor for both Windows and Mac OS users, plus the Chrome and Firefox browsers for both Windows and Mac OS users. This appendix also shows you how to download and install the source code for this book.

As you read these descriptions, please remember that most websites are continually upgraded. As a result, some of the procedures in this appendix may have changed since this book was published. Nevertheless, these procedures should still be good guides to installing the software.

How to install Aptana Studio 3

If you're already comfortable with a text editor that works for editing HTML, CSS, and JavaScript, you can continue using it. But otherwise, we recommend that you use Aptana Studio 3. It is a free editor that offers many features, it runs on both Windows and Mac OS systems, and chapter 1 presents a quick tutorial on it that will get you started right.

On a Windows system

Figure A-1 shows how to download and install Aptana Studio 3 on a Windows system.

On a Mac OS system

Figure A-1 also shows how to download and install Aptana Studio 3 on a Mac OS system.

The website address for downloading Aptana Studio 3

http://www.aptana.com/products/studio3/download

How to install Aptana Studio 3 on a Windows system

1. Go to the website address above.
2. Click on the Download Aptana Studio 3 button near the bottom of the page.
3. If a dialog box is displayed asking if you want to run or save the exe file, click on the Save button.
4. If a Save As dialog box is displayed, identify the location where you want the exe file saved.
5. When the Download finishes, use Windows Explorer to find the exe file, and double-click on it to start it.
6. As you step through the wizard that follows, you can accept all of the default settings that are offered.
7. After Aptana Studio 3 is installed, start it. Then, if you don't have a Git application installed on your system, Aptana will ask you if you want it to install a Portable Git application. Accept that option because Aptana won't run without it.

How to install Aptana Studio 3 on a Mac OS X system

1. Go to the website address above.
2. Click on the Customize Your Download button, and select Mac OS X.
3. Click on the Download Aptana Studio 3 button, and click on the Save File button in the resulting dialog box.
4. When the Download finishes, double-click on the dmg file in the Downloads folder to display the Aptana Studio 3 window.
5. Double-click the Aptana Studio 3 Installer folder to start the installation.
6. When the installation is complete, start Aptana Studio 3. Then, if you don't have a Git application installed on your system, Aptana will ask you if you want it to install a Portable Git application. Accept that option because Aptana won't run without it.

Description

- Aptana runs on Windows, Mac, and Linux systems.
- Git is a source code management tool that Aptana requires. If necessary, Aptana will install it for you when you start Aptana for the first time.
- Chapter 1 of this book presents a tutorial that will get you off to a fast start with Aptana.

Figure A-1   How to install Aptana Studio 3 as your text editor

How to install Chrome and Firefox

When you develop JavaScript and jQuery applications, you need to test them on all of the browsers that the users of the application are likely to use. For a commercial application, that usually includes Chrome, Internet Explorer, Firefox, Safari, and Opera. Then, if an application doesn't work on one of those browsers, you need to debug it.

As you do the exercises and work with the applications in this book, though, you can test your applications on just two browsers. Windows users should use Internet Explorer plus Chrome, and Mac OS users should use Safari and Chrome. Then, if you need to debug an application, you can use Chrome's developer tools as described in chapter 4.

The first procedure in figure A-2 is for downloading and installing Chrome. As you respond to the dialog boxes for the installer, we recommend that you make Chrome your default browser. Then, you can follow the second procedure in this figure to download and install Firefox so you can use it for any additional testing you want to do. If you want to install Opera or Safari, you can use a similar procedure.

The website address for downloading Chrome

`https://www.google.com/intl/en-US/chrome/browser/`

How to install Chrome

1. Go to the website address above.
2. Click on the Download Chrome button.
3. Review the Google Chrome Terms of Service that are displayed. Then, indicate if you want Chrome to be your default browser and if you want to automatically send usage statistics and crash reports to Google.
4. Click the Accept and Install button.
5. If a dialog box is displayed with a security warning, click the Run button.
6. If you're asked if you want to allow the program to make changes to your computer, click the Yes button.
7. The installer is downloaded and Chrome is installed and started.
8. When the Welcome to Chrome dialog box is displayed asking you to set the default browser, click the Next button and then select a browser.
9. When the Set up Chrome tab is displayed, you can log in using your email address and password so your bookmarks, history, and settings are updated on all the devices where you use Chrome. Or, you can click the "Skip for now" link to skip this step.
10. A tab is displayed with the Google home page.

The website address for downloading Firefox

`http://www.mozilla.com`

How to install Firefox

1. Go to the website address above.
2. Click on the Download Firefox - Free button.
3. Save the exe file to your C drive.
4. Run the exe file and respond to the resulting dialog boxes.

Description

- Because Chrome is the most popular browser today, we suggest that you test all of the exercises that you do for this book in this browser.
- If you have a Windows system, Internet Explorer will already be on it and you should test with it as well.
- If you have a Mac, Safari will already be on it and you should test with it too. You won't be able to install Internet Explorer because it doesn't run on Macs.
- Because Firefox, Safari, and Opera are also popular browsers, you may want to install them too. To install Safari and Opera, you can use a procedure similar to the one above for installing Firefox.

Figure A-2   How to install Chrome and Firefox

How to install and use the source code for this book

The next two figures show how to install and use the source code for this book. One figure is for Windows systems, the other for Mac OS systems.

On a Windows system

Figure A-3 shows how to install the source code for this book on a Windows system. This includes the source code for the applications in this book, the starting files for the exercises, and the solutions for the exercises.

When you finish this procedure, the book applications, exercises, and solutions will be in the three folders that are listed in this figure, but the exercises will also be in the second folder that's shown. So, when you do the exercises, you use the subfolders and files in this folder:

    c:\jquery\exercises

but you have backup copies of these subfolders and files in this folder:

    c:\murach\jquery\exercises

That way, you can restore the files for an exercise to their original state by copying the files from the second folder to the first.

As you do the exercises, you may want to copy code from a book application into a file that you're working with. That's easy to do because the applications are in this folder:

    c:\murach\jquery\book_apps

When you finish an exercise, you may want to compare your solution to ours, which you'll find in this folder:

    c:\murach\jquery\solutions

You may also want to look at a solution when you're having trouble with an exercise. That will help you get past the problem you're having so you can continue to make progress. Either way, the solutions are an important part of the learning process.

The Murach website

www.murach.com

The Windows folders for the applications, exercises, and solutions

```
c:\murach\jquery\book_apps
c:\murach\jquery\exercises
c:\murach\jquery\solutions
```

The Windows folder for doing the exercises

```
c:\jquery\exercises
```

How to download and install the source code on a Windows system

1. Go to www.murach.com, and go to the page for *Murach's jQuery*.

2. Scroll down the page until you see the "FREE downloads" tab and then click on it. Then, click on the DOWNLOAD NOW button for the exe file for Windows. This will download a setup file named 2qry_allfiles.exe onto your hard drive.

3. Use Windows Explorer to find the exe file on your hard drive. Then, double-click this file. This installs the source code for the book applications, exercises, and solutions into the folders shown above. After it does this install, the exe file copies the exercises folder to c:\jquery so you have two copies of the exercises.

How to restore an exercise file

- Copy it from its subfolder in
  ```
  c:\murach\jquery\exercises
  ```
  to the corresponding subfolder in
  ```
  c:\jquery\exercises
  ```

Description

- The exe file that you download stores the exercises in two different folders. That way, you can do the exercises using the files that are stored in one folder, but you have a backup copy in case you want to restore the starting files for an exercise.

- As you do the exercises that are at the ends of the chapters, you may want to copy code from a book application into the file you're working on. That's easy to do because all of the applications are available in the book_apps folder.

- In the solutions folder, you can view the solutions for the exercises.

Figure A-3   How to install the source code for this book on a Windows system

On a Mac OS system

Figure A-4 shows how to install the source code for this book on a Mac OS system. This includes the source code for the applications in this book, the starting files for the exercises, and the solutions for the exercises.

When you finish this procedure, the book applications, exercises, and solutions will be in the three folders that are listed in this figure. Then, before you start the exercises, you should copy the exercises folder from:

```
documents\murach\jquery
```

to

```
documents\jquery
```

That way, you can restore the files for an exercise to their original state by copying the files from the first folder to the second.

As you do the exercises, you may want to copy code from a book application into a file that you're working with. That's easy to do because the applications are in this folder:

```
documents\murach\jquery\book_apps
```

When you finish an exercise, you may want to compare your solution to ours, which you'll find in this folder:

```
documents\murach\jquery\solutions
```

You may also want to look at a solution when you're having trouble with an exercise. That will help you get past the problem you're having so you can continue to make progress. Either way, the solutions are an important part of the learning process.

The Murach website

www.murach.com

The Mac OS folders for the book applications and exercises

```
documents\murach\jquery\book_apps
documents\murach\jquery\exercises
documents\murach\jquery\solutions
```

The Mac OS folder for doing the exercises

```
documents\jquery\exercises
```

How to download and install the source code on a Mac OS system

1. Go to www.murach.com, and go to the page for *Murach's jQuery*.

2. Scroll down the page until you see the "FREE downloads" tab and then click on it. Then, click on the DOWNLOAD NOW button for the zip file for any system. This will download a setup file named 2qry_allfiles.zip onto your hard drive.

3. Move this file into the Documents folder of your home folder.

4. Use Finder to go to your Documents folder.

5. Double-click the 2qry_allfiles.zip file to extract the folders for the book applications, exercises, and solutions. This will create a folder named jquery in your documents folder that will contain the book_apps, exercises, and solutions folders.

6. Create two copies of the exercises folder by copying the exercises folder from
   ```
   documents\murach\jquery
   ```
   to
   ```
   documents\jquery
   ```

How to restore an exercise file

- Copy it from its subfolder in
  ```
  documents\murach\jquery\exercises
  ```
  to the corresponding subfolder in
  ```
  documents\jquery\exercises
  ```

Description

- This procedure stores the exercises in two different folders. That way, you do the exercises using the files that are in one folder, but you also have a backup copy.

- If you want to copy code from a book application into an exercise file that you're working on, you can find all of the applications in the book_apps folder.

- In the solutions folder, you can view the solutions for the exercises at the end of each chapter.

Figure A-4   How to install the source code for this book on a Mac OS system

Appendix B

A summary of the applications in this book

This appendix summarizes the applications that are presented in this book. That will make it easier to find an application when you want to review or copy its code.

Section 1: JavaScript essentials for jQuery users

Application name	Starting figure	Description
Future Value	2-21	Gets user entries from text boxes, displays the result in a disabled text box, and displays errors using the alert method.
Email List	3-4	Gets user entries from text boxes, validates the entries, and displays error messages in span elements.
FAQs	3-6	Uses collapsible div elements to hide and show answers beneath questions that are in h2 elements.
Image Swap	3-10	Swaps large images when thumbnail images are clicked. To do that, it cancels the default action of the <a> elements, and it preloads the images.
Slide Show	3-14	Uses a timer to display images in a slide show.

Section 2: jQuery essentials

Application name	Starting figure	Description
Email List	5-8	Uses jQuery to simplify the Email List app of section 1.
FAQs	5-14	Uses jQuery to simplify the FAQs app of section 1.
Image Swap	5-15	Uses jQuery to simplify the Image Swap app of section 1.
Image Rollover	5-17	Changes the image in an image element when the mouse hovers over it.
FAQs with Effects	6-2	Two versions of the FAQs app of chapter 5 but with effects.
Slide Show	6-3	Two versions of the Slide Show app presented in section 1 that use jQuery and effects.
Slide Show	6-5	A Slide Show app that provides for stopping and starting the show.
FAQs and Animations	6-9	Like the earlier FAQs app but with an animated heading and easings.
Carousel	6-11	Uses animation to implement a carousel of books.
Lightbox	7-4	Demonstrates the use of the Lightbox plugin.
Carousel	7-5	Demonstrates the use of the bxSlider plugin.
Slide Show	7-6	Demonstrates the use of the Cycle 2 plugin.
Menu Highlighter	7-8	Illustrates a custom plugin that highlights menus.
Vecta Corp	7-10	Shows how you can use multiple plugins (two) for one web page.
Membership Form	8-6	Data validation of the entries in a membership form using JavaScript and jQuery.
Membership Form	8-10	Data validation of the entries in a membership form using the Validation plugin.
TOC	9-5	Generates a TOC in a sidebar from the headings in an article.
Enhanced TOC	9-9	Like the earlier TOC app, but with the TOC moving next to the heading in the article that has been accessed.
Employee List	9-11	Uses the on method to attach event handlers to employees that are added to the list as the app runs.
Slide Show	9-15	Two versions of a slide show that uses the DOM traversal methods to implement it.

Section 3: jQuery UI essentials

Application name	Starting figure	Description
Accordion	10-7	Demonstrates the Accordion widget.
Tabs	10-8	Demonstrates the Tabs widget.
Button and Dialog	10-9	Demonstrates the Button and Dialog widgets.
Autocomplete	10-10	Demonstrates the Autocomplete widget.
Datepicker	10-11	Demonstrates the Datepicker widget.
Slider	10-12	Demonstrates the Slider widget.
Menu	10-13	Demonstrates the Menu widget.
Vecta Corp	10-14	Shows how you can use multiple widgets (five) for one web page.
Draggable and Droppable	11-2	Demonstrates the Draggable and Droppable interactions.
Resizable	11-3	Demonstrates the Resizable interaction.
Selectable	11-4	Demonstrates the Selectable interaction.
Sortable	11-5	Demonstrates the Sortable interaction.
Individual effects	11-7	Demonstrates individual effects.
Color transitions	11-8	Demonstrates color transitions.
Class transitions	11-9	Demonstrates class transitions.
Visibility transitions	11-10	Demonstrates visibility transitions.

Section 4: Ajax, JSON, and APIs

Application name	Starting figure	Description
XMLHttpRequest	12-4	Shows the use of the XMLHttpRequest object for Ajax.
Load HTML	12-6	Shows the use of the Ajax load method.
Load XML	12-7	Shows the use of the Ajax $.get method with XML data.
Load JSON	12-8	Shows the use of the Ajax $.getJSON method.
Load data	12-11	Shows the use of the $.ajax method to get XML data.
Flickr API	12-13	Shows how to retrieve data using tags.
	12-15	Shows how to work with the description that's returned for each photo in a JSON feed.
	12-16	Shows how to search for photos using one or more tags entered by the user.
Google Maps API	13-3	Displays a Google map on a page.
	13-5	Adds markers to the map.
	13-7	Adds messages to the markers on the map.
	13-8	Adds custom messages to the markers on the map.
	13-9	Adds custom messages that contain Flickr images.
	13-11	Adds driving directions between two points on the map.
Geolocation API	14-4	Shows a user's position on a Google map.
Web Workers API	14-7	Uses a web worker to display elapsed seconds.
	14-8	Loads JSON data using a web worker and Ajax.
Book List	14-10	Uses a web worker to load book data from a JSON file and store it in session storage.

Section 5: jQuery Mobile essentials

Application name	Starting figure	Description
Vecta Corp	15-15	A mobile application that uses the basic features of jQuery Mobile.
Vecta Corp	16-14	An enhanced version of the chapter 17 application that uses some of the other features of jQuery Mobile.

Appendix C

How to resolve $ conflicts

A *$ conflict* occurs when two or more libraries or plugins require the use of the $ sign, and they aren't written in ways that prevent the conflict. Then, the browser doesn't know which library or plugin the use of the $ sign refers to, and that will cause a debugging problem.

Before you go any further, you should know that a $ conflict shouldn't ever occur because libraries and plugins are supposed to be written in ways that prevent these conflicts. For instance, chapter 7 shows how to create a plugin that won't cause a $ conflict. As a result, $ conflicts are extremely rare, and you probably won't ever encounter one. That's why you can think of the solutions that are presented in this appendix as "measures of last resort".

How to avoid $ conflicts

If you are using one or more libraries or plugins in addition to the jQuery, jQuery UI, and jQuery Mobile libraries and you suspect that you may be experiencing a $ conflict, figure C-1 presents two solutions for resolving the conflict. To understand these solutions, you need to know that you can use either the $ sign or "jQuery" to refer to the jQuery library.

As a result, one easy way to resolve a $ conflict is to change all of the $ signs that refer to the jQuery library to "jQuery". This is illustrated by the first example in this figure. That's also a quick way to find out if your debugging problem is a $ conflict. The only trouble with this method is that it can be cumbersome if your code includes many references to jQuery.

The second solution in this figure not only solves the problem but also lets you use the $ sign to refer to jQuery. With this solution, you use the $.noConflict method to relinquish jQuery's control of the $ sign. After that, you use "jQuery" instead of the $ sign to start an event handler for the ready method with $ as the only parameter for the handler. Once you've done that, you can use the $ sign within the ready event handler to refer to jQuery. You can also use the $ sign outside of the ready event handler to refer to other libraries or plugins.

Two ways to refer to jQuery

- $
- jQuery

jQuery code that uses jQuery instead of the $ sign to refer to jQuery

```
jQuery(document).ready(function() {
    jQuery("#selected_item").jqueryMethod();
});
```

jQuery code that uses the $.noConflict method to avoid $ conflicts

```
$.noConflict();                    // relinquishes control of the $ sign
jQuery(document).ready(function($) {
    // code that uses the $ sign to refer to jQuery
    $("#selected_item").jqueryMethod();
});
// code that uses the $ sign for other libraries or plugins
```

How to write JavaScript code that avoids $ conflicts

- Code the $.noConflict method.

- Use jQuery instead of the $ sign to select the document and create an event handler for its ready event.

- In the parameter for the ready event handler, code $. Then, you can use the $ sign within the ready event handler.

- Write the code for any libraries or plugins that require the $ sign outside of the ready event handler.

Description

- A *$ conflict* can occur when a jQuery application uses other libraries or plugins that require the use of the $ sign. Then, the $ sign can inadvertently refer to a library or plugin other than the one you intended.

- To refer to jQuery, you can use either the $ sign or "jQuery". As a result, you can avoid $ conflicts altogether by using "jQuery" instead of the $ sign to refer to jQuery.

- Another way to avoid $ conflicts is to use the $.noConflict method as shown above.

Figure C-1   How to avoid $ conflicts

Index

XYZ

100% Guarantee

When you order directly from us, you must be satisfied. Our books must work better than any other programming books you've ever used...both for training and reference...or you can send them back within 60 days for a prompt refund. No questions asked!

Mike Murach, Publisher   *Ben Murach, President*

Ready to expand your JavaScript skills?

Then *Murach's JavaScript* is for you! It shows you how to do the type of client-side programming that jQuery doesn't provide for, like how to use regular expressions, how to create and use your own objects, and much more.

Books for web developers

Murach's HTML5 and CSS3 (3rd Ed.)	$54.50
Murach's Dreamweaver	54.50
Murach's JavaScript (2nd Ed.)	54.50
Murach's PHP and MySQL (2nd Ed.)	54.50

Books for Java programmers

Murach's Beginning Java with NetBeans	$57.50
Murach's Beginning Java with Eclipse	57.50
Murach's Java Servlets and JSP (3rd Ed.)	57.50
Murach's Android Programming	57.50
Murach's Java Programming (4th Ed.)	57.50

Books for database programmers

Murach's MySQL (2nd Ed.)	$54.50
Murach's Oracle SQL and PL/SQL for Developers (2nd Ed.)	54.50
Murach's SQL Server 2012 for Developers	54.50

Books for .NET programmers

Murach's C# 2012	$54.50
Murach's ASP.NET 4.5 Web Programming with C# 2012	57.50
Murach's Visual Basic 2012	$54.50

Prices and availability are subject to change. Please visit our website or call for current information.

We want to hear from you

Do you have any comments, questions, or compliments to pass on to us? It would be great to hear from you! Please share your feedback in whatever way works best.

 www.murach.com

 1-800-221-5528
(Weekdays, 8 am to 4 pm Pacific Time)

 murachbooks@murach.com

 twitter.com/MurachBooks

 facebook.com/murachbooks

 linkedin.com/company/
mike-murach-&-associates

What software you need for this book

- To enter and edit JavaScript, HTML, and CSS, you can use any text editor, but we recommend Aptana Studio 3 for both Windows and Mac OS users. It is a free editor with many excellent features.
- To help you get started with Aptana Studio 3, chapter 1 provides a short tutorial.
- To test the JavaScript and jQuery applications that you develop on a Windows system, we recommend that you use Internet Explorer and Chrome. On a Mac OS system, we recommend that you use Safari and Chrome. Then, to debug your applications, you can use Chrome's developer tools. All of these browsers are free.
- To help you install these products, appendix A provides the website addresses and procedures that you'll need.

The downloadable applications and files for this book

- All of the applications that are presented in this book.
- The starting files for the exercises in this book.
- The solutions for the exercises.

How to download the applications and files

- Go to www.murach.com, and go to the page for *Murach's jQuery (2nd Edition)*.
- Scroll down the page until you see the "FREE downloads" tab and then click on it.
- If you're using a Windows system, click the DOWNLOAD NOW button for the exe file to download a file named 2qry_allfiles.exe. Then, find this file in Windows Explorer and double-click on it. That will install the files for this book in this directory: c:\murach\jquery.
- If you're using a Mac, click the DOWNLOAD NOW button for the zip file to download a file named 2qry_allfiles.zip onto your hard drive. Then, move this file into the Documents folder of your home folder, use Finder to go to your Documents folder, and double-click on the zip file. That will create a folder named jquery that contains all the files for this book.
- For more information, please see appendix A.

www.murach.com